P9-CQJ-660

Joe Louis

JOE LOUIS

The Great Black Hope

Richard Bak

DA CAPO PRESS • NEW YORK

Library of Congress Cataloging-in-Publication Data

Bak, Richard, 1954–
   Joe Louis: the great Black hope / Richard Bak.—1st Da Capo Press
ed.
      p.   cm.
   Originally published: Dallas, Tex.: Taylor Pub., c1996.
   Includes bibliographical references and index.
   ISBN 0-306-80879-X (alk. paper)
   1. Louis, Joe, 1914– . 2. Boxers (Sports)—United States—Biography.
I. Title.
[GV1132.L6B35 1998]
796.83′092—dc21
[B]   98-6772
                                                                CIP

First Da Capo Press edition 1998

This Da Capo Press paperback edition of *Joe Louis* is an unabridged
republication of the edition first published in Dallas in 1996,
with a few minor textual emendations. It is reprinted by
arrangement with Taylor Publishing Company,
1550 West Mockingbird Lane, Dallas, TX 75235.

Copyright © 1996 by Richard Bak

Published by Da Capo Press, Inc.
A Subsidiary of Plenum Publishing Corporation
233 Spring Street, New York, N.Y. 10013

For Mary, Hilary, and Rosemary

Contents

Acknowledgments

$\mathcal{H}$aving been born and raised in Detroit, I developed an interest in Joe Louis at an early age. This is hardly shocking. After all, one can barely escape his name or image around town. Over time my interest developed to a point where I knew I would someday write a book about Detroit's legendary Brown Bomber. I'm grateful to the powers-that-be at Taylor Publishing for finally affording me that opportunity.

I'm also grateful to the family members, prize fighters, writers, and others associated wih Joe Louis whose reminiscences were instrumental in helping me to create his world: Alberta Barksdale, Joe Louis Barrow Jr., Eddie Batchelor Jr., Mark Beltaire, Ben Bentley, Jimmy Bivins, Saul Davis, Truman Gibson, John Glover, Freddie Guinyard, Edgar Hayes, Tommy Henrich, Vunies Barrow High, Bill Hines, Charles "Red" House, Marshall Miles, Ken Offet, Shirley Povich, George Puscas, Leonard Reed, Billy Rowe, Nello "Rocky" Sensoli, Jackie Sherman, Walter Smith, Clyde Sukeforth, Ron Teasley, Tommy Tucker, Jesse Walker, James Ware, Fred "Sunnie" Wilson, and Lacy Wilson. The relatives of some of Louis's opponents graciously provided me with information and illustrative material concerning their careers. Thanks to Johnny Paychek's grandson, David Levien; Johnny Miler's nephew, Richard Buckheim; Tami Mauriello's nieces, Theresa and Deborah Mauriello; and Bob Pastor's daughter, Roberta Sansiveri.

Several collectors, archivists, artists, photographers, and boxing historians lent assistance along the way, including Michelle Andonian, Joanna Britto of the National Portrait Gallery, Phil Desind of Capricorn Galleries, Orlin Jones, Rosemary Jones of Pug Shots, Hank Kaplan, Kristine Krueger of the National Film Information Service, Margaret Kurtz of Caesars Palace, Martin Paul, Dave Poremba of the Burton Historical Collection, Bob Sampson of the Brewster Old Timers, Sally Stassi of the Historic New Orleans Collection, and Bert Sugar. Dr. Laurence F. McNamee, the last person to have a comprehensive interview with Max Schmeling, shared the fruits of his meeting and provided pertinent sections of the German fighter's autobiography, which he is in the process of translating into English. Special recognition is due ring historian Angelo Prospero, who came through in championship style in the late stages of this project. Two friends and fellow writers, Brett Forrest and Veronica White, facilitated my research.

Finally, I owe my greatest debt of gratitude to my wife of nineteen years, Mary, and our daughters, Hilary and Rosemary. For a long time they have magnanimously shared their living space with a writer. We all know that it hasn't been easy.

Prologue

From "The Prize Fighter," *The Crisis* (August 1914):

Boxing is an ancient sport. It is mentioned in Homer's Iliad and Virgil's Aeneid and was a recognized branch of the celebrated Olympic games. During the middle age boxing went out of style among most nations, the preference being given to various sorts of encounters with weapons. In England it was revived in the Seventeenth Century, and fighting with bare fists became a national sport in the Eighteenth Century. Boxing gloves were invented late in that century, and in the beginning of the Nineteenth Century, John Jackson (note the prophecy!) became champion and teacher of Lord Byron and other great and titled personages.

Gradually the more brutal features of the sport were eliminated and the eighth Marquess of Queensbury drew up a set of rules in the sixties which have since prevailed. . . .

Despite all this, boxing has fallen into disfavor—into very great disfavor. To see publications like the *New York Times* roll their eyes in shivery horror at the news from Paris (to which it is compelled to give a front page) makes one realize the depths to which we have fallen.

The cause is clear: Jack Johnson, successor of the Eighteenth Century John Jackson, has out-sparred an Irishman. He did it with little brutality, the utmost fairness and great good nature. He did not "knock" his opponent senseless. Apparently he did not even try. Neither he nor his race invented prize fighting or particularly like it. Why then this thrill of national disgust? Because Johnson is black. Of course, some pretend to object to Mr. Johnson's character. But we have yet to hear, in the case of white America, that marital troubles have disqualified prize fighters or ball players or even statesmen. It comes down, then, after all to this unforgivable blackness.

Chapter One

From 'Bama to Black Bottom

I'm goin' to Detroit, get myself a good job
I'm goin' to Detroit, get myself a good job
Tried to stay around here with the starvation mob

I'm goin' to get a job, up there in Mr. Ford's place
I'm goin' to get a job, up there in Mr. Ford's place
Stop these eatless days from starin' me in the face

—BLIND BLAKE, "DETROIT BOUND BLUES" (1926)

*A*t first it was a trickle, a few brave souls tired of dragging their hoes across the inhospitable dirt of Texas and Georgia and Mississippi, weary of the capricious ways of the white man and the boll weevil. They were overwhelmingly young, male, single, and black—pioneers in the same sense that those who had once headed west in covered wagons or braved the ocean in leaky boats were pioneers. Encouraged by labor agents talking of Henry Ford's five-dollar day, influenced by postcards describing such wonders as electric lights, moving pictures, and indoor plumbing, and inspired by dreams of what the new promised land of the great industrialized North might hold in store for them, they just had to go.

When a world war suddenly slammed the door shut on the millions of European immigrants who had historically manned the country's foundries, factories, mills, and mines, the trickle became a veritable flood, with Chicago's South Side alone taking in fifty thousand blacks during one eighteen-month period. Daily trains snaked north from the Cotton Belt. Eighteen or twenty dollars was generally enough to take a hopeful from Atlanta to Detroit or from Birmingham to St. Louis. These newcomers, said

John Dancy of the Urban League, arrived with "little or no education, little or no money—nothing much, really, except the clothes on their backs and a grim determination to find some place where they could work and make better lives for themselves than they had previously known."

Within a few short years these transplanted sharecroppers had formed the nucleus of the emerging black ghettos of Chicago, St. Louis, Detroit, Pittsburgh, Cleveland, Philadelphia, and other smoke-belching metropolises. By the end of 1930, more than 1.2 million blacks had migrated north, irreversibly changing the face—and complexion—of modern America.

Left behind was a South of rigidly enforced segregation, seething racial animosity—and long memory. In nearly every one of the thirteen states that comprised the former Confederacy, the Stars and Bars were either prominently featured on the state flag or proudly flown alongside it. Theoretically, blacks had become free citizens in the wake of the Civil War, and they had actually made some substantial gains during Reconstruction. But by the early 1900s a mushrooming network of Jim Crow ordinances and customs had effectively stolen their right to vote, gain an education, and earn a decent living.

Indeed, their very humanity was being bled from them by a thousand and one daily humiliations. "Colored Only" and "Whites Only" signs appeared on virtually every public convenience from telephone booths and ticket windows to drinking fountains and lavatories, while most restaurants, hotels, parks, art galleries, and libraries were completely off limits to blacks. In Mobile, Alabama, all blacks were required to be off the streets by 10 P.M. Inside Atlanta's courts, black witnesses kissed separate Bibles and rode their own elevators. A Florida law required schoolbooks to be segregated even when in storage. Seating arrangements inside waiting rooms, schools, streetcars, and circus tents were strictly circumscribed. Blacks traveled via Jim Crow Pullman cars and steamboats. The city of Birmingham, Alabama, required separate entrances at least twenty-five feet apart and "well defined physical barriers" in every "room, hall, theatre, picture house, auditorium, yard, court, ball park, or other indoor or outdoor place." In New Orleans, black and white prostitutes were required to ply their trade in separate districts. In at least one corner of Dixie the doctrine of "separate and unequal" continued into the hereafter, as a Mississippi state law prohibited blacks from being buried in the same cemeteries as whites.

As the courts increasingly turned a deaf ear towards cries of mistreatment, injustice, and disenfranchisement, the practical running of society was left to the bullies. Jim Crow, observed historian C. Vann Woodward, "put the authority of the state or city in the voice of the street-car conductor, the railway brakeman, the bus driver, the theater usher, also into the voice of the hoodlum of the public parks and playgrounds." The Ku Klux

Klan, which had faded away after Reconstruction, was revived in Georgia in 1915, and once again the white-sheeted night riders became the scourge of dark country paths and isolated farmhouses.

The rising tide of violence shocked former Alabama governor William C. Oates into proclaiming that the public wanted "to kill [the Negro] and wipe him from the face of the earth." That seemed to be the object of white rioters in East St. Louis, Illinois, who in 1917 burned the Negro quarters to the ground, routing six thousand blacks from their homes and killing perhaps as many as two hundred. Matters worsened when black servicemen, hungry for the democracy fought for in France, returned to their homes after the First World War. In 1919 alone, more than twenty deadly race riots broke out in cities from Longview, Texas, to Washington, D.C. The toll didn't include the seventy or so blacks lynched in the first year after the Armistice. Several of those found twisting under branches were veterans still in their uniforms.

In this environment religion "soared to a shout," as Langston Hughes described it. Revival hymns and spirituals begat the blues (as well as its instrumental cousin, jazz)—cultural tom-toms, said Hughes, that expressed "pain swallowed in a smile." Whether the music was being issued by a back-woods amen congregation or the "Empress of the Blues," Bessie Smith, its rhythms told the story of a race, awash in suffering, bravely struggling to keep its head above the torrent.

The paradox of America's separatist society was that an air of strained civility and paternalism characterized much of the everyday social interaction between blacks and whites. But this could continue only for as long as members of the subordinate race remembered to mind their proper place. It all made for an uneasy coexistence.

Richard Wright, the respected author of such autobiographical works as Native Son and Black Boy, described through one of his best-known characters, Bigger ("bad nigger") Thomas, how he was made to feel "conscious of every square inch of skin on his black body" while in the presence of white people. And the good Lord help those who got too "uppity" in their behavior, said Wright, whose anecdotal encounters on coming of age in the turn-of-the-century South spoke to the universal experience of his race. He was once beaten and fired from his job in a Jackson, Mississippi, eyeglass factory after committing "the worst insult that a Negro can utter to a southern white man": failing to preface his name with Mister.

"When I told the folks at home what had happened," he later wrote, "they called me a fool. They told me that I must never again attempt to exceed my boundaries. When you are working for white folks, they said, you got to 'stay in your place' if you want to keep working."

Wright kept that advice in mind as he moved on to another job as a

porter in a clothing store. He remained quiet one morning while the propri-
etor and his son dragged a screaming black woman off the street and into a
back room. She emerged a short while later, clutching her stomach and
trailing blood and tufts of hair and clothing—whereupon a policeman
picked her up on charges of being drunk and disorderly.

"Boy," the storeowner told Wright, "that's what we do to niggers when
they don't want to pay their bills."

Later at lunch, Wright described the incident in terrified tones to his
fellow porters. Nobody expressed shock or surprise. "Man, she's a lucky
bitch!" one said between sandwich bites. "Hell, it's a wonder they didn't lay
her when they got through."

Wright's Jim Crow education deepened when he found another job as
a hall-boy in a hotel. Once a black bellhop was caught in bed with a white
prostitute. Angry white men sent the whore on her way, then held her partner down as one of them tore off the offending organ with a straight razor.
Again, some thought the victim had gotten off easy—they could've just as
easily killed the castrated fool was the thinking—but Wright, who had
spent the whole of his young life watching his race being figuratively emas-
culated, was sickened. As soon as he could, he moved to Chicago.

>‹

Of course, not everybody headed for the North, and those who did
leave did not all go at once. Against a backdrop of general segregation and
discrimination, lives of relative harmony and simple satisfaction continued
to play out even as the phenomenon that came to be known as the Great
Migration gathered speed. This was especially true in the more remote rural
sections of the South where a common poverty and economic interdepen-
dence allowed relations between the races to develop along more tolerable
lines than in such crowded urban areas as Atlanta and Birmingham.

Sometime at century's turn, a pair of illiterate country blacks, Munroe
Barrow and Lillie Reese, came together and sought to carve out a life in
Chambers County in eastern Alabama, at the foot of the Buckalew Mountains and close to the Georgia border. In their time and place this typically
meant sharecropping, an economic system that was not too far removed
from the old slave-and-master ways of their parents' day.

Under this system a landowner gave the sharecropper and his family a
parcel of land to cultivate, a horse or mule to pull the plow and wagon, and
a drafty cabin to live in. The size of the plot usually ranged between fifteen
and forty acres, depending on how many family members were available to
work in the fields. In exchange the sharecropper promised the farmer half
of his crop at harvest time. Because the sharecropper was advanced such
essentials as food, clothing, fertilizer, equipment, and other supplies

throughout the year—the payment to be deducted from his share of the crop—a poor harvest or dishonest bookkeeping could place him in the planter's debt year after year. In effect, he and the other unlucky sharecroppers working the plantation "owed their soul to the company store." At that point they usually had no choice but to sneak off in the middle of the night, to be replaced during the following year's planting season by a new set of croppers who were themselves fleeing onerous debts elsewhere. To hundreds of thousands of uneducated and perpetually indigent croppers (the majority of whom were white, by the way), sharecropping was a form of involuntary servitude only slightly less odious than slavery.

For those who could afford their own equipment, stock, and supplies, a more desirable method was tenant farming. In exchange for a set fee—say, a five-hundred-pound bale of cotton—a renter was allowed to cultivate crops on a landowner's property. Ideally this arrangement gave the tenant more independence, a larger share of the harvest, and greater say in his destiny. Trouble came with the absence of formal contracts, which opened the door to endless disputes, misunderstandings, and charges of piracy. Munroe and Lillie Barrow, like most of their barefoot and straw-hatted brethren eking out a living among the furrows, moved constantly from farm to farm, alternating between sharecropping and renting.

Although he would later suffer a breakdown, Munroe Barrow initially seemed up to the task of raising crops and a family. He was an impressive physical specimen, standing more than six feet tall and weighing about two hundred pounds. Both of Munroe's parents had been slaves, taking the surname of the man who owned the plantation they worked on, James Barrow. Munroe's mother was half Cherokee, and his father had some white blood in him.

Lillie Reese Barrow, six years younger than Munroe, had been born in 1886 to a pair of former slaves. As had been the case with her parents, she spent her life in the fields, stooping to pluck and bag the wispy balls of cotton until at times her aching back felt like someone had placed a small boulder upon it. Marriage compounded her work load. As the maternal head of a growing family, she added sewing, cooking, and cleaning to her field chores.

She was a big, fleshy woman—about five-foot-six and 170 pounds—with tough, calloused hands. She could work a plowhorse over rough, broken ground as effectively as most any man. Her size, coupled with a deeply devout Baptist faith, made her a formidable disciplinarian. She raised her children to respect their elders, believe in the Almighty, care for their fellow man, and always tell the truth. "I'm not whipping you for what you did," she'd say in the midst of meting out some punishment. "I'm whipping you for lying about it."

But Lillie Barrow was also a loving, giving person who did much to shape the personalities of her eight children, all of whom were born in about a twelve-year period ending in 1916. In order of appearance, they were Susie, Emmarell, Alvanious, Ponce deLeon (known as deLeon), Alonzo (Lonnie), Eulalia, Joe, and Vunies. A mixture of white, black, and Native American blood coursed through all of their veins.

Her seventh and most famous offspring, Joseph Louis Barrow, came along on May 13, 1914. About eight o'clock that morning, while the rest of the family worked putting in that season's seed, an elderly midwife named Susan Radford helped Lillie deliver the eleven-pound baby in the front bedroom of the Barrows' four-room cabin. He was named for his father's brother-in-law, Joe Louis Nichols.

His birthplace, a ramshackle dwelling, still stands on Bell Chapel Road, about a mile off Route 50. LaFayette, the nearest town and the Chambers County seat, is about six miles to the southeast. Although king cotton has since fallen off its throne, natural wonders continue to rule the area: red clay, sixty-foot pines, and enough rattlesnakes and water moccasins to make outsiders slightly nervous when traipsing about.

Up until a couple of years ago a second cousin, Turner Shealey, lived inside the sagging, century-old cabin. Shealy had added a dining room and bathroom and covered the aging clapboard with sheets of particle board painted the color of apricots.

Shealey was twelve years old when Joe was born. At the time the Barrows were renting the land, large enough for a two-mule farm, from Shealey's family. Asked by the occasional visitor about the area's most famous product, he'd respond that, as an infant, Joe could "holler as loud as a wildcat." At times the incessant crying drove Shealey, an orphan who moved in with the Barrows when Joe was about five months old, right out of the house.

"I loved to 'possum hunt," said Shealey. "Get a dog and go in the woods at night and catch 'possum. I'd get my dog and go in the woods to keep from hearing him holler."

Compared to his brothers and sisters, Joe was a slow developer, not starting to walk until he was eleven months old and preferring not to talk much. When he did speak, the words came out slightly garbled. "When I went to school," Joe recalled years later, "the teacher made me say my words over and over, and by and by I got stubborn, I guess, and wouldn't say them at all." As a result, said Joe, "It got to be my habit not to talk much, even out of school."

Except for a severe earache when he was six or seven, Joe was a remarkably healthy child. "He's always been healthy and strong 'cause I fed him plenty collard greens, fat back, and corn pone," his mother once explained. "He didn't talk 'til he was six. He always like to sleep too much. It was worth my life to get him outta dat bed."

No photographs exist of Joe's twelve years in Alabama. Probably none were taken. This is disappointing but not surprising. The itinerant photographers of the day rarely tramped the back roads in search of black customers. Not that these farmers weren't willing to leave the fields for a few minutes to sit for a portrait; they simply didn't have the money.

There is, however, a grainy portrait of Joe's father, taken shortly after his fourth child, deLeon, was born. Joe's birth was still several years in the future, but the photograph reveals that he would inherit many of Munroe Barrow's facial features as well as his size.

Joe never really knew his father. In 1916, when he was two years old, Munroe Barrow was committed to the Searcy Hospital for the Criminal Insane in Mount Vernon, Alabama, an institution at which he had been hospitalized off and on since 1906. For years Munroe had been spending short periods of time at the asylum before escaping back to his family. No one ever fixed the exact cause of his deteriorating condition—genetics, epilepsy, syphilis, toxic moonshine, a blow to the head, or simply his hardscrabble life—but it's a fact that he never emerged from his final confinement. He died in 1938, when he was fifty-eight, unaware that his youngest son had grown up to become the most famous black man in America. Long before then Joe and the other young Barrow children had accepted Pat Brooks as their real father.

Pat Brooks came into the Barrow family's life at the critical moment. After Munroe Barrow went away for good, Lillie had moved her clan repeatedly, farming parcels of land in nearby Red Grove, Waverly, and Canaan. As the family and its neighbors understood the situation, she was a widow, word having come from Mount Vernon that Munroe had died. Widowed or not, Lillie Barrow faced the hardship of single-handedly feeding and clothing eight children. Joe later recalled the succession of tumbledown shacks they lived in and how cold they could get at night.

"A lot of people were real nice to us" during this period, he remembered. "They knew Momma was a widow with a big farm and a lot of children. People would send me on errands and give me pennies and sometimes nickels. I'd give it all to Momma. Even though these were real poor people, they'd share a little bit of food with us when the crops didn't come through like they should."

Lillie Barrow, acting on the assumption that her husband was dead, began keeping company with the slender, fair-skinned Brooks. According to Joe's youngest sister, Vunies, Brooks "worked for the richest man in Alabama; at least that's what we always said. His boss was a white man who had something to do with building bridges."

Brooks, a widower with eight children of his own, was a good man who recognized a good woman in Lillie Barrow. They married and moved their combined brood into a larger house near Camp Hill, deeper into the Buckalew Mountains.

"Because of my stepdad, our situation improved," said Vunies. "It was better than what we had known. He had a Model T Ford. On Sundays we'd travel to church in it. I remember that car very well. It had a plastic top that snapped on. You could drive over big holes in the road and still go on. We had an organ in our living room and rugs on the floor."

Joe gained a playmate his own age, Pat Brooks Jr. The two youngsters were usually kept out of the fields except to act as messengers or to deliver lunch and cold water to the rest of the family.

"We got along good when his daddy married my mother," Joe said. "We liked to lay in the cotton when it went to the cotton gin. The mules would go slow down the dirt road and we would bounce on the cotton in the cart."

Joe's most pleasant memories of Alabama revolved around Saturday trips to Camp Hill, whose packed-dirt main street featured a variety of storefronts. Although Joe and Pat had to stay in the wagon while Poppa Brooks conducted his business, they were given cheese and crackers, "and that made a kind of holiday." Real holidays, such as Easter and Christmas, were celebrated with egg hunts and stocking-hanging. "What you'd find in your stocking would be apples and oranges and big red peppermint candy," he recalled.

Such meager pleasures were the order of the day. The world then was still primarily rural and heavily agricultural. In fact, it wasn't until 1920, about the time the Barrow and Brooks families combined forces, that the official United States census finally showed more Americans living in towns and cities than on farms. If not exactly blissful, life in the Alabama countryside was necessarily simple. Kerosene lamps, not electricity, provided light. Water for bathing, washing, and cooking was hauled in from outside, while an outhouse, equipped with the standard issue of catalogs and flies, sat in the back. Wood needed to be chopped to feed the large cast-iron stove. Meals were not fancy but filling: lots of home-grown potatoes, corn, peas, milk, and chicken. As a youngster Joe ate so many pork chops that, once an adult, he quit eating them for the rest of his life.

Recreation was primitive by today's organized standards, but possibly more fun because of it. There were always swimming holes and snake-hunting expeditions to fill idle hours. "I hunted join-y snakes," recalled Joe. "Down there they said if you cut these little snakes apart in the swamps, they would join together by themselves and be a whole snake again."

Occasionally his older sister, Eulalia, would play "fire ball" with him in the evenings, soaking a balled-up bundle of rags in kerosene and lighting it. They'd toss it back and forth. "You had to be quick to get rid of it before it'd burn you," she said.

One game Joe especially enjoyed was called "skin the tree," which he described as "a country kind of hide-and-seek."

As Joe explained: "One boy would be it. He'd have a chance to close his eyes and count to ten. The rest of us would then shinny up a tree and hide in the branches. You usually picked a tree that was a slender sapling, so it would bend. If the fellow who was it found you, he had to tag you by climbing the tree. If he got near you, you'd get a good hold on that sapling and bend it down 'til you dropped to the ground. Sometimes we'd just swing in the trees like little Tarzans. It sure was good for the development of shoulders and arms."

These formative years in the back country also accounted for Joe's adult pastimes of fishing and horseback riding, as well as for his troubling habit, after he became famous, of taking off by himself and disappearing for days at a time. Shoehorned into a household overflowing with people, sometimes sleeping three or four to a bed, Joe grew up craving his solitude.

The best times were after most of the family left the house for the fields. Sharecroppers labored from sunup to sundown, leaving Joe plenty of time as a youngster to explore his world. On one memorable occasion he happened upon a bottle of white lightning.

"Of course I drank it," he said, "and of course I got drunk. I wandered around stumbling until I fell asleep under a tree. Momma found the bottle and me under the tree, asleep. She didn't spank me, but, worse, she gave me a lecture on the evils of drink. She won. It was many decades before I touched a drink of alcohol."

Ducking chores has always been a necessary element of a young boy's life, and in this regard Joe was no different. Other times, with a burst of energy and anxious to gain his mother's approval, he would scrub all of the floors in the house. "When Momma came home and saw what I had done," he remembered, "she'd grab me and give me a big kiss for it. Then I could have floated clear up to the sky."

In Momma's view of the world, that would have put him in very good company. Lillie was a God-fearing woman who absolutely believed the hardships of the here and now would one day be rewarded with a generous spot in the hereafter. To that end she bore life's cruel blows with the same kind of quiet equanimity for which Joe would later be universally admired.

The Mount Sinai Baptist Church, an unpainted, one-room wooden building about three miles from where Joe was born, was where Lillie reen-

ergized her soul and where her children learned about salvation and, hopefully, the alphabet. On Sundays Joe would put on his only pair of shoes and
a clean pair of overalls and join his siblings in fidgeting through a long day
of worship. And on those days when the family could spare him from
chores, he would sit in these very same pews and painstakingly chalk his
lessons onto a small slate board. A big iron stove provided heat on cold
mornings while on warm, muggy days the two large batten windows were
thrown open to capture any stray breeze. The church school, open to children of all ages, generally was in session from October through April to
coincide with the planting and harvesting seasons. Sharecroppers' offspring
would attend irregularly and after several years leave with an education
only marginally better than the one with which they had entered.

Which is exactly the way those who ran society liked it. If there was
one thing legislators in every southern state feared, it was an educated black
populace. The hostile white majority implicitly agreed no good could come
from lifting the colored race, especially at the expense of white taxpayers.
Thus the public school system in Alabama, which Joe attended once his
mother remarried, was not only segregated, it was inequitable. Generally
speaking, for every dollar spent on public education in the South during
this period, only a dime went to black schools. Most were little better than
overcrowded shacks with four or five youngsters trying to study out of the
same book while ignoring the roof leaking above them. The teachers often
were second-rate and always poorly paid in comparison to their counterparts in the white schools. Alabama's school year was considerably shorter
for blacks (115 days compared to 167 for whites), and many districts ended
black children's primary education after seven years to guarantee that the
only high school in the area would remain white. College or professional
training for blacks was practically unheard of throughout the South.

Even so, maintained Vunies, conditions at the public schools were
better than those at Mount Sinai Baptist Church. "For the first time," she
said, "we weren't being taught by people who were mostly illiterate because
they'd had a limited education themselves."

Joe never took to books in any situation. One reason was his natural
reticence, which was compounded by a slight stammer; another was his
wanderlust, which made any excuse to skip class a valid one. Sometimes he
fell in with the Langley boys, George and James, who were on their way to
the area's whites-only school. The youngsters would play hooky, shooting
marbles or chasing each other through the countryside. "Since none of us
wanted to go to school," said Joe, "it was a good interruption."

Such casual friendships with the Langleys, whose father owned the
country store in Camp Hill, as well his stepfather's employment with the
bridge contractor, reinforced Joe's color-blind view of his limited world. He

later insisted that he never heard about lynchings and was never called a nigger all the time he lived in Alabama.

"My folks seemed to get along with the white people in the area," he said. "Maybe it was because, 'You got your place and I got mine.' Probably we never crossed the line to cause the angers and hurts and lynchings that took place all over the South." Joe occasionally heard black folks boasting about their white or Indian ancestry, "but hardly anybody would talk about how much black blood they had."

Pat Brooks's servile reputation saved his life. Late one night in 1925 he and Lillie were driving home after spending the day sitting with the relatives of a deceased friend. Suddenly several riders in white hoods and gowns appeared in the road. Brooks's heart jumped into his mouth as the men on horseback menacingly circled the Model T. They were just about to pull him out of the car when one of the masked men recognized him.

"That's Pat Brooks," he said. "He's a good nigger." The Klansmen let them pass.

Shaken by the experience, Brooks made up his mind that his family would leave the South. Even without the Klan, the decision was easy to make. Although Brooks served as the contractor's right-hand man, farming still was a primary source of family income. But the voracious appetite of a grayish, quarter-inch-long insect known as the boll weevil, combined with the area's played-out soil, had made working the land a Herculean task, especially with many of the older children leaving the fields. Joe's two oldest sisters, Susie and Emmarell, had found husbands and moved to Alexander City, about forty miles away. DeLeon had hired on at a local lumber mill, handing over half of his weekly, twelve-dollar salary to his mother to help make ends meet. Joe, big for his age, had as much enthusiasm for farming as he did for schooling.

A year earlier, some of Brooks's relatives had visited from Detroit, and talk around the kitchen table centered on the high wages paid to factory hands in the booming Motor City. "They said the Ford factory didn't mind hiring Negroes," said Joe, "and for once we'd have hard solid money we wouldn't have to share with the landowner." If there was ever a time to make the move, Brooks ultimately decided, this was it. As soon as they could make arrangements, he and Lillie and several of the older boys traveled to Detroit in hopes of carving out a foothold for the rest of the family.

Joe and the younger children were left behind in the care of his older sisters and stepsisters and Lillie's brother, Peter Reese. News came back to them over the next several months that life actually would be better in Detroit. Papa Brooks had gotten a municipal job sweeping streets for fifty cents an hour and hoped to get hired at Ford. The others had also found work. Joe, who missed his mother and stepdad terribly, got caught up in the excitement of joining them in this new world of opportunity and adventure. "All of a sudden," he said, "I was not as happy catching snakes, shooting marbles, fishing, and playing skin the tree."

Finally, one day in 1926, Joe slipped on his new shoes and overalls, then joined his brothers and sisters for the emotional journey to the train station. There they said their goodbyes to relatives, neighbors, and friends, then boarded the railroad's colored car, filled with apprehension and barely contained excitement. The dining car was off limits, but they thought nothing of it. They had wax-papered shoeboxes and baskets jammed with biscuits, fried chicken, smoked ham, and sausage, which helped make the eight-hundred-mile journey seem like a long picnic.

>‹

The path to Detroit was a well-beaten one. As the center of auto production in the world, the industrial boom town had been transformed into the nation's fourth largest city. Between 1899, when its first auto plant opened, and the mid 1920s, by which time four million vehicles a year were rolling off the assembly lines, Detroit's population had exploded sixfold to some 1.5 million people. During this time peasants had come from almost every point of the globe to fill the factories, making Detroit an ethnic tossed salad where two-thirds of the citizenry were either foreign-born or the children of immigrants.

No metropolis was as intimately tied to one industry as Detroit, which even during the up-tempo twenties suffered periodic depressions based on the fickle mood of the economy. When the rest of the country caught a cold, the old joke went, Detroit got pneumonia. But when the assembly lines were humming along at full speed, times were awfully good.

At the time of Joe's arrival some eleven thousand blacks were working in Detroit's auto plants. Ten years earlier there had been none. The First World War had brought about the change in attitude. With many white workers called into military service and the country's shores closed to immigration, industrialists had no choice but to import blacks. Henry Ford, who enjoyed tinkering with social problems as much as he did mechanical ones, had emerged as the paterfamilias of Detroit's rapidly expanding Negro community. Between 1917 and 1925 the creator of the Model T hired about ten thousand blacks at his sprawling Rouge plant, the greatest industrial complex in the country. What set Ford apart from other bosses was that he allowed blacks into all job classifications and paid them the same salaries as whites (though the majority of blacks still were assigned by less benevolent department heads to such dirty and dangerous areas as the foundry and paint shop). The paternalistic billionaire was regularly seen meeting with Baptist preachers and national race leaders like Booker T. Washington. In the eyes of many blacks, he was their greatest white advocate since Abraham Lincoln.

James Dancy, director of the Detroit Urban League, helped hook newcomers up with employers. Some had barely stepped off the train at the Michigan Central Station when they found themselves being rounded up and shipped off to some shop to put in a twelve-hour day. The migrants, an increasing number of whom were urbanized southerners, were highly desirable, although their reputation as tireless manual laborers was owed to stereotype and limited opportunities.

"The percentage of Negroes who are rugged physically is probably no greater than the percentage of whites, if indeed it is as great," Dancy remarked in his autobiography. "For a white man, however, there were plenty of occupations that did not require exceptional strength and stamina; for the Negro newcomers to Detroit there were very few such jobs. If you had the ability to stand on your feet all day, to lift heavy things, to withstand the stifling heat of a foundry, there was perhaps a place for you. If you lacked these qualifications, and still were determined to break away from the oppressions of life in the South, Detroit offered a rather slim chance for improving your condition. It *was* a chance, however, and increasing numbers of Negroes took it."

Between 1910 and 1920 Detroit's black population ballooned from 5,700 to 41,000, a sevenfold increase that was the greatest in the country. By 1930 that number would triple to 120,000, then nearly quadruple again, reaching 450,000 by the end of the 1950s. Today 90 percent of the city's one million residents are black, a remarkable racial transformation that has its roots in the countless soot-stained shops and factories that dominated Detroit's landscape after the turn of the century.

DeLeon Barrow's experience was typical of an autoworker caught in the boom-or-bust cycles of Detroit's golden age of auto production. Joe's brother was hired by Ford in 1928 and, despite layoffs caused by depressions, model changeovers, labor unrest, and prejudiced foremen, managed to work the next forty-five years, two months, and twenty-one days in the Rouge's steel mill.

"Ford paid well," said the old pensioner, now near ninety and living in declining health in Detroit. "You only had to work eight hours a day for five dollars a day. Nobody was paying that kind of money. Then we got raised to eighty cents an hour. After sixty days, you got a raise to one dollar. I worked up to eight dollars a day. When the Depression came, they knocked me all the way back to four dollars a day. It was 'take it or leave it.'"

In Detroit the colored population was crowded into a sixty-square-block area on the near east side called Black Bottom. A large part of the district was paved over in the "urban removal" frenzy of the late fifties, by which time the striking down of illegal housing covenants had allowed many blacks to abandon the crumbling neighborhood for other parts of the city.

The area had gotten its name in the eighteenth century when French farmers had tilled the rich, black topsoil. By the early 1900s Black Bottom was in transition, the Jewish families being displaced by Greeks, Poles, Syrians, and other recent immigrant groups. Soon thousands of southern blacks were also being squeezed into what officially became known as the East Side Colored District. Typically two or three families joined forces to meet the exorbitant rents. Other households took in boarders. A housing study conducted after the war revealed tenants paying for the right to sleep inside outhouses, on the dirt floors of alley shacks, and on top of pool tables. The overcrowding and lack of hygiene produced sky-high rates of communicable diseases, particularly tuberculosis and syphilis. Additionally, the rates of infant mortality and sterility among blacks were nearly triple those of whites. As a result, during the booming twenties, the number of deaths in Black Bottom actually exceeded births.

Joe and his family first lived in the upper floor of a two-family flat they rented on Macomb Street, between McDougall and Joseph Campeau. Across the street was the Duffield Elementary School, which all of the younger children attended. The flat quickly proved to be too cramped for comfort. About two or three months later, towards the end of 1926, the family moved four blocks away to a rented house at 2700 Catherine (now known as Madison), between Chene and Joseph Campeau. They stayed there several years, until hard times forced them to move one block over to a house on Mullett.

The size and energy of the big city nearly overwhelmed Joe.

"You can't imagine the impact that city had," he recollected. "I never saw so many people in one place, so many cars at one time; I had never even seen a trolley car before. There were other things I had never heard of—parks, libraries, brick schoolhouses, movie theaters. People dressed different, and then I realized that even with those brand-new overalls and country shoes, I wasn't dressed right. But one thing I knew, Detroit looked awfully good to me."

The main avenues of this city within a city were St. Antoine and Hastings, streets that snapped and sizzled as 80,000 more blacks—most of them unattached men—poured into the ghetto during the decade. Legitimate businesses such as the 250-seat Crisis Cafe and Biltmore Hotel coexisted with back-room joints set up to satisfy every kind of urge with booze, jazz, drugs, women, and various games of chance. A newcomer didn't have to look far to find a wide range of experiences. He could sign up for a factory job at the Urban League office on St. Antoine, then mosey three storefronts over for a cheap, filling meal of biscuits and sausage gravy at John Brosher's restaurant. Afterwards, the self-styled Biscuit King could steer the newcomer fifty feet in any direction to one of the 711 "disorderly houses" the the American Social Hygiene Association had uncovered within a one-mile radius of city hall. Authorities felt little pressure to eliminate the rampant vice that characterized this strip dubbed Paradise Valley. They were satisfied to contain it—and, from time to time, to sample a taste of it themselves.

The Valley was only the flashiest part of a ghetto that was home to every hustle, scam, and temptation under the sun. Certainly things were not always what they appeared to be. Everitt Watson's realty office was a front for his numbers racket. Ike Portlock's tailor shop always had a crap game going. Whiskey was being brewed in Dave Winslow's sweet shop. Even local Negro-league pitcher Jack Marshall ran a two-bed brothel. Joe and his stepbrother Pat couldn't stroll down Catherine Street without noticing "the best little whorehouses in Detroit, with *les girls* sitting demurely in the front windows, ostensibly reading books but really waiting for customers," one person fondly recalled. Inside certain other doorways, "muggles"—marijuana cigarettes—could be purchased for a dollar apiece. Someone innocently wandering into the wrong shoeshine parlor risked getting slapped around and tossed out; didn't the dummy know he was interrupting a round-the-clock poker game? Prohibition, the law of the land from 1920 to 1933, had the effect of making countless citizens into criminals. A visit to a friend's flat might reveal the entire family busily engaged in bootlegging, which in terms of gross revenues was estimated to be the city's second leading industry behind automaking. Mother would be scrubbing bottles, father would be tending his still in the closet, and the children would be packing the hooch, not intended for home use, for delivery to neighborhood clients.

Coleman Young, whose family had left Alabama three years before Joe's, was one of the many impressionable youths torn between two role models: "the hustlers, with their flashy clothes and money clips, and the Ford mules, as they were called, straggling home from work all dirty and sweaty and beat."

"All over the streets," recalled Young, who grew up to serve a record twenty years as Detroit's first black mayor, "you'd see black guys with their pants neatly pressed and their fingernails manicured and their yellow leather shoes shined so bright it made you squint. Most of those guys came from the South. . . . The object was to remain unsullied by hard labor, and the young smartasses of Black Bottom seemed to have it knocked. Naturally, I aspired to be one of those fine gentlemen. I thought they had all things figured out. They were so sure of themselves that they'd sit along the street and make jokes when the buses came through to recruit men for the Ford plants. They'd laugh and point and shout things like 'Bring the job to me! I want to see it!' They were even so brazen as to taunt the Ford men about having their wives while the husbands were off bolting bumpers. Their motto was 'You feed 'em, we fuck 'em!'"

A proper upbringing in this kind of environment depended upon strong and regular doses of discipline. All of the Barrow and Brooks children still living at home were given early curfews. The girls were forbidden from attending dances and not allowed to date until they were sixteen and a half years old. Sundays were given over almost entirely to religious instruction and worship.

"We'd spend practically the entire day at church," said Vunies. "We'd go to school in the morning, and then services started as soon as Sunday school was over, at eleven. In the evening we'd attend the Baptist Youth Program."

These Sunday marathons, she insisted, coupled to a solid home life, accounted for Joe being a religious person, at least in his own way. "I'm not trying to make an angel out of him, but he really was an all-around good person. He always believed in helping out his fellow man. That was one of his faults, really. There's such a thing as being too generous."

Freddie Guinyard, a lifelong recipient of Joe's largesse, first met his future benefactor on the Duffield playground. Guinyard—short, willowy, and three months younger than Joe—had moved with his family from South Carolina when he was nine. "For all his skinny self, he was tough and slick," Joe remembered. "We made a good team."

The two became close companions, playing ball, exploring forbidden cracks of the neighborhood, and getting into minor trouble together, such as sneaking into the Catherine Theater to watch Tom Mix and Buck Jones shoot-'em-ups. Because Guinyard's parents were rock-solid Baptists, they also saw each other at the Calvary Baptist Church. Joe would tease his friend over the sailor's cap with the long silk ribbon that he was forced to wear.

"Occasionally Joe and I would help ourselves to some fruit at Eastern Market," Guinyard said. "Our parents didn't approve of that. We'd have to eat all the fruit before we came home. If they caught us with a banana, they'd ask, 'Did you work for that?' I'd think, 'Yeah, we worked for it. We had to run like hell.'"

Toward the end of his days Guinyard grew miffed at suggestions that he was a bit of an operator, though it was clear that he had long ago mastered the art of getting over. For a good chunk of his life, his primary source of income was either his best buddy Joe or some vaguely defined enterprise. Upon his death in the spring of 1994, it was revealed that the 80-year-old Guinyard, who in his later years was always careful to distribute business cards identifying himself as a travel consultant, had for some time actually been running the largest whorehouse in downtown Detroit.

Joe took good care of his pal. When he got three dollars for shoveling snow, he gave a buck to Guinyard, whose string-bean arms were either unable or unwilling to lift a shovel. As teenagers, they worked for a time for the Pickman & Dean Company, delivering coal in the winter and ice in the summer. Joe would use a giant set of tongs to pull a fifty-pound block from the sawdust in the back of the horse-drawn wagon, then lug it up two or three flights of stairs to the waiting kitchen. In addition to building up Joe's muscles, this arrangement led to one of his most frequently repeated quips. "That's how I learned the meaning of the word 'manager,'" he'd say. "Freddie would holler 'Ice!' and I'd deliver it."

The boys also shared a love of baseball, a pastime split along racial lines. They played the game on sandlots and, whenever they could, watched the professionals go at it. The lily-white Tigers of the American League entertained 23,000 fans at Navin Field, a modern concrete and steel facility a few blocks west of downtown. Meanwhile, the Negro National League's Detroit Stars played home games at Mack Park, a cramped, wooden facility on the far east side that could usually be reached by hopping onto the back of a produce truck. Thus the boys had the opportunity to watch the greatest black and white stars of the era, including Babe Ruth, Lou Gehrig, Charlie Gehringer, Turkey Stearnes, and Satchell Paige. If both teams were in town at the same time, Joe usually opted to watch the Tigers, even though they were some thirty years away from fielding their first black player.

Joe's choice was small but revealing. As a youth he rarely thought one way or the other about race. A segregated society was the only one he had ever known. Like his stepdad, most blacks followed its rules and customs with a mixture of forbearance, resignation, and humor. One didn't always have to scrape and bow to get by, but neither was it particularly wise to get as overwrought as W. D. Fard, the mysterious street-peddler-turned-prophet who set up the University of Islam inside an abandoned Detroit school during this period. The founder of the Black Muslims denounced the white race as devils and spread the gospel of racial pride and black separatism.

Pat Brooks's coming to Detroit coincided with a surge of white-on-black crime. In 1925 the local chapter of the rejuvenated Ku Klux Klan swore in thousands of new members, burned a cross on the lawn of city hall, and barely missed having a Klan-backed candidate elected mayor. The activity was partially in response to the ongoing Ossian Sweet case, which was drawing national attention. The black dentist and members of his family were being tried for murdering a white man after a mob tried to force them out of their neighborhood. Sweet contended that a Negro had a right to defend his property—an argument that had traditionally failed to sway juries. In 1926 Clarence Darrow's impassioned defense won an acquittal, but the verdict in the landmark case did nothing to stem the rising racial tensions as migrating blacks and whites competed for jobs and housing. The nearly all-white police force continued to be the final arbiter in too many disputes. In an eighteen-month period spanning 1925-26, Detroit cops shot to death twenty-five blacks. This compared with just three such deaths in New York whose black population was twice as large. Joe's experiences were more benign but still significant. For the first time in his life he heard the word nigger casually tossed his way.

One of Joe's contemporaries, John Glover, remembered too well the deep-seated frustration of the period.

"The schools were integrated, but everything else in the city was seg-regated," said Glover, another Alabama transplant who lived on Catherine Street. "In a way that was good. We had our own businesses—hotels, restaurants, shops, our own baseball team. The same dollar would get spent six or seven times in Black Bottom. But we couldn't patronize most white places. Monday night usually was colored night, like at the Graystone Ballroom on Woodward Avenue, since the owners figured the white folks were still recovering from the weekend. Sure, it was annoying and belittling and you were made to feel less than human. You'd take a girl to the movie, and your white classmate in the ticket booth would be only too happy to direct you to the balcony. But we didn't cry too much about it."

A wisecrack from Freddie Guinyard got Joe reflecting. One day a white teacher explained to a group of black students that those with good grades would get a chance to shine shoes on weekends at J. L. Hudson, downtown's most exclusive department store.

This caused Guinyard to jump out of his seat. "Why should you need good grades to shine shoes?" he asked. He was promptly tossed out of school for the day. "It was the first time I started thinking about racial mat-ters," Joe said.

His mother would have preferred him concentrating on his classwork. Beginning with the masters who had punished their slaves for reading the Bible, blacks had historically been deprived of education, which is precisely why so many craved it. Tens of thousands of them had come to the North not for economic reasons, but rather to obtain something other than a sham education for their children. One of Lillie Barrow's proudest moments would be when Vunies, just two generations removed from slavery and the most knowledge-hungry kid in the house, graduated from college and returned to Duffield as a teacher.

Joe showed as little desire for learning in the Motor City as he did in Alabama. Of average intelligence and with little formal learning under his belt, he was initially assigned to the third grade at Duffield. This in itself wasn't unusual, as children from inferior school systems in the South or foreign countries often were set back two or three grades until they could catch up in their studies.

But school, with all of its assemblies, fire drills, and endless lessons, bored him. Years later he admitted, "I'd rather have been anyplace else than in that classroom trying to listen to something I didn't understand." The only part he liked was when the teacher allowed him to carry the flag at assembly. For those special days his mother made sure he had on a freshly starched white shirt and a blue tie. "No way I could mess that up," he said of his flag-carrying duties.

The more difficult tasks continued to vex him. By the time he was fifteen he was seriously behind in basic reading, writing, and math skills, a situation made even more embarrassing when Vunies was promoted past him. He felt self-conscious, a husky country kid squeezed into a too-small desk and stuck for eternity inside a sixth-grade classroom. Even when by chance he knew the answer to a teacher's question, he had a hard time expressing it. His speech impediment, which had caused him a good share of grief down South, inspired the same kind of teasing at Duffield. He'd already decided the best course of action was simply to clam up.

One day a classmate was asked by her father, "What's Joe Barrow do in school?"

"Pop," she replied, "he just looks out the window."

Chapter Two

A Punch In
Either Hand

*We worked out in the ring plenty of times. We
were in the same age bracket, all of us young
guys. Joe had a good left hook and left hand. He
had a punch we called the D.O.A.— a left hook
to the stomach and a right cross to the head. If
you couldn't get out of the way of both of them
at the same time, you'd be dead on your ass . . .
that's what it really stood for.*

—WALTER SMITH

$\mathcal{I}$t was a well-meaning teacher named Vada Schwader who gently suggested that Joe Barrow might be better off educating his hands instead of
his mind. So, when he was sixteen, the decision was made to enroll him
into the Bronson Trade School, an all-boys vocational school. For the next
year or so he made shelves, cabinets, tables, and assorted knickknacks,
pieces that he brought home to furnish the family's rather spartan quarters.

Looking back on his Bronson days, Joe concluded that he was a "pretty good" cabinetmaker. Unfortunately, the family couldn't eat wood. The
Depression had kicked Detroit, and especially Black Bottom, right in the
teeth. Between 1929 and 1932 auto production fell by three-quarters, cost-
ing tens of thousands of workers their livelihoods. Blacks, the last hired and
first fired even when the economy was rolling along, suffered a disproportionate share of the layoffs. At one point an estimated 80 percent of
Detroit's black workers were idle, including every male member of the
Barrow-Brooks family. To make matters worse, hard times here were different than in the South. In Alabama, no matter how rough things got, you
could still raise your own vegetables and hogs. Not so in Detroit where the

homestead was surrounded by acres of concrete. As much as it must have pricked Pat Brooks's pride to do so, the family accepted relief checks.

For the first time in memory Joe, whose limited wardrobe included hand-me-downs donated by sympathetic teachers at Duffield, was hungry. When he wasn't working a lathe at Bronson, he was out doing odd jobs, delivering groceries, shoveling coal, and doing whatever else he could to contribute to the family welfare.

Not long after Joe entered Bronson, his mother came up with another use for his hands: the violin. It seems incredible in retrospect, but Lillie Barrow had convinced herself that her budding heavyweight had the makings of a musician—this despite the fact that Joe's only acquaintance with an instrument was fooling around with a mouth harp when he was a little boy. Somehow she scraped together the change needed for weekly lessons and instrument rental.

How many lessons Joe took is anyone's guess—anywhere from just one to twenty, depending on who is telling the story—but it's a fact that he never even bothered to learn the scale. He felt awkward with the violin placed in his big mitts, and the sound that he produced stood hair on end. He took a good deal of teasing as he lumbered, shamefaced, to and from his lesson at a small music school at Woodward and Warren Avenues. If Joe wasn't exactly the next Fritz Kreisler, there was a tenuous connection between him and America's most popular concert violinist. One day about the time that Kreisler was making a splash with his new operetta, *Sissy*, some wiseguy called violin-toting Joe the same; fed up, he crashed the instrument over the fellow's head.

Given the circumstances, it would have been easy for Joe to drift into the same life of petty crime and small-time hustle that claimed so many of his contemporaries during Prohibition and the Great Depression. Big for his age, facing an uncertain future, needing to make money, and inclined to be a follower, not a leader, he was ripe for exploitation.

Joe's formative years coincided exactly with the ascendence of the Purple Gang. This loose affiliation of Jewish thugs centered around several sets of brothers who had grown up together on the lower east side. Beginning in the early twenties the Purples were involved in a variety of notorious activities including kidnapping, extortion, bootlegging, labor racketeering, prostitution, and—their specialty—contract murder. Before the gang fell apart in the middle thirties, it had committed an estimated five hundred murders. Members were generally suspected of having participated in the quintessential tommy-gun slaying of the era, the St. Valentine's Day Massacre.

"They only used colored people to do the really dirty jobs," said Joe. "Their connections went all the way down to Louisiana and out to Al

Capone in Chicago. They operated from the Detroit River. We'd see police stop trucks—bootleg liquor and stolen goods. Sometimes we saw the police take bodies away after a murder. Hastings Street was a bad street."

Although reading the sordid tales of crime that filled the dailies "twisted" his stomach, Joe hung around corners with a group of less lethal wanna-bes known as the Catherine Street Gang. While apparently never a full-fledged member, he sometimes was recruited into fist fights when the honor of the neighborhood allegedly was at stake. "I got a reputation as a good hard puncher, and they were always after me to join them," he said. "I didn't want to because those guys would play some pretty bad tricks on people."

On one occasion gang members tried to convince Joe to grab somebody so they could rob him. Luckily, another set of eyes was trained on Joe. They belonged to a black patrolman named Henderson "Ben" Turpin. With his stocky build, shaved bullet-shaped head, and brace of pearl-handled revolvers, the brutal and ignorant Turpin, a former shoeshine boy from Kentucky, commanded respect. According to Pearl Johnson, who was raised in a family of fourteen on Sherman Street, he usually got it.

Johnson would attend evening shows at the Catherine Theater and find the off-duty Turpin holding court in the lobby. "He'd sit in a chair at the entrance doors and observe people as they came in. If the line in front of the candy counter needed to move, he'd say, 'Hey, fella, move up there!' And if someone had their hat on, he'd say, 'Hey, let's get that hat off!' He wasn't paid for it. He was just fulfilling his role as neighborhood guardian."

Turpin's exploits, which ranged from acts of bravery to outright buffoonery, could fill a book. An example from his service jacket is typical of the many complaints filed against him. One spring day officers were dispatched to break up a ruckus caused when Turpin and a female friend were caught *flagrante delicto* inside his car. Three passersby, "suspecting that sexual intercourse was taking place," remarked, "Give it to her, big boy." Turpin, trousers and revolver in hand, held the trio of citizens at gunpoint until he was convinced that they had learned "they could not get away with their smart remarks."

Such complaints failed to deter Turpin, who was respectfully called Mister Ben by wary youths. Nobody knows for sure how many people he killed during his quarter century of service. Estimates run as high as twenty, including the well-publicized shooting of a Purple Gang bodyguard, Louie Bryant, gunned down one night outside a drugstore on St. Antoine.

When he wasn't manhandling loiterers or chasing down thugs, Turpin, who liked his sports, enjoyed dropping in at the Brewster Center. The two-story red brick building, still standing at 637 Brewster between St. Antoine and Hastings, was the Bernard Ginsberg branch of the Detroit

Public Library until an addition and a name change converted it into the city's first community center for black citizens. It opened October 25, 1929, just eleven days after Turpin had dispatched Louie Bryant to that great speakeasy in the sky.

Today the building is named the Wheeler Center in honor of its first director, Leon "Toy" Wheeler, a one-time basketball standout from Indianapolis, who in 1919 had become Detroit's first black recreation worker. Wheeler was aided in his efforts by Atler "Kid" Ellis, a former sailor and Philadelphia prizefighter whose skill in sewing sail canvas had led him to repairing gym equipment and, ultimately, to the job of athletic trainer. Inside the basement gym, hundreds of black youths participated in a range of athletic programs including basketball, track, swimming, and boxing.

Turpin paid particular attention to one of Ellis's pupils, a big, strong kid whose threadbare clothes had inspired the good-natured nickname of Joe Bare from his fellow boxers. Turpin, aware that few young blacks ever climbed out of the ghetto, had always made it his business to watch out for the neighborhood's promising athletes. On that evening when the Catherine Street Gang was trying to talk Joe into participating in a robbery, the bearlike cop hustled over and intervened in his usual strong-armed fashion.

"Thank God," Joe remembered in his autobiography, "he had some kind of policeman's instinct, and he chased me away from the gang and took me home. I'll never forget the thankful look my mother had on her face that night when he pushed me through the door."

Most of the Catherine Street Gang, added Joe, wound up in jail.

➔❮

After Joe became famous, any number of people swore that they had seen it coming, that he had always exhibited the kind of behavior that made them think, "Someday Joe Barrow will be champion of the world." Tall tales abounded. Relatives in Alabama entertained reporters with stories of young Joe sometimes beating up three or four kids in succession.

To the best of Joe's recollection, however, he rarely fought as a child. Once he and his stepbrother, Pat Brooks Jr., got into an argument, and Joe wound up getting beaned in the head with a brick; he carried the scar to the end of his life. Other times he felt obliged to stand up for his sisters in some petty spat or played a game of "knocking," where the idea was to dare someone to knock a chip of wood off your shoulder. Joe's most memorable scrap was when he got into a schoolyard altercation with a classmate when they lived near Camp Hill. A teacher rushed over to break it up. "She whipped me for it," Joe recalled in his typically dry humor, "but she didn't whip him. I guess that gave him the decision."

After moving to the city, Joe started messing around with his fists, as teenaged boys are wont to do. According to deLeon Barrow, there was a barn in the back of the house on Macomb Street. The boys built a boxing ring in its attic. "That's where Joe really started out," he insisted. Joe later recalled how he and a good friend, Amsey Rinson (later a champion amateur lightweight) "used to spar around my backyard every time we got a chance. He'd said that if we went over to the gym, maybe we could borrow some boxing gloves. We just never got around to it, then."

Joe's childhood heroes included Jack Dempsey, heavyweight champion of the world from 1919 until losing to Gene Tunney in 1926. The Manassas Mauler, who enjoyed an amazing public following, retired from the ring in 1932, having lost just five of sixty-nine fights and attracting million-dollar gates. "We listened to his fights on the radio," Joe said. "It was always Dempsey does this, Dempsey does that."

Vunies, a temperamental sort who some family members described as "a red-headed peckerwood," saw absolutely no foreshadowing of future greatness in Joe as a young teen.

"I've always been amazed over how he turned out to be such a great fighter," said the youngest Barrow, "because he never exhibited the kind of tendencies you'd expect a fighter to have. Joe didn't have an aggressive personality. We were taught that you get along with people, you don't fight them. I was the fighter in the family. He was always calm, gentle, and I honestly never knew him to have a single fight."

As proof, Vunies recounted the day when she noticed some commotion outside their Catherine Street home. "Someone was running around the house, and it was Joe. He was running from some boys and he couldn't get into the house fast enough. He said, 'Open the door the next time I come around.' So he took one more turn around the house, and by that time someone had opened the door for him."

Joe had put on some size between then and the time he entered Bronson. He loved baseball and was a playground terror during soccer matches, his heavy work boots threatening to splinter the shins of anyone unlucky enough to get in the way of one of his powerful kicks. He had also continued to dabble in boxing. One day inside the Bronson gym, he tugged on the gloves and, moments later, floored his opponent with a single left-handed punch. The swift execution caught the attention of an older student, a good-looking ladies' man and promising amateur named Thurston McKinney.

"Man," McKinney reportedly said in awe, "throw that violin away!"

Like so many other young men trapped in the depths of the Great Depression, McKinney was looking toward a ring career as his ticket out of his environment. He produced dog-eared issues of *The Ring*, boxing's bible, and showed Joe stories of the money and adulation enjoyed by top fighters. Even as an amateur, McKinney explained, a fighter got merchandise checks redeemable at local merchants. The talk turned Joe's head. He journeyed down to the Brewster Center and joined Atler Ellis's day class in the fall of 1930. He did it on the sly, borrowing the money from one of his sisters and not telling his folks what he was up to. Later he used the money he was supposed to be spending on his music lessons for his amateur dues and locker rental. Legend has it that Joe left the house every day with his gloves hidden inside his violin case.

Ken Offet, a bantamweight on his way to turning pro in July 1931, transferred from the night class in November 1930 and was soon placed in the ring with the awkward sixteen-year-old, who reportedly had some potential.*

At five-foot-ten and 150 pounds, Joe had four inches and twenty-five pounds on his ring opponent. Nonetheless, Offet almost tore the newcomer's head off. "I hit Joe upside his jaw," he remembered. "He went into the ropes, and I swarmed all over him. Then they called time and broke it up." Fourteen years later, Offet ran into Louis during an exhibition tour in England. "He hit me so hard," Joe told an audience of servicemen, "I thought he was the heavyweight champion of the world."

At first Joe was just another face in the crowd. Detroit's gyms were overflowing during the dirty thirties. Blame it on hard times or the universal press coverage of such popular prizefighters as Dempsey, but just about every boy in the sadly out-of-gear Motor City was at one time or another throwing phantom haymakers in his bedroom.

"This was a fight town," Offet stressed. "It seemed like everybody wanted to be a boxer." Scores of schools, churches, rec centers, and neighborhood clubs offered instruction. Lovers of the fight game could watch amateurs for twenty-five cents at places like Arena Gardens or Sullivan's Athletic Club; a buck bought a seat at Olympia Stadium on Grand River to watch the pros go at it. Brewster's basement gym was packed wall-to-wall with young men shadow boxing, skipping rope, and attacking the speed bag.

The growth of organized amateur competition helped fuel their dreams of fistic glory. The Amateur Athletic Union had been staging tournaments since its establishment in 1888, awarding champions on local, state, and national levels. Starting in 1923, these competitions were supple-

---

* Between 1910 and 1970 boxing authorities in the United States and Great Britain recognized nine weight divisions: heavyweight (over 175 pounds), light-heavyweight (up to 175), middleweight (up to 154), welterweight (up to 142), lightweight (up to 133), featherweight (up to 122), bantamweight (up to 116), flyweight (up to 112), and paperweight (up to 105). Since 1970, five other weight divisions (cruiserweight, super-middleweight, super-bantamweight, super-flyweight, and light-flyweight) have been created. Then, as always, young fighters typically moved up several classes as they matured. Today the heavyweight class includes any fighter over 195 pounds.

mented by the Golden Gloves, an annual tournament created by the *Chicago Tribune* (the name was first used in New York in 1927) and introduced to Detroit in 1931. The *Detroit Mirror*, destined to fold one year later, was the original local sponsor, followed by the *Free Press*. Champions received a tiny jeweled pair of boxing gloves. These symbols of fighting primacy were as treasured as the Ford work badges many of their fathers and uncles proudly pinned to their suit lapels on Sunday.

Golden Gloves applicants typically were solicited beginning in October (though more serious aspirants trained and fought year-round). Those who were interested simply filled out an entry form printed in the sponsoring newspaper, cut it out, and mailed it in. The only requirements were that applicants be at least sixteen years old, in "good physical condition," and registered with the Michigan Amateur Athletic Union. Those with no boxing experience were entered in the novice class; those with at least one victory in an AAU-sanctioned bout competed in the open class. Most entrants were affiliated with an athletic club, ethnic society, or church group. Those who weren't fought as "unattached."

Promoters and participants recognized the Golden Gloves as a stepping stone to the professional ranks. They all knew of the great lightweight Barney Ross, who had been a Golden Gloves champ in New York and Chicago in 1929. In the thirties there were sometimes as many as a couple of thousand entries, divided into east and west sections of the city. Pairings were determined by draw, with members of the same athletic association or boxing club often squaring off against each other.

The attraction for young competitive blacks was that the Golden Gloves did not discriminate. According to one alliterative Detroit reporter, "The Golden Gloves might be billed as an All-Nations show. There were milling Maltese and pugnacious Poles, iron-fisted Irish and scrappy Scots, impulsive Italians and energetic English, clever Czechs and daring Dutchmen—a real cosmopolitan bunch of guys." Conspicuously absent from this rundown of ethnic stereotypes is any mention of black boxers, who usually were described in newspaper accounts as "satchell-footed Negroes" or "brown pineapple tossers."

The six-week single-elimination tournament began the first week of January. The Naval Armory on East Jefferson Avenue was an especially busy spot, though venues ranged from simple clubhouses and church basements to high school gyms and YMCAs all over the metropolitan area. The climactic event, the finals, was held in mid-February at "the big place," Olympia Stadium. It was easily the biggest boxing show of the year in Michigan.

At the end there were only sixteen champions—novice- and open-class winners in eight weight divisions—which meant that there were considerably more disappointments than successes. Many entrants were fighters in name only, as they lacked the proper skill, training, or disposition to knock another fellow's head off. (In fact, fear, laziness, or a lack of transportation accounted for one-third of them never reporting to their assigned arena on fight night.) A few were so intent on trying to remember how to properly arrange their hands and feet that they never got off a punch. Some disregarded their textbook and geared their entire strategy around letting loose one haymaker; others flailed away for the entire three rounds. Most of the knockouts were of the technical kind, a referee rushing in to stop a bout before an obviously overmatched beginner could be seriously hurt.

Marian Berman Kohlenberg, who grew up in the Jewish neighborhood bordering Black Bottom, remembered how her older brother Irv bought a pair of gloves at this time, filled out an application, and fantasized about joining the ranks of famous pugilists:

> We sparred around our living room on Clairmount Street (between 12th Street and LaSalle). We pivoted, we ducked. A jab with the right, guarding the face with the left.
>
> Irv kept his gloves on his dresser. When he was away, I, the youngest of eight children, would tenderly touch them, not daring to try them on.
>
> Then it happened: Irv was scheduled to fight in a tournament. I thought my world was going to end. But I wasn't alone. My older sisters huddled and whispered a lot that day. And my father, Morris, smoked and coughed more than ever.
>
> The boxer, my dad, brother Dave, and cousins Joe and Sam Hein drove off to the arena. Mother Hilda and the rest of us anticipated a long day waiting at home for them. But shortly thereafter, the car drove up. The fight was described as "brief." One blow and it was over. My brother hit the floor. The next thing he knew, he was lying on the bench in the dressing room. That ended Irv's professional boxing aspirations.

The better boxers, whether or not they were Golden Glovers, were grabbed by promoters to fill local fight cards. The bouts, typically between three and six rounds duration, provided action for bettors, copy to fill out spare inches on the sports pages, and a forum by which prospects could be judged. Amateurs were compensated with merchandise checks, ribbons, medals, and trophies, but that was just hardware to someone desiring the sweeter things in life.

For a select few, the payoff was a potentially lucrative professional career, although the odds of making it anywhere near the top or surviving on ring earnings alone were terribly long. The experiences of a pair of

Detroit boxers, one white and the other black, are representative of their era. Both were middleweights who entered the pro ranks in 1932, the absolute bottom of the Depression.

As a boy Jackie Sherman lived in the same Jewish neighborhood as the Purple Gang. Today, Parkinson's disease has affected the old fighter's speech, but not his guys-and-dolls style of recall. "I grew up with those guys," said Sherman, who was eighteen when he began fighting for money. "I was a pretty rough kid. I didn't back off from nobody."

Like so many other aspirants, Sherman became a club fighter, eking out a living battling other ham-and-eggers in smokey basements for a few bucks a fight while waiting for a shot at a ranked contender. That opportunity never came.

At its worst professional boxing was a sad, subterranean world of flattened noses, cauliflower ears, and mashed brains, populated by hoods, hustlers, unscrupulous managers, and a handful of powerful promoters who determined the pairings. Sherman told the story of his older and more talented brother, Morrie, a former state champion who was reduced to throwing a fight to Barney Ross in order to get a payday. "The way the deal was worked out, Morrie would go down in six. Instead, he took a dive in the second. 'Why'd you do that for?' I asked. He said, 'I knew I was gonna get paid, so why take all that punishment?' Morrie was a very practical guy."

Sherman's manager was Eddie Fletcher, the ring name of this failed fighter who had carved out a second career as a kingpin of the Purple Gang. Sherman denies ever being pressed into strong-arming for the Purples or being asked to throw a fight (others aren't so sure), but that just may be a case of having been saved by the bell. In late 1933, Fletcher and another top Purple, Abe Axler, were found machine-gunned to death in the back seat of a car parked on a lonely country road. This ended their relationship, said Sherman, whose varied post-ring career included being an extra in a Joe Palooka movie, running a gambling hall that fronted as a veterans club, and working as a pit boss in Las Vegas.

Holman Williams had a considerably longer and more noteworthy career than Jackie Sherman. In fact, some observers have called this forgotten product of the Brewster gym one of the best fighters, pound for pound, who ever lived—"the perfect fighter," said one.

Born in Florida in 1912, Williams moved to Detroit and began training at the Brewster Center as soon as it opened. It wasn't long before he was helping Atler Ellis train other young boxers, including Joe Barrow. In a sixteen-year career that finally flamed out in 1948, Williams had 187 fights in three weight divisions (moving up to challenge middleweights and light-heavyweights) and lost just thirty of them. A scientific, defense-minded boxer, he was knocked out only three times. His victims included some of the biggest names in the sport, notably Charlie Burley, Louis "Kid" Cocoa, and Archie Moore. His speed, ring generalship, and strong chin resulted in his being ranked a top-ten contender by *The Ring* for several years.

"Williams was a good puncher but he fractured his hands all the time," observed Ken Offet. "His knuckles would always be split. The bad hands kept him from going for the head. Instead he'd cut a man up with uppercuts."

But even someone as skilled as Williams endured a lifetime of paltry purses and dashed hopes. The reason? In addition to being the wrong color, he was *too* good. No topflight white fighter would risk his ranking against a Negro, especially one as talented as Williams. As a result he and other gifted black fighters were forced to the outer edges of boxing's big-time circuit, typically taking turns battling each other several times in the same year. Williams entered the ropes against the Cocoa Kid fourteen times alone.

The sadly unheralded Williams died in 1970, having never come close to a title fight. "You'd almost cry to see his hands when he got old," said Offet. "His hands were broken, and the bones had mended wrong."

Williams's greatest contribution to ring history may be the instruction he provided young Joe Barrow. Atler Ellis was known for being strong on conditioning and discipline, said Offet. "You had to come to the gym, you had to train hard. Conditioning was very important to him." But it was Williams who worked closely with Joe on footwork, combinations, and strategy.

Joe was intoxicated by the saunalike air and *whap-whap-whap* of the speed bag. He enjoyed doing his roadwork on nearby Belle Isle, gulping in the early-morning air and relishing the solitude as he rumbled along the pathways of the scenic park. He loved the rough camaraderie and singleness of purpose that characterized workouts. Having grown infatuated with the idea of developing into a professional fighter, he followed McKinney's example and dropped out of Bronson after a year to concentrate on training. He did it with the blessings of his mother, who had received a visit from his music teacher.

Vunies recalled the scene. "Of course, my mother believed in discipline, and she was ready to discipline him to the heights. But he convinced her that he just didn't like the violin and that he wanted to be a boxer. Nobody in our house ever did anything that she didn't believe in." Joe, who was known for his persistence, got his way.

One member of the Brewster crew, Charles "Red" House, a talented middleweight, was also a good enough ballplayer to later play a season in the Negro leagues. Joe, who sometimes shagged flies for the Detroit Stars, occasionally mused about switching sports, but Holman Williams kept him on track. His earning potential as a prizefighter far outweighed any he may have had as a lumbering, lefthanded first sacker, Williams reminded him.

Joe, tired of being used as just a sparring partner, was itching to test himself. The growing youngster had passed 154 pounds, the ceiling for middleweights, and moved into the light-heavyweight class. The Christ Church Athletic Club, one of the city's premier centers for boxing instruction, was managed by Billy Stewart, whose several Golden Gloves champions included his twin sons. One day Joe discovered that he had been scheduled to meet one of Stewart's other prize pupils, Johnny Miler, in a three-rounder at the Naval Armory.

House and Williams and the rest of the Brewster crew knew that Miler was one tough cookie. "Are you afraid?" House asked Joe.

"No," he replied.

He should have been. Miler, born Johnny Miletich in Hocking, Iowa, in 1910, had dropped out of tenth grade to follow his father into the coal mines. When he was twenty he moved to Detroit and got a short-lived job on the assembly line. Laid off and with nothing better to occupy his time, the six-foot-one, 175-pounder rattled the speed bag under Stewart's instruction. Miler (as he was known after an announcer mangled his Croatian surname) quickly acquired a reputation as a hard-nosed craftsman. At the time he was to face Joe, he'd already had as many as twenty amateur fights.

"He was no knock-out artist," Stanley Evans, another promising fighter of the time, said of Miler. "He was tough, but he was cagey—a bee on a horse's rump. He wasn't about to stand in there and punch it out; his tactic was to bite and scram."

Joe fought Miler in the early part of 1932. He was seventeen years old, four years younger than his infinitely more savvy opponent.[*]

"Fought" is a generous term. "Survived" would be more precise.

---

[*] There has always been considerable confusion in trying to fix the date of Joe's amateur debut. No accounts of it could be found in the surviving sports pages of the period. Relying strictly on vague memories, Louis and his biographers typically placed it in late 1932 or early 1933, but this appears to be off by about a year. The key is that Miler is always described as having already represented the United States in the 1932 Olympic Games at the time of his historic tête-à-tête with Joe, making their confrontation appear to be an even greater mismatch than it actually was. However, Miler's nephew, Richard Buckheim, has a scrapbook of mostly undated clippings which suggest Miler had to have fought Joe either several weeks before winning Detroit's 1932 Golden Gloves light-heavyweight title (possibly in the first round of elimination fights in that year's tournament), or soon afterwards as a tune-up for the Olympic trials in San Francisco.

In any event, the summer games opened in August with Miler, the first Detroit boxer ever to compete in the Olympics, losing a controversial decision to favorite James J. Murphy of Ireland. After the games Miler sparred with former heavyweight champion Max Schmeling (who had just lost the title to Jack Sharkey), then broke into the professional ranks with a $250 payday against Leon Jasinski in Grand Rapids. In early 1933, about the time given by some for the Louis fight, Miler was pummeling Flash Riser in front of three thousand fans at Olympia Stadium to become Michigan's new heavyweight champion; meanwhile, Joe had already captured the local Golden Gloves crown.

According to Freddie Guinyard, one of several friends in attendance that night, the novice confidently thought his size and sledgehammer right hand would slow Miler down.

At the bell, Joe moved in slowly, shot a left jab, then crashed a right across Miler's jaw. Joe stepped back to watch him fall. But instead of toppling over, Miler was all over Joe, finally depositing him on his bottom.

As Joe later recalled, his head was "going around like a top" when the bell ending the round sounded. "They must have poured half of Lake St. Clair on me at intermission."

At the beginning of the second round, a right hand "landed on the only unbruised spot on my chin," said Joe, who was knocked down six more times. At the bell his handler "picked up the pieces that used to be me and dropped them on the stool in my corner. Miler must have been arm-weary by the third. I stayed on my feet, but he won. He was too far ahead of me in everything."

Miler collected a twenty-five-dollar merchandise check and moved on to the Olympic Games in Los Angeles before starting a four-year professional career that included a title shot against "Slapsie" Maxie Rosenbloom. He left the ring in 1937, started a new career as a policeman and a state agent in Iowa, then retired to a farm where he died in 1976. Nobody suspected that the old bachelor quietly tending his petunia garden had once knocked the stuffing out of the great Joe Louis.

Which, by the way, is what Joseph Louis Barrow was soon to become known as. There are variations of the story of how and when he acquired his ring name. The most accepted version is that he ran out of room while painstakingly filling out, in giant letters, a fight application form, possibly for the Miler bout. At some point during his amateur days, one of his sisters presented him with a satin jacket with *Joe Louis* stitched on its back. Some have said the dropped surname also was designed to fool his mother, who supposedly didn't know or approve of his fighting. In reality, at the time of the Miler fight, Lillie Barrow knew and halfheartedly supported Joe's decision. It was Joe's stepdad who preferred he find himself a steady factory job. At any rate, the name change soon became permanent, although newspapers continued to spell it "Joe Lewis" through most of his amateur career.

Miler had battered Joe's ego and body. Joe was "all skinned up," remembered one of his friends. He handed his seven-dollar merchandise check to Poppa Brooks and got a lecture in return. Surely there were better and easier ways to make a living, his stepfather said. Not long afterward Joe and his brother Lonnie woke early one morning to join a long line of similarly hungry and dispirited men looking for work at Briggs Manufacturing.

"When it came to noontime we were like dead," Joe recalled. "Alonzo took the dollar we got from my mother and went out to buy some hot dogs while I held his place in line. We didn't know any other kind of meat but hot dogs in those days. Finally in the late afternoon, we got to the employment window. Lonnie didn't get a job, but I was lucky. They hired me for twenty-five dollars a week. Our feet were aching so we thought they'd fall off by the time we got home."

Briggs, which built bodies for several automakers, was nicknamed "the slaughterhouse" by the thousands of blacks toiling inside its several plants. Joe was assigned one of the traditional "Negro jobs": pushing truck bodies to the paint sprayer on the assembly line. It was hot, grueling work. "The tape would come off the body-covers and land on the floor, sticky side up. The tape would gum onto the dolly wheels, and you'd get a real workout pushing those truck bodies. I would leave the factory around five o'clock, go home for dinner, and then go over to the gym."

It's unclear how long Joe worked at Briggs and whether he quit or was laid off. In any event, Holman Williams and Thurston McKinney, both of whom emerged victorious in the 1932 Detroit Golden Gloves, encouraged Joe to stick with boxing. Sometime that summer Williams helped arrange a three-rounder with Otis Thomas, a local black with a growing reputation. In his first bout since the Miler debacle, Joe employed one of Williams's combinations and quickly put away Thomas with a left hook and a right to the jaw.

"It was my first official knockout," he said. "I was on top of the world."

His next thirteen opponents were at the bottom. Each hit the canvas, the victim of one of his powerful straight-arrow punches. "I could punch you and knock you out, if I could catch you," he later said of this period. "I had a lot to learn—there's no such thing as 'natural.'" He understood that he had to "train damn hard" in order to be a success.

To a considerable degree, the growing stable of Brewster boxers helped train each other. Although they fought for a variety of neighborhood clubs, thanks to Ellis and Williams they had a similarity of style that allowed them to tear up the amateur ranks. In 1933, for example, six Golden Gloves finalists were products of Brewster's gym. All but one emerged as champions.

According to Walter Smith, who broke in under Ellis and Williams in 1930, the Brewster style consisted of "left jab, right hand, left hook. Boxing all the time. Moving back and forth. This is the Detroit style. You gotta have a good left hand. That's the Detroit style."

Joe was considered a top prospect, but no more so than the others. "He used to struggle to win our club championship," said Eddie Futch, a Golden Gloves champ in the lightweight class, "that's how many good fighters we had." Featherweight Curtis Shipp and middleweight Clinton

Bridges joined McKinney, Futch, and Williams as highly regarded boxers. There also were such up-and-comers as the baby-faced welterweight Dave Clark, lanky heavyweight Lorenzo Pack, and Joe's one-time backyard sparring partner Amsey Rinson, a middleweight who had learned to handle his dukes while selling newspapers on the street corner.

James Ware, a frequent observer of workouts at Brewster's gym, was asked if he thought at the time that Joe was bound for greatness. "No, I didn't," he responded. "He was a slow, awkward fellow. They'd put him in against flyweights to improve his speed. That's how he got quick hands. He was already a heavy hitter."

Smith, a welterweight, often worked with Joe. "He liked to spar with guys in a lower weight class," said Smith, who went on to train such future Detroit champions as Thomas Hearns at the world-famous Kronk gym. "He believed their quickness made him move faster and hit harder."

Futch, a beelike 130-pounder, was another sparring partner whose Brewster experience resulted in a long career tutoring such notables as Ken Norton, Joe Frazier, Larry Holmes, and Alexis Arguello. At first Futch put off Joe's overtures. But Joe rarely took no for an answer.

"I never knew anybody so persistent," Futch told Dave Anderson. "If you had an apple, he'd beg and beg for a bite until you gave him a bite. So he always got me into the ring to spar with him. But I told myself, if he wants me to work with him, I've got to know when those punches are coming. I've got to know the moves he makes before he punches, because he never telegraphs anything. The left hook came out of nowhere. Bang. If he hit you with a shot, you never saw the punch coming. You just saw a light in your head. Like a camera flash going off. Bang."

As word spread of how he dented the punching bag, Joe began to enjoy his first taste of notoriety and hero worship. Local followers of the fight game nodded their heads when his name was mentioned, and kids started following him around.

One was a slim youngster named Walker Smith—known around the neighborhood as Junior (and not to be confused with Walter Smith)—who would wait every day for Joe to stroll past on his way to working out. To Joe's embarrassment, Junior would insist on carrying his bag to the gym, which naturally prompted some ribbing about Joe's rough skills already commanding a personal valet.

Joe liked the boy's iridescent smile and sense of style—Junior could walk a city block on his hands—although he really didn't know anything about him. Joe lost his juvenile porter when the boy and his mother moved to New York in November 1932. But the two would become reacquainted in the army a decade later, by which time Junior had grown into a promising welterweight named "Sugar Ray" Robinson.

In his first full year as an amateur, Joe slugged his way to the local light-heavyweight championship in the novice class. His Golden Gloves debut was January 11, 1933, at Detroit Stadium, an overblown name for a drafty facility located at East Forest and Hastings. Representing the Detroit Amateur Association, the organization for which most Brewster boxers fought, he disposed of Joe Baldyga in the first round in front of one thousand fans. Joe's event was just one of eighteen elimination bouts that Wednesday evening. Many left talking about another black Lewis, John Lewis, a member of the 1928 Olympic track team and "a fair boxer for a beginner," observed a reporter.

Two weeks later, John Lewis was beaten and quickly forgotten while Joe scored two first-round knockouts. In the semifinals, Joe flattened Robert Campbell in the last round to advance to the finals. On February 22 in front of a packed house of 13,000 at Olympia, Joe stepped into the ring late in the evening wearing the blue and gold silks given to all finalists.

His opponent was Joe Biskey. As the *Free Press* decribed it, "Biskey, strong man from the Naval Armory, refused to heed the advice of his seconds to 'get in close and mix it' with Joe Louis. . . That permitted Lewis, a terrific puncher, to get a clean shot at Biskey's chin."

Joe's third-round KO, his sixth straight as a Golden Glover, gave him the light-heavyweight title and earned him a silver trophy as the most promising novice of the tournament. Joe, one reporter wryly noted, had "started out in the footsteps of Fritz Kreisler but he abruptly switched to the path of Jack Dempsey. . . . He's been in the boxing ring instead of on the concert stage ever since."

Despite his crowd-pleasing string of knockouts, Joe was not considered invincible, at least not yet. The *Free Press* sent him to Chicago for the nationals where he was outpointed by the heavier and more experienced Clinton Bridges, a Brewster stablemate. That spring he also fought for the AAU championship in Boston, losing in the title bout with Max Marek. Marek, a former end on the Notre Dame football team, skillfully avoided Joe's heavy punches while delivering enough hits of his own to win the battle of the scorecard. (Years later Marek squeezed his victory for all it was worth, operating a tavern in Chicago that had a sign encouraging passersby to drop in, buy a cold one, and shake the hand of the man who beat Joe Louis.)

Traveling to distant cities in the company of other young fighters, away from the security blanket of his family, was an eye-opening experience, Joe said later. "I saw things I wanted that I had never really known about. I met important people and wanted to be important, too. Doctors, lawyers, big time gamblers would come up and talk to me and encourage me."

As Joe progressed through the amateur ranks, his knockout magic made him an increasingly popular choice for local fight cards. But his ferocity in the ring continued to belie a remarkably even temperament. Girls were attracted to his shy sweetness. Adults commented on his diffidence. His friends liked his quiet sense of humor, evident even when the teasing was at his expense. "He'd laugh at the jokes, the same as we would," a companion recalled. "We all liked Joe. He had a hell of a disposition."

A family friend, Jesse Walker, remembered an illuminating incident from this period.

"We were all at Joe's house on Mullett," he said, "getting all dressed up to go to the Graystone Ballroom. Joe liked to borrow clothes from his brother, Lonnie, who worked at the A & P on Joseph Campeau and liked to buy nice clothes with his money. Just before we left, Lonnie spotted Joe wearing his socks and demanded that he remove them. We all went to the Graystone that night, including Joe—without his socks."

Joe's success was remarkable in light of his impoverished situation. He trained on a diet of hot dogs and ice cream, two of his favorite (and cheapest) junk foods, and ran roadwork in ratty sneakers. He followed an on-again, off-again schedule in the gym, depending on what outside jobs he was working.

Meanwhile, he was suffering a management crisis. Atler Ellis quit the Brewster Center after a dispute with Toy Wheeler, shifting his instruction to Mount Olivet Baptist Church and eventually convincing several top athletes to compete for the club he had formed there. Holman Williams, who had turned professional in August 1932 after accompanying Johnny Miler to the Olympic trials, needed to focus on his own career and had less time for tutoring. Ellis was back in Joe's corner for his pursuit of the 1934 Golden Gloves title, but left his coaching duties of the Detroit Amateur Association temporarily, putting Joe in the hands of his replacement, George Slayton.

Slayton, described in various versions of Joe's life as his trainer, "never had a pair of gloves on in his life," sniffed Ken Offet. Slayton, who also went by the name of George Moody, was the prototypical Hastings Street hustler, dabbling in the usual activities—pimping, bootlegging, running numbers—before finally settling into a career as a bail bondsman. As a coach, Slayton was in over his head, but his connections would prove invaluable. It enabled him to introduce his nineteen-year-old pupil to the man who would exert the greatest influence on his professional aspirations.

In the summer of 1933, Slayton booked a three-rounder with Stanley Evans, who at the time was widely considered the town's finest light-heavyweight. "I had watched him train and I knew if he hit you, you were down," Evans said of his opponent. "I had to outsmart him. I had to have more ring generalship. I'd block his punch and counter, or beat him to the punch." Evans didn't knock Joe down, but he outpointed him for the decision. It was the last fight Joe would lose as an amateur.

Afterward Slayton brought a well-groomed, well-fed, middle-aged visitor into the dressing room. Joe later recorded his first impression of his patron-to-be, John Roxborough.

"This man had real class. He was a very light-skinned black man about six feet tall, and he weighed about 190 pounds. He didn't seem flashy, but stylish and rich-looking. He had a gray silk suit, the kind you don't buy off the rack. It made me look twice. His attitude was gentle, like a gentleman should be. Mr. Roxborough told me he liked the way I fought and he was interested in me. I couldn't understand why—hell, I'd just lost the fight. He told me to drop by his real estate office within the next couple of days."

→←

John Roxborough was a respected and well-known figure in Black Bottom, although Joe's mother undoubtedly frowned on how he made his living. Along with Everitt Watson, his partner in the real estate office they shared on St. Antoine, he operated the largest numbers racket in Detroit.

Numbers and similar lottery-like games had been a popular pastime among poor urban blacks long before Roxborough got into it in the 1920s. It was simple and inexpensive to play, a bettor putting down as little as a penny on a specific three-digit number. Each day the winning number was determined by stock market transactions or the pari-mutuel handles at a race track. Winners typically were paid off at odds of 600 to 1. Because bettors faced odds of 999 to 1, the difference gave bankers like Roxborough their profits. Publishing "dream books," dope sheets, and other gambling aids was an additional source of income.

It was hard to find someone who didn't play numbers. Every day salesmen (many of whom were listed as realtors in the city directory) fanned out over the neighborhood, collecting bets from a wide strata of society: maids, barbers, porters, housewives, the unemployed, even an occasional minister. The official protectors of the black community, people like patrolman Ben Turpin and Urban League director John Dancy, either regularly wagered themselves or simply looked the other way. "As I saw it," said Dancy, who willingly accepted large cash donations from racketeers for various charitable causes, "the gambling situation was only one of the little troubles affecting the Negro community." It was better to concentrate on the larger ones, he added.

That had always been Roxborough's view. The son of a New Orleans lawyer, he had moved to Detroit in 1899 when he was seven years old. He had light skin, the result of his mixed Scottish, Spanish, Creole, and Jamaican ancestry, and spoke nothing but Spanish and French when he arrived. He learned English and a good deal of Polish while growing up in an all-white neighborhood. According to Roxborough, "those Polish people were wonderful. I never knew I was a Negro until I made my first trip downtown."

Looking to follow in the footsteps of his brother Charles (who would become Michigan's first black legislator), he pursued a law degree at the University of Detroit. But he soon concluded that long years of study produced little payoff for even the most urbane and educated Negro. Tell a prospective employer that you were a college graduate—a rarity for members of any race in those days—and you'd be told that, oh yes, there was a porter's position available.

"To hell with education" was Roxborough's response. "What good would it do me? I made up my mind that when I got a chance to make money, no matter how, I'd take it. I would avoid embarrassing situations, like asking for a job when I was qualified. I also promised myself I'd help myself first and then I'd help my black brothers."

Roxborough became a bail bondsman, a color-blind profession that was responsible for him finding his true calling. One night he climbed out of bed to bail out a numbers operator from Kansas City. To show his appreciation, the racketeer invited Roxborough to Kansas City, where he filled him in on the workings and possibilities of his line of work. Detroit, he told Roxborough, was a gold mine. "The way Ford is bringing Negroes into the city, you can't miss."

And he didn't. His illicit income, when added to his above-board interests in real estate and insurance, allowed him to become that most treasured of black citizens—a "race man." He enriched not only himself but those far less fortunate, lending his time, money, and influence to benevolent organizations like the Young Negroes Progressive Association and acting as a financial guardian angel to struggling students and athletes. This kind of involvement wasn't unique to Roxborough. During the 1930s nearly every team in the Negro baseball leagues was bankrolled by black racketeers, including the Detroit Stars, who were kept afloat by Everitt Watson. Roxborough's partner in crime also underwrote the career of local heavyweight prospect Roscoe Toles.

Roxborough, a fine basketball player in his youth, recognized Joe's potential. Altruism aside, he knew that if the young fighter turned out to be a success, he stood to make a good deal of money managing his career. He took his protégé on a shopping spree, buying him bandages, rubbing alcohol, socks, shoes, trunks, and professional boxing gloves. He donated some of his old shirts and suits, which were altered to fit. He gave him pocket change when he needed it and switched his eating habits from junk food to a proper fighter's diet of steak, vegetables, and potatoes.

"Sometimes he'd invite me to his house for dinner," Joe remembered. "It was a beautiful house, and he had a good-looking and gracious wife. I loved it. I never saw black people living this way, and I was envious and watched everything he did."

When a divorce put a dent in Roxborough's resources, he used his connections to get Joe a job at the Rouge plant for $6.80 a day. But soon Joe took a leave of absence from Ford to concentrate on training for several upcoming tournaments.

He never returned. Instead, empowered by Roxborough's largesse and inspired by the fine things he saw attached to success, he marched through a half-dozen young men to become Detroit's 1934 Golden Gloves light-heavyweight titleholder in the open class.

This time around Joe and several of his friends fought for Mount Olivet Baptist Church (an association that must have pleased his mother). He started his quest by bombing Chico Golden with an opening-round left hook that the *Free Press* described as "a masterpiece." Golden, "a strong rugged lad, was out for quite a while."

Mark Beltaire, then a prep school student, was at the Naval Armory that night. "He hit the guy so hard, they didn't even bother to count him out," recalled Beltaire, who later worked for the *Detroit News* and the *Free Press*. "I remember the sound of his head hitting the floor. He laid there like a pancake while the doctor climbed over the ropes to help him.

"He eventually came around, but what I remember best is thinking, 'Holy God!' and then the fight being over. It was incredible. I've been to a lot of fights before and since, but I've never seen anything quite like it. I was absolutely amazed that anybody could hit that hard."

Over the next several weeks Joe and his nemesis, Stanley Evans, zipped past the elimination rounds, both knocking out all of their opponents through the semifinals. On the cold evening of February 16, they met at Olympia Stadium for the title.

Evans, who worked at Briggs when he wasn't representing the Highland Park Amateur Boxing Club, went into the fight as a slight favorite, due mainly to his victory over Joe the previous summer. He was described as "a rugged mauler who can take a punch as well as deliver one."

But "cool, skillful" Joe prevailed, reported the next day's *Free Press*. "Louis got the jump on Evans. Boxing carefully, he won the first round. In the second he landed a terrific left hook to Evans' jaw while the two were in the midst of a heated exchange. A right followed and Evans slipped to the floor. He was up without taking a count, however, and battled gamely for the remainder of the round.

"In the third round Evans, evidently realizing that he was behind, came out of his corner determined to slug it out with Louis. Joe, knowing he had won the first two rounds, played safe. He lost the final round after much hard slugging, but still had enough of an advantage to take the decision at the finish."

Joe then carried his lethal wallop to Chicago where he and seven other Detroit Golden Gloves winners participated in the Tournament of Champions. Golden Glovers had descended on Chicago Stadium from nine midwestern states, with the first night's program alone featuring 140 bouts. Seven thousand people watched two rings in action continuously from 6:30 P.M. to the wee hours of the morning.

Joe won his opening matches, flooring Ray Wozniak four times and then outpointing Harry Swanson. The next evening 15,000 howling fans watched him put away Cooney Tucker, a sturdy blond kid from Fort Wayne, Indiana, with a second-round TKO. "When the official intervened the Hoosier was receiving a severe beating," reported the *Free Press*'s Charlie Ward. "In the first round one of Louis's right head shots almost dropped him. In the second Joe rocked him several times with right crosses, left hooks, and right uppercuts. It isn't likely that he could have finished the round, and the referee performed an act of mercy in ending hostilities when he did."

Joe blasted his way to the national Golden Gloves title when the tournament concluded in early March. In the semifinal match he almost punched Ario Soldati of Rockford, Illinois, out of the ring. He easily handled Cleveland's Joe Bauer in the title bout, winning over the crowd of nearly 22,000 with a display of skill and sportsmanship. "Louis was given a tremendous ovation as he left the ring," wrote Jack Carveth. "He established himself here as the greatest amateur in the country. His clean-cut victory might have ended in a knockout had not Louis refused to cut loose when he had his opponent on the ropes."

An injured hand kept Joe out of the intercity competition between Chicago and New York Golden Glovers. Missing the event, which drew a remarkable crowd of 19,467 to Madison Square Garden (and outgrossed the recent heavyweight title fight between Primo Carnera and Tommy Loughran), cost him considerable publicity in the influential New York dailies. He recovered sufficiently to be crowned the national AAU champion in St. Louis the first week of April, though several boils on his right side affected the force of his punches. Boils or not, Stanley Evans took no chances. At the weigh-in he wisely placed weights in his pocket in order to move up to the heavyweight class and avoid facing Joe.

On May 23, 1934, nine days after celebrating his twentieth birthday, the young man Charlie Ward had started calling "the Brown Bomber" entered Chicago Stadium for what was expected to be the capstone of his amateur career: being proclaimed the world's light-heavyweight champion in an international Golden Gloves competition against a strong squad from Poland.

Instead, he wasn't permitted to toss a single punch. At the weigh-in, officials announced that he was two ounces over the 175-pound limit. An innocent drink of water upon arrival was the culprit. Franciszek Baranowski, secretary of the Polish Boxing Union, was deaf to suggestions that he waive the miserly difference. Some secretly thought Baronowski might have been more sportsmanlike had the boxer in question been white. Others suspected the scales had been rigged. The *Chicago Tribune* Golden Gloves committee had no choice but to substitute Ario Soldati, who had recently lost to Joe in AAU and National Golden Gloves meets. Joe was introduced to the crowd, then given a seat at ringside to watch a substitute steal a moment of triumph that should have been his.

He didn't even get the satisfaction of seeing the entire fight. During the action, some men approached him and introduced themselves as deputy sheriffs from South Bend, Indiana. They were looking for a man named George Smith, who was wanted for having murdered his spouse three years earlier in Gary. Joe fit the description of the suspect, they said. He was quietly led from the stadium to the Eleventh Street Police Station for questioning.

Joe—"scared shitless," he later admitted—tried to convince the authorities that at the time in question he had been a fifteen-year-old living in Detroit. After a short while he was released. He soon learned his arrest had been a ruse. Some Chicago fight fans, their money on the Polish boxer, had arranged to have Joe put out of the way in order to give their man a chance. (It was to no avail; Soldati won in Joe's place.)

Arch Ward, sports editor of the *Chicago Tribune*, was impressed with Joe's even response to these twin blasts of adversity. That night, he observed, Joe "took two of the toughest raps that could have been thrown against him and never put up a squawk. What happened to that kid that night could have soured him against boxing and the world had he not been made of the timber champions are cut from."

The response among the Brewster brethren to Joe's trouble was a collective shrug of resignation. So what else was new? Machinations by gamblers and bigoted officials were part of a sport controlled by whites. "There wasn't a single black official or referee in the state," said Ken Offet, who started fighting for money in the summer of 1931. "In a crowd of one thousand people, maybe fifty were black. So if the fight is close, who do you think is going to get the decision?"

The previous December, Offet had been robbed of a decision against a white fighter, Johnny Mitchell, in a ten-round event in Mount Clemens,

Michigan. The Associated Press writer had scored seven rounds in Offet's favor, but it was Mitchell's hand that was hoisted in victory. This caused "a near riot" among bettors in the stands, reported the following day's paper.

Despite the disappointment over having a loss registered in his ring record, Offet had to look first and foremost at the purse. When the hungry professional won the state bantamweight title in 1932, he had received forty-four dollars—a fortune to his friends back in Black Bottom, he remembered. "With that I spent ten dollars for a suit, bought a hat, and paid $2.98 for a pair of shoes, and I still had some change in my pockets. I never lived so well."

It was the chance to make some real dough that caused Joe to approach Roxborough one day that spring and tell him that he wanted to turn professional. Roxborough tried to talk him out of it. It would be better to wait another year or so, until he had filled out some more, moved up to heavyweight, and captured the 1935 Golden Gloves in that class. Asked to explain his haste, Joe replied, "Mr. Roxborough, I want the money."

"That I could understand," Roxborough admitted. "That was why I was in the numbers racket—and I've never been ashamed of it—and I said 'Okay, Joe, I'll find you a good manager and a good trainer.'"

On June 12 Joe returned home to whip old foe Joe Bauer in an inter-city tournament with Cleveland at Ford Field. In less than ninety seconds it was all over—the fight *and* Joe's amateur career. In an era where a black fighter usually had to lay out a white opponent to assure a fair decision, he'd won fifty of fifty-four bouts. All but seven of them had been by knock-out. He was already practicing what Jack Blackburn, soon to be his trainer and destined to be a major factor in his professional success, had always preached as his credo:

Let your fist be the referee.

Chapter Three

The Long Shadow of Papa Jack

Amaze an' Grace, how sweet it sounds,
Jack Johnson knocked Jim Jeffries down.
Jim Jeffries jumped up an' hit Jack on the chin,
An' then Jack knocked him down agin.

The Yankees hold the play,
The white man pulls the trigger;
But it makes no difference what the white man say,
The world champion's still a nigger.

—DITTY SUNG BY NORTH CAROLINA BLACKS, 1910

*J*ohn Roxborough made good on his promise to find Joe a manager and trainer. First, however, because Joe was still a year from turning twenty-one, Roxborough needed to secure permission from his legal guardians in order to sign contracts on his behalf.

Joe brought his mentor over to the family's rented house on Mullett Street (where the Barrow-Brooks clan had moved in the early 1930s) to talk to his mother and stepfather. They listened carefully as Roxborough discussed his plans for Joe's future. "You take him, keep him a good boy," Lillie Barrow told Roxborough. "You'll do fine for him."

Roxborough, who lacked boxing connections and was hurting for cash, turned to an old friend in Chicago. Julian Black was a chunky numbers racketeer with a slight limp and shiny hair combed straight back. The Wisconsin native had studied to be an embalmer but fell into a considerably more lively line of work, operating a speakeasy called the Elite Number 2. Unlike the warm and refined Roxborough, Black was cold and calculating. "He was friendly enough to me," Joe said, recalling their first meeting, "but I knew he was basically a tough guy."

Black, who put up two thousand dollars for his half-interest in Joe, knew exactly who he wanted for his trainer. He and Roxborough went to George Trafton's gym. The gigantic Trafton, who was a former star center with George Halas's Chicago Bears and had been dubbed Beast, actually knew little about the sweet science and had never boxed himself. But his crowded, smoke-filled joint on Randolph Street was the place to train for most local fighters in the 1930s and a popular hangout for promoters, managers, writers, and ex-pugs.

Black introduced Roxborough to a wiry, scar-faced trainer named Jack Blackburn. Then they got down to business. Would he like to handle their young fighter, Joe Louis?

"Bring around this white boy, and I'll look him over," Blackburn answered. Told that Joe was black, he quickly had a change of heart. "I won't have no truck with a colored boy," he said. "Colored boys ain't got much chance fighting nowadays—unless they just happen to be world-beaters."

Roxborough laughed and told him his boy fit that description. The balding, leathery Blackburn, then handling a pair of mediocre white fighters, grudgingly agreed to a look-see. Should he agree to take Louis on, his initial pay would be thirty-five dollars a week for four weeks. By that time Joe would be ready to make his pro debut. After that, assuming Joe did well, the financial arrangement would be adjusted.

"This will be the best job I ever had," Blackburn told his gentlemen callers the following day, as Joe hit the bag under the old trainer's gimlet eye. "Usually got to whip my man to collect my pay. I got to tell you, you'll never make a success of this kid, but I need the job. He ain't going to make no money worth shaking your finger at. Remember he's a colored boy."

While Black and Roxborough were more optimistic, they still had to consider the trainer's pessimism, for both knew the unlettered Blackburn possessed the equivalent of a doctorate in street smarts. He had been born in Versailles, Kentucky, in 1883 and raised in Indiana where he began fighting when he was sixteen. He ran away from home and continued his violent way of life in Pittsburgh and Philadelphia, boxing as often as two or three times a week for a few dollars a bout. Boxing was still illegal in many parts of the country then, so Blackburn had to suffer fly-by-night promoters who frequently took off with the gate receipts. To combat this, Blackburn wore shoes two sizes too large, got his money up front and stuffed it into the toes.

In his prime the five-foot-nine Blackburn weighed between 135 and 145 pounds, but that didn't deter him from taking on all comers, even heavyweights. His record included four draws and two no-decisions against Sam Langford, the mighty Boston Tar Baby, who Jack Johnson and Jack

Dempsey both carefully avoided during their championship reigns; and two draws and a loss to Joe Gans, the first black lightweight champion. The 1904 loss to Gans was Blackburn's sole setback in the first eight years of his career. During this period no one had been able to knock the tough crafts-man to the canvas. In Philadelphia in 1907, Blackburn fought six one-rounders in one evening and kayoed three of his opponents. The following year he bloodied Jack Johnson's nose during a sparring session, precipitating a lifetime feud between the two men.

Blackburn had a fair number of scrapes with the law, most stemming from his lifelong struggle with the bottle. Acquaintances remember him as a beer drinker who was "wholly unnatural" when he'd had too many. His most distinctive feature, a long scar that creased the left side of his face from ear to lip, was a souvenir from a knife fight at a Philadelphia bar.

One January night in 1909, Blackburn went berserk with a gun, killing a man named Alonso Polk during a heated argument. He also shot Polk's wife and his own "white wife or paramour," Maude Pillion. For this Blackburn received a fifteen-year prison sentence. Inside the stone walls, he instructed the warden and his three sons in the fine art of self-defense, pos-sibly the reason he was paroled in 1913 after serving just four years. Another decade of fighting followed. When Blackburn wrapped up his career in 1923, his official record showed only two losses among his 167 fights. (Blackburn reckoned he'd actually fought closer to four hundred times.) Most of the rest were no-decisions—common in those days—but nobody disputed Blackburn's ability. "Fearless, clever, snappy puncher, good jabber, and had a powerful left hook," *The Ring* once described him.

Later he trained several Philadelphia-based fighters, helping to make champions out of bantamweight Bud Taylor and lightweight Sammy Mandell. Unfortunately, Blackburn never could get a handle on his drink-ing and his murderous temper, which usually went hand in hand. In late 1935 he reportedly killed a man in Chicago, although the case was quietly dropped.*

"A lot of people were afraid of Blackburn," recalled one of his pupils, Joe Gramby. "He was a nice person, but when he was drinking, he was hell. We used to come up on the elevator, and if we heard him talking loud and all, we wouldn't train that day."

---

* On March 3, 1936, Blackburn was tried inside a packed Chicago courtroom for the murder of Enoch Hauser, a Negro caught in the crossfire as Blackburn and two other men argued over the purchase of a South Side garage the previous fall. Shots had been fired, killing Hauser and wounding a child. Six days after the trial started, the prosecution abruptly decided not to pursue its case against Blackburn. Exactly whose influence or money was at work here is unknown, but it certainly didn't hurt matters that Blackburn was needed to train his now-famous fighter for his upcoming bout with Max Schmeling or that the murder victim was black.

When Joe first met Blackburn, the world-weary trainer had just turned fifty-one and was showing the effects of arthritis and alcoholism. Nonetheless, said Freddie Guinyard, who would later share a room with Blackburn after becoming a member of the entourage, "he was the man who made Joe great."

Blackburn's initial impression of his new charge—"a big, easy-going Negro boy with high water pants and too much arms for his coat sleeves"— was far from overwhelming.

"So you think you can get somewhere in this fighting game?" he asked Joe. "Well, let me tell you something right off. It's next to impossible for a Negro heavyweight to get anywhere. He's got to be very good outside the ring and very bad inside the ring. Mr. Roxborough, who has known you quite a while, is convinced that you can be depended on to behave yourself, but you've gotta be a killer, otherwise I'm getting too old to waste any time on you."

"I ain't gonna waste any of your time," Joe solemnly responded.

After having lived the last eight years in Detroit, Joe's home was now Chicago's South Side, which was replacing New York's Harlem as the capital of black America. Here resided a large and prosperous black middle class, including such nationally known figures as gospel singer Mahalia Jackson, Congressman Richard Dawson, and Reverend J. H. Jackson, pastor of the largest black congregation in the country. The race's most influential newspaper, the *Chicago Defender*, was based here, as was the powerful American Giants of the Negro National League. Even the Black Muslims had moved from Detroit to the South Side. The names of institutions like the Savoy Ballroom, Regal Theater, and the Hotel Grand were recognized around the country, but many locals preferred to frequent one of the numerous neighborhood taverns where Saturday nights dissolved with the help of a three-piece blues band and a mason jar of moonshine. Whether one was looking to gain money and dignity or simply searching for the wild side of life, the South Side offered it all: substantial homes and slums, night clubs and blind pigs, elegant shopping districts and street-corner hustlers. Its high energy always appealed to Joe, who over the coming years would divide much of his time between the South Side and its seamier cousin Harlem.

Joe moved into the apartment of Bill Bottoms, who served as a combination watchdog and cook. The tenement, on Forty-sixth Street near South Parkway, was five blocks from Washington Park, where Joe did his roadwork each day. For the first time in his life, he had a bedroom to himself, but that only accentuated his loneliness. His managers were anxious for him to concentrate on boxing, so initially they prohibited visits from old friends, especially those they considered a bad influence, such as Freddie Guinyard. Guinyard, in town after somehow wrangling a job as a gofer for the Mills Brothers, was forced to sneak through the backyard and up the back stairs to see Joe. Eventually he and Thurston McKinney were allowed into camp after Black and Roxborough noticed how much Joe's spirits picked up when they were around.

Joe settled into a routine. Blackburn got him up at six o'clock each morning to run twice around the park, a total of six miles. Afterward Joe returned to bed and slept until eleven when Bottoms made him a hearty breakfast. Joe let the meal digest for a couple of hours before heading over to the gym where he spent the balance of the afternoon. Evening hours were spent eating a big dinner and loafing around the apartment until it was time to hit the sack. Occasionally he was allowed out to see a movie. Girls were strictly off limits.

It took about a week, but Blackburn began to see something in the rawboned youngster. Joe was a shade over six feet tall and weighed 175 pounds—about twenty pounds shy of where they wanted him to be as a heavyweight—but Bottom's carbohydrate-rich meals and Blackburn's vigorous daily workouts were steadily putting some meat on his still-growing frame.

If prizefighting can be considered an art form—and many creative types insist it can—then on the basis of his style Joe might be called a minimalist. Throughout his ring career he preferred to throw no punch rather than a bad one. As a result, he was extremely accurate. He also exhibited impressive hand speed. The oft repeated observation that he could level an opponent with a six-inch punch from either hand was not mere hyperbole. "You can beat anyone you can hit," Blackburn told him, "but I have to teach you how to get in the proper position to do so."

The hard-boiled teacher quickly took a liking to his pupil. Joe proved to be an earnest student of the ring who genuinely enjoyed the long hours of gym work and instruction. He was also respectful and, at times, charmingly naive. Once, early in their relationship, Blackburn told Joe that he must go to the stockyards and drink two quarts of hot beef blood. "You got to do that every day," he said. "That's the only way you'll put on weight. You hear?"

It was meant to be a joke. But that night Joe dejectedly showed up at Blackburn's apartment door. "Mr. Blackburn," he said, "I've been thinking about drinking that blood. I just can't drink it, Mr. Blackburn, and I thought I'd better come 'round and tell you."

Joe addressed his comanagers as Mr. Roxborough and Mr. Black. But as a sign of how close he and Blackburn became, the two called each other "Chappie," a term of endearment that would last until the trainer's death in 1942.

One aspect of Joe's makeup troubled Blackburn, however. He seemed to lack a killer instinct. He "didn't have any blood in his eye," he once told an interviewer. "He didn't go out to murder the boys in the gym. Didn't have the killer's instinct. So I knows right then what I got to do and I does it."

Blackburn revamped Joe's mobile, defense-oriented philosophy, a legacy of Holman Williams's instruction. "You can't get nowhere nowadays trying to outpoint fellows in the ring," he instructed. "It's mighty hard for a colored boy to win decisions. The dice is loaded against you. You gotta knock 'em out and keep knocking 'em out to get anywheres. Let your right fist be your referee. Don't ever forget that. Let that right fist there be your referee!"

Blackburn converted Joe into a more aggressive fighter who stalked his foe—a relatively easy task since Joe was more comfortable shuffling flat-footed than trying to dance around on the balls of his feet. Over time he became highly effective in crowding his opponent, slicing the ring into a small kill zone and blocking all escape routes.

Blackburn also worked to improve Joe's left jab, which had been a hallmark of Blackburn and all of the fighters he'd coached. Joe had always demonstrated a powerful hook coming from that side, but with Blackburn's help he developed a pistonlike lead with which to create an opening in his opponent's defense. Blackburn spent hours sparring with Joe, showing him how to block punches without ducking and stressing balance at all times. He preached that a fighter, properly balanced, could pick off a punch and fire off two, three, or more of his own in return. Joe developed into a terrific counterpuncher.

"Whatever he told me to do in the ring, I did," said Joe. "I used to be clumsy-footed when I was a kid in Alabama. When I began with Blackburn, he saw things I didn't know about myself. He saw I couldn't follow a left hook with a right without picking up one foot. He said it was no good, that a fighter had to keep both feet planted on the canvas to get power, or to take a punch. He soon had me throwing a series of punches. He was the best teacher anybody ever had."

As all astute managers do, Roxborough and Black selected Joe's opponents carefully. The idea was to build up their fighter's confidence and record by matching him with progressively tougher foes. Late in June, Joe was told that his first rival would be Jack Kracken, a local white heavyweight. Because of Joe's outstanding amateur record, the scheduled ten-rounder would be the main event of the Independence Day show at the Bacon Casino, a modest-sized facility located on Forty-seventh Street on Chicago's South Side.

A week before his professional debut, Blackburn warned Joe just how remote his chances of success as a heavyweight were—and why.

"You know, boy," he said as they took a breather one afternoon at Trafton's gym, "the heavyweight division for a Negro is hardly likely. The white man ain't too keen on it. You have to really be something to get anywhere. If you really ain't gonna be another Jack Johnson, you got some hope. White man hasn't forgotten that fool nigger with his white women, acting like he owned the world."

At that point in his life, Joe knew next to nothing about Jack Johnson. But over the coming months and years, he would find himself intimately acquainted with the legacy of the infamous Papa Jack, the first black man to wear the heavyweight crown.

>←

If Jack Johnson had come along today instead of when he did, he would be welcomed with open arms by white corporate America. Think of all those fast-food commercials and made-for-television boxing "events" featuring the fight game's phenomenon of the 1990s, George Foreman, and one gets a rough sense of how Madison Avenue would have packaged the similarly affable, large-souled, shaved-headed Papa Jack. But owing to the racial and social conventions of his times and his own churlish conduct, Johnson was destined to be anything but a media darling during his tumultuous tenure as boxing's top dog.

John Arthur Johnson, the son of a religious school janitor, was born into a poor family of nine in the port city of Galveston, Texas, in 1878. He worked as a stevedore on the docks and also as a part-time gym attendant. Both occupations provided him with a rudimentary education in handling his fists. His first experiences included participating in the infamous "battle royals," back-alley spectacles where eight or more blacks were thrown into a ring and fought amongst themselves until only one was left standing.

Johnson saw the world as so many adventuresome young men did in those days, hopping freight trains and living in hobo jungles. His travels took him to cities like San Francisco, Chicago, Boston, and New York, where he filled in the time betweeen his sporadic appearances on fight cards by working at odd jobs and finding occasional work as a sparring partner. Contrary to his later reputation as some kind of superman, Johnson could be beaten during his early years. In 1901, he fought the aging but still dangerous Joe Choynski, a storied performer who had once broken the great Jim Jeffries' nose. Choynski knocked out Johnson, at which point Texas Rangers raided the place and tossed both fighters in jail. This turned out to be a stroke of good fortune for Johnson, because he used his jail time sparring with Choynski and soaking up all that the old master could teach him.

During this period, professional prizefighting was alternately gaining and waning in popularity, depending in great measure on who the reigning heavyweight champion was. John L. Sullivan, a colorful and outspoken knockout artist who took on all challengers ("I can lick any sonofabitch in the house" was his trademark boast), rose from modest beginnings to become America's first great sports hero and the acknowledged father of modern prizefighting. The mustachioed son of Irish immigrants won the American heavyweight championship in 1882 and held it for the next ten years, bringing a fresh excitement and a certain legitimacy to what had long been considered a brutal pastime. He thoroughly enjoyed his fame, wearing a $10,000 championship belt studded with more than four hundred diamonds and appearing in top hat and cane in a variety of stage productions.

The gaslight era that the melodramatic Sullivan so perfectly personified also marked the transition from the old London Prize Ring Rules, under which bareknuckled boxers could employ fouls, delays, and wrestling holds, to the new Marquis of Queensbury Rules, which stipulated the use of five-ounce gloves and three-minute rounds separated by a minute of rest. Sullivan, who fought successfully under both codes, emerged victorious in history's last bareknuckle heavyweight title fight. One broiling July morning in 1889 in Richburg, Mississippi, he beat Jack Kilrain in a seventy-five-round grudge match that lasted an astounding two hours and sixteen minutes in 104-degree heat. Technically, prizefighting was illegal in all thirty-eight states then, but through the early 1920s, promoters often got around the law by either advertising bouts as "exhibitions" with no announced winner (although the next day's sports pages often carried an unofficial decision for the benefit of bettors) or by staging them in some out-of-the-way locale like Richburg. (River barges were a popular alternative.) The Sullivan-Kilrain duel attracted unprecedented interest in all parts of the country and helped persuade some municipalities to either revise the law or to not enforce it so vigorously in the future.

On September 7, 1892, in New Orleans, Sullivan met challenger "Gentleman Jim" Corbett ("the Adonis of the Fistic Arena," said the *New York Illustrated News*) in the first heavyweight title fight governed by the Queensbury Rules. It was the most famous boxing match of its time. Corbett, a refined and finely chiseled young man from San Francisco, knocked out the older and heavier Sullivan in the twenty-first round, establishing him as the first U.S. heavyweight champion of the modern (gloved) era. Sixteen months later he became the first fighter to be recognized as champion on both sides of the Atlantic when he defeated England's Charley Mitchell. In this era of heightened nationalistic fervor, when Americans were throwing off the last vestiges of English influence, Corbett's victory was seen by jingoistic citizens as further proof of England's decline and yet another example of this young country's emergence as a world power. It wouldn't be the last time that the heavyweight champion would be employed as some sort of geopolitical symbol.

Gentleman Jim launched what some historians have termed the golden age of the American ring (roughly 1895 to 1905) when some of the sport's greatest names laced up gloves. On St. Patrick's Day, 1897, Corbett lost his title to Bob Fitzsimmons, an elongated, knock-kneed, generously freckled fighter who had gained his remarkable upper-body strength through years of swinging a blacksmith's hammer in New Zealand. Two years later Fitzsimmons was displaced by Jim Jeffries, a powerfully built product of California's copper mines. Jeffries defended his title for five years. Not only did he never lose a fight, he was never knocked off his feet. He finally retired in 1905, having saved enough money to buy a farm.

Jeffries's retirement brought up the question of succession. All other heavyweight champs had lost their titles in the ring; Jeffries was the first to simply surrender his. Jeffries agreed to referee a bout between two undistinguished fighters, Jack Root and Marvin Hart, the winner to be appointed champion. Hart won, but no one considered him king of the hill. Hart's claim became moot when he was beaten by Tommy Burns in Los Angeles in early 1906. Jeffries, again the referee, proclaimed that the short, barrel-chested Burns had earned the vacated title.

Burns, a Canadian born Noah Brusso in 1881, had learned the fight game from Jim Burns in Detroit. Jim Burns, a saloonkeeper and the brawling owner of the Detroit Tigers at the turn of the century, had once been the state's boxing and wrestling champion. He liked what he saw in the feisty youngster Brusso, who had an exceptionally long, seventy-four-inch reach for his size. In honor of his tutor, Brusso changed his name to Burns when he began his boxing career in 1900.

As had been the case with Marvin Hart, few people considered the equally colorless Tommy Burns the true champion. Boxing was in decline now that old favorites like Corbett and Jeffries had left and Fitzsimmons (who wouldn't quit until he was fifty-two) had passed his prime. Moreover, it was evolving into a western sport, legal only in California and Nevada and unofficially tolerated in few places east of the Mississippi River. New York, rocked by several scandals, repealed its short-lived law allowing prizefighting. Between 1901 and 1915 every heavyweight title fight on United States soil was held west of the Mississippi, in places like Reno and San Francisco, further distancing the sport from the major population and media centers of the East.

Looking to earn some respect, as well as some dollars, Burns welcomed all challengers, defeating "Fireman Jim" Flynn and earning a draw and a victory in two fights with "Philadelphia Jack" O'Brien, another top contender. With only second-raters left on the scene, Burns announced a self-managed world tour. It began in London, where he won twice, and continued on to Dublin, where he demolished the big Irish champ, Jem Roche, in just eighty-eight seconds. At the time it was the quickest heavy-weight title bout in history.

This is when Jack Johnson started to make his considerable presence loudly known. Nearing thirty, he had been polishing off boxers of both races for nine years, using his size, quickness, and reach to devastating effect. He was a marvelous defensive boxer, possibly the best that ever was. According to Ed "Gunboat" Smith, a leading heavyweight and one-time sparring partner, "Johnson was a fellow that used to stand flat-footed and wait for you to come in. And when you came in, he'd rip the head off of you with uppercuts, cut you all to pieces." When people remarked that Burns had cleared the heavyweight field of all worthy contenders, they meant of course *white* contenders. Talented Negro pugilists like Johnson and Sam Langford were treated as if they were invisible. This was in keep-ing with the unspoken but implicit color bar that was an integral part of American sports. There were no blacks in organized baseball, nor were there any in tennis or golf. Just a handful of blacks played collegiate football or competed in track and field. Even horse racing, once dominated by Negro jockeys, had become practically an all-alabaster affair.

Still, it was hard to ignore the claims of Johnson, whose lopsided vic-tories over Jim Flynn and Bob Fitzsimmons logically made him the number-one challenger. To drive home his case, Johnson literally chased Burns around the globe, showing up in every country—England, Ireland, France, Australia—during Burns's world tour. Burns denied that he was avoiding Johnson, saying that it was all a matter of money, not race. Veteran observers knew this not to be the case. John L. Sullivan had publicly pro-claimed that he would not fight Negroes as a matter of principle, and subse-quent heavyweight champions had followed his lead. Shortly before Burns died in 1955, he admitted that at the time the "idea of a Negro challenging me was beyond enduring." However, money proved thicker than blood. When promoters approached Burns with an offer of $30,000 to meet Johnson (who would receive $5,000), he readily accepted. It was the first time a black man had been allowed a crack at the heavyweight title.

The fight was held December 26, 1908, inside a wooden amphithe-atre on the outskirts of Sydney, Australia. Bettors installed the incumbent as a 3-to-1 favorite. Burns was not afraid of the much bigger Johnson, who stood a shade over six feet tall and weighed 205 pounds. In fact, he dis-played the customary arrogance in such matters, assuming the superiority of the Caucasian race would prevail. He told the press that Johnson had "a yellow streak."

Joe Louis's father, Munroe Barrow, was photographed several years before Joe's birth with his first four children. From left: Susie, Alvanious, deLeon, and Emmarell.

Jack Johnson in 1910, two years into his reign as world heavyweight champion. The prizefighter inflamed public opinion with his open dalliances with white women, including his second wife, Etta Duryea, pictured here. (Library of Congress)

A typical Alabama sharecropper during the time of the Great Migration. (U.S. Department of Agriculture)

Detroit's Black Bottom in 1925, a year before the Barrows arrived from the South. (Manning Brothers)

While Jack Dempsey was heavy-weight champ from 1919 to 1926, legitimate black contenders such as Harry Wills and Sam Langford were denied a shot at the title. (Pug Shots)

Two Detroiters who displayed no fear of young Joe Louis Barrow. Patrolman Henderson "Ben" Turpin ruled the neighborhood with an iron hand, while Johnny Miler knocked Joe down seven times in Joe's first organized fight. (Richard Buckheim)

Max Marek, seen here in front of his Chicago bar and grill in 1948, never let the world forget that he had beaten Louis in an amateur title fight in 1933.

Joe (top, center) and his fellow Golden Gloves champions gather in Chicago in 1934.

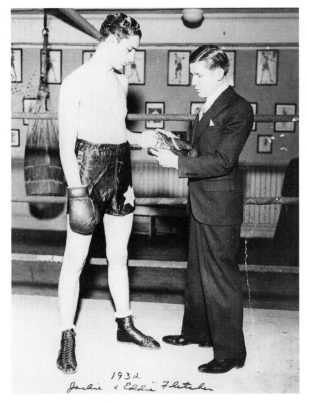

Organized crime was deeply involved in the fight game. In this 1932 shot, welterweight Jackie Sherman gets some help from his manager, Eddie Fletcher, inside a Detroit gym. Fletcher, a former boxer and one of the leaders of the city's notorious Purple Gang, was found shot to death a few months after this picture was taken. (Jackie Sherman)

Holman Williams was just one of several notable graduates of Detroit's storied Brewster Center. The superb middleweight helped train Louis early in his amateur career. (Angelo Prospero)

Joe and his management team: Julian Black (center) and John Roxborough. Both men had made their money in the numbers racket—Black in Chicago, Roxborough in Detroit. (Detroit Free Press)

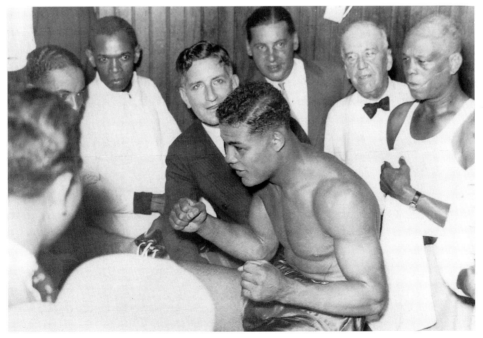

Trainer Jack Blackburn (far right) watches his prize pupil celebrate his 1935 knockout of King Levinsky. Despite their menacing images, Blackburn and Louis forged an affectionate relationship, calling each other "Chappie." (Hank Kaplan)

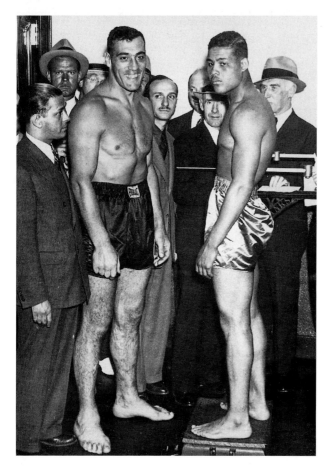

Louis's first experience as a racial symbol came when he fought Primo Carnera, the giant Italian heavyweight, in the summer of 1935. At the time Italy was drawing tremendous criticism from the international community for its invasion of tiny Ethiopia. As this cartoon in the *Washington Post* illustrates, the boxers represented something much larger than themselves. (National Archives)

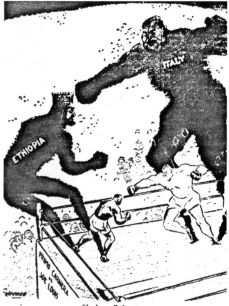

Shadows Before?

The Brown Bomber greets Harlem for the first time in 1935.

Family members celebrate the victory over Primo Carnera. From left: deLeon, Emmarell, Lonnie, Eulalia, Vunies, and mother, Lillie. (Wide World)

Joseph Golinkin sketched Louis's final knockdown of Max Baer on September 24, 1935. "I could have struggled up once more," Baer said. "But when I get executed, people are going to have to pay more than twenty-five dollars a seat to watch it." (National Portrait Gallery)

Lillie Barrow is the center of attention inside her new home as friends and relatives rejoice over yet another of her son's victories. The $9,000 house was the first major purchase Joe made with his ring earnings.

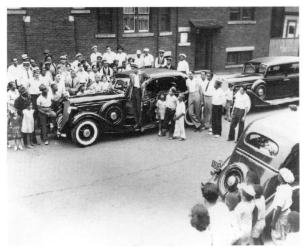

The widely acclaimed and financially prosperous fighter returned to Black Bottom in the fall of 1935, just after the Baer fight.

One stop included having his portrait taken at Greenfield Village's tintype studio. (Henry Ford Museum)

About this time Joe was pictured with another black athlete making a name for himself, track star Jesse Owens. The two became fast and lifelong friends.

Louis in Lakewood, New Jersey, while training for his first fight with Max Schmeling. (Freddie Guinyard)

Schmeling, who held the heavyweight title from 1930 to 1932, was a 10 to 1 underdog when he met Louis on June 19, 1936. But the German shocked the sporting world and thrilled officials of the Third Reich with his unexpected twelfth-round knockout. It would be Joe's only professional defeat before his 1949 retirement. (Library of Congress)

James Braddock, boxing's Cinderella Man, had rebounded from the relief rolls to capture the heavyweight title. On June 22, 1937, at Comiskey Park, the championship changed hands on Joe's right cross. (Pug Shots)

Two days after becoming the first black champion since Jack Johnson, Joe settles in for a meal of fried chicken at his mother's house. His wife Marva pours him a glass of iced tea in a photograph that was typical of his public image during the 1930s. (National Archives)

Louis's first of an eventual twenty-five title defenses was against British champion Tommy Farr, a "bulldog" who gamely went the full fifteen rounds but lost the decision. (Pug Shots)

A few days after the Farr fight, Louis was back in a far less dangerous sporting arena: Detroit's Navin Field, where he and friends Freddie Guinyard (left) and Holman Williams watched Joe's beloved Tigers. (Detroit News)

An avid horseback rider, Joe for a time owned several horses as well as a popular riding stable in the Detroit area.

As this 1936 Decca ad indicates, Joe Louis was the greatest blues hero since the mythical John Henry. Blacks took to the streets whenever he won a fight. But all of the vicarious victories did little to change the lot of ordinary blacks, who continued to live in a separate and unequal society throughout Joe's career.

To nobody's surprise, Joe's first Hollywood role cast him as a boxer in *The Spirit of Youth*, a low-budget movie loosely based on his life.

Despite the possible harm to his public image, Louis had discreet affairs with many white women, including actresses Sonja Henie (above) and Lana Turner.

One of Louis's most intense relationships was with entertainer Lena Horne, who admired him for being "the one invincible Negro, the one who stood up to the white man and beat him down with his fists." (Hollywood Museum Collection)

"Who told you I was yellow?" Johnson yelled at the start of the fight, just before he leveled Burns with a left uppercut. It turned into a slaughter, Johnson toying with his overmatched opponent. The sun glinted off Johnson's gold-capped teeth as he smiled and kept up a constant obscene banter. Burns, sputtering expletives through bloodied lips, never quit, but finally police jumped into the ring and stopped the debacle in the four-teenth round. Novelist Jack London, then covering the fight for the *New York Herald*, characterized it as a battle between "a pygmy and a colossus . . . a playful Ethiopian at loggerheads with a small white man." His ringside report ended: "But one thing now remains. Jim Jeffries must emerge from his alfalfa farm and remove the golden smile from Jack Johnson's face. Jeff, it's up to you. The White Man must be rescued."

And thus began the quest for the great white hope to unseat the swaggering, grinning Johnson. As the public implored the retired Jim Jeffries to shed years of accumulated blubber and put on the gloves one more time, it also became more intimately acquainted with the new Negro champion. In addition to being bombastic and boastful, Johnson liked fast cars, good times, and white women—the last the most egregious affront then imaginable. Johnson defended his preference this way: "I didn't court white women because I thought I was too good for the others. It was just that they always treated me better. I never had a colored girl that didn't two-time me."

That was at least partially true. His first wife, a fair-skinned Negro, divorced him in 1901 after he refused to abandon prizefighting. Later, a second black woman he was living with ran off with a white man, taking all of Johnson's clothes and cash in the process. Fed up, he turned to white women. Accompanying him on his worldwide chase of Tommy Burns was Hattie McLay, an Irish gal from New York who was the daughter of a respectable jeweler.

Today, of course, interracial dating and marriage do not have any-where near the same forbidden caste, especially among celebrity athletes. Barry Bonds, O. J. Simpson, and Charles Barkley are just a few of the many modern black sports figures who have had white wives. But in the superheated racial atmosphere of turn-of-the-century America, sex was at the very core of Jim Crow. If the races were allowed to mingle freely, sepa-ratists argued, it could only lead to widespread intermarriage and the even-tual mongrelization of America. Therefore, legal segregation was needed to enforce social segregation.

"In the panoply of white fears about blacks, this sexual one was not only the most important but also the most wholly misplaced . . . ," Nicholas Lemann pointed out in his masterful study of the Great Migration, *The Promised Land*. "Everything flowed from their idea that if blacks and whites were allowed to deal with each other as equals, sex would be the result. That was why blacks were always called by their first names and whites, from the age of ten or eleven, by 'Mister' or 'Miss.' It was the reason a black person could not enter a white person's house by the front door, or sit next to a white person in a public place, or go to school with whites."

What inflamed the public was how the stubbornly proud boxer flaunted his conquests. Back in Chicago after beating Burns, he dropped Hattie McLay for a German girl named Belle Schreiber, who was described as "the prettiest whore in Chicago." Schreiber worked at the Everleigh Club, an elegant brothel that featured cashmere blankets and gold tubs, and catered to such personalities as actor John Barrymore, writer Ring Lardner, and Gentleman Jim Corbett. She usually received fifty dollars a toss, but offered to donate her services to Johnson. Soon they were living together. She accompanied him to San Francisco where, to Johnson's horror, he discovered Hattie McLay had checked into the same hotel seeking a reconciliation. The two women got into some name-calling and hair-pulling over the object of their desire, who brokered a truce by promising to make both happy.

Johnson's solution was to make love to Belle and Hattie each night in their respective apartments, then climb down a rope into his own room to avoid reporters. One evening, however, the hotel manager's young daughter reached out a window and grabbed him as he was making his rounds. "She wanted the sight and feel of my privates," Johnson said. "Like she thought I was built of leather down there. I've never seen a girl get so frantic."

In order to pacify the groupie, Johnson slept with her. However, the following day she demanded he return to her room, at which point Johnson declared that enough was enough. He couldn't make love to three women every night, he said. Crushed, she accused Johnson of rape. The hotel manager confronted the fighter, blaming him for "ruining his poor little baby, with his gigantic, oversized thing." A large bribe kept the angry father from going to the police.

A little later Johnson fell in love with a twenty-eight-year-old blonde divorcee, Etta Terry Duryea, and presented her with a $2,500 engagement ring. Their marriage in 1909 created an uproar, a din that grew louder as Johnson continued to humiliate a succession of great white hopes. George "Tex" Rickard, a former Klondike gold prospector and soldier of fortune turned promoter, capitalized on the heightened racial tension by arranging the eagerly anticipated match between Johnson and Jeffries, who was finally lured out of retirement with a promise of the largest purse of his life.

The fight was held in Reno, Nevada, on a hot, sunny Fourth of July afternoon in 1910. Rickard, a master at public relations, had unashamedly played the race card in his promotion, and thus "The Fight of the Century" was treated as front-page news across the country. Twenty-five thousand fans packed the wooden stands; millions more followed the action via telegraph. Although Jeffries was overweight, rusty, and out of shape, gamblers had made him a 10 to 7 favorite to uphold the honor of the white race.

Instead, Johnson cuffed the former champ around at will. "Hardly had a blow been struck when I knew that I was Jeff's master," he later wrote. Johnson easily avoided Jeffries's wild swings and peppered him with short punches and a nonstop string of insults. "Package being delivered, Mister Jeff," he gloated before driving home his fist. At one point he half-carried the battered Jeffries to the corner where Jim Corbett sat hurling not-so-gentlemanly invectives at Johnson. "Where do you want me to put him, Mister Corbett?" asked Papa Jack. That shut Corbett up.

Jeffries, silently absorbing blow after blow, was bleeding and staggering by the fifteenth round. When it became clear that he was on his way to being knocked out, his supporters cried for Rickard, who was refereeing, to stop the fight. But Johnson administered the ultimate humiliation, sending Jeffries to the canvas for the first time in his life. Jeffries staggered to his feet, was promptly knocked down again, rose once more, then was sent crashing to the floor for a third and final time. End of fight. That evening stunned supporters maintained that Jeffries had been poisoned the day before; others pointed to his poor physical condition as the reason for his defeat. Hardly anyone wanted to admit that he had been beaten fairly and squarely by a black man.

Except Jeffries. "I could never have whipped Jack Johnson at my best," he said, his shattered pride assuaged somewhat by the big bundle of cash he took back to his alfalfa farm. "I couldn't have hit him in a thousand years."

Johnson's victory was like touching a match to kindling. Violence erupted from coast to coast. In New Orleans, ten-year-old Louis Armstrong was walking down Canal Street when he saw a group of his black friends running at him. "You better get started, black boy," the future musician recalled them yelling. "Jack Johnson has just knocked out Jim Jeffries. The white boys are sore about it and they're going to take it out on us." Armstrong beat feet for home.

In Brooklyn three whites confronted a black man who had called out to a dog, "Lie down there, Jeffries."

"Why don't you call it Johnson?" they demanded to know.

"Because Johnson is black and this dog is yellow," he responded, starting a fight.

These were mild episodes. In Little Rock, Arkansas, angry whites killed two blacks; in Washington, D.C., a pair of whites were stabbed to death by suddenly brazen blacks. A riot in Pueblo, Colorado, caused thirty injuries; violence in Shreveport, Louisiana, accounted for three deaths. Nationally, the bloody aftermath of the Johnson-Jeffries fight included nineteen deaths, 251 injuries, and five thousand cases of disorderly conduct. Social reformers and elected officials across the map screamed for the abolishment of prizefighting. Within days, showing film of the fight was declared illegal in hundreds of communities, all of which feared its inflammatory impact. Two years later a federal law prohibited the interstate transportation of all fight films—a direct result of the Johnson-Jeffries precedent.

Meanwhile, Johnson continued to thumb his nose at the white establishment. In the vernacular of the day he was considered to be a "bad nigger," a dangerous, independent cuss too crazy to submit to the accepted code of conduct governing blacks' behavior in mixed society. This made him popular with many members of the black lower classes who vicariously reveled in his outlaw ways. More refined blacks like educator W. E. B. Du Bois, however, distanced themselves from the controversial champion. To them, he was just a crude prizefighter, certainly not the kind of individual destined to lift the race out of its doldrums.

Looking to yank the white man's chain whenever he could, Johnson came upon a form of intimidation sure to keep bigoted blood aboiling. Before going out to spar, he would carefully, lovingly, wrap his penis with gauze. Several orbits of tape had the desired effect on his critics. With one eye on his crotch and the other on public morality, they demanded that he wear baggy shorts instead of the skintight trunks then in vogue. The venerable John L. Sullivan finally helped put an end to the controversy by proclaiming, "The size of a nigger's penis is not to be discussed in public."

Papa Jack's oversized genitalia corresponded perfectly with his larger-than-life persona. Stories abounded of his diamond stickpins, gold straws, and six luxury automobiles. He was a fixture on the vaudeville circuit and could usually be found leading the singing at some cabaret into the wee hours of the morning. But the salacious details that the press seized upon obscured the fact that he was a marvelous fighter, losing just seven of his 113 recorded bouts. Although comparing fighters from different eras is always problematic, no less an expert than Nat Fleicsher, founder and long-time editor of *The Ring*, regularly called him "the greatest heavyweight of all time."

In the two years following the Jeffries fight Johnson beat several more challengers, usually with minimal training. He was too busy carousing and living the high life, particularly at the Everleigh Club, where he was welcomed as the brothel's first black patron, and at his own nightclub, the Cabaret de Champion. However, matters outside his control soon had a dramatic impact. On September 11, 1912, his wife Etta, depressed by years of controversy and her husband's philandering, shunned by both white and black society, shot herself in the temple. Her suicide led to a failed legislative attempt to pass a Constitutional amendment banning mixed marriages. Leading the charge was Georgia Congressman Seaborn Roddenberry, who predicted unions between "fallen white women" and the "sombre-hued, black-skinned, thick-lipped, bull-necked, brutal-hearted African" would ultimately lead to a bloody race war if not stopped.

Scandal followed scandal. Shortly after Etta's suicide, Johnson hired Lucille Cameron, a nineteen-year-old white girl from Minneapolis, as his secretary. When Lucille's mother found out that the two were sleeping together, she demanded that authorities arrest the fighter for kidnapping her underage daughter. The outrage was so great that a lynch mob of one hundred Texans prepared to travel north to administer justice. The ever defiant Johnson married Lucille shortly after he was indicted for violating the Mann Act. Strictly interpreted, the law made it a federal offense for any man to cross a state line with a woman other than his wife for the purposes of sex. Belle Schreiber, still mad over being jilted several years earlier, testified against her former lover. In the spring of 1913, the all-white jury considered the tissue-thin evidence and convicted Johnson. He was fined one thousand dollars and sentenced to a year in prison. Rather than surrender to authorities, Johnson fled the country disguised in the flannels of the touring Chicago American Giants baseball team.

For the next seven years Johnson moved around Europe and South America, sampling women, fighting matches, and winning and losing tens of thousands of dollars. He interrupted his dissipated fugitive lifestyle long enough to fight the latest white hope, Jess Willard, in Cuba on April 5, 1915.

Willard was a dim, plodding Kansas cowhand whose greatest asset was his enormous size: he was nearly six feet seven inches tall and weighed about 260 pounds. His reach was an incredible eighty-four inches. It was virtually impossible to knock the rawboned giant out, as Gunboat Smith, a terrific hitter, had found out in an earlier bout. Smith had thrown his best punch at him, and "his hair wiggled a little bit. That's all," he said.

Purely for reasons of indestructibility, Willard was selected to battle Johnson under the broiling Havana sun. In the twenty-sixth round, Willard finally put an end to America's longest-running morality play. A right to Johnson's jaw dropped him to the canvas; he rolled over and was counted out. Years later, a nearly destitute Johnson sold his "confession" to Nat Fleisher, maintaining that he had actually taken a dive in exchange for admittance back to the United States. Film footage reveals that the flabby old warrior had simply been tagged a good one by his younger, stronger, and—to America's relief—infinitely duller opponent.

Johnson finally returned to the United States in 1920. By then the charismatic Jack Dempsey had supplanted Willard as champion, helping to restore some of the glamor, excitement, and respectability that had been lost during Johnson's madcap reign. After serving his sentence at Leavenworth, the aging, fleshy Papa Jack—he was now forty-three—challenged Dempsey, but nobody in their right mind honestly believed a Negro would ever again be allowed to contend for the heavyweight crown. That was the unfortunate legacy he had created.

Initially Johnson had not seen himself as a standard-bearer for his race. By his own admission, he thought of little else than simply satisfying his own voracious appetite for novelty and adventure. The Jeffries fight changed that, he claimed. "He was firmly convinced that he had a mission in life," the British liberal Trevor Wignall maintained. "He told me this in so many words—he believed it was his duty to 'lift the black race,' that it would be superior to the white. . . ."

Johnson was not above making self-serving statements. The depth of his sincerity can best be plumbed by his refusal to meet another member of his race for the title. About three years after the Jeffries fight, he declined an invitation by London's National Sporting Club to square off against Sam Langford for $5,000. It would have been a historic event: the first time two Negroes had contested for the heavyweight belt. It would have guaranteed that, no matter the outcome, a black man would continue to own prizefighting's greatest jewel—a consideration that would have swayed a true race man. A victory by the phlegmatic Langford, in fact, would have created a champion more acceptable to whites and may have resulted in some doors opening ever so slightly to other blacks.

But Johnson decided he could make more money continuing to meet white hopes far less threatening than Langford. When Joe Louis came across the deprived Boston Tar Baby a quarter century later, he was nearly blind and scratching out a living shining shoes. Even an admirer like Wignall had to admit that Johnson "did considerable harm to boxing, but the men to whom he rendered the greatest disservice were pugilists of his own hue."

Ever mindful of the damage Jack Johnson had wrought, John Roxborough from the start lectured his young fighter on the conduct he needed to display if he was to climb out from under Johnson's considerable shadow. Later, as a public relations gimmick to win favor with the white press, Roxborough's informal advice was released as a written set of commandments:

- Joe was to never have his picture taken with a white woman.

- He was to never enter a nightclub alone.

- He would not participate in any soft fights.

- He would not participate in any fixed fights.
- He was to never gloat over a fallen opponent nor speak negatively about him before or after a fight.
- He was to maintain a deadpan expression in front of the cameras.
- He was to live and fight clean.

The white press, just as anxious to distance itself from Papa Jack, welcomed this refreshing set of personal values. In a typical treatment, Richards Vidmer of the *New York Herald-Tribune* soon wrote: "Joe Louis is as different a character from Jack Johnson as Lou Gehrig is from Al Capone. It seems to me that the Brown Bomber is just what the doctor ordered to restore life in the business of boxing. He is a God-fearing, Bible-reading, clean-living young man, to be admired, regardless of creed, race, or color. He is neither a showoff nor a dummy. Modest, quiet, unassuming in his manner, he goes about his business, doing the best job he can every time he climbs into the ring."

Characteristically, Joe would always refuse to judge Papa Jack, who was destined to die in the same hell-bent fashion in which he had lived, driving his car too fast and running off a North Carolina road one afternoon in 1946.

"When I got to be champ," Joe said years later, "half the letters I got had some word about Jack Johnson. A lot was from old colored people in the South. They thought he disgraced the Negro. I just figured he did what he wanted to do, and what he did had no effect on me."

Chapter Four

No Ordinary Joe

*Joe isn't as smart as Einstein; there are things
    beyond his scope;
He never will sing like a Melchior or speak like a
    Bayard Swope.
But of all the men in all the world, J. Louis wins
    the crown
For throwing a leather thunderbolt and blasting a
    rival down.*

—JOHN KIERAN, "OWED TO JOE LOUIS" (1935)

*J*oe stepped through the ropes on July 4, 1934, for his professional debut with a fluttering stomach and a good deal of trepidation. Would he give a good account of himself? Would he be able to remember everything that had been crammed into his head over the past four weeks? Would he have the stamina to go ten rounds after never having fought anything longer than a three-rounder?

He studied his older opponent. Jack Kracken, a black-haired fellow in white shorts, was a veteran club fighter. His impassive face gave the impression of supreme confidence.

"He looked like he had it made," Joe said, "and that bothered me a lot."

The opinion of some of the crowd at Trafton's gym was that Joe's handlers had made a mistake. "Those guys must be nuts," said one manager. "Kracken will kill that boy. Louis is in over his head."

Jack Blackburn tried to soothe Joe's nerves with a stream of talk. "One clean punch is better than a hundred punches," he said. "Bide your time. Place your punches and knock your opponent out." It was simply noise until the fight started.

At the bell the two boxers drew to each other like magnets. At 181 pounds, Joe had a six-pound advantage over Kracken. As Blackburn had instructed, Joe went straight to the body. Less than two minutes into the fight, a flurry of body blows caused Kracken to drop his arms and cover his stomach. Joe hit him on his unprotected jaw, and just like that it was over, a first-round knockout. Joe and Freddie Guinyard whooped it up like two youngsters on the playground.

Not everybody was happy. The victor had looked sluggish, his management team agreed. The reason was a mystery until Joe innocently mentioned that he had eaten a dozen bananas before the fight! His startled handlers, who let him keep the entire fifty-nine-dollar purse, could only stare and sigh. "After that," said Joe, "everybody watched me like a hawk before every fight."

Seven days later Joe earned an additional sixty-two dollars by knocking out, in the third round, Willie Davis, a black fighter whom he had befriended after coming to Chicago. (Davis later became one of Joe's sparring partners.) Because Joe was starting to get a small following, the venue for his third fight shifted from the cozy Bacon Casino to the larger, 2,100-seat Marigold Gardens. On July 29, he popped Larry Udell on the chin in the second round of a scheduled eight-rounder. The referee counted Udell out, and Joe left the arena with a check for $101.

The fight business was looking almost too easy to Joe, who next fought Jack Kranz on August 13. However, Kranz unexpectedly lasted the full six rounds. Joe got the decision and a piece of advice from his trainer. "Don't worry," counseled Blackburn. "Fights like that give you experience. You can't knock them all out." But he could try. Two weeks later he kayoed Buck Everett in the second round for his fifth straight victory.

The prize money continued to grow: $125 for taking on Kranz and $150 for Everett. For these first several fights his managers allowed him to keep the entire winnings; their 50-percent share of the pot (after expenses had been deducted) would come out of the much larger purses they trusted would be down the road. Upon Roxborough's suggestion, Joe sent most of the money home. Pat Brooks, his eyes growing wide over the several hundred dollars his stepson had made in just a few short weeks, began to become a fight fan.

After starting his pro career with five fights in Chicago, Joe returned home for a match with Alex Borchuk at Detroit's Naval Armory. The match was put together by the *Detroit Times*, a Hearst-owned daily not exactly known for its coverage of the black community, except for the usual crime stories.

"We didn't cover much black news," said Edgar Hayes, then a sports reporter for the *Times*. "Blacks were kind of invisible as far as newspapers were concerned. We had one editor who came out of Knoxville, I believe, or somewhere down south. Anyway, he was bitterly opposed to giving coverage to any blacks. Of course it was wrong, but that's the way things were run in those days." Joe Louis was something else, though, he admitted. "It was kind of hard to ignore him."

A large number of friends and family members turned out on the night of September 11, 1934, for their first look at Joe as a pro. Nervousness may have played a part in his mediocre performance. Borchuk, an aggressive 180-pounder from across the river in Windsor, Ontario, carried the action from the get-go and looked as if he would spoil the homecoming. In the second round the Canadian rocked Joe to his heels with a right to the point of his jaw, shattering his tooth in the process.

But Joe, who weighed in at 191 pounds, his heaviest yet, dropped Borchuk three times in the fourth frame. The final knockdown in the last half minute brought a towel flying from Borchuk's corner. The hard-gained victory earned Joe $106. He celebrated by staying over in Detroit for a couple of days and taking his friends bowling.

There was some back-room drama accompanying Joe's return to Detroit. According to John Roxborough's reminiscences, he had a closed-door meeting with Bingo Brown, the state boxing commissioner, and five white fight managers. There Brown reportedly tried to convince Roxborough that it would be in everybody's best interests if he took on a white comanager. When Roxborough refused to consider Brown's increasingly strident suggestions, the commissioner warned him that he would see to it that in the future Louis fought nothing but black boxers in the state—a threat that guaranteed small purses, since promoters viewed such matches as box-office duds.

"Then Joe won't fight in this state," Roxborough responded. "We sure as hell don't need Michigan. But when people start yelling to see the home-town boy, I'm going to tell them exactly what happened."

Detroit Free Press sportswriter Eddie Edgar, the only other person in attendance, vacillated in his recollection of events. Sometimes he maintained the meeting was friendly, not antagonistic, just some fellows sitting around drinking and talking. On other occasions he assigned himself a role as Roxborough's only ally in a room filled with white oppressors. The truth probably lies somewhere in between, Brown and his cronies trying to persuade Roxborough to cut a deal but stopping short of actually blacklisting him. The proof is that over the next eight months Joe would have five more fights in Michigan, including three in Detroit. After that he would fight almost exclusively in New York and Chicago.

In his next time out, Joe went the full ten rounds with Adolph Wiater at the Arcadia Gardens in Chicago. Wiater, who hailed from Green Bay,

Wisconsin, proved as rugged as the weather back in his hometown. He crowded Joe all night and was the first fighter to really bloody him. But Joe rallied to win the last three rounds to get the decision.

Joe's performance against Wiater had Roxborough crowing. Nine days later he took Marshall Miles, a member of a well-to-do Buffalo family that had made its money in the numbers racket, to his office to meet Joe. "Come on," said Roxie, "I want you to meet the next heavyweight champion of the world."

Miles, in town to watch Joe's treasured Tigers take on St. Louis's "Gas House Gang" Cardinals in the opener of the World Series, thought, "My gosh, they're certainly jumping the gun." Miles and Joe hit it off, discovering a mutual interest in horses and showgirls. With more money and time than he knew what to do with, Miles became one of Joe's primary "running buddies," making the circuit of nightclubs and training camps with him. After the war he would become his manager.

On October 24, by which time Dizzy Dean had broken Joe's heart by stopping the Tigers in the seventh game of the fall classic, Joe returned to the Arcadia Gardens to go toe to toe with Art Sykes. Sykes was knocked cold in the eighth round and remained unconscious for thirty minutes. Joe fretted, vowing to quit if his traumatized opponent didn't recover. Sykes finally was revived in the hospital. Joe, much relieved, went on to flatten his next three opponents—each of them in less than three rounds—running his five-month professional record to a perfect 11-0. The fact that two of the victims, Stanley Poreda of Hoboken and Charley Massera of Pittsburgh, were knockout artists of some ability failed to catch the attention of the eastern sporting press.

Poreda's manager, Mushky Jackson, knew why. "The fight itself was something nobody ever heard of," he said. "My fighter took a count of thirty-nine in one round. The first punch from Louis put him down for nine, the second punch for another nine. The third punch knocked Poreda out of the ring, and the referee kept counting until he got back. He got up to twenty-one.

"When I got back to New York, I tell everybody what a fighter that Louis is. But nobody paid any attention. He was colored, and colored fighters were a dime a dozen."

Despite the lack of publicity, Joe's reputation within the sport's inner circle was growing. Ray Arcel, the legendary trainer whose career stretched from the 1920s through the 1970s, was in Charley Massera's corner when he fought Louis in Chicago in late 1934.

"I didn't know how good Louis was," Arcel said a half century later. He remembered talking with his old friend, Jack Blackburn, before the fight. "I don't want to discourage you, Ray," Blackburn told him. "I'm glad to see you. But I got me a fighter!"

Massera took a right cross to the chin and was counted out in the third round. Afterwards, Blackburn asked Arcel what he thought of Joe.

"You got a fighter," Arcel agreed.

Joe's purses picked up. The Massera fight brought him $1,200, up from the $300 he had received for knocking Poreda halfway back to Hoboken. For his twelfth and final fight of 1934, a hard-fought, eighth-round knockout of Lee Ramage on December 14 in Chicago, Joe earned $2,200. It was an amount equal to what he had made for his first eleven money fights combined, and it represented about a year's salary for the average workingman. With his newfound wealth he sent money home, bought snappy new suits, and plunked down some cash for his first car, a black Buick with whitewall tires. That Christmas he spent freely on family and friends: "I was happy and they were happy. I knew there was no place for me to go except up."

Joe's victory over Ramage, a tough, clever boxer who was considered the best heavyweight on the West Coast, pushed him into the rankings. At the start of 1935 *The Ring* rated him as the ninth-ranked contender for the crown, then worn by Max Baer. This boosted Roxborough's and Black's confidence enough for them to call James J. Johnston, the boxing promoter at Madison Square Garden. Before doing so, Joe's managers asked Jack Blackburn what he thought.

"Yeah, he's ready for New York," he agreed. "But New York ain't ready for him."

Sure enough, Johnston turned Roxborough and Black away. There was no money to be made booking a colored fighter, he explained. Unless, of course, his boy was willing to take a fall. "I told you so," said Blackburn.

Joe's first fight of 1935 was on January 4 against seventh-ranked Patsy Perroni, who'd been fighting professionally for six years. The fight went the full ten rounds at Detroit's Olympia. Joe knocked Perroni down three times, was staggered with several hard hits himself, but managed to stay on his feet. He earned the hard-fought decision and $4,227 to go with it. One week later at Pittsburgh's Duquesne Gardens, he disposed of Hans Birkie, an interior decorator turned boxer, with a knockout at one minute and forty-seven seconds in the final round.

In February Joe traveled for the first time to California, bringing along Vunies, for whom the trip was a high school graduation present. Once again, his opponent was Lee Ramage, and once again Joe knocked him out, this time taking less than two rounds to do so.

The rematch with Ramage was notable for a couple of reasons. It

inspired Scotty Monteith, a Detroit manager and promoter, to call
Roxborough and suggest what became Joe's most famous moniker.

"The kid can't miss," Monteith said. "He's going to be a champ. He's a
bomber. Come to think of it, that boy is a real brown bomber." Soon sportswriters were referring to Joe Louis in print as the "Brown Bomber" (including Charles Ward of the *Detroit Free Press*, who has also been credited with
coining the nickname).

Of greater importance, the fight was attended by the man who would
do the most to further Joe's career. Together, the newly christened Brown
Bomber and "Uncle Mike" Jacobs would make millions of dollars, pull boxing out of its doldrums, and give the American public some of history's most
memorable ring battles.

>‹

Mike Jacobs had endured a youth as impoverished as Joe's. He was
born in 1880 to Jewish parents who had emigrated from eastern Europe via
Ireland, which made their decision to settle in the tough Irish west side of
New York, Hell's Kitchen, instead of the Jewish district on the east side of
the city, a bit more understandable. Jacobs learned to ball his fists early,
fighting off competitors as a ten-year-old newsboy determined to hold onto
his stock of papers.

He also worked as a digger, selling opera and theater tickets for organized scalpers, then going into business for himself when he was just twelve.
When he wasn't hawking tickets, he was selling refreshments on excursion
boats. Always looking for an edge, he would sell overly salted peanuts at
cost, then make his profit selling overpriced lemonade to his thirsty customers. Another trick was to casually toss candy into the lap of a woman
enjoying the sea breezes with her male friend, as if it was a free sample. A
few minutes later he would approach the lady's escort for payment; in
almost every instance the flustered gentleman was too embarrassed not to
pay up. He also peddled his own special seasick remedy, which when broken
down turned out to be nothing more than tea with lemon.

As a teenager Jacobs pounded the sidewalks so hard selling tickets to
the Metropolitan Opera that his feet actually bled. Through his connections at the theater, he eventually signed Enrico Caruso to a series of one-
night performances that guaranteed the impresario $1,000 an evening.
Jacobs cleared $80,000, his first fortune. Later he arranged successful tours
for Ethel and Lionel Barrymore and suffragette Emmeline Parkhurst, brokered World Series tickets, and created a concessions empire at military
posts that he sold for $1 million just before the First World War ended.

In 1916 Jacobs joined forces with Tex Rickard, advancing the flamboyant promoter the money he needed to stage the Jess Willard-Frank

Moran heavyweight title fight. In exchange Jacobs got blocks of choice seats, which he sold for a big profit. Five years later Jacobs put together a syndicate of ticket brokers to bankroll Rickard's championship match between Jack Dempsey and George Carpentier. Eighty thousand people paid a total of more than $1.7 million for seats at a makeshift wooden bowl constructed on land outside Jersey City, New Jersey. Jacobs's share of boxing's first million-dollar gate amounted to a cool $250,000.

Although Rickard was the matchmaker at the new Madison Square Garden, which opened at Eighth Avenue and Forty-ninth Street in 1924, Jacobs's promotional expertise literally made him a hidden power. While he had an office at the Forrest Hotel a block away, he actually conducted much of his business inside a secret, windowless storage room at the Garden. When Rickard died of pneumonia in 1929, Jacobs seemed to be the obvious choice to succeed him. Instead, arena executives chose a dapper, slightly built ex-fight manager named Jimmy Johnston.

Johnston's monikers—the Boy Bandit and Little Larceny—hint at how he liked to handle the business of arranging fights at the Garden, which during Rickard's tenure had become the number-one fight venue in the country. Champions and contenders were made and broken there, and not always on the square. Through contracts and connections, the Garden controlled the lucrative heavyweight division, but it was Johnston's bad luck that he got the job just as the Great Depression hit. Aggravating the problem, observed John Kieran of the *New York Times* in 1930, was that when Jack Dempsey "went over the hill, the ring lost most of its drama." Gene Tunney, who had defeated the Manassas Mauler in a pair of memorable bouts, had been a dud of a champion in the public's eyes. When Tunney retired in 1930, it created a free-for-all among several uninspiring candidates, none of whom figured to wear the crown as smartly as the magnetic Dempsey had.

On June 12, 1930, a Dempsey look-alike, German boxer Max Schmeling, fought Jack Sharkey for Tunney's vacated title. The unpopular Sharkey, of Lithuanian extraction (his real name was Joseph Paul Zakauskas), was dubbed "the sobbing sailor" because he had complained long and hard after he had lost a title fight when Dempsey socked him in the groin in their 1927 meeting. A low blow once again did Sharkey in. In the fourth round he floored Schmeling, but as the German was being counted out, officials ruled that Sharkey was guilty of hitting below the belt and thus disqualified. The underdog Schmeling, apparently a fine actor (films revealed no low blow), won the title while writhing on the canvas.

The smell of this fight further reduced public confidence in the sport. Schmeling, who drew criticism from his own country's press for his unconvincing win, defended his title twice before meeting Sharkey again in 1932.

In what has been described as the worst decision in ring history, Sharkey was declared the victor. It astonished everybody, particularly Schmeling's manager, Joe Jacobs, who earned a tiny slice of sports immortality by screaming into an open microphone, "We wuz robbed!"

Into this odoriferous environment plodded a giant of a man who proved to be the most offensive of them all. Primo Carnera —"Da Preem" to his largely Italian fanbase, the "Ambling Alp" to amused sportswriters— weighed twenty-two pounds when he was born near Venice in 1906. Leaving home as a youngster with his canoe-sized feet wrapped in burlap, he eventually found work in Paris as a circus strongman. Standing six and a half feet tall and weighing upwards of three hundred pounds, Carnera entertained audiences with his prodigious strength. A favorite stunt was to grab ropes attached to two cars, their motors running, and prevent them from racing off in opposite directions.

Carnera's manager, Leon See, brought him to the United States on New Year's Day, 1930. The naive, trusting fighter—whose pathetic story would one day inspire Budd Schulberg's novel, *The Harder They Fall*— immediately became the tool of racketeers Owney Madden and Dutch Schultz and engaged in a long series of fixed bouts and setups that padded his record and brought him to the threshold of the heavyweight crown. In one such outing against Elziar Rioux, Carnera knocked his opponent to the floor six times within the first forty-seven seconds of the opening bell, although nobody in the large crowd had seen him land a single blow. One member of the entourage, "Good Time Walter" Friedman, conceded that many of Carnera's bouts were "mischievous." In early 1933, in an elimination match to determine who would meet Jack Sharkey for the championship, he killed a promising Boston fighter, Ernie Schaaf, at Madison Square Garden. Compounding the tragedy was the heavy suspicion that Schaaf, whose financial backers included Sharkey, had been instructed to throw the fight anyway. (Cries of "Fake! Fake!" had accompanied Schaaf's fall to the canvas.) Four months later, on June 29, 1933, Carnera capped his byzantine climb to the title by knocking out Sharkey with a shadow punch.

Schaaf's death was probably more attributable to a beating he had taken earlier from Max Baer than from Carnera's soft left jab. If so, it meant that Baer was responsible for the deaths of two boxers during his career, which perhaps accounted for his erratic approach to the sport.

Baer, born in Nebraska and raised in California, started boxing professionally in 1929 when he was twenty years old. He owed his well-muscled physique to genetics (his parents each measured six feet and 230-plus pounds) and his early work swinging a meat axe in his father's slaughterhouse. In 1930 in San Francisco, Baer knocked out Frankie Campbell, who later died of his injury. Distraught, Baer took three months off and moved to New York. Ironically, the first man he met in his return to the ring in early 1931 was Ernie Schaaf, who won their bout but then was seriously injured when they met again in August 1932. Six months later, when Carnera dealt the brain-damaged Schaaf a deadly blow, most doctors agreed that the Italian giant had merely finished off what Baer had started.

At heart, Madcap Maxie was more clown than killer. He had a certifiably murderous punch, but he'd always preferred spending his time in the glare of neon and klieg lights than in the dankness of the gym. He married movie actress Dorothy Dunbar, made the rounds of nightclubs and studios, and reportedly needed ten trunks to transport his considerable wardrobe. "What a ham!" was how he frequently described himself. His greatest ambition was to become a star on the big screen; the high-profile world of prizefighting was simply the bloody means to achieving that end.

Baer, of Jewish, German, and Scottish extraction, often wore the Star of David sewn onto his trunks, a minor publicity gimmick. When he beat Max Schmeling in the spring of 1933 enroute to meeting Carnera for the championship, he innocently believed—as did millions of other Americans in the early 1930s—that Nazi Germany's intense nationalism could be defined more by its love of sport than its hatred of any particular ethnic group. While in training for the Carnera bout, he poked fun at the German government's decision to ban the movie, *The Prizefighter and the Lady*, in which he'd had his acting debut. "They didn't ban the picture because I have Jewish blood. They banned it because I knocked out Max Schmeling. It doesn't make much difference to me, but I'm sorry for the women and children of Germany. Too bad they won't get a chance to see the world's greatest lover and the world's greatest fighter in action."

Baer treated his title shot as a big joke. At the weigh-in he plucked hairs off Carnera's chest, saying in a singsong voice, "He loves me; he loves me not." He even tried tickling the bewildered boxer, saying, "Boo, you big palooka." The night of the fight, June 14, 1934, Baer had no trouble handling the inept Carnera, flooring him eleven times while laughing and talking to people at ringside. At one point both fighters fell together, prompting Baer to say, "Last one up is a sissy." When the tangle-footed Carnera stumbled while backing up, Baer roared with laughter.

Earlier, New York boxing commissioner Bill Brown had called Baer "a bum" as he watched him play the fool in training. After his final knockdown of Carnera, Baer leaned over the ropes and asked Brown, "Well, Mr. Commissioner, what do you think of me now?"

"You're still a bum," Brown said disgustedly. Then he added: "And so is Carnera."

Frauds, clowns, stiffs, and bums. Such was the state of boxing as Joe Louis embarked on his professional career. Not long before Baer reduced the mountainous Carnera to an anthill of ash, syndicated columnist Paul Gallico had witnessed another stinkeroo of a match between two alleged heavyweight contenders, Walter Neusel and King Levinsky.

"I thought that the whole fight industry was magnificently summed up one second after the bell rang," he wrote. "In one corner was the big, burly, powerful Levinsky. In the other, his equal in size and strength though not in build, was Neusel. As you sat and looked at these two bruisers you thought—'boy, oh boy, when they meet something must fall.' Then the bell rang, they got up out of their chairs and walked right into a clinch without a blow being struck. They COULDN'T have been tired at that point, unless they were both born tired . . . maybe it's just a general grouch. But if Levinsky and Neusel are championship contenders, 'eaven 'elp the promoters."

Mike Jacobs, a religious man in his own way, wasn't banking on divine intervention to pull the fight game out of its mess. Instead, he capitalized on a major misstep by Jimmy Johnston. In 1933 Johnston canceled Madison Square Garden's participation in charity events in which the arena donated a share of the receipts to some worthwhile cause. Left in the cold was the Milk Fund for Babies, a favorite charity of Mrs. William Randolph Hearst, wife of the newspaper tycoon.

Jacobs was approached by three Hearst reporters: Edward J. Frayne, sports editor of the *New York American*; Bill Farnsworth, sports editor of the *New York Journal*; and columnist Damon Runyan, who also was one of the country's best-known short-story writers. As the principal writers and editors of the Hearst flagship papers, they controlled the sports section. Until the Garden severed its relationship, they had cranked out reams of free publicity for the arena and its fighters.

Now the trio proposed to form a corporation that would promote boxing events in direct competition with Johnston and the Garden. The arrangement would be similar to the one struck with the Garden. The corporation, to be called the Twentieth Century Sporting Club, would make sure the Milk Fund got a percentage of the gate in exchange for blanket coverage of the new club's events. The major difference was that under this new scheme Runyan, Frayne, and Farnsworth would share in the profits, unbeknownst to their employer. Of course, this was highly unethical, so the writers needed to be silent partners—*extremely* silent. Jacobs would be the highly visible head of the corporation, handling the details of sales and promotion, and protecting his partners' identities. The four men signed partnership papers and leased the aging New York Hippodrome at Forty-fourth Street and Ninth Avenue for fights.

What the Twentieth Century Sporting Club needed now was a fighter that could excite the public. Several people pointed Jacobs in Joe's direction, including Sam Pian and Art Winch, comanagers of middleweight champion Barney Ross, and *Ring* editor Nat Fleischer, who also did some freelance publicity work for Jacobs. Uncle Mike was at Wrigley Field in Los Angeles the night Ramage went down in two. Afterwards he paid a visit to the victor's dressing room.

"Joe, you can fight on the level when you fight for me," he promised, lisping through his poorly fitting false teeth. "You don't have to drop a fight to anybody. I'll make a lot of money for you."

And, of course, for himself. During his twelve years as head of the Twentieth Century Sporting Club, Jacobs grossed an estimated $10 million staging Joe's fights alone. All told he arranged sixty-one championship fights and 1,500 shows in all divisions. Dan Parker of the *New York Mirror* felt Uncle Mike should be called "Uncle Wolf" for his business dealings, which included arranging cards for mob-controlled fighters.

Joe always saw Jacobs in a different light.

"There's been a lot of talk about Mike Jacobs using me for a sucker, but that's all wrong," Joe said in a two-part autobiography published in *Life* magazine in 1948, five years before Jacobs's death. "If it wasn't for Mike Jacobs I would never have got to be champion. He fixed it for me to get a crack at the title, and he never once asked me to do anything wrong or phony in the ring. When I was in the army and out of cash he was always good for a loan. He never wanted interest. It was a friendly thing. I like 'Uncle Mike.' I knew he took a gamble on me. He made a lot of money through me, but he figured to lose, too."

Jacobs got the publicity mill cranking. In late March of 1935, he arranged for about thirty sportswriters to travel from New York to Detroit to view Joe in action against Natie Brown. The Jewish boxer didn't figure to present much of a challenge to Joe, whose previous fight against Donald "Reds" Barry went beyond the first round only because of Joe's empathy for a local sportswriter, Harry Smith, who had predicted a third-round knockout. Joe liked Smith, so he carried Barry. He enlightened his puzzled trainer at the end of the second stanza.

"Well," said Blackburn, "it's round three now, so don't fuck up." Joe didn't. Rising from his stool at the bell, he proceeded to quickly finish off Barry. Prediction fulfilled.

Things didn't proceed as smoothly against Natie Brown, however. Brown fought defensively, and Joe failed to pierce his guard. Joe won the ten-round affair but left the ring disappointed in his performance.

Not to worry, he was told later by Jacobs, who had joined Joe's handlers for a victory celebration at the Frog Club, a Paradise Valley black-and-tan joint catering to members of both races. Uncle Mike assured Joe that the writers had been unanimously impressed. After a hard night of partying at Jacobs's expense, they would return to their respective papers and write generally glowing stories about the Brown Bomber from Detroit.

As the merrymaking grew more boisterous, Jacobs laid out his plan to make Joe the first black heavyweight to have a shot at the title since Jack Johnson. Over the next several weeks Joe would fight regularly to keep himself in the public eye. Meanwhile, the Hearst papers would do their part, drumming up publicity for a projected fight with Primo Carnera. Where they went from there depended on how hungry a fighter Joe proved to be.

Jacobs produced a contract that gave the Twentieth Century Sporting Club the exclusive right to promote Joe's fights for the next three years, with an option for renewal. In return Joe would get $37 \frac{1}{2}$ percent of the gate receipts. The management crew of Roxborough, Black, and Blackburn would stay intact. Satisfied with the terms, Joe retreated into a lavatory, the only quiet spot available, and signed.

Joe and his team understood that New York was the beginning of the big time and big money. Through April and May he eagerly polished his fists on five journeymen fighters in such towns as Dayton, Peoria, and Kalamazoo, knocking out each of them. Only one lasted past the third round. The paychecks were small, but they enabled him to finally fulfill a dream. For a year he had been secretly hoarding his prize money to buy his mother a new house. On Easter Sunday, he surprised Lillie Barrow by presenting her with a four-bedroom brick bungalow at 2100 McDougall, near Elmwood Cemetery. It cost $11,500, including repairs, and Joe kicked in an additional $3,000 to furnish it. "I was prouder of this than anything I had ever done," said Joe, who also made down payments on homes for his sisters, Susie and Emmarell, and stepbrother, Pat Brooks Jr.

Word soon came that Jacobs had made arrangements for Joe and Carnera to meet in June. The Louis entourage left for New York in the middle of May. The bright lights and quickened pace nearly left Joe's head spinning. First was a press conference at Mike Jacobs's office, which was packed with reporters, photographers, and newsreel cameramen. Although Uncle Mike handled most of the questions, the bashful boxer still felt awkward. "I couldn't talk as fast as those reporters were talking," he remembered.

Next stop on the promotional merry-go-round was the Harlem Opera House, where Roxborough and Black had booked Joe to do a boxing skit with Dusty Fletcher. For four shows a day for an entire week, Joe skipped rope and punched a speed bag while Fletcher told jokes. The packed houses loved it. Joe ended the skit by blasting the bag into the seats. "That's what you're gonna do to Carnera!" members of the audience invariably would yell.

Joe was housed at an apartment house at 381 Edgecombe, an address that jazzman Duke Ellington would soon make his, too. Evenings were spent at Small's Paradise on Seventh Avenue at 135th Street. Here he met show people like dancer Bill "Bojangles" Robinson and chorus girl Marion Eggberg, with whom he would carry on an affair for several years. At the Cotton Club he was introduced to a young singer named Lena Horne, another future flame. Lillie Barrow's antennae may have picked up her son's nocturnal frequency. Just before leaving for his training camp at Pompton Lakes, New Jersey, Joe received a giant Bible from his mother. Mike Jacobs made sure the photographers got plenty of shots of his humble, God-fearing fighter reading it.

In addition to his growing legion of admirers, Joe's success was bringing the usual bloodsuckers out of the woodwork. Atler Ellis, his former trainer at the Brewster gym, sued to get a piece of Joe's contract, but the suit was settled in Roxborough's favor in April 1935. A short while later Jack Johnson visited camp and unsuccessfully tried to persuade Roxborough to jettison Blackburn and hire him in his place.

White gangsters and promoters also tried to muscle in. While it's impossible to get the particulars of these stories straight, it appears that the Purple Gang was involved—for good or bad, however, cannot be firmly established. One variation has the gang trying to intimidate Roxborough through an intermediary named Lefty Clark, a well-known bootlegger who ran a gambling joint in a downriver suburb of Detroit. Roxie supposedly held his ground and wasn't bothered again, possibly because he knew that the repeal of Prohibition and the imprisonment of several top Purples had caused the gang to lose much of its teeth. The positive version of events has the Purples interceding on Joe's behalf after Owney Madden, the white bootlegger who owned Harlem's Cotton Club and controlled several fighters, invited Roxborough to the nightspot and informed him that he wanted to buy his fighter's contract for $50,000. A phone call from Detroit reportedly got the New York gangster to back off.

Joe's first fight in New York gave those members of the eastern press who had not been part of Mike Jacobs's junket to Detroit the chance to see for themselves the kid that Uncle Mike and his cronies had been raving about.

"My first impression of Louis was how young and strong he was and how he could punch," recalled Shirley Povich, longtime sports columnist for the *Washington Post*. "But here was Carnera, a mastodonic guy, with great height and reach and outweighing Joe by fifty or sixty pounds. There was a great curiosity as to how he would fare against him."

Normally that would have been enough to produce a healthy gate. But world events were transforming the ring at Yankee Stadium into a surrogate battlefield. Italy's fascist dictator, Benito Mussolini, was preparing to invade tiny Ethiopia, one of the few independent black countries in the world. Although the average American, black or white, knew little of Ethiopia (also known as Abysinnia), the symbolism of barefooted black patriots bravely battling jackbooted white imperialists was too hard to resist. The actual invasion wouldn't take place until October, when a quarter million of Il Duce's troops crossed the border and were stubbornly resisted by an ill-equipped army one-tenth their size. But in the late spring of 1935 Emperor Haile Selassie already was a hero to American blacks, and Joe was a convenient metaphor to rally around.

The press played up the David vs. Goliath comparison. Cartoonists typically portrayed the smaller, darker Louis as representing Ethiopia, overshadowed by the towering, glowering Carnera (who had been personally received by Mussolini and was a reservist in the Italian army).

City officials were concerned about aggravating racial unrest. William Randolph Hearst talked of canceling the bout, now scheduled for June 25 at Yankee Stadium. Their fears were not unfounded: in March, rumors of a white shopkeeper shooting a black youth had sparked a minor riot in Harlem. Columnists like Westbrook Pegler and Arthur Brisbane irresponsibly fanned the flames of discord with dire warnings of possible large-scale altercations between Italian and Negro spectators. This revived memories of the race riots that had broken out in the wake of Jack Johnson's victories and helped support segregationists' arguments as to why blacks should remain in their place, inside and outside the prize ring.

Joe began to feel the pressure as various black nationalists visited his camp and made him aware of his role as a racial ambassador. This was a wholly unexpected part for Joe to play, something for which he did not feel the least bit qualified. For the first time, but certainly not the last, he would be fighting for something much larger than himself. In his words, "They put a heavy weight on my twenty-year-old shoulders. Now, not only did I have to beat the man, but I had to beat him for a cause."

The dinosaur-sized Carnera, categorized as *Carnivorous Horribilis* by the *New York Times's* erudite sportswriter, John Kieran, represented a challenge of size, if not ability. To prepare, Joe had worked with the three largest sparring partners his managers could find. The trio of Seal Harris, Ace Clark, and Leonard Dixon averaged six-foot-four and 250 pounds.

Jack Blackburn devised the strategy. "Chappie told Joe to use his fists like an axe," remembered Freddie Guinyard, who was in Carnera's corner as the Louis camp's official observer. "He said to chop Carnera down—not to be whittlin' away at him, but to hit him hard, like he was swinging an axe."

Joe stepped into the brightly lit ring that evening at Yankee Stadium and felt almost naked under the gaze of some 62,000 people. Thirteen hundred policemen, as well as three hundred plainclothesmen sprinkled throughout the stands, were on hand to handle any outbreaks of violence.

Special trains had delivered black fans from Baltimore, Chicago, Detroit, Indianapolis, New Haven, Philadelphia, Pittsburgh, and Toledo. Four hundred reporters, the largest press congregation since Dempsey fought Carpentier fourteen years earlier, hunched over their typewriters and telegraph keys.

Tuxedoed ring announcer Harry Balogh began the main event by appealing to a universal sense of sportsmanship. "Tonight," he said into the microphone, "we have gathered here to watch a contest of athletic skill. We are Americans. That means that we have come from homes of many different faiths, and we represent a lot of different nationalities. In America we admire the athlete who can win by virtue of his skill. Let me then ask you to join me in the sincere wish that regardless of race, color, or creed the better man may emerge victorious."

Balogh's words had barely stopped echoing through the packed stadium when the identity of the better man was firmly established. A series of lefts and rights to Carnera's head drove his lower teeth through his upper lip, causing him to spurt blood. The second round was more of the same. Blackburn, flashing hand signals like a catcher, directed Joe throughout. Fingers pointed downward meant to attack the midsection; fingers pointed toward the sky meant to go for the head.

To his credit, Carnera hung on through a merciless thrashing, but he knew he had met his master when Louis actually lifted him off his feet as they struggled in a clinch late in the fifth round. Through his shredded lips, the astonished Carnera said, "I should be doing this to you."

In the sixth round he absorbed a savage bombardment. A right to the jaw sent him spiraling to the deck. "He went down slowly, like a great chimney that had been dynamited," wrote John Kieran. He wobbled to his feet and soon was smashed back to the floor. A combination knocked him down a third time. He struggled back up, but referee Arthur Donovan had seen enough. He signaled the fight was over.

Joe was the toast of Harlem. So as not to cut into the gate, there had been no local radio broadcast, but 20,000 people gathered at the Savoy Ballroom on Lenox Avenue quickly got word of the result via a telephone call. Bojangles Robinson, rushing back from Yankee Stadium in order to participate in the revelry, announced, "I'm so happy I could eat a mud sandwich." Between the snake dancing and gin guzzling, the multitudes repeatedly called for a personal appearance by the man of the hour. Joe, who insisted that he was too sleepy, finally decided to calm the Savoy's nervous managers and placate the raucous crowd. He showed up at 2:30 in the morning, mumbled a few words into a dead microphone, and everybody eventually went home happy.

Especially Joe. Although he had been his usual expressionless self as

Balogh directed him to the center of the ring and raised his right hand in victory, he confessed that, deep inside, he felt a warm sense of satisfaction and joy. It "was the night I remember best in all my fighting," he said. "If you was ever a raggedy kid and you come to something like that night you'd know. I don't thrill to things like some people. I only feel good. I felt the best that night."

Contributing to his happiness was the realization that he was probably already the best heavyweight in the world. Twelve days earlier, he and Blackburn had taken the one-hour trip from Pompton Lakes to Madison Square Garden to watch Max Baer listlessly lose the heavyweight crown to James Braddock. It was one of the biggest upsets ever in a title fight. Joe, whose win over Carnera advanced his unblemished record to 23-0 with nineteen knockouts, couldn't believe that Braddock, who had lost twenty-six professional bouts, was now the champion.

"How come not me?" he asked his managers, who assured him his time would come. Looking back at his impatience, an older Joe Louis recalled in his autobiography: "I was still young and still black. I had to wait my turn."

➤❖

So much was written about Joe's lethal punches after the Carnera fight that some opponents actually grew rubber legged in the locker room thinking about them. Harry "Kingfish" Levinsky, a onetime fish peddler managed by his equally picturesque sister, Leapin' Lena, provided comic relief between Joe's bouts with Carnera and Max Baer.

Joe and Levinsky went at it on August 7, 1935, at Chicago's Comiskey Park. Sensing that Kingfish might bolt for the dressing room door at any minute, Mike Jacobs ordered officials to start the fight a half hour sooner than scheduled.

"Why?" argued one. "It's too early."

"It's gonna rain," said Jacobs, ignoring the clear, star-studded sky.

The apprehensive Kingfish, a hard puncher who had previously squared off with the likes of Carnera, Baer, and Sharkey, practically had to be shoved into the ring for his ninety-eighth professional fight. A straight right sent him hurling towards the apron. He got up and took a left hook to the head. That was it. At the end, Levinsky was sitting on the ropes, begging the referee, "Don't let him hit me again." In two minutes and twenty-two seconds Joe had earned $53,000, slightly less than what he had gotten for the Carnera fight. Afterward the normally deadpan victor allowed himself what Newsweek described as his "first sincere smile to the cameras." The reason was that he had made a bet with his handlers that they would all go on the wagon for six months if he took care of Levinsky in one round.

The following day Jacobs announced that the matchup the sporting public was demanding would take place September 24. Max Baer, recently deposed champion, had signed to fight boxing's new sensation at Yankee Stadium. To the disappointment of thousands of young women, the date would also be Joe's wedding night.

Joe had been seriously courting Marva Trotter since spring, even inviting her to Detroit to meet the family. Marva had been introduced to him the previous December at Trafton's gym by Al Monroe, a writer for the *Chicago Defender*. She had been part of a crowd watching Joe prepare for the first Lee Ramage fight.

"Marva was a lovely girl," said Truman Gibson, a young Atlanta-born lawyer who worked for the Chicago firm representing Julian Black. "She came from a family of very beautiful sisters. She was very smart and assertive, but not obnoxiously so. She was gregarious if she knew you."

The nineteen-year-old secretary, who was five feet and six inches tall and lightly complected, definitely wanted to know Joe. "I gave the big man a once-over," she said. "It was love at first sight."

Joe was similarly smitten. She was the type that he always fell for: independent-minded, elegantly dressed, a ready smile. "Oh, I was crazy about those other beauties," he admitted, talking of all the young ladies available to him, "but I loved Marva."

At that time a fighter's love life was often put on hold. Blackburn preached sexual abstinence leading up to a fight, believing as most trainers and coaches did then that an orgasm kept an athlete from achieving his physical peak. When Joe first met Marva, he had a girlfriend of several years, Bennie Franklin, a small, perky Alabama transplant with long shiny hair. They had been seeing each other, best as they could, since Joe was fourteen. The relationship was doomed because she was the stepdaughter of one of his sisters. Since Joe coyly described their long-term relationship as being "as close as a relationship can get," there's a good chance that she represented his first sexual conquest, though he also confessed to "a little fooling around here and there." While their affair was not technically incestuous, it was close enough to warrant severe reproach if they had been caught by a family member at one of the several lover's lanes they liked to frequent on Belle Isle.

The first sexual experience that Joe was willing to admit occured in the fall of 1934 after he had moved in with Bill Bottoms. It involved a middle-aged woman who lived in the same apartment building. She seduced the virile twenty-year-old fighter a week or so before the Massera fight. Joe felt so guilty about breaking training that the next day he ran ten miles instead of five and boxed six rounds instead of three. Blackburn, mystified by this excess energy, finally asked, "Chappie, what the hell is wrong with you?"

Raging hormones accounted for Joe's and Marva's sudden decision to tie the knot. Marva, a teenager brought up in a proper household, was a virgin, and Joe was like a snorting bull.

"When Marva came out, my blood started throbbing," Joe said of the small, quick wedding ceremony which took place at 7:45 P.M. at a friend's apartment at 381 Edgecombe. "She looked like something you'd see in a fairy-tale book, with a white-silk velvet gown, a long train in the back trimmed with ermine, and a bunch of little white flowers in her hand." Marva's brother, a minister, officiated. Her sister Novella was the maid of honor, and Julian Black was the best man. A few other friends were there to watch Joe kiss the bride, then rush out the door, across a sidewalk packed with well-wishers, and into a limousine for the hectic ride to the ballpark. A motorcycle escort, sirens wailing, got him through the jammed streets. Once dressed and in the ring, he glanced at his new bride stationed in a front row.

"I wanted this to be a quick fight," he said. "I wanted to start being a married man as soon as possible, but I put all those thoughts out of my mind and concentrated on Baer."

Earlier in the day, the Merry Madcap had gotten Joe smiling at the weigh-in. The tale of the tape, reproduced here, shows Joe's measurements as they were in his prime and how they stacked up against those of his chief rival:

	BAER	**LOUIS**
Age	26	21
Weight	210 lbs.	199 lbs.
Height	6 ft., 2 $1/_2$ in.	6 ft., 1 $1/_2$ in.
Reach	81 $1/_2$ in.	76 in.
Neck	17 in.	16 in.
Biceps	14 $3/_4$ in.	13 in.
Wrist	8 in.	7 $3/_4$ in.
Chest (normal)	44 in.	41 in.
Chest (expanded)	47 in.	43 in.
Waist	33 in.	34 in.
Thigh	18 in.	20 in.
Calf	13 in.	15 in.
Ankle	8 $1/_2$ in.	10 in.

The only numbers Mike Jacobs concerned himself with were ticket sales. The hype helped produce a crowd of 88,150 that paid $1,000,832, the largest gate since the second Dempsey-Tunney fight in 1927. In addition, Jacobs sold the radio rights to Buick for a reported $27,500.

The fight didn't come close to matching the hoopla. Baer, swinging wildly, left himself wide open to Joe's left jabs, which he later described as feeling "like a bomb bursting in your face." After the first round Blackburn told Joe, "You got him. Just keep up like you're doing. He won't last."

And he didn't. Joe worked over his head and body, and by the start of the fourth round Baer wore the look of someone who would have much rather been somewhere else than inside this fistmill. A hard left and a hard right knocked Max off his feet for the first time in his career. He rose to one knee, shaking his head back and forth while tens of thousands of leather-lunged spectators screamed for him to get back up.

But Baer, the faces of Frankie Campbell and Ernie Schaaf possibly swimming through his rattled noggin, remained on bended knee while the referee counted him out. The crowd hooted and yelled that he was a quitter. Afterward he showed that Joe's thunderous blows hadn't dislodged his sense of humor. "I could have struggled up once more," he said, "but when I get executed, people are going to have to pay more than twenty-five dollars a seat to watch it." *

In what had now become a postfight ritual, black neighborhoods from coast to coast erupted in spontaneous celebration. Harlemites partied until dawn. "Milling thousands of Negro men, women, and children turned the district into bedlam as they surged through the streets, howling gleefully, blowing horns, dancing madly, pounding on pots and pans," the *New York Sun* reported.

Joe received immediate national acclaim. By beating the man generally considered to be his only competition, he had become boxing's uncrowned champion. And his knockouts had brought excitement and the magical million-dollar gate back into the sport; writers called him "a boon to boxing." Most observers agreed that it was just a matter of time before Joe met—and defeated—Braddock to make it all official.

"Louis, a boxer still two years removed from his peak, is being pronounced as a greater fighter than John Lawrence Sullivan, James J. Corbett, Robert Fitzsimmons, James J. Jeffries, and Jack Dempsey," Harry Salsinger wrote in the *Detroit News* two days after the fight. "Nothing like this has ever happened before. No heavyweight champion in history was ever considered as anything more than a good prospect after eighteen months of professional boxing. Louis should continue flattening the heavyweights of

---

* Baer would fight another six years. Unlike the other clown champion of the thirties, Primo Carnera, who was forced to turn to wrestling and vaudeville to make a living, Baer didn't wind up a pauper. He invested his ring winnings shrewdly and parlayed his connections into subsequent careers as a disc jockey and public relations man. Considering his aspirations, it's somewhat fitting that he died of a heart attack inside his Hollywood hotel room in 1959 while he was in town to film a television commercial. A few years later Max Jr. followed in his father's buffoonish footsteps, portraying the dim-witted Jethro Bodine in the hit comedy series, *The Beverly Hillbillies.*

the world and by the time he retires he undoubtedly will be nominated the greatest fighter of all time by acclamation."

America's blacks weren't about to wait. This quiet, stone-faced youth, who had divided his life between the cotton fields and the ghetto, was beating the white man at his own game in as decisive and unambiguous a manner as legally possible. The growing number of whites who knew of Joe Louis generally admired his talent and sportsmanship. Many talked patronizingly of his deferential nature: he seemed to be "a good nigger." No serious call for a new wave of great white hopes went out, showing that many weren't threatened by Joe thrashing the best white boxers around. After all, the racial climate was not nearly as volatile as when Jack Johnson was swaggering across the front pages a quarter century earlier. But how much had the country really changed? In 1935, the year of Joe's smashing wins over Carnera and Baer, mobs lynched another eighteen blacks with impunity. Jim Crow still ruled practically every facet of American life. Frustrated shoeblacks, maids, waiters, and Pullman porters were ever ready to revel in Joe's knockdowns of a system that continued to be stacked against them from the moment they drew their first breath.

Richard Wright, who had left Mississippi for Chicago's South Side, experienced the heady if fleeting feeling of empowerment that Joe's fists wrought. The fledgling writer's first literary effort, which appeared in the socialist paper, *New Masses*, two weeks after Baer's dismantling, described the public celebration that erupted in Chicago in the wake of Louis's victory:

> Two hours after the fight the area between South Parkway and Prairie Avenue on 47th Street was jammed with no less than twenty-five thousand Negroes, joy-mad and moving so they didn't know where. Clasping hands they formed long writhing snake-lines and wove in and out of traffic. They seeped out of doorways, oozed from alleys, trickled out of tenements, and flowed down the street, a fluid mass of joy. White storekeepers hastily closed their doors against the tidal wave and stood peeping through plate glass with blanched faces.
>
> Something had happened, all right. And it had happened so confoundingly sudden that the whites in the neighborhood were dumb with fear. They felt—you could see it in their faces —that something had ripped loose, exploded. Something which they had long feared and thought dead. . . .
>
> As the celebration wore on, the younger Negroes began to grow bold. They jumped on the running boards of automobiles going east or west on 47th Street and demanded of the occupants:

"Who yuh fer—Baer or Louis?"

In the stress of the moment it seemed that the answer to the question marked out friend and foe.

A hesitating reply brought waves of scornful laughter. Baer, huh? That was funny. Now, hadn't Joe Louis just whipped Max Baer? Didn't think we had it in us, did you? Thought Joe Louis was scared, didn't you? Scared because Max talked loud and made boasts. We ain't scared either. We'll fight too when the time comes. We'll win, too.

Similar scenes played out in black neighborhoods across the country. From Joe's strength, America's Negroes found their own strength, and millions of black biceps flexed in synergistic splendor. "Here's that *something*, that pent-up folk consciousness," Wright trumpeted. "Here's a fleeting glimpse of the heart of the Negro, the heart that beats and suffers and hopes—for freedom. Here's that fluid something that's like iron. Here's the real dynamite that Joe Louis uncovered!"

Chapter Five

Tan Tarzan, Black Messiah

Louis, the magnificent animal. He lives like an animal, untouched by externals. He eats. He sleeps. He fights. He is as tawny as an animal and he has an animal's concentration on his prey. Eyes, nostrils, mouth, all jut forward to the prey. One has the impression that even the ears strain forward to catch the sound of danger. He enters the arena with his keepers, and they soothe and fondle him and stroke him and whisper to him and then unleash him . . . He lives like an animal, fights like an animal, has all the cruelty and ferocity of a wild thing. What else dwells within that marvelous, tawny, destructive body?

—PAUL GALLICO, 1935

*J*oe's victory over Primo Carnera made him a newsworthy subject internationally, while his bashing of Max Baer hastened his transformation from a minor celebrity to a genuine folk hero. At the start of 1936, by which time he had concluded a remarkable year of achievement with an easy fourth-round knockout of Paulino Uzcudan at Madison Square Garden, Joe's picture had appeared in newspapers in Bulgaria, Canada, China, Czechoslavakia, England, France, Germany, India, Portugal, Russia, and Spain, as well as throughout Africa. The *Barbados Herald* proclaimed him "the greatest," while Cuban businessmen mourned that his fight there against Isadoro Gastanaga was canceled because of political unrest. Moreover, his skill, decency, and sportsmanship had largely won over even the most suspicious members of the American public. On the night of the

Baer fight, a white man in Cordele, Georgia, shocked his neighbors by naming his newborn baby Joe Louis. Earlier in June, the National Association for the Advancement of Colored People indicated Joe's acceptance by the black middle class by featuring him on the cover of their monthly magazine, *The Crisis*.

Those predicting a white backlash were sorely disappointed. "There has been no great umbrage, no severely ruffled pride among the great body of whites," Shirley Povich wrote in the *Washington Post*. "Never did the public as a whole show a greater tolerance for the black man. If it did not care to see Joe Louis beat Max Baer and thus pave the way for the return of the title to the black race, then, at least, it did not kick up a great fuss about it . . .

"At Yankee Stadium the other evening, the cheers that greeted Louis almost shamed in volume the applause that greeted Baer's introduction. It seemed that the crowd wanted the better man to win. Twenty-five years ago, even less, it would not have been a question of skill or conduct, but color. Baer had not been a popular fellow. A consummate braggart, a playboy and clown, he had profaned the popularity that was his after his conquest of Carnera. Yet, he was white. But it seems that didn't make any difference."

Southern newspapers, initially wary of building up a black fighter for fear of antagonizing the races, saw that the young Detroiter was not the second coming of Jack Johnson and praised him for breathing life into a dying sport. Of course, they hesitated in hailing him as any kind of racial savior. The *Raleigh News and Observer* warned against the "danger of overestimating the significance of a socker." In the paper's opinion, "wise Negroes—as wise white men—will not put their pride in a prizefighter, but will watch the race's advance in the more important, less dramatic, things by which in the long view any race or any people must be judged." By the spring of 1936, the *Atlanta Journal's* Harry Stillwell Edwards was remarking that "the now famous prizefighter . . . has the sympathy of the south." While admitting that it was not "a loudly declared sympathy," Edwards felt the significant point was that "all 'white hope' sentiment, which once went with any kind of white man who fought a black champion in the ring, is, at this time, altogether missing."

As encouraging as the reaction of the white media was, it paled alongside that of the black press. Much to his astonishment, Joe was starting to be cast as a messiah by his own people, who overwhelmingly decided that, yes, they *would* put their pride in a prizefighter.

Even before vanquishing Carnera and Baer, Joe had come to dominate the black press like nobody before him. As early as December 22, 1934, the *Pittsburgh Courier* had proclaimed him the "New Black Hope"—surely a heavy burden for someone so young. The *Chicago Defender*, which like the *Courier* served as an influential black weekly, almost never published sports news on its front page. But between 1933 and 1938, it mentioned Joe in front-page headlines or ran his photograph on its cover a total of eighty times. This included an attractive nine-by-twelve-inch color portrait, published a few days after the Baer fight, that immediately found itself tacked to countless kitchen walls from Shreveport to Philadelphia. The runner-up cover subject was Ethiopian leader Haile Selassie, featured twenty-four times. The only American Negroes to even remotely approach Joe's level of prominence were Oscar DePriest, Chicago's fearless Congressman, and Jesse Binga, a banker whose home had been bombed when he dared move outside the city's ghetto. During this same period, DePriest was featured twenty times, Binga sixteen.

Further evidence that Joe had transcended the roped boundaries of the squared ring was that his exploits had become the stuff of sermons in black churches. On September 30, 1935, Joe took his new wife to Sunday services at the Calvary Baptist Church, the family's place of worship since moving to Detroit. More than two thousand people were jammed into the church while another five thousand frustrated souls stood outside. Joe sat slightly discomfited during the sermon as the pastor, J. H. Maston, did everything but fit him for a robe and a sceptor.

"He's doing more to help our race than any man since Abraham Lincoln," shouted the reverend.

"Amen to that, brother," answered the congregation.

"He don't smoke."

"Amen."

"He don't pour no red-hot liquor down his throat."

"No, sir. Amen to that."

"He fights clean and he shall stand before Kings. That's what the Bible say."

"Amen to all that," said the congregation. "Amen."

The pastor also told his flock that America's first great black hero had confided in him that he was one of "the Chosen," selected to use his fists to uplift his race, to show the whole world that "Negro people were strong, fair, and decent."

Given Joe's natural reticence and the literary license employed by most preachers, it can be safely assumed that Joe never said anything resembling the above. Which is not to say that his victories did not already have a quasi-religious aura about them.

"It was like a revival," Richard Wright said of the jubilation that accompanied Joe's victories. "After one fight, really, there was a religious feeling in the air. Well, it wasn't exactly a religious feeling, but it was *something*, and you could feel it. It was a feeling of unity, of oneness."

The celebrations themselves were becoming news items. The revelry in Memphis after the Baer fight lasted until dawn, prompting the press to say that Joe had "driven the blues from Beale Street." In Baltimore, four men were arrested and fined between five and twenty-five dollars for "assault with tomatoes." In Detroit, fire trucks chased after false alarms while reporters remarked about the number of young black boys suddenly seen throwing phantom punches on street corners. And on Harlem playgrounds, a few days after an estimated 150,000 Negroes had stopped traffic on 7th Avenue from 130th to 150th Streets, little girls skipped rope and sang:

> I went down last Tuesday night
> To see Joe Louis and Max Baer fight
> When Joe Louis socked, Max Baer rocked
> Dream of a viper
> Yeah man, Tee man
> Dream of a viper

As the young fighter unintentionally helped to raise the level of black consciousness, writers, musicians, and artists began to use him in their work. Some were just looking to cash in on Joe's celebrity; others saw in him the embodiment of the "New Negro," one for whom personal dignity and racial pride had become paramount. Within a few months of his toppling of Carnera, composer Claud Austin had made him the subject of an operetta, and several phonographic recordings had been released. The 78s included Carl Martin's "Joe Louis Blues," George Dewey Washington's "Joe Louis Chant," and Memphis Minnie McCoy's two-sided tribute, "Joe Louis Strutt" and "He's in the Ring Doing the Same Old Thing." In Houston, bluesman Joe Pullum recorded "Joe Louis is the Man":

> Joe Louis is a battlin' man,
> The people think his fame will always stand.
> He's the brown bomber of this land,
> He's supposed to whop 'most any man. . . .
> I said Joe is the battlin' man,
> Bought his mother a brand new home and some brand
>   new land.
> You can gather his intentions must be good,
> 'Cause he's doing the things for his mother a boy really
>   should.
> He's makin' real good money and it doesn't swell his
>   head,

He throws his fist like a 45 throwin' lead.
He throws them heavy and he throws them slow,
Then you know it's powerful Joe,
And boy if he hits you, you sure bound to hit the floor.

Over the years, few have described Joe's cultural impact as eloquently as poet Maya Angelou did in her memoir, *I Know Why the Caged Bird Sings*. The scene is her uncle's store in a small southern town sometime in the 1930s, where scores of blacks are glued to the broadcast of the Louis-Carnera fight:

> The last inch of space was filled, yet people continued to wedge themselves along the walls of the Store. Uncle Willie had turned the radio up to its last notch so that youngsters on the porch wouldn't miss a word. Women sat on kitchen chairs, dining-room chairs, stools and upturned wooden boxes. Small children and babies perched on every lap available and men leaned on the shelves or each other. . . .
>
> "A quick jab to the head." In the Store the crowd grunted. "A left to the head and a right and another left." One of the listeners cackled like a hen and was quieted.
>
> "They're in a clinch, Louis is trying to fight his way out."
>
> Some bitter comedian on the porch said, "That white man don't mind hugging that niggah now, I betcha. . . ."
>
> "He's got Louis against the ropes and now it's a left to the body and a right to the ribs . . . It's another left to the body and it looks like Louis is going down."
>
> My race groaned. It was our people falling. It was another lynching, yet another Black man hanging on a tree. One more woman ambushed and raped. A Black boy whipped and maimed. It was hounds on the trail of a man running through slimy swamps. It was a white woman slapping her maid for being forgetful. . . .
>
> This might be the end of the world. If Joe lost we were back in slavery and beyond help. It would all be true, the accusations that we were lower types of human beings. Only a little higher than the apes. True that we were stupid and ugly and lazy and dirty and, unlucky and worst of all, that God Himself hated us and ordained us to be hewers of wood and drawers of water, forever and ever, world without end. . . .
>
> "And now it looks like Joe is mad . . . Louis is penetrating every block. The referee is moving in. . . ."

Champion of the world. A Black boy. Some Black mother's son. He was the strongest man in the world. People drank Coca-Colas like ambrosia and ate candy bars like Christmas. Some of the men went behind the store and poured white lightning in their soft-drink bottles. . . .

It would take an hour or more before the people would leave the Store and head for home. Those who lived too far had made arrangements to stay in town. It wouldn't do for a Black man to be caught on a lonely country road when Joe Louis had proved that we were the strongest people in the world.

The deep and far-reaching symbolism of his fights had escaped Joe at first. Up until the Carnera bout, "I just wanted to fight and make some money and have some fun with pretty girls," he said. Now, as he relaxed in the afterglow of his ring triumphs and tried to settle into a new routine as a husband, he was belatedly understanding just how others outside his immediate circle perceived him. The responsibility of being accountable to an entire race instead of just himself worried him. He later confessed that his reaction to Reverend Maston's rousing sermon was to think, "Jesus Christ, am I all that?"

He was, but not always to his own family. According to sister Vunies, "There was never any fuss made over Joe in the house. I don't ever remember any of our brothers or sisters making a big deal over him. He was just Joe, our brother, and that was it."

Still, it was hard for even family members who remembered Joe as a nappy-haired kid in overalls not to get swept up in all of the commotion that suddenly surrounded his every move. His sister Eulalia, watching a crowd follow him down a Detroit street, started running after him, too. She came to her senses a few seconds later: *Wait a minute. What in the world am I running behind him for?* This pied-piper magnetism was often commented on. Soon even *Time* was describing him as "a black Moses, leading the Children of Ham out of bondage."

→←

The white press, unconcerned about black pride, painted Joe in the racially tinged language of the period. While it's safe to assume that many, if not most, reporters then were bigots, theirs was an everyday, unthinking prejudice that owed more to ignorance than malice. So infrequent was the mention of a black person in the mainstream press that the journalistic conventions of the time called for the designation "Negro" or "colored" to be attached to the person's name. Joe obviously was no ordinary black man, but he would continue to be referred to as a "colored fighter" or "Negro boxer" for the next several years.

In the extremely competitive world of daily newspapering, a small army of thirty-dollar-a-week reporters couldn't be professionally satisfied with uniformly referring to Joe as the Brown Bomber. They tripped over themselves dreaming up new nicknames and appellations. All of the following popped up at one time or another in press reports during the 1930s: The Detroit destroyer, the African avenger, the colored pugilist, the Alabama twister, the Alabama assassin, the heavy-fisted Harlemite, the chocolate chopper, the mocha mauler, the dark angel, young black Joe, the immutable brown sphinx, the mahogany maimer, the dark dynamiter, the Bible belter, the Ethiopian explorer, Uncle Mike's pet pickaninny, the dusky downer, the sepia slugger, the sable cyclone, the shufflin' shadow, the brown cobra, the tawny tiger cat, the tan-skinned terror, the zooming Zulu, and the tan Tarzan of thump.

There were many more. Some were so contrived as to make even the most seasoned reader wince. "The coffee colored kayo king," "the murder man of those maroon mitts," and "K.K.K. (Kruel Kolored Klouter)" stand out as examples of alliterative excess and simple bad taste.

At its worst the sports pages then were a gumbo of poor puns, classical allusions, manufactured quotes, pretentious verse, and pseudoscientific theories. This painful style, in vogue for a generation, was in the process of being phased out, the result of better-educated reporters, a more sophisticated readership, and a growing sensitivity to ethnic and racial stereotypes. But in the middle thirties, it was still going strong. An example was this report of the Louis-Carnera fight, filed by Lou Sabol of the *New York Evening Journal*:

> The dead-panned dusky David from Detroit dealt the gawky Goliath four deadly wallops to his kolossal kisser in the 6th of a series of sulky stanzas, and 1,500 gendarmes immediately rushed to the center of the ring and looked foolish because all the widely-ballyhooed anticipated trouble just wasn't. . . .

Joe wasn't the first or the last athlete to be written about in such fashion. Stories of athletes in all sports often included some stereotypical references to ethnicity, particularly when the athlete was just breaking into print and needed to be "introduced," so to speak, to the public. The New York Yankees' star center fielder, Joe DiMaggio, another sports sensation whose playing career (1936–1951) paralleled Louis's, was regularly described in his early years as being "olive skinned" and having "descended from the race of the Romans." Game accounts referred to him as "Giuseppe," "the deadly dago," and "the wallopin' wop" while his physical talents were attributed in part to his love of pasta dishes.

Such casual stereotyping died hard. In 1939, as the now nationally known DiMaggio was leading the Yankees to a record fourth straight world title, *Life* magazine still felt compelled to inform millions of readers that the country's greatest ballplayer (who had been born in San Francisco) "speaks English without an accent." Furthermore, instead of "olive oil or smelly bear grease he keeps his hair slick with water. He never reeks of garlic and prefers chicken chow mein to spaghetti. . . ." One of the photographs accompanying the text showed America's two most famous Joes together. The caption read: "Like Heavyweight Champion Louis, DiMaggio is lazy, shy, and inarticulate."

Unlike DiMaggio and other white sports figures, Joe frequently was quoted in colloquial black speech, another unfortunate but pervasive literary convention. An example was a cartoon that appeared in the *New York Evening Journal*. "Use the word 'defeat,' Joseph," the caption read. "Sho," Joe's cartoon image said. "I pops 'em on de chin and dey drags 'em out by de feet." Many writers continued to employ this Uncle Remus dialect ("Ah'm a goin' to run right into dat Schmelin' an' tear him a paht") throughout his career. While it was true that Joe had imperfect grammar, occasionally slurred his syllables, and retained a trace of his Alabama accent, there definitely was a double standard at work. During the Louis-Carnera buildup, black reporters complained that their white counterparts routinely quoted the Italian fighter in perfect English even though his knowledge of the language was limited and he spoke in a heavy accent. The Negro press understandably depicted Joe in far more literate language. An example was this quote from the August 10, 1935, issue of the *Cleveland Gazette*: "If I reach the goal I have set for myself . . . I'll walk out and leave the other fellows to argue over the spoils."

It was difficult for some whites to shed their deeply ingrained prejudice. By employing Uncle Remus dialogue and working into their stories references to his lack of education and flat-footed fighting style, reporters subconsciously succeeded in portraying Joe as the stereotypical sleepy-eyed, shuffling "darkie." Many of them innocently subscribed to the throwback theory; that is, Joe was the perfect end product of a biological chain stretching back to the primitive days of loincloths and spears. Comments from learned sources lent that theory a veneer of respectability. An eye doctor named Walter H. Jacobs examined Joe and speculated that his perfect occlusion was the result of his being a "throwback to a primitive human species." Leroy Atkinson theorized in *Famous American Athletes of Today* that "back in the deep jungle, there must have been a fighting ancestor," to whom Joe owed his physical prowess.

By constantly describing Joe in bestial terms, writers were able to recognize his stature while simultaneously dehumanizing him. The lead sentence from a wire service account of the Carnera fight was typical: "Something sly and sinister and perhaps not quite human came out of the African jungle last night to strike down and utterly demolish the huge hulk that had been Primo Carnera, the giant." One famous scribe, Grantland Rice, a Georgia native who often was called the dean of American sportswriters, liked to call Joe a "bushmaster" and a stalking "black panther of the jungle" in print. In private, remembered New York journalist Barney Nagler, Rice always referred to Joe as simply "the nigger."

Even a liberal like Paul Gallico, a Columbia graduate who would soon quit sports to write novels in Europe, could be just as guilty as his less enlightened counterparts in the press box. In 1935 the nationally syndicated columnist of the *New York Daily News*, perhaps the most cultured and influential sportswriter in America, made this observation of Joe in training: "I felt myself strongly ridden by the impression that here was a mean man, a truly savage person, a man on whom civilization rested no more securely than a shawl thrown over one's shoulders, that, in short, here was perhaps for the first time in many generations the perfect prizefighter. I had the feeling that I was in the room with a wild animal."

It didn't help matters that Joe, ever mindful of Jack Johnson's golden smiles as he vanquished his white opponents, maintained a deadpan expression in the ring. This inevitably led to such descriptions as "avenger," "bomber," "destroyer," and, worse of all, "killer." Joe hated these characterizations and rebutted them in a 1935 interview with the *New York World Telegram*. He'd had many occasions to hurt a man in the ring, he said, but had never done so unnecessarily. All the same, the "jungle killer" image was one that Joe would not be able to shake for several more years.

Some, anxious to preserve the myth of white superiority, questioned his heritage. Floyd Tillery insisted that Joe barely qualified as a Negro. According to his article in the May 1936 issue of *The Ring*, Joe had three-quarters white blood; the remaining quarter was more Indian than African. So much for Joe being some kind of Negro superman, Tillery seemed to imply.

It was a sign of the press's sometimes patronizing attitude towards Joe that his mother became a minor celebrity. Lillie Barrow was a stereotype that whites on both sides of the Mason-Dixon line could feel comfortable with. She was fat, loved to talk, and reminded them of their favorite Hollywood mammy, Hattie McDaniel (who in a few years would become the first black to win an Academy Award, portraying Scarlett O'Hara's maid in *Gone With The Wind*). The press ate up the story of how Joe had saved his money from his first year of fighting to buy his Bible-thumping mother a house, then later bought her a chicken farm. While photographs of Joe being served plates of fried chicken by his mother nearly became a cliche, they certainly compared favorably with those of a quarter century earlier, when shots of Jack Johnson squiring white prostitutes around Paris dominated newspapers.

The public delighted in reading stories of Joe's generosity. The Sunday of Reverend Maston's sermon, he dropped one hundred dollars in the collection basket, and his three companions added five dollars each. This accounted for $115 of the $118.34 collected during the service. Later that year he visited the offices of the Detroit Welfare Board to repay the $269 his mother had collected when the family had been on relief a few years earlier. Then he donated $6,800 to the Cleveland Christmas Fund.

Although Joe didn't do these acts to garner publicity, his handlers made sure most of them got into print. Thanks to Mike Jacobs and his three Hearst henchmen, the country was reminded several times that 10 percent of the gross receipts from the Baer and Carnera bouts had been given to the Free Milk Fund for Babies. This amounted to a whopping $93,294.40 donation from the Baer fight alone. A great cause, but even greater publicity.

Most of all, Americans could appreciate the rags-to-riches tale of an Alabama sharecropper who had, in classic Horatio Alger fashion, pulled himself out of poverty and made something of himself. Better yet, success obviously had not gone to his head. His image was that of a humble, modest, hard-working, and thankful young man. Who in depression-ravaged America couldn't thrill to his story? The Associated Press sportswriters voted him the 1935 Athlete of the Year, with Joe outpolling the reigning heavyweight champ, James Braddock, 184 votes to 7. The following spring *Ring* publisher Nat Fleischer presented him with a gold belt for his contributions to the sport, the first of three Boxer of the Year Awards he would receive from the magazine in six years. Even Jack Dempsey, to whom occasional racist comments were attributed over the years, admitted in a September 1935 interview with the *New York Times* that Joe was both a great fighter and a credit to his race.

That seemed to be the prevailing opinion. In fact, many liberal-minded whites seemed eager to pull Joe to their bosom—a salve, perhaps, for their own guilty consciences. Just prior to the Carnera fight, a veteran fight manager named Jack Weske sat down to write Joe a letter:

Dear Joe,

I presume that like all young fellows you will cast this letter aside without giving it a moment's thought. However, that isn't going to keep me from writing it.

Let me introduce myself. My name is Jack Weske and for five years I was manager of that grand little fighter, Johnny Coulon, bantamweight champion of the world. In all, I was connected with boxing for seventeen years but finally severed my connection with the game because of the sickening crooked tactics of the outstanding managers in the business.

Today, through your gentlemanly conduct, you are as highly regarded by the whites as you are by members of your own race, possibly more so. That in itself is remarkable. You can by your fine boxing, your ability, and your good behavior continue to be the good will ambassador of the Negro race to the rest of the world. This will do more to help your race and make it respected than anything I know of.

Someday you may be champion of the world. There have been Negro champions whose conduct reflected nothing but discredit on their race. What a wonderful opportunity you have!

Be true to your own people and to yourself.

Frank D. Fitzgerald, the Democratic governor of Michigan, also took time to drop a note of encouragement:

Dear Joe:

Don't be too greatly impressed by this stationary. I happen to be Governor of Michigan but I'm talking to you as a man more than twice your age just to give a little advice to a young fellow who has a real chance to do something for his people. . . .

Destiny seems to have pointed you for a high rank in pugilism. Your ability to overpower others by skill and physical force is something of which you may be proud. It's going to make you a lot of money, too; more money than is made by those who excel, let us say, as artists or surgeons, or poets. You'll have world prominence and money.

They will mean little, Joe, if you do not use them as God intended that gifts bestowed by Nature should be used.

Your race, at times in the past, has been misrepresented by others who thought they had reached the heights. Its people have been denied equal opportunity. Its obstacles and its handicaps have been such that it has been saved only by its own infinite patience and its ability to endure suffering without becoming poisoned by bitterness.

The qualities which may soon make you a world champion should call to the attention of people the world over, that the good in you can also be found in others of your race, and used for their own welfare, and the welfare of humanity at large.

So, Joe, you may soon have on your strong hands the job of representative-at-large of your people.

From the start Joe's handlers understood that it was crucial to develop and maintain a favorable public image in order to win acceptance by white America. It's the reason they released these letters to the press, as well as Roxborough's informal code of conduct for his fighter, and why they never complained about the frequently racist press coverage. Even crusty, cynical Jack Blackburn cooperated as best he could. When an overzealous black fan started chanting "Kill him, Joe!" during the Baer fight, he immediately told the man to shut up.

All of which is not to suggest that Joe was a phony. He came across exactly as he was. The fact that he openly deplored his lack of education and was doing something about it made him even more appealing. In 1935 Russell Cowan, a sportswriter and college graduate from Detroit, was hired to tutor Joe in math, English, and other basic subjects. The daily, two-hour tutorials eventually helped Joe feel more at ease around white writers, most of whom had already been won over by his genuineness.

"I thought Joe was a very high-class kind of guy," said Edgar Hayes of the *Detroit Times*. "He wasn't boastful or keen on confrontation, the kinds of things sportswriters often have to deal with. He was always very accomodating to those around him. All that goes a long way in this world, and it really doesn't matter if you're black or white, or famous or not."

There is no denying that as a young man Joe did conform to certain racial stereotypes. He did love to eat such traditionally southern foods as fried chicken and black-eyed peas, he could go to sleep on a moment's notice, and he did shuffle (at least in the ring) and mumble. Moreover, his quiet and unassertive manner could easily be misinterpreted as a display of the kind of automatic deference many whites of that period had been raised to expect from blacks.

However, in his own understated way, he refused to be molded into prizefighting's equivalent of the foolish, foot-scraping Stepin' Fetchit, another stock version of the Hollywood Negro. He never forgot the day at Trafton's gym when Jack Blackburn showed him a bug-eyed, thick-lipped "eight ball" doll.

"I got the message," said Joe. "Don't look like a fool nigger doll. Look like a black man with dignity."

Freddy Guinyard recalled an incident that happened at Pompton Lakes while Joe was in training for the Carnera fight. A photographer approached Joe and asked if he would mind posing with a watermelon. It would be "a great shot," the photographer offered, one certain to go out over the wires and be picked up by hundreds of newspapers.

That, as Joe quickly analyzed the situation, was the problem. Guinyard, who had spit out more than a few seeds with Joe during their childhood days at Eastern Market, watched with amusement as his friend told the photographer he couldn't because he didn't like watermelon.

"Joe could've fooled me, 'cause I know he loved watermelon," said Guinyard. "But he understood how to take care of the situation, how to say no, without making a big fuss about it. Nobody had to tell him. He was just smart enough to know how to take care of that foolishness himself."

Chapter Six

Champion of All, Save One

This is it, Chappie. You come home a champ tonight.

—JACK BLACKBURN TO JOE LOUIS, JUNE 22, 1937

At the end of 1935, a hard-working journeyman named James Braddock held the heavyweight crown, and Joe was the obvious number-one challenger. Neither Braddock nor Jimmy Johnston, however, were inclined to schedule a title fight anytime soon. Braddock, not too far removed from the relief rolls, understandably preferred to keep his title on ice, looking to enjoy the adulation, endorsements, exhibitions, and other perks for as long as he could. And Johnston, who controlled the champ through the Madison Square Garden Corporation, was hesitant to surrender the Garden's influence over big-time boxing to Mike Jacobs. But sooner or later, for the sake of a big gate and to satisfy public demand, Johnston would have to settle with Jacobs and Braddock with Louis.

There was another fly in the buttermilk: Max Schmeling. "The Black Uhlan" was still an attractive property with many friends in America. The beetle-browed German, whose dark good looks and pile-driver right hand had reminded many people of Jack Dempsey, had first come to the United States in 1929 after capturing the European light-heavyweight championship. Over the next several years his fights had grossed more than $4 million, much of it due to the savvy promoting of his Jewish manager, Joe Jacobs (who was no relation to Mike Jacobs). Schmeling, who had won the championship in 1930 on a foul by Jack Sharkey and then lost it in their rematch two years later, returned to Germany in early 1934 after losing to Max Baer and a second-rater named Steve Hamas. While Louis was dominating the headlines in America, the former titleholder quietly, methodically rehabilitated his image in Europe. He kayoed Walter Neusel, knocked out Hamas in a return engagement, then won a twelve-round decision against Spanish heavyweight Paulino Uzcudan. Schmeling's handlers announced that their man was ready to reclaim the championship.

The German fighter's unexpected return to prominence coincided with Hitler's rise to power. Employing spellbinding oratory and an army of brown-shirted thugs, Hitler had wrested control of the fatherland and jacked its citizens to new heights of nationalistic fervor. By the middle of 1933, he had abolished the republic, eliminated rival political parties and free speech, and launched a systematic persecution of Jews, Communists, and intellectuals. The Dachau internment camp was opened in 1934, a year that also saw widespread, violent anti-Semetic demonstrations. In 1935 the Nuremberg Laws stripped Jews of their legal and property rights; a year later, German troops marched into the Rhineland, reoccupying land that had been lost in the Treaty of Versailles that formally ended the First World War.

Although Schmeling had no real affection for this brutal regime, he had little choice but to publicly embrace *Der Fuehrer*. Even Joe Jacobs thought it wise to give the Nazi salute in the ring following his fighter's defeat of Steve Hamas in Hamburg. "You gotta do it there or else," he said. "Anyway, I had my fingers crossed. I'm 560 percent Jewish."

If most Americans seemed disinterested in what was going on in Germany, New York Jews were not. Through the spring of 1935, they loudly promised to boycott any domestic fight between Max Baer and Schmeling. Baer, who was Jewish only when it benefitted the gate, challenged the Germans to allow a rematch with Schmeling in Hamburg, but Hitler wouldn't hear of it. Another defeat in the ring, this time on German soil, would be an embarrassing setback for his claims of Aryan superiority. Such a fight, if held, would have to take place in some country other than Germany or the United States.

According to Schmeling's memoirs, German promoter Walter Rotenburg "was cherishing a dream of bringing Max Baer to Europe for a heavyweight championship match. And after [Rotenburg] had agreed to put $300,000 up front, Baer agreed to defend his title in Amsterdam. Then of course, all these plans fell through when Baer was upset by Jimmy Braddock." Now the representative of the Third Reich would have to first get past another fighter of undesirable blood—this time a black man—in order to get a crack at the title. Schmeling arrived in New York on December 6, 1935, and made his way to Mike Jacobs's office. There it was officially announced that he would fight Joe Louis the following June at Yankee Stadium.

One week later, on December 13, Joe entered the ring with Paulino Uzcudan. Jacobs, looking to stir interest in the upcoming Louis-Schmeling affair, had paid $19,000 to Schmeling's last opponent to cross the Atlantic for a scheduled fifteen-rounder. It was a sign of Uncle Mike's muscle and his fighter's status that he was able to bypass Jimmy Johnston and arrange a deal directly with Col. John Reed Kilpatrick, chairman of the board of Madison Square Garden Corporation. It was the first time the Garden had ever been leased to a rival promoter, but Kilpatrick had pragmatically recognized who the new players in the heavyweight division were and acted accordingly.

Joe was initially frustrated by Uzcudan's "peek-a-boo" style, which consisted of keeping his gloves close together in front of his face as he manuevered bent over at the waist. In the fourth round he finally penetrated the Basque's exaggerated defense. Uzcudan momentarily opened his mitts and—Bam!—Joe shot in an overhand right. It was a tremendous wallop, one that drove two of Uzcudan's teeth through his bottom lip and sent the 200-pound boxer sailing across the ring. His head bounced off the bottom rope. Although he was able to get back on his feet by the count of nine, referee Art Donovan took a close look at Uzcudan's battered, bewildered face and stopped the fight. For the first time in his long career, the veteran fighter had been knocked out. Twenty minutes later, Uzcudan rose from his bench in the dressing room and fell over in a heap. "I can't begin to describe that punch," said one of the writers in attendance.

Also in the crowd that night was Schmeling. While impressed by his future opponent's power, he was heartened by what he saw as a serious flaw in Joe's style. According to boxing legend, Schmeling mysteriously said afterward, "I see something."

Actually, the Uzcudan fight only confirmed what Schmeling already knew. "I had studied clips of Louis's fights and detected a weakness," he told Dr. Laurence F. McNamee in a 1992 interview in Hamburg. "When he would throw a left, he would drop that left before throwing a second one. I saw he was open for my right. So, I made a special trip just to watch Louis fight—and knock out—Paulino and look for that weakness. It was there. I was jubilant. I knew I'd win after that."

This defect, which left Joe especially vulnerable to a strong counterpuncher like Schmeling, wasn't exactly news—the reason, perhaps, that Schmeling didn't mind sharing it with reporters. One of Joe's sparring partners, Frank Wotanski, had mentioned it to the press. *New York Daily News* reporter Jack Miley had also declared that Joe was "a sucker for a right hand punch." Jack Johnson, old Papa Jack, made a similar observation after watching Joe train.

Joe's last fight before squaring off with Schmeling was January 17, 1936, against Charlie Retzlaff. He floored his man twice, the second time for keeps, receiving $23,065 for less than two minutes of work.

"We were rather disappointed in the length of time that it took Joe Louis to dispose of Charlie Retzlaff in what was laughingly termed their 'fight' in Chicago," observed Detroit sportswriter Eddie Batchelor. "We had assured our large and trusting public that Retzlaff wouldn't last out the first minute. . . . So when the affair dragged along to one minute and twenty-five seconds we felt that the Chocolate Clouter either didn't have his mind on his work or else is beginning to slip."

Although Batchelor was simply being sarcastic, he was on to something. After his poundings of Uzcudan and Retzlaff, Joe enjoyed the same aura of invincibility that Mike Tyson would fifty years later carry into his fight with an unheralded third-rater named Buster Douglas—and with the same disastrous consequences. Louis's climb to fame had been the most meteoric in ring history. In his first eighteen months as a professional, he had fought twenty-seven times and won them all. He had knocked out twenty-three of his opponents including his last ten in a row and two former world champions. Sixteen of his fights had lasted less than the three full rounds that constituted a Golden Gloves match. Although he was not yet the heavyweight champion, the title was all but a foregone conclusion. But first Schmeling.

In early May, when Joe left the fashionable six-room apartment in Chicago for the rigors of preparing for Schmeling, he forgot to pack one important item: focus. The Louis camp was installed at Lakewood, New Jersey, a resort town popular with New Yorkers. But gone was the monastic dedication of earlier camps. As the overwhelming favorite, Joe found it hard to bring his skills to a competitive peak. Roadwork became a drudgery, sparring an unnecessary dress rehearsal to what promised to be a short fight. As a bonafide celebrity, he found it difficult to ignore all the demands on his time, including a newfound passion, golf. And as a newlywed, he found it impossible to keep his hands off his wife—as well as all the other attractive women hovering nearby.

Ray Arcel watched Joe in training and was shocked at his sluggishness. "Chappie," Arcel asked Blackburn, "what's wrong with your fighter?"

"Ray," answered Blackburn, "he's here on his honeymoon, and she's here with him."

"Enough said, buddy," responded Arcel.

Partial blame for Joe's lack of condition could be laid at the feet of Ed Sullivan, a popular New York columnist who was to later gain fame as host of the long-running television variety show bearing his name. Like many of his friends in the entertainment industry, Sullivan was a golf nut, and he got Joe hooked on the sport. Joe often cut his training short to take to Lakewood's links with sportswriters Hype Igoe and Walter Stewart.

Blackburn warned him. "Chappie, that ain't good for you. The timing's different. And them muscles you use in golf, they ain't the same ones you use hitting a man. Besides, being out in the sun don't do you no good. You'll be dried out."

The other problem was women. Joe bunked at a stucco house called the Albert Mansion while Marva stayed just two blocks away at the Stanley Hotel. When he wasn't getting away for a rendezvous with his wife, he was sneaking away for a tryst with some fine-looking camp follower. Labeled a distraction, Marva soon was sent back to New York, but Joe continued his irresponsible ways, including regular trips to Atlantic City to consort with a lady whose name he couldn't even remember. Good friends like Freddie Guinyard and Marshall Miles tried to talk some sense to Joe, but he dismissed them—literally, in Miles's case. Miles drove to Lakewood one night to check in on his buddy, only to discover that he was out nightclubbing instead of getting some sleep. The two later exchanged angry words, with Joe ending the argument by throwing Miles out of camp.

"Lord knows I didn't mean to be fresh to Chappie, Roxy, and Black and certainly not Marva," Joe later apologized. "I kept excusing myself because I was twenty-two. People crowding all around me, getting a kind of respect I never anticipated, doing things real grand—like I never expected. Sometimes you have to excuse youth—but it nearly cost me my career."

The fight, originally scheduled for June 18 at Yankee Stadium, was postponed a day because of rain. The extra day didn't help the gate, which barely reached half of the million-dollar level Jacobs had hoped for. When some ticketholders asked for refunds, Jacobs instructed his assistants, "Tell 'em to go to hell. I didn't sell tickets for a date. I sold them for a fight." Officially, 45,000 fans paid a total of $547,531 for the expected privelege of seeing the Brown Bomber sock "the terrific Teuton" senseless.

Despite a partially successful boycott by Jewish merchants, few writers considered the pairing to be a racial or political confrontation. For one thing, the Nazi Party assumed Schmeling would lose, so it distanced itself from the proceedings. The party's official *Reich Sport Journal* had observed that there was "not much interest" in the fight, while propaganda minister Joseph Goebbels had written an editorial criticizing it. Asked by American reporters if Hitler had wished him luck upon his departure from Germany,

Schmeling replied, "Why should he come down to the boat to see me off? He is a politician."

Another factor working against the fight being used for ideological purposes was Schmeling's popularity. It was true that the NAACP and the Anti-Nazi League protested. But when some writers predictably dubbed him the "Heil Hitler hero" and "the Nazi nudger," there was no real derision or hate attached. One reporter's opinion that "Almost every sports writer in this country likes Max, who is good natured, gentlemanly, sportsman-like, polite, thoughtful and almost every good thing imaginable," was typical coverage. The only other feeling the press expressed for the German was pity: too bad a nice guy like Max had to get his face caved in. The Louis camp did get steamed up about Jake Jacobs's calling Joe "Mike Jacobs's pet pickaninny," but that was about the extent of the animus between the two sides.

The sole Nazi correspondent covering the bout naturally viewed it differently. "The racial factor is placed in the foreground," Arno Hellmis told readers of the *Volkischer Beobachter*, "and it is hoped that the representative of the white race will succeed in halting the unusual rise of the Negro. In fact there is no doubt that Max Schmeling, when he enters the ring on Thursday evening, will have the sympathy of all white spectators on his side, and the knowledge of this will be important moral support for him."

Acting on conventional wisdom, Helmis stopped well short of predicting victory for his fellow countryman. After all, Joe entered the ring the evening of June 19 a 10-to-1 favorite. But Blackburn, concerned over his fighter's conditioning, had confessed to Edward Van Every of the *New York Sun* that Joe, who had weighed in at 198 pounds, three under where Blackburn wanted him, might be in trouble if the fight went longer than a few rounds. Schmeling, eight years Joe's senior, was past his prime. But he had considerable ring savvy and unshakable confidence.

Even Joe expressed some mild concern. "That German was sure a pretty cool bird," he told Blackburn after the weigh-in.

"Chappie," said Blackburn, "it looks to me like you got a fight on your hands this time."

Blackburn's strategy was for Joe to use his left jab to keep Schmeling off balance and unable to use his right hand, and then to gradually move in for the knockout. It worked well enough for the first three rounds, Joe scoring points on Schmeling's face and the scorecard. But he was beginning to drop his left. "Keep your guard up, keep your guard up," Blackburn told him between the third and fourth rounds.

Schmeling, his right fist tucked in tight to his chin and his left acting like a prod, patiently waited for an opening. In the fourth, Joe threw a left hook, and Schmeling swiftly countered with a right to the jaw. Joe jabbed, and Schmeling came back with a right to the chin. Swelling with confidence, the German absorbed another hard jab and retaliated with a short right cross that caught Joe full in the face. Surprised and staggered, Joe covered up. A few seconds later Schmeling delivered a pile-driver right that sent Joe to the floor for the first time in his professional career. The Yankee Stadium crowd was in an uproar.

Joe, stunned, got up at the count of three and kept his attacker at bay with his left jab. But in the fifth, he lowered his guard a fraction of a second too soon. The bell rang just as Schmeling was uncorking a right; Joe dropped his gloves, and the punch hit him in the jaw. His handlers had to help him back to his corner, while Schmeling was issued a warning by referee Arthur Donovan

That, in effect, was the fight, agreed practically everybody who was there. "It was after the bell," Donovan said of the late blow, "but you can't withhold a punch once it goes. And the way I saw it, Louis never recovered from the shot." According to Freddie Guinyard, "Joe fought the rest of the fight on instinct. He told me that, later. He was out on his feet, and that's why he took such a licking."

In the sixth round, Schmeling's arm grew weary bouncing rights off Joe's chin. Lillie Brooks, watching her son fight for the very first time, grew hysterical. "She started screaming, 'They're killing my boy! They're killing him!'" recalled Guinyard, who had to forcibly remove her from the stadium. "Because of that, she never went to another of Joe's fights." Marva was also sickened and wanted to leave, but friends convinced her that Joe would rebound and win.

Instead, Joe continued to take a pounding as Schmeling came in time and again with solid right-handed shots. Joe stayed on his feet and continued to throw punches, but his arms and legs were feeling the effect of too many hours spent chasing women and little white balls around Lakewood. Disoriented, he hit Schmeling with several low blows.

Before the twelfth round, Edwin C. Hill, broadcasting the fight with Clem McCarthy, told millions of listeners: "There isn't a trace of that which so many people have been afraid of, racial feeling or anti-Nazism, anything of that kind. These people here in this Yankee Stadium are realizing we've got two great athletes. One may be a little darker than the other, perhaps, that is, but there's no question of anything else." Hill went on to say that there was "no booing or hissing" of either fighter, but Schmeling later said he heard some in the crowd yelling, "Kill him!" when he had Joe on the ropes.

The final flurry consisted of a right to the jaw, an uppercut, and then a roundhouse right that exploded against the left side of Joe's battered, swollen face. He slumped to his knees, his limp arms hanging like untied shoelaces over the middle strand of the ropes. Then he fell backward, rolled over, and covered his head with his glove. "When the referee counted," he recalled later, "it came to me faint, like somebody whispering."

Afterward Joe wept long and hard in the locker room. His mis-shapened face had been bludgeoned blue, purple, and yellow, his left eye was closed, and both of his thumbs were sprained.

"His face was all one-sided," remembered Dave Clark, the former Golden Glover from Brewster who had fought on the card as a light-heavyweight. "He didn't do much talking about it. It was just one of those things. The next day we caught a train into the Union Station. But we had the train slow down before it got there to let us off. Joe wanted to avoid the crowd and the reporters."

White America was astounded by Schmeling's victory, but not upset. They gave Schmeling all due credit and empathized with the loser, giving Joe high marks for not coming up with excuses. There was considerable chortling from the South, including O. B. Keeler's opinion in the *Atlanta Journal* that "the Pet Pickaninny" was "just another good boxer who had been built-up."

But given Joe's lofty status among American blacks, his mauling was predictably perceived as being a symbolic defeat for the race. There were scattered reports of looting and black-on-white violence as some disap-pointed followers looked for ways to vent their frustration. Outside Yankee Stadium, buses were stoned, windows were broken, and a man was shot. The *New York Times* reported that thirty blacks had kicked a fifty-year-old white man unconscious and a teenaged girl had attempted suicide by swal-lowing poison. Harlem pawn shops did a brisk business as those who had wagered on Louis hocked rings and watches to pay off their bets. The *New York World Telegram* estimated that Harlem businessmen had lost a half mil-lion dollars because of Joe's loss. For weeks afterward there was talk that Joe had been doped or that Schmeling's gloves had been loaded. The truth was too painful to bear.

"Man, Harlem was a sad and sorry place," one resident recalled. "Not only was it a sad place, it was a dangerous place to be in. People were dis-traught and very, very edgy. You were subject to being really hurt if you crossed anybody in the wrong way. Man, Joe Louis was such an idol, and it was assumed he could not lose."

Lena Horne was singing with the Noble Sissle Orchestra at Cincinnati's Moonlight Gardens that night. Between sets she and band members listened with growing despair to the broadcast until finally all were crying over the outcome—much to the disgust of Horne's mother, who refused to accept the notion of an uneducated prizefighter somehow being a black messiah.

"How dare you?" she scolded. "You have a performance. The show must go on. Why, you don't even know this man."

"I don't care, I don't care," Horne shouted back. "He belongs to us."

Garvin Bushell was in Dallas blowing sax for Cab Calloway's band when the headliner came out on stage to announce that Schmeling had knocked out Louis.

"And the crackers stood up and said, 'Here! Here!'" Bushell recalled. "The Negroes just slid down in their seats. You could hardly see them. They were so stunned they almost disappeared."

Bushell, who like most black Americans was a fight fan only on those nights when Louis was in the ring, was astounded by the radically different responses to the decision. "Do you see what I see?" he asked his companions. "Here a foreigner beats an American champion, and the crackers stand up and applaud."

To make matters worse, the date of the fight happened to be Emancipation Day, which many blacks still observed with vigor. Instead of having a double reason to celebrate, they "just scrunched down in their seats; their heads were dropped," said Bushell. "You can't imagine the human reaction to that extent over an athletic event, but it happened."

It surely did. But why? The technical explanation was Joe's dropped left hand. The kneejerk excuse was Schmeling's "Sunday punch" after the bell. The real reason was Joe's misplaced sense of invincibility. Some thought his head was swollen to twice its size long before Schmeling accomplished the task literally, including his most severe critic—himself.

"It was all my fault, entirely," he reflected. "I was too damn sure of myself. Didn't train properly, and between the golf and the women and not listening to what Chappie said, it's a wonder I wasn't killed in the ring. I let myself down, I let a whole race of people down because I thought I was some kind of hot shit."

As if matters weren't bad enough, he discovered that his stepfather had been paralyzed by a stroke two days before the fight. The family had decided against telling him because they were afraid the news would affect his concentration. Within a few weeks Pat Brooks died, with Joe at his bedside, bawling like a baby. If there was any consolation, it was that the only father Joe had ever known was never told the results of that disastrous evening at Yankee Stadium. He left this world believing his famous stepson was still undefeated and unbowed.

Despite his hurt pride, aching body, and sorrowful soul, Joe managed to keep his dry sense of humor. Asked by one of his managers if he'd like to watch film of his performance against Schmeling, he replied, "No, I saw the fight." One day in Detroit, where he had his wounds salved by his mother and family members, he stopped by the Brewster gym to renew acquaintances. He watched Thurston McKinney go at it with a sparring partner.

"Thurston," Joe yelled, "you better keep your left hand up or you'll get tagged."

"You ought to know," responded McKinney.

Joe's still puffy face broke into a grin. "I sure do," he admitted.

>‹

Within eight weeks of his defeat by Schmeling, Joe had recovered to the point that he was able to dispatch aging Jack Sharkey with a third-round knockout at Yankee Stadium. Among those watching Louis repeatedly knock the blubbery former champion to the canvas was the new number-one heavyweight contender, Schmeling, back in the States to prepare for his scheduled title fight with James Braddock.

Schmeling, who had been given practically no chance to beat Louis by his countrymen, suddenly was the new darling of the Third Reich. "Congratulations," Joseph Goebbels had telegraphed immediately after Schmeling's sensational knockout. "I know you won for Germany. Heil Hitler." The German dictator cabled "Most cordial felicitations on your splendid victory" and sent flowers to Schmeling's movie actress wife, Annie Ondra. Schmeling returned to Germany as a special guest on the zeppelin *Hindenburg*. After landing to a huge crowd in Frankfurt, he was whisked off to Berlin to enjoy a private reception with Hitler, where they watched film of the fight. Later the footage was expanded into a full-length feature called *Max Schmeling's Victory, A German Victory*, which played to enthusiastic audiences in theaters throughout Nazi Germany.

The Third Reich was in a sports tizzy. On August 2, just six weeks after Schmeling's unexpected triumph, the Olympic Games opened in Berlin. The Nazis politicized the world's premier amateur athletic event as no host country had since the modern games began in 1896. Germany proclaimed to have "won" the Olympics by accumulating more medals, beginning the now familiar scoreboard approach to judging competing nations' relative performance. But it also had to swallow the ignominy of American blacks dominating the track and field competition, including four gold medals won by Jesse Owens alone.

Owens, just a month shy of his twenty-third birthday, had been born in Alabama and raised in Cleveland, where as a high schooler he had set his first track record by running the hundred-yard dash in ten seconds flat. On one incredible spring afternoon in 1935, he set five world records and tied a sixth while competing for Ohio State University in the conference championships. "The world's fastest human" shared Joe's humble background—like Joe, Owens's father had been a sharecropper and his grandparents had been slaves—as well as his benign public image. They met for the first time in 1935 and became quick and lifetime friends.

Hitler pointedly snubbed Owens at the awards ceremonies, exposing the hypocrisy of a fascist regime that had tried to camouflage its policies of racial prejudice from the world press. But in accepting Owens as a national celebrity who had succeeded in twisting *Der Fuehrer's* mustache, white America found itself uncomfortably forced to face its own attitudes towards prejudice. As was the case with Joe, many reporters and commentators skirted the issue by attributing the performance of America's black Olympians to some primeval natural gift such as longer heels or the ability to withstand junglelike heat. "Owens runs as easily as Bill (Bojangles) Robinson tap dances," reported *Newsweek*. Newspapers referred constantly to the U.S. Olympic team's "Ethiopian troops" and "black auxiliaries," as if they were somehow hired mercenaries rather than American citizens.

Considering the second-class citizenship of American Negroes, this was essentially the case. But an increasing number of progressive white journalists, jarred by the official governmental policies of Germany, Italy, and Japan, and influenced by the liberal, humanistic tilt of the country during Franklin Roosevelt's first years, were joining the black press in questioning their own country's racial practices. Sports, because they were so much in the public eye, became a favorite battleground and a suggested laboratory for change. If blacks of good, sound character could excel in track and prizefighting, shouldn't it follow that, given the chance, they could make their mark in such still-segregated sports as football, basketball, and baseball? And if a more tolerant white America was willing to acknowledge their achievements in athletic competition, why couldn't it take the next step and extend first-class citizenship to the workplace, classroom, and voting booth? By the middle 1930s there was a growing clamor among a handful of influential white sportswriters and social commentators, including Westbrook Pegler, Paul Gallico, and Harry Salsinger, that even that most sacred of all-white competitive strongholds, organized baseball, should open its doors to blacks and become a truly national pastime.

Although real change in sports or any other element of American life was still a ways off, liberal organizations such as the NAACP recognized the unique contributions of Louis and Owens in forcing the kind of dialogue that hopefully would one day help all blacks. "If these two mere boys have done nothing more than just awaken curiosity in Negroes in millions of white minds," the organization stated in its magazine, *The Crisis*, "they have served their race well."

While Jesse Owens was becoming a household name for beating the Nazis, Joe contended with the aftershocks of his first professional loss. Marva continued to have vivid nightmares of her husband, his face swollen and his eyes closed, being pummeled over and over again by Schmeling's right fist. And newspapermen pestered him with the same question: Did he feel that he had let his people down by losing?

Joe tried to downplay the significance. "There are just as many Negro doctors, lawyers, and politicians as before I was whupped," he insisted. "And none of the poor ain't suddenly rich either." He might have added that Owens's recent triumphs had done nothing to improve the lot of the millions of ordinary blacks who couldn't long jump twenty-six feet or sprint one hundred yards in 9.4 seconds.

Joe's managers felt that a lot of work would keep his mind off his defeat, fine tune his skills, and restore the luster to his name. On September 22, five weeks after dispatching Sharkey, Joe flattened Al Ettore, a promising Philadelphia fighter, twenty-eight seconds into the fifth round. Two left hooks and a right uppercut did the trick. Joe was once again taking his preparatory work seriously. Eddie Batchelor wrote at this time:

> He knows now that he can be licked and that the best way to avoid getting licked is to put himself in the best possible condition and fight with what brains he has—not too many at best. It is perfectly easy to understand why Joe's handlers find him trying. In the space of a few months he went from the estate of a struggling colored boy to that of a world-famed figure. Until he achieved his sudden success as a fighter, Joe never had known even complete comfort; all of a sudden he was up to his ears in luxury. He had money, admiration, and an attractive wife, things that he never even had dreamed of two years ago. No wonder he preferred enjoying life to training for a fight, especially as the world kept telling him that he was so good he could lick any man alive without half trying. Joe has no great mentality, but he probably realizes now that the world's heavyweight championship is worth the temporary sacrifice of a lot of the pleasures that his money has made available.

While Jack Blackburn continued to work with Joe in the gym, Mike Jacobs was maneuvering behind the scenes. The Braddock-Schmeling title fight was postponed when the champion developed arthritis in his right hand. Because open-air stadiums were the only venues large enough to hold the king-sized crowds needed to make such matches profitable, important bouts could be held only when the weather was expected to be reliable—typically early June through the middle of September. Braddock and Schmeling wouldn't be able to meet until the following spring, at the earliest.

Jacobs tried to interest Schmeling's handlers in a rematch, dangling a $300,000 guarantee in front of them. But the German fighter knew he had a better chance of whipping Braddock, gaining the championship in the process, than tangling with the younger, revenge-minded Louis in a nontitle bout. The answer was no.

Cynics didn't believe Braddock's claim of injury. They thought that his manager, Joe Gould, was holding out for the best deal. Although Gould and his fighter were contractually bound to Madison Square Garden, he was entertaining overtures from Jacobs about a title fight with Louis. Gould, who had traveled the same hard road up from poverty that Jacobs had, only with considerably less financial success, understood that his ring-rusty fighter's first title defense would probably be his last. In which case, he and Braddock were going to squeeze every nickel he could out of whoever they were going to surrender the crown to.

Jacobs joined forces with a Philadelphia promoter named Herman Taylor to offer Gould a $500,000 guarantee if his man would fight a twelve-round exhibition with Joe in Atlantic City. Calling the fight an exhibition, which meant it was a no-decision bout, would technically free Gould from his contract with the Garden. However, because a fighter who knocked out the champion in an exhibition was then considered the champion himself, Joe stood a terrific chance of lifting Braddock's crown, albeit in a back-door kind of way.

While Gould mulled over Jacobs's proposal, Joe kept on fighting. He went on a six-week exhibition tour, then traveled to Cleveland for a scheduled bout with Johnny Risko for the *Cleveland News* Christmas Fund. After Risko fractured his ribs training, a second-rater named Eddie Simms was put on the card. On December 14, 1936, Joe popped Simms with a left hook just seconds after the opening bell. Simms sank to the floor. As he regained his feet, he grabbed referee Arthur Donovan by the arm.

"Let's go someplace," Simms told him. "Let's get out of here. Let's go on the roof or someplace."

"Jesus," said Donovan, "he's out of it if he thinks I'm some girl." He signaled the bout over at twenty-six seconds of the first round. It remains one of the shortest heavyweight fights on record.

At the same time, Max Schmeling was returning to New York aboard the *S. S. Bremen*. All the talk of a possible Louis-Braddock fight had him up in arms. The New York Boxing Commission sided with Schmeling. It ruled against a possible exhibition between Joe and Braddock and got Schmeling and Braddock to each put up $5,000 as a guarantee that they would meet on June 3, 1937, at the Madison Square Garden Bowl (an outdoor arena the Garden operated in Long Island City) for the championship. Gould was forced to sign an agreement with the

Garden stating that under no circumstances would his fighter meet Louis before fighting Schmeling.

The politicking continued into the new year. On January 27, 1937, sixteen days after he had kayoed Steve Ketchell in the second round in Buffalo, Joe got into the ring with Bob Pastor at Madison Square Garden. Jimmy Johnston, who managed Pastor, hoped to rattle Joe and make him look bad. He partially succeeded. Minutes before the fight was scheduled to start, Johnston and several armed men burst into the dressing room, accusing Joe of having loaded his fists with quick-drying cement. A stare-down between Joe's bodyguards and Johnston's men ensued while John Roxborough angrily threatened to call off the fight. Johnston left, but he still had a surprise left in the ring.

The fight that night more closely resembled a bicycle race. Pastor, a former Golden Gloves champion from the Bronx who had once played blocking back for the New York University football team, was a hard-nosed fighter of some ability. But on Johnston's instructions he spent the evening dancing away from Joe, who bettors had made a 2-to-1 favorite to register a knockout.

Joe admitted his frustration. "I felt like a goddamn fool trying to chase this mosquito. Chappie kept telling me to try and trap him in a corner. Impossible. I never fought anyone like him. I was clumsy—when I reached out to give him a good punch, I might just graze him. I didn't get in one crack, except a right to his collarbone. But he bumped me with his head and stuck his thumbs in my eyes. That's all the damage he did. He must have run twelve miles that night. At the end of the tenth round, he run to his corner jumping up and down with his arms raised in the air."

Pastor had fired enough harmless jabs to make him and a good share of the partisan crowd think that he had won, but referee Arthur Donovan awarded eight of the ten rounds to Joe. The crowd booed the decision for a full thirty minutes. In the aftermath most writers praised rather than criti-cized Pastor's tactics. It wasn't so much that the underdog had run away, but that Joe had failed to catch him. It fed the prevailing belief that Joe could not adapt to the strategy of "smarter" boxers such as Schmeling and now Pastor.

Joe looked to dispel this myth his next time out. He met Natie Brown on February 17 at the Municipal Auditorium in Kansas City. Six months earlier, the state of Missouri had reversed its long-standing ban on interra-cial prize fights, a reversal that was due in great part to Joe. Brown had managed to go the distance with Joe two years before in Detroit, but this time around he lasted only forty-two seconds into the fourth round. A flur-ry of lefts and rights drove Brown to the canvas; as he tried to pull himself up by the referee's legs, he brought the official tumbling down as well. Prone on the canvas, the referee counted the fallen boxer out.

Two days later, Mike Jacobs and Joe Gould rocked the boxing world. They announced that they had signed a contract for their fighters to meet June 22, 1937, for the world's heavyweight championship. Jacobs, who knew that the New York State Athletic Commission would oppose the fight on the grounds that Schmeling had earned first crack at Braddock's title, scheduled it for Chicago.

It was a neat bit of boxing intrigue. Gould, having twice rejected guarantees of a half million dollars to put Braddock up against Louis, had tried to intimidate John Roxborough into giving him a half interest in Joe in exchange for a twelve-round exhibition. Gould had pitched his proposal after sending a pair of thugs to pick up Roxborough one winter evening in New York. The underworld small fry had silently driven Roxborough around the city for an hour before finally delivering him to the nightclub where Gould was waiting.

The nerve-wracked Roxborough, who up until a few moments earlier had been convinced that he was being taken for the proverbial one-way ride, refused to be intimidated. He turned down Gould's offer. "No fifty percent, not even fifty cents," he said. "Nothing. We don't need Braddock. If he had ten fights, he couldn't make as much as Joe can in one. He needs us. You need us. No deal and no exhibition."

Roxborough continued to say no as Gould dropped his demand to 25 percent, then 20 percent. At last Roxie suggested Gould talk to Jacobs about getting a slice of Uncle Mike's future earnings. As champion, Joe would be worth a bundle, and Jacobs would control the heavyweight division. His nerves on edge, Roxie walked out, then found the nearest bar and ordered a double scotch on the rocks.

Gould acted on Roxborough's suggestion. Soon he and Jacobs worked out a compromise. In exchange for giving Louis first shot at the title, Gould and Braddock would receive $500,000 or half the gate and broadcast revenues, whichever was greater—and 10 percent of Jacobs's net profits from promoting heavyweight title fights over the next decade, should Louis win. Even if Joe subsequently lost the championship (a likely scenario, since no heavyweight had ever held it for more than seven years), Jacobs, who would continue as the division's kingmaker, would still have to hand over one-tenth of the money he made promoting title fights. Braddock later estimated that through 1947 he and Gould received annual payments totaling about $150,000 from this agreement, "which wasn't a bad annuity." But it turned out to be mere pocket change when compared to the money Jacobs grossed during Joe's unprecedented reign as champion.

To make the Braddock-Louis deal more savory to the public, Jacobs helped stir up anti-Nazi sentiment. Protest groups warned of the likelihood of the heavyweight championship being held hostage for propaganda purposes by the Third Reich, which would happen if Schmeling, as expected, defeated Braddock. The Anti-Nazi League, whose vice presidents included New York Mayor Fiorello LaGuardia, was Jacobs's most vigorous ally, blanketing the New York State Athletic Commission and Madison Square Garden with angry telegrams and threatening to boycott any fight featuring the German fighter.

As expected, Schmeling and Jimmy Johnston were outraged by these machinations. A lawsuit was immediately filed by Madison Square Garden, seeking an injunction against the Louis-Braddock fight. But Jacobs's lawyer, Sol Strauss, had examined the fine print of Braddock's contract. He discovered that while Braddock was obligated to make his first title defense with Madison Square Garden, there were no conditions imposed on the Garden itself to put on such a fight, therefore, in his view, the contract was inequitable and thus invalid. As Schmeling stubbornly continued training, the case wound its way through the legal system. In a federal court in Newark, New Jersey, Judge Guy L. Fake ruled against the Garden, but that didn't stop the New York State Athletic Commission from staging a weigh-in ceremony for what the papers jokingly referred to as Schmeling's "phantom fight" with Braddock.

As for the real fight, preparations were proceeding at full steam. Jack Blackburn—finally convinced that his man, a *black* man, was actually going to be allowed to fight for the heavyweight championship—packed away his skepticism. "All right, you son of a bitch," he told Joe, "you made it all the way to here, and I'm going to see you make it all the way. When I finish with you, you're gonna be a fucking fighting machine!" As proof of his dedication, Blackburn swore off drinking until the fight was over.

After spending a couple of weeks in the western Michigan resort town of Stevensville, relaxing and "buildin' up energy" (as Blackburn described it), the Louis entourage set up camp in Chiwaukee, Wisconsin, in early May. His quarters were magnificent, a ten-room Spanish-style stucco summer home owned by Fred Fisher, a Chicago bed manufacturer. It was situated on Lake Michigan, five miles south of Kenosha.

There was little of the fooling around that had marked previous camps. Joe kept to a rigorous schedule. He got up at five o'clock each morning and ran ten miles through the dewy, half-lit countryside. Blackburn and bodyguard Carl Nelson crawled behind him in a car, measuring his distance on the odometer. Then it was back to bed, where he would sleep until awakened for a ten o'clock breakfast consisting of prunes, orange juice, and liver or lamb chops. The next several hours were his to relax. Then on alternate afternoons he sparred, this time helped by Harry Lenny, a veteran white trainer who coached Joe on fending off his opponent's right-handed punches. Blackburn had no quarrel with the arrangement, saying, "If it helps Chappie become champ, it's good."

After the afternoon session Bill Bottoms cooked Joe a large dinner, including plenty of chicken, fish, vegetables, and ice cream. For his twenty-third birthday, Bottoms baked him a giant cake. Joe, who had a notorious sweet tooth but needed to shed ten pounds to get into fighting trim, restricted himself to a single piece—as good a sign as any of his commitment. He spent the evening playing cards or ping-pong with members of his entourage, reading the newspaper and listening to his favorite jazz recordings, or simply taking in the cool Lake Michigan breezes, before turning in at nine o'clock.

Joe was brought along slowly—so slowly, observers thought he was seriously off his game. This was part of Blackburn's plan to have Joe peak at the right time. "Joe is working along just the way he should be—that is to get himself right at the right time and not just to put on a training camp show," Blackburn explained. "Just before the fight, I'll let Joe go to town and that's the way you'll know better how ready Joe really is."

But it also evolved that the press was the victim of a disinformation campaign designed to make Joe appear as lethargic and overconfident as he had been before the Schmeling fight. Mike Jacobs knew that if the public suspected the truth—that the fight probably would be a lopsided affair—ticket sales would be seriously affected. To generate interest, he had a press agent at Braddock's camp at Grand Beach, Michigan, issue enthusiastic accounts of the champ's workouts. At the same time his publicist at the Louis camp, Jersey Jones, hinted to reporters that the challenger was indifferent or distracted.

The result was a slew of stories like the one filed by Bill Corum of the *New York Journal*. "There isn't an ounce of killer in him," Corum said of Joe. "He's a big, superbly built Negro youth who was born to listen to jazz music, eat a lot of fried chicken, play ball with the gang on the corner, and never do a lick of heavy work he could escape. The chances are he came by all those inclinations naturally." Other writers described him as the "hulking, lazy brown boy" and "uncommunicative, unimaginative."

Joe's loss to Schmeling and his poor showing against Pastor combined with these fresh portrayals of his supposed sloth and empty-headedness, were causing many members of the press to re-appraise him, often in stereotypical terms. The *Literary Digest* wrote of Joe's "inherent laziness" while Jack Miley of the *New York Daily News* opined that Joe "performs by instinct and nobody will ever be able to pound anything through his kinky skull." In his drive to sell tickets Jacobs had helped drop Joe's public image to its lowest point since he turned pro three years earlier. The whites who lined up behind Braddock began to believe that their man, painted as the smarter and more aggressive of the two combatants, had a chance.

Ben Bentley, a native Chicagoan who has hung around the fight game for many years as a ring announcer and public relations hand, wasn't one of them. "The money was all on Joe," remembered Bentley. "Everybody realized that he was a comer. Braddock was regarded as a good fighter, but he didn't belong in the same ring as Joe Louis."

Maybe not, but Braddock deserved high marks for his perseverance and sportsmanship. The thirty-two-year-old underdog was the sentimental choice of many writers—some because of the color of his skin, but most because of his inspirational climb to the championship.

Braddock had been born in Hell's Kitchen, a rough-and-tumble neighborhood just a few blocks from Madison Square Garden, and grew up in northern New Jersey. He dropped out of school when he was thirteen and within six years had become both the state light-heavyweight and heavyweight amateur champ. He joined the pro lists in 1926 and three years later lost his bid for the world light-heavyweight championship when Tommy Loughran decisioned him in fifteen rounds. A long slide into mediocrity followed. His right hand, first injured in 1928 and repeatedly battered afterwards, accounted for him losing sixteen of twenty-six fights between 1930 and 1933. With a wife and three children to feed, Braddock supplemented his meager ring earnings by working on the docks and then later for the Works Progress Administration, one of FDR's New Deal programs, for seventeen dollars a week. Like Louis, once he became solvent, he paid back every cent of the money he had received on relief.

During these gloomy years, Braddock had favored his left hand in order to allow his right to mend; the unintended side effect was that both hands became equal in strength. His manager, Joe Gould, who had stuck with him through the Depression, was able to persuade Jimmy Johnston to put him on the card against a young Georgia heavyweight named Corn Griffin for the same night Max Baer would punish Primo Carnera for the championship. Braddock was considered to be no more than a rung on the ladder for the up-and-coming Griffin, but he stunned everybody by knocking him out in the third round. "I did that on stew and hamburgers," Braddock told Gould afterwards. "Get me some steaks and see what I do."

The hungry boxer, who stood a shade over six-foot-two and weighed about 190 pounds when he was eating well, proceeded to win decisions over two highly rated fighters, John Henry Lewis and Art Lasky. His reward was being named the number-one challenger to heavyweight champ Max Baer. Oddsmakers made Baer a 10-to-1 favorite, but Braddock was confident. He called his wife and vowed that he would "bring home the title." His three children were excited; they thought Daddy had promised to bring home a turtle.

On June 13, 1935, at Madison Square Garden Bowl, Braddock craftily outboxed Baer for fifteen rounds, gaining a decision so shocking Damon Runyon annointed him "the Cinderella man." Through sheer pluck and determination, Braddock had returned from oblivion to capture the richest individual prize in sports.

Having dethroned Baer, Braddock was reluctant to offer up the crown himself. The custom of the times allowed him to profit through endorsements, testimonials, and personal appearances before risking his title. When he stepped into the ring with Joe Louis, he had not fought professionally for two years and nine days.

Unlike Jack Johnson's fights a generation earlier, almost nobody regarded this fight as a showdown between a black man and a white man, with the fate of either race hanging in the balance. Just two years earlier, Joe's skin color had caused many to comment and wonder at length about a Negro's place in the prize ring, but his conduct had made the issue seem almost quaint. On October 31, 1935, in St. Louis, a black man, John Henry Lewis, had beaten a white fighter, John Olin, for the world's light-heavyweight championship. Lewis's win came on the heels of Joe's victories over Carnera and Baer, which accounted in part for the lack of any white backlash. "Maybe things were breaking through," reflected Joe, who was there cheering on Lewis.

Also helping to make race a nonissue was Braddock's sense of fair play. Unlike Baer, Jack Sharkey, and other of Joe's opponents, he did not make any racially offensive prefight comments. "I never thought about whether a fighter was white or not," Braddock said. "What you were interested in was your own ability." George Nicholson, a black heavyweight who served as a sparring partner for both Joe and Braddock during his career, vouched for Braddock's equanimity. "He was a wonderful guy," Nicholson said. "Always treated everybody the same. When we put rocks in the beds of guys at training camp, we would put them in his too. We ate together, showered together, all equals." Joe was always grateful to Braddock for not drawing the color line. For the rest of his life, whenever their paths would cross, he would always warmly address Braddock as "Champ."

Shirley Povich spoke to the absence of racial animus: "If, perchance, Joe Louis should come into the heavyweight championship of the world this evening at Chicago and Nordic Supremacy in the prize ring is ended for the time being, there is no reason to believe it would be a national calamity. . . . None of the blatancy that characterized the arrogant Jack Johnson has been noticed in Louis's conduct. He has proved himself just a big, playful brown boy who happens to be deadly serious when he's in that ring."

→←

On the evening of June 22, 1937, the champion and the challenger made their separate ways to the ring pitched in the outfield grass of Comiskey Park. Under his lucky red-trimmed blue bathrobe, Joe was wearing purple trunks with the initials *JL* embroidered on them. As a tribute to his Irish heritage, Braddock wore a green robe with a white shamrock on its back. The champ had weighed in that morning at 197 pounds, one-quarter pound less than Joe.

Joe, a 2-to-1 favorite, looked around at the crowd. Forty-five thousand people filled the park. Most of the 20,000 blacks in attendance had scraped together $3.75 to squeeze into the bleachers. "They must have saved real hard to get that money together," he thought. "Half of them must have been on welfare, but Lord knows what they sacrificed to see me. I had a responsibility to them." At ringside black professionals rubbed shoulders with racketeers and gamblers, expecting to see history made. "Most of the black folks, though, were sitting around their radios, making little parties, chipping in on beer or booze, and waiting to cheer for me or cry for me."

After the customary prefight introductions of all the former and current champs in attendance—Jack Dempsey, Gene Tunney, John Henry Lewis, Sixto Escobar, and Barney Ross—the two fighters were read instructions by referee Tommy Thomas. Then it was back to their respective corners to wait for the opening bell. Jack Blackburn leaned over to Joe. "This is it, Chappie," he said. "You come home a champ tonight." Braddock, sitting on his stool a few feet away, made a sign of the cross with his gloved right hand.

A couple of minutes later, that same right hand deposited Joe on the seat of his pants. The short uppercut to Joe's jaw had come after the two boxers had come out of a clinch and Braddock had parried a right.

Joe, his head clear, quickly scrambled to his feet. He wasn't hurt, just mad. Just before the bell, he socked Braddock with a left hook and a right cross. Between rounds Blackburn admonished him: "Chappie, when you is knocked down, you stay there until the count of nine. You can't ever get up so fast they can't see from the bleachers that you was down."

Joe later maintained that he could have finished off Braddock anytime after the opening round. But Blackburn instructed him to play it safe, sticking and countering until Braddock ultimately unraveled. "I'll tell you when to shoot," Blackburn said.

By the fourth round, Braddock was visibly sapped. He was absorbing blow after blow while his own punches lacked steam. Years later, Braddock

The fight of the century: Louis vs. Schmeling, 1938. (Pug Shots)

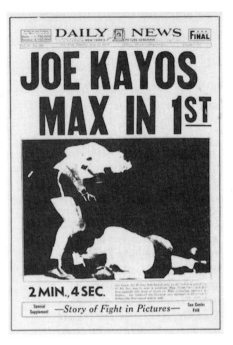

JOE KAYOS MAX IN 1ST

2 MIN., 4 SEC.

Special Supplement —*Story of Fight in Pictures*— *See Center Fold*

Newsreels and headlines told the story of the Schmeling rematch, which was over before many at Yankee Stadium had a chance to settle into their seats.

Scant minutes after the fight had started, Joe's right hand was raised in triumph. "It was a long time coming," Joe later said, "but now I felt like the 'real' champion. I'd gotten my revenge." (UPI/Bettmann Newsphotos)

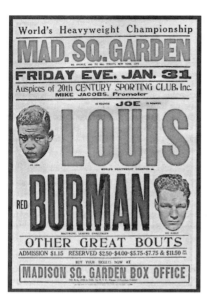

Louis's post-Schmeling opponents were collectively known as the "Bum-of-the-Month Club." Victims included Red Burman, who didn't get much closer to the champ than this on-site poster, and checkers-playing Johnny Paychek, who went down for keeps in the second round. (David Levien)

The most colorful of Joe's opponents was Tony Galento, a brawling saloonkeeper who coined the phrase, "I'll moider da bum!" before their 1939 bout. Galento, who trained on frankfurters and beer and took on an occasional kangaroo in the ring, amazed everyone by flooring Louis before finally being beaten to a pulp by the embarrassed champion. (Angelo Prospero)

Anatomy of a fight. Heavyweight contender Bob Pastor is pictured inside his New York home with daughter Roberta and son Albert, then shown training in Saratoga for his 1939 fight with Louis. Alas, the bout ended as it so often did for Joe's opponents. Pastor kissed the canvas in the eleventh round at Briggs Stadium in Detroit. (Roberta Sansiveri)

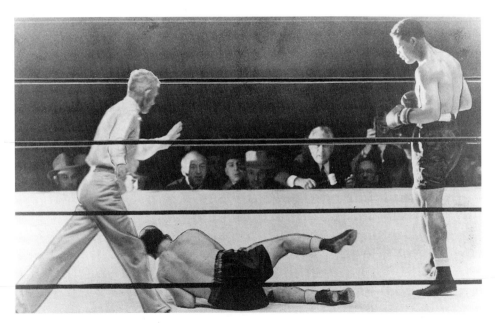

Billy Conn, a light, fast, and clever Irishman from Pittsburgh, nearly stole the title from Louis in their famous 1941 match.

Sugar Ray Robinson's friendship with Louis stretched back to his childhood days in Detroit when he would tote Joe's equipment bag to the gym. (Pug Shots)

Louis's reputation soared to new heights during the Second World War. Among those recognizing his service to his country and his profession were the Boxing Writers Association of New York and the *Ring* magazine. (Hank Kaplan)

"The man who had knocked out Hitler" was used principally for propaganda purposes, including an appearance in Irving Berlin's *This Is The Army*. (Angelo Prospero)

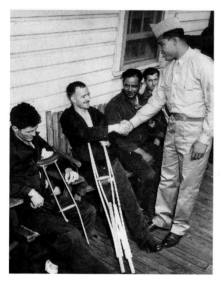

His main duty was touring military installations in the United States and overseas, staging boxing exhibitions, and visiting the wounded. (National Archives)

Louis crowns Jimmy Bivins of Cleveland the "Duration Champ" in 1943. Seven years later Bivins would lose a ten-round decision to his boyhood idol. (Hank Kaplan)

The much-anticipated rematch between Louis and Billy Conn was the first big fight of the postwar years. Although the bout was disappointing, Joe's eighth-round KO allowed the merrymaking to go on as scheduled at Harlem victory parties.

In the dressing room afterwards, Joe took a celebratory swig with his beaming manager, Mannie Seamon. Seamon replaced Jack Blackburn, who had died while Louis was in the army. (Hank Kaplan)

Branch Rickey, seeking a man with the athletic skill and dignity of Joe Louis to break baseball's color line, found him in Jackie Robinson.

Promoter Mike Jacobs looks on as Louis and Tami Mauriello come to terms on their 1946 fight. Joe later mused that his victory over the lumbering Mauriello was his "last great fight." (Hank Kaplan)

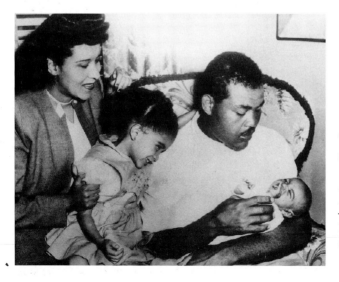

The fighter holds his infant son, Joe Louis Barrow Jr., in 1947 in the company of his wife Marva and daughter Jacqueline. Despite warm pictures like these, Louis was a failure as a family man. (National Archives)

Jersey Joe Walcott floors Louis in their first fight, December 5, 1947. Louis won a controversial decision, but came back six months later to knock out Walcott in the rematch. (Gjon Mills)

Reporters crowd into Toots Shor's restaurant on March 8, 1949, shortly after Louis announced his retirement as heavyweight champion. He had held the title for nearly twelve years, longer than anyone else. (National Archives)

Ezzard Charles (left) succeeded Louis as heavyweight champion, but had difficulty being accepted by the black community. (National Archives)

Louis works the speed bag during his comeback. He won eight straight fights before Rocky Marciano drove him back into retirement with an eighth-round knockout at Madison Square Garden on October 26, 1951. (Hank Kaplan)

After the war Louis was secure enough in his public image to lend his name to alcohol and tobacco products, which he had previously refused to endorse. This shipment of Joe Louis Kentucky Straight Bourbon Whiskey is being loaded in New Orleans in 1952. (Historic New Orleans Collection)

By 1956 the former champ owed the government $1.2 million in back taxes. In an attempt to pay just a fraction of this staggering debt, he worked with a circus, refereed wrestling matches, and went on tour as a professional wrestler. "It was like seeing the President of the United States washing dishes," said one observer. (Angelo Prospero)

In 1955 Louis married Rose Morgan, who owned a cosmetics business in Harlem. Her attempt to settle Joe down failed, as did their marriage. (UPI/Bettmann Newsphotos)

Louis, who was a partner in a New York public relations firm, drew heat for having the Cuban government as a client. He is shown with dictator Fidel Castro at a New Year's party in Havana in 1959.

Martha (Malone) Jefferson, Louis's third wife, was a successful Los Angeles attorney who stuck by her troubled husband for twenty-two years. "There's a soul about this man, and a quietness that I love," she once explained.

Caesars Palace put Louis on its payroll as a "greeter" in 1970. His unofficial duties included playing golf, gambling with house money, posing for snapshots, and rehashing just one more time for casino guests his fights with Max Schmeling and Billy Conn. (Caesars Palace)

In 1977 Joe suffered a heart attack and cerebral hemorrhage, severely affecting his speech and confining him to a wheelchair until his death on April 12, 1981. (Caesars Palace)

Joe Louis lies in state inside the boxing ring at the Caesars Sports Pavilion before his burial at Arlington National Cemetery.

Statuary has helped America's Brown Bomber remain part of the public environment. This solid marble tribute stands in the entrance of the Olympiad Sports Book in Caesars Palace. (Las Vegas News Bureau)

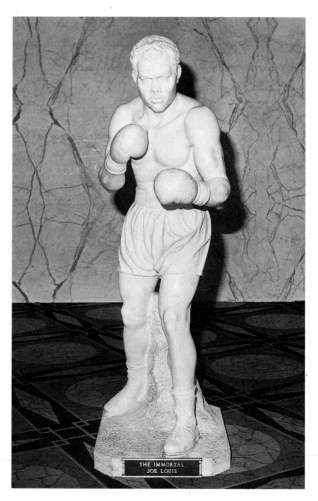

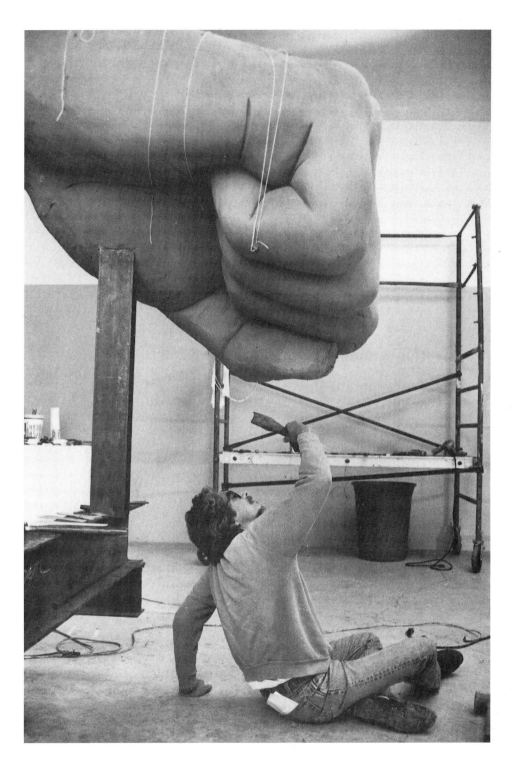

Robert Graham works on his giant bronze, *Tribute to Joe Louis*. (Anne Kresl)

In Detroit, the city most closely associated with Joe Louis's life, his memory is kept alive in various ways. The most controversial is Robert Graham's two-ton fist hanging menacingly downtown. (Michelle Andonian)

In 1988 Freddie Guinyard posed with the bronzed glove his old playground pal had used to knock out Max Schmeling fifty years earlier. (Michelle Andonian)

recalled the fusillade: "In the four rounds from the fourth to the eighth round, I got hit with more punches that night than I got hit with in the other eighty-seven fights I had." When he plopped down on his stool after the seventh round, his face was so ripped and bruised Joe Gould told him he was throwing in the towel.

"If you do," Braddock sputtered through his bloodied lips, "I'll never speak to you again as long as I live."

Braddock came out for the eighth round, his hands held high. This was the sure sign of a tired fighter, Joe knew. A boxer kept his gloves at normal height until he was no longer fresh; fatigue caused a man to make an exaggerated effort to keep them raised. It didn't help Braddock, either, that he was suffering from arthritis in his left arm. He simply had nothing left. He pawed the air as Joe bore in. Finally, a thunderous right hand to the face "about blowed half my head off," Braddock later said. The force of the blow drove a tooth through his mouthpiece and into his lip. It sent him crashing to the canvas where he sat dazed and bleeding, his right hand supporting him, his left splayed useless to the side. Then he rolled over. "When he knocked me down," he said, "I could've stayed down three weeks." *

Joe never looked at Braddock. As the referee began to count him out, the new world's heavyweight champion walked to a neutral corner. There he stood for several seconds gazing out over the sea of bobbing black faces. Unlike the expressionless mask he wore, these were torn wide open with joy.

Joe Louis Barrow, the first black heavyweight champion in a generation and its youngest titleholder ever, was on top of the world. "Harlem Holds Maddest Revel" screamed the headline in the *New York Sun*, which told of jubilant blacks leaning out hotel windows and yelling, "How do you like that, white man?" British journalist Alistair Cooke, caught inside a cabaret in Baltimore's Darktown, said the celebration "looked like Christmas eve in darkest Africa," with "cops barking and women screaming and men going down grabbing their toes and snarling oaths." In Chicago it was "bedlam, sheer bedlam," remembered Joe's wife, Marva. South Side blacks commandeered elevated trains and taxis and rode around for free. Others disconnected trolley cars and burned bonfires on street corners. The *Chicago Defender* devoted almost its entire front page to

---

* Despite being the short-ender, Braddock always expressed satisfaction with his effort. "You always got to figure you're not the best man in the world, there might be somebody better. That's the way it was. That's the way boxing is. The champion don't always stand up. There's always somebody coming up to take him. That's a part of life." Braddock fought only once more before retiring to the comfortable house he'd bought in 1937 in North Bergen, New Jersey, across the river from Manhattan. He died there thirty-seven years later, his postboxing income comfortably padded for a decade by his share of the new heavyweight champion's ring earnings.

the fight; the only other item deemed to be important enough to share space with Joe's win was a two-column story reporting the U.S. Senate's vote favoring an antilynching bill. The makers of Sweet Georgia Brown Hair Dressing announced they would give away a free nine-by-twelve-inch photograph of the Brown Bomber with every product sold.

Within a half-hour of the fight's conclusion, newsboys were hawking fight extras. Over the coming days, the press would shower an almost inordinate amount of compassion and affection on the gallant, overmatched Braddock, who needed twenty-three stitches to repair the damage to his face. There would be universal praise for Joe, as well, though the violent and impersonal nature of the beating he had administered inspired a fresh round of jungle-killer imagery. Nonetheless, the victory restored his reputation. In the emotional dressing room, Joe sat exhausted, his hands throbbing, and talked of one last challenge.

"I don't want nobody to call me champ," he said, "until I beat that Schmeling."

Chapter Seven

Knocking Out Hitler

*So the next Fight of the Century was moving into the
center ring, clenched fists across the sea. When Max
Schmeling returned to America to challenge Joe Louis
for the championship of the world, the Wehrmacht was
goose-stepping across the Austrian border. Neville
Chamberlain was buying time with other people's land
and lives. There was a Berlin-Rome-Tokyo Axis. The
concentration camps . . . were now filling up with victims of bureaucratic madmen tooling for war and drooling for conquest. Nobody on either side of the Atlantic
viewed Louis and Schmeling II as anything less than the
personification of Good vs. Evil. If Schmeling won, the
shadow of the swastika would darken our land. If Louis
triumphed, Negroes, Jews, anti-Nazis, pacifists, and
everyone who yearned for an order of decency without
violence would feel recharged and reassured.*

—Budd Schulberg

After his demolition of James Braddock, Joe was feted far and wide.
The morning after the fight he awoke to an avalanche of congratulatory
telegrams and stage, movie, and radio offers. "About $500,000 was put up
for grabs," recalled Joe, who soon fled Chicago to see his family in Detroit.

The crush of humanity was even greater at his mother's house. While
Joe polished off a couple of baked chickens and all the ice cream he could
handle, his wife, mother, and boydguard were kept busy trying to sort out
the people who streamed nonstop through the house. All claimed to be a
friend or relative of the champ. It was worse when he tried to leave the
house. Hundreds of people swarmed around him, calling his name, clapping
him on his shoulders, warning him not to be another Jack Johnson. Joe,

peeling off five- and ten-dollar bills, jammed money into well-wishers' hands and soaked in all of the adulation.

One day not long after he became champ, he was eating dinner at the Brown Bomber Chicken Shack with Marva, his friend Freddie "Sunnie" Wilson, and Wilson's fiancee, when the urge to flee hit him. Earlier, auto tycoon Henry Ford had presented the local hero with a new luxury Mercury.

"Let's go and try this car out," Joe suggested to Wilson. The two piled in and, leaving the girls behind in the restaurant, proceeded to disappear for the next several days.

"I had about eight or nine hundred dollars in my pocket and Joe, I guess he had a couple thousand," recalled Wilson, a South Carolina native who had come to Detroit to study law but fell in love with show business instead. In the thirties he produced shows at places like the Harlem Cave and the Chocolate Bar, and also managed the Golden Gloves program at the tiny gym at Mount Olivet Baptist Church. His and Joe's mutual interest in chorus girls and boxing made them good buddies and business associates and accounted for their impulsively taking to the highway in pursuit of good times and leggy women.

"We followed this show to Toledo," continued Wilson. "Nothing was happening there. So we went to Cleveland and caught up with those chorus girls there. We went out to this farm, so nobody could find us, and stayed out there for awhile. By now we'd run out of money, so we borrowed some from this friend of ours. Bought some new clothes, new underwear, put 'em on and followed the show to Pittsburgh. Then we came back to Cleveland. We get some more money, get a change of clothes, and go on to Buffalo. Get some money from Marshall Miles, who had a cabaret there. By now the F.B.I.'s looking for us.

"That's when we looked up and here comes that sneaky-pete, Freddie Guinyard. He said, 'Goddamn, everybody's been looking for you.' We said, 'Goddamn, you ain't supposed to be looking for us. We're just traveling.' That's when they caught us. Mike Jacobs called, Roxborough called, they were all mad as hell. The girls are worried, everybody's worried. Those who knew where we were didn't tell. We're just having fun, living out of the back trunk of that Mercury. We just shook down everybody on that trip. We paid 'em back eventually. Well, maybe we did and maybe we didn't, but we did have a lot of fun."

Episodes like this put an early strain on Joe's marriage, which was less than two years old when he won the championship.

"Joe was never a constant husband," said Chicago attorney Truman Gibson. "Especially in the early years when he'd be away so much. Marva wouldn't be around, and he'd be attracted to the girls. They were always slipping him pieces of paper with their names and phone numbers on them and chasing after him. Of course, we all know Joe couldn't run too fast. . . .

The fact that he was gone so much and exposed to so many women made it hard to have the kind of marriage that Marva desired."

Marva, whose family had moved from a farm in Muskogee, Oklahoma, to Chicago when she was five, had spent her entire life trying to improve her station. When she first met Joe, she was attending the Vogue School of Designing in Chicago with hopes of being a designer. She also was taking English classes at the University of Chicago. Her ambitions of middle-class respectability got an enormous boost when she married Joe. Now she was seen strolling down Harlem's Lenox Avenue on the arm of the most famous and desirable black man in the country. "In the beginning I felt like Cinderella," she said. "I was exposed to so much. It was just travel, travel, travel. It was really exciting, different, and fun."

It wasn't too long before Marva started dreaming of trading in their glamorous whirlwind of a life for a more settled, gracious domestication. She innocently believed that once her husband became champion, he would continue fighting for only another year or so before retiring. By then they would have all they would ever need. They would be only in their early twenties and could look forward to spending a long life together, raising a family free from financial worries. She convinced Joe to buy an apartment building at 43-20 South Michigan Avenue instead of continuing to pay rent. The $15,000 purchase, which Marva happily spent several months and several thousands of dollars more decorating, turned out to be one of the few wise investments Joe ever made. He particularly liked the seven-foot-long, king-sized bed Marva had custom built for them.

Joe was living royally long before he gained the heavyweight crown, though of course he could afford to. In 1935 alone his purses totaled $429,682; his eleven fights in 1936–37 produced an additional $538,200. More was down the road. Although Joe's training expenses and his managers' shares had to be deducted, the balance still represented a staggering amount of money. At the time only one in a hundred Americans had an annual salary of more than $10,000. When most families got by on between $1,500 and $2,500 a year, Joe frequently dropped that much gambling on a single game of golf.

Joe, who only a few years ago was walking the streets of Black Bottom in clunky work shoes and nondescript pants, spent money almost as fast as he made it. He was a clotheshorse, ordering expensive, custom-fitted wardrobes from Broadway tailor Billy Taub. He was not the pretentious type, but he did exhibit a good deal of personal vanity. He dressed stylishly and elegantly and often criticized Marva's fashion selection when they were getting ready for a night out. He was immaculate in his personal hygiene, as well.

Marva may have been Joe's only legal dependent, but he also was responsible for supporting dozens of people, in full or in part. There was Bill Bottoms, who would remain his cook until the war; his bodyguard,

Chicago detective Carl Nelson; and his tutor and private secretary, Russell Cowan, who, tired of the constant traveling, would leave for a newspaper job in early 1938. In addition, Joe's entourage in the 1930s included mostly old and new friends from Detroit: Pat Brooks Jr., Freddie Guinyard, Thurston McKinney, Sunnie Wilson, and Leonard Reed, among others. They filled a variety of roles, depending on whether he was in training (when they received as much as a thousand dollars a month) or between fights (in which case they got "walking around" money). But most of the time their function was simply to provide companionship and amusement and to keep the wrong elements away.

"He was our meal ticket," Wilson acknowledged. "We kept bad things from happening to him. We kept the scandals away. Gangsters, certain kind of women, people who might want to get him off into different directions. We might not have broken cameras or something like that, but then Joe wouldn't have allowed it, because he was always a gentleman."

Joe was the center of attention at every nightclub, theatre, or bowling alley he visited. He didn't smoke or drink, and when in a certain mood, he could be slightly puritanical about those who did. He might playfully crumple someone's pack of cigarettes or gently chastise someone about their bad habit. Ever the gentleman, he didn't allow cursing when ladies were around (which was practically always) and picked up every tab, which was expected. He'd sip orange juice or a soft drink, listen to music and tell stories, and shake hands with an endless stream of strangers.

"He was the kind of guy who always knew what he wanted," said Billy Rowe. The theater critic for the *Pittsburgh Courier* first met Joe in 1935 and became one of his closest friends and a business associate. Rowe agreed with Wilson that one of the benefits of hanging with Joe was the spillover effect of his celebrity.

"You never had to push yourself on women," said Wilson, "because you've only got so many celebrities and big fellows and you got a thousand women out there."

Joe was a source of ready capital at a time when bankers were unwilling to make loans to blacks. In January of 1936 he was approached by Pittsburgh numbers king Gus Greenlee about bankrolling a Detroit-based team in the Negro National League. Although the idea of being a baseball owner appealed to Joe, John Roxborough successfully argued that his public image would take a beating if he was involved in an enterprise so brazenly run by racketeers.

Friends recognized him as a soft touch. Leonard Reed, who produced shows at the Plantation Bar inside the Norwood Hotel, convinced Joe to open the Brown Bomber Chicken Shack at 424 East Vernor Highway in Detroit. The Chicken Shack, staffed with several of Joe's unemployed friends, opened to great hoopla one New Year's Eve. Unfortunately, in all of the excitement, management forgot to order enough chickens. Joe eventually gave his half share of the wobbly business to Sunnie Wilson, who later induced his generous buddy to become his partner in a downtown hotel and a Paradise Valley bowling alley. Joe lost money on all of these ventures.

One of Joe's worst investments, if it can even be called that, was the Brown Bombers softball team he organized in the summer of 1935 as a way of helping some of his down-and-out Detroit buddies. It was also a way for Joe to indulge one of his favorite fantasies: becoming a big-league ballplayer. When he could manage to get away, he would join the team on tour or suit up for a game at Detroit's Mack Park.

"He could've been fighting exhibitions for a lot of money," recalled Jesse Walker. "Instead, he played first base. I never made the team, but I know he gave his friends the receipts to split. He didn't take any money himself. That's the kind of man he was."

The team existed for several years and lost a bundle of money, maybe as much $50,000. At one point cash-strapped Thurston McKinney sold the tires off the team bus, but Joe just shrugged his shoulders and bought some new rubber.

His greatest joy was helping out his family. In addition to the cars and houses he bought for various family members, there was the hat shop he purchased for his sister Emmarell. His stepbrother Pat was his well-paid chauffeur. He also helped his other older sister, Eulalia, turn her life around.

Eulalia, described by Joe as "a good-looking woman" who was "an out-and-out swinger," had had her head turned by some of the hangers-on in Chicago. She drank too much, borrowed money constantly, and at one point even stole Marva's fur coat. That's when Joe had her committed to a private hospital. There she discovered the Bible. Later she finished her high school education and took up the Baha'i faith, traveling throughout the United States and Africa and preaching against racial prejudice up until her death in the spring of 1995. "Thank God I had the money to help her," Joe once reflected. "That's what money is all about, isn't it?" *

His brother Lonnie and sister Vunies represented opposite extremes of

---

* Eulalia (Barrow) Taylor's passing on May 14, 1995, was followed two days later by that of another Bible-toting beneficiary of Joe's generosity, Dave Clark. Joe had taken the former Golden Gloves champion under his wing, convincing Roxborough and Black to manage his career, as well as that of another old Brewster buddy, Holman Williams. Unfortunately, Joe's handlers had to devote most of their attention to him, to the detriment of solid performers like Williams and Clark. Although Williams never got the title shot he so richly deserved, Clark made it to the cusp of the big time. In 1939 the jolly light-heavyweight was scheduled to face John Henry Lewis in a championship bout. But that was canceled because of Lewis's vision problems. A year later Clark's career ended when his own eye was severely injured in an automobile accident. Half blind, Clark became a cornerman and trainer. Somebody once saw him reading the Bible between bouts and joked, "Stealing Joe Louis's stuff, eh, Clark?" To which the even-natured boxer answered, "I've always read the Bible, even before I took up boxing." Clark and Joe's sister both were buried at Detroit's Memorial Park Cemetery.

the Barrow family's response to Joe's windfall of cash. Joe always was a little envious of Lonnie, who he thought garnered a disproportionate share of their mother's love and attention. The heavyweight champion of the world was also more than a little afraid of his oldest brother, who had a well-deserved reputation for being tough and argumentative. It seemed that Joe and Lonnie were always fussing over something. Once, tired of her sons' cross words with each other, Lillie Barrow "hauled off and gave me a right to the jaw that shut me up," said Joe. "She said she didn't care what kind of world champion I was, she was the champion in her home."

According to deLeon Barrow, Lonnie and their cousin Albert ran together. "Everywhere Joe went, them two were there also. I remember one time when Joe was fighting an exhibition in St. Louis. They went—driving their car to somewhere in between St. Louis and Chicago and catching the bus the rest of the way. When they got there, Joe gave them $500 apiece and a ticket to see the fight. They sold the ticket and got back on that bus and come on back to Detroit."

Marshall Miles, a "running buddy" who served as Joe's manager after the war, knew Lonnie constantly leaned on his famous brother for money. Late in his career, about 1948, Joe gave Lonnie $30,000, which he promptly dissipated. He then hit Joe for an additional $7,500, half of which was to buy a bar and the other half for an alimony payment, he explained. Joe, by now wrestling with cash-flow problems of his own, nonetheless made out two checks to the respective parties. The next day Lonnie was once again broke, having illegally cashed the checks and lost the entire amount playing blackjack. "He always liked blackjack" was Joe's only recorded comment on the matter.

The free ride would screech to a halt with Joe's retirement, after which Lonnie became involved in a variety of minor schemes and scams. He lived in an apartment over a shoeshine parlor that was a front for gambling. One day in 1960 he was found dead, asphyxiated by fumes from a gas heater. Detroit police noted that a section of the exhaust pipe was missing. Whether the death was accidental, suicide, or a murder was never established.

Vunies, on the other hand, kept to the straight and narrow. Today the retired educator lives in a high-rise apartment building overlooking her former Black Bottom neighborhood.

"Joe didn't have much of an education himself," said Vunies, who spent twenty-five years in the Detroit public school system, "so that's probably why he was so eager to see us go as far as we could through school."

Vunies graduated with honors from Cass Tech, a predominantly white high school with a tough admission policy and a formidable curriculum. Joe paid her tuition to Howard University and then the University of Michigan, where she received her master's degree. Vunies joined Joe in stating that the biggest thrill of their lives was when they walked arm in arm with their mother across the Howard University campus after Vunies had become the first family member to graduate from college. All three couldn't help thinking of how far they had traveled since their days in Alabama.

It was hard to find anyone who didn't benefit from the champ's largesse. He pulled strings to get friends jobs at the Rouge plant and got Roxborough and Julian Black to manage a pair of his Brewster stablemates, Holman Williams and Dave Clark. Coleman Young remembered that after a fight Joe would always come back to Black Bottom to visit and to pass out dollar bills on the street corner. "Everybody would gather around him, and the champ would dole out money according to his own system—the most for older men and friends, and on down the line. Since I was four years younger than Joe, I was probably a punk in his eyes. That made me a two-dollar man."

The handouts and business loans put a drain on Joe's resources, especially as more and more people ("sycophants," Marva called them) attached themselves to the champ. But Joe didn't mind. "It gave me pleasure to be able to do it," he said. "I had a ball spending money."

>‹

While Joe was busy indulging himself, his manager, who many in the fight game considered a snake, added to his reptilian reputation. In late 1937, Mike Jacobs was named the boxing promoter at Madison Square Garden, replacing Jimmy Johnston, who had been fired as a result of the fiasco surrounding the failed Schmeling-Braddock title fight. By the following summer Uncle Mike had consolidated his power by leaking word of his three silent partners' involvement in the Twentieth Century Sporting Club to the Scripps-Howard chain. The three Hearst reporters, their conflict of interest revealed to the world, quickly sold their interest to Jacobs for a paltry $25,000 apiece.

Jacobs knew he had a gold mine in his fighter. He and his comanagers also realized that in order to be fully accepted by the press and the public, a black champion had to be willing to take on all comers. Joe accepted this. "I will fight whenever and whoever Mike Jacobs wants me to," he said.

Joe's first choice was Max Schmeling. He burned for revenge, but Schmeling wasn't particularly eager for a rematch—at least not at Jacobs's price. Jacobs offered a fight in New York at the usual challenger's share: 20 percent of the gate. Schmeling insisted on 30 percent. When Jacobs said no, the German fighter made plans to meet Tommy Farr, champion of the British Isles.

But once again Jacobs submarined Schmeling. He guaranteed Farr $60,000 and a quarter share of the radio and movie rights if he would agree to fight Joe in New York. Farr, who looked to earn twice as much as he would fighting Schmeling, signed to meet Joe on August 26, 1937, at Yankee Stadium.

The fight wound up being delayed four days by bad weather, which may have taken some of the edge off Joe's preparedness. Farr, a Welsh miner who was relatively unknown in the States, proved a gritty competitor. He crowded Joe all night and, armed with "only cleverness, courage, and a fair sort of left hook," said the *New York Sun*, doggedly managed to last fifteen rounds. British fans stayed up until 3 A.M. in order to listen to the short-wave broadcast of the great American fighter's first title defense.

Joe got the unanimous decision, though he was anything but satisfied. Farr won six rounds on one of the judges' scorecards and five on another. Afterward Joe needed to place his badly bruised right hand in a plaster cast for two weeks. He had injured it while breaking Farr's nose with a punch in the fourth round.

But his spirits soon soared. Three days after he fought Farr, Jacobs announced that a deal had been reached with Schmeling. The German fighter, fearing Jacobs would act on his threat to stage an elimination tournament to create a number-one contender, thus pushing him to the back of the line, agreed to face Joe the following June. Jacobs had also sweetened his original offer of 20 percent of the gate by throwing in the same percentage of the radio and movie rights.

Joe was so antsy to get at Schmeling he would have fought him for the seven-dollar merchandise check he used to get as an amateur. As he told reporters over and over again, he would never consider himself the true champion until he had licked the only man to have beaten him. Now the fight was on, but he would have to wait nearly ten months. During this long interval, the press and world events would help create the most politicized buildup to a fight ever seen.

In mid-December of 1937, Schmeling came to New York to fight Harry Thomas at Madison Square Garden. Thomas was a mediocre fighter, and the Anti-Nazi League staged a boycott, but the affair still drew the largest indoor fight crowd in the city in two years—a measure of the growing interest in Louis-Schmeling II. One paper described Schmeling's eighth-round knockout: "Seven times Thomas went down under that short, flashing, paralyzing right-hand punch to the jaw with which Schmeling hammered Louis into submission."

Joe was made constantly aware of his antagonist's right fist, whether it was reading the newspapers or going out in public. "People with smart remarks is what really got Schmeling whipped," insisted Freddie Guinyard. "For two years, Joe'd be in a crowd and someone would yell out, 'Look out, Joe, here comes Schmeling!' I'd notice Joe acting kind of sulky afterwards."

On February 22, 1938, at Madison Square Garden, Joe tuned up for Schmeling with a third-round kayo of Nathan Mann. Then, on April 1, he put Harry Thomas on the floor in the fifth round. Meanwhile, Schmeling had returned to Hamburg where he decisioned Ben Ford in January and registered a fifth-round knockout of Steve Dudas in April. On May 9, Schmeling completed a six-day transatlantic voyage back to New York aboard the S. S. Bremen. "Schmeling Arrives Confident He'll Beat Louis and Be First to Regain Title" was one of the banner headlines announcing his arrival to train for the big fight. "Schmeling Go Home" was one of the slogans carried by the picketing demonstrators who turned out to jeer him.

"It gave me a bad feeling because I always thought I was liked in America," he said later. "I found out later that the propaganda wasn't against Max Schmeling, the fighter, but against Max Schmeling, the German. Every German, even if it wasn't true, was at this time thought to be a Nazi by Americans."

For good reason. In the two years since Schmeling's first fight with Joe, Nazi Germany had grown increasingly belligerent. Hitler had unilaterally annexed Austria, was threatening a move on Czechoslovakia, and continued to help the fascist rebels in Spain. A year earlier, Hitler had shocked the civilized world by sending German bombers to level the Spanish city of Guernica. In the States, German Bund rallies and the inflammatory rhetoric of demagogues like "Radio Priest" Father Charles Coughlin incited anti-Semitic sentiment. Polls revealed that the majority of Americans, despite their sympathies, wished to remain neutral in the event of another all-out war in Europe. In this climate of fear, hostility, and helplessness, the role of sports as a vicarious form of political expression—first seen in the 1936 Olympic Games and Joe's fights against Carnera and Schmeling—continued to grow in importance.

One of Joe's favorite ballplayers, Detroit first baseman Hank Greenberg, took tremendous abuse as baseball's first Jewish star. Greenberg would later remember the summer of 1938 as one of tremendous responsibility, pressure, and personal vindication. In September, as Hitler bullied England and France into surrendering Czechoslovakia and Jews continued to be rounded up by the tens of thousands, Greenberg chased Babe Ruth's single-season home run record with one eye on the front page. "Being Jewish did carry with it a certain responsibility," he said. "After all, I was representing a couple of million Jews among a hundred million gentiles. . . . As time went by, I came to feel that if I, as a Jew, hit a home run, I was hitting one against Hitler."

Schmeling had received a gala send-off from the Hamburg dock, but he represented a problem for the Nazi party. For years Jack Dempsey had been trying to get him to defect; to insure against that possibility, propaganda minister Joseph Goebbels refused to allow Schmeling's wife and mother to accompany him to America.

Goebbels's propaganda machine cranked out ficticious quotes as the representative of the Aryan race went into training. "The black man will always be afraid of me," Schmeling was reported to have said. "He is inferior." Schmeling didn't say or believe this rubbish, but with his family held hostage, he could hardly deny the inflammatory statements attributed to him. He did his best to downplay the political overtones, telling the reporters who continually peppered him with questions of Nazi race policies that "I am a fighter, not a politician. . . . I am no superman in any way."

Coincidentally, the premier issue of *Action Comics* was on the stands, beginning the saga of "Superman, champion of the oppressed, the physical marvel who had sworn to devote his existence to helping those in need!" Those in the know believed that the real Man of Steel was not to be found in Germany or Smallville, but in Pompton Lakes, New Jersey, where the black *ubermensch* Joe Louis was resolutely working himself into peak condition, both physically and mentally.

"Ordinarily, you know, Joe doesn't care who the other fellow is," Roxborough explained. "It's just another fight for Joe. But this Schmeling—on account of that other fight and what everybody has been saying—well, it's sorta got under Joe's skin. This time it isn't just another fight; it's a chance to catch up with Schmeling and square an account."

"He was mean," observed Dave Clark, "so mean that three days before the fight he'd lock himself away so nobody could bother him. He'd just lay on a training table and think about that fight."

Fight talk and war talk were interchangeable in all of the dailies as June 22, the date of the bout, grew nearer. As groups like the Anti-Nazi League and the American Jewish Committee picketed Mike Jacobs's office, wrote letters to the editors, and otherwise did their best to slow ticket sales, rumors flew all over the place. Hitler was going to make Schmeling the minister of sport for the Third Reich if he won. Schmeling's trainer, Max Machon, had a full Nazi uniform hanging in his closet at camp. Storm troopers would be part of the group of German fans sailing over on the *Hamburg* and *Europa*. German correspondent Arno Helmers informed his homeland that the Jewish governor of New York, Herbert Lehman, was part of a conspiracy to make sure Louis won.

Earlier that spring, the Washington press corps had done its best to politicize the fight. In a meeting between Joe and President Roosevelt at the White House, FDR had asked him to lean over so he could feel his muscles.

"Joe," he said, "we need muscles like yours to beat Germany."

Of course, newspapers improved on the president's words, reporting his comment as, "Joe, beat Schmeling to prove we can beat the Germans."

To protesters like Benjamin Solomon of Port Jervis, New York, buying a ticket to watch Schmeling fight was tantamount to buying German-made goods. "I don't see how anyone with a sense of decency would willingly do anything that helps the continuance in power of this regime of mass lying, mass tyranny, mass torture, and mass murder!" he editorialized in the *New York Times*.

As the betting action picked up between Harlem and Yorkville (Manhattan's predominantly German neighborhood), writers produced their share of doggerel. John Kieran, who had picked wrong in the first match, spelled out his position in "On Second Thought."

> They warned me of an ancient day
> —Before the first Joe-Max affair—
> When odds ran wild the other way,
> And yet the Tortoise beat the Hare.
> So Schmeling would—and were they wise!—
> Beat Louis down. But even though
> It happened right before my eyes,
> I still like Joe.
>
> They told me that the Persian host,
> Who later ran to hell-an'-gone,
> Were 1 to 10 in book and boast
> To beat the Greeks at Marathon.
> But sunset saw them on the lope,
> As moonlight saw Joe Louis low.
> Greek-like, Herr Schmeling crossed the dope.
> I still like Joe.
>
> They argued eke, in rising wrath,
> That little David, brave and bold,
> Unplayed at 8 to 1 in Gath,
> Rose up to knock Goliath cold.
> From this they judged—and were they right!—
> That Max would land the winning blow.
> But this is yet another night.
> I still like Joe.
>
> I've had due warning, loud and long,
> Of what must come when clangs the bell,
> And how again I will be wrong;

A state in which I often dwell;
Of how, once more, will Joe recline,
And how they'll shout: "We told you so!"
But here I lay it on the line:
I still like Joe.

Kieran wasn't alone in liking Joe. Bookies had Joe as a 2-to-1 favorite to keep his crown and avenge his sole professional defeat. James Braddock visited Joe in camp and predicted a seventh-round knockout. "Joe seems to be concentrating on infighting and body punishing," he explained. "Those are the tactics that should whip a veteran like Schmeling."

Most writers, while giving the champion the edge over his thirty-three-year-old opponent, still weren't convinced that Joe was a cerebral fighter, one who could adapt his strategy to beat a man who had previously defeated him. If Joe won, it would be because of his superior natural ability. If Max won, it would be because of his craftiness and brainpower.

Ironically, Joe would retire with a reputation for always having fared better the second time around with an opponent, proof of his analytical mind. During his career he would fight ten different fighters twice; each time he followed up a so-so effort with a superior one.

This time the strategy called for Joe to attack from the opening bell. As Blackburn observed during the 1936 fight, when Joe was on the offensive, following up his jab with combinations, Schmeling had been forced to retreat. But when Joe failed to follow up, Schmeling had been able to counter his right over Joe's left, with devastating effect. The plan was to keep the pressure on and not to allow Schmeling the chance to deliver his right.

The pressure on Joe, who had turned twenty-four during training, was suffocating. Marva recalled, "Everywhere we'd go before the fight, all we heard was, 'We want you to get Schmeling.' It seemed his whole life hinged on that one fight."

The morning of the fight, a Wednesday, Joe woke at nine in the morning and, accompanied by his managers and three state troopers, rode to the office of the New York Boxing Commission for the official weigh-in. He and Schmeling acknowledged each other with a silent nod. Schmeling's scale read 193 pounds, five and a half less than Joe's. After that, Joe went to a friend's apartment where Bill Bottoms fed him a steak and salad at three o'clock. In that day's comic page, which Joe read faithfully, Jeff told Mutt that he was prepared to take on Louis and Schmeling at the same time. Looking to work off the meal and some nervous energy, Joe took a walk along the Harlem River with Blackburn and Fred Wilson, John Henry Lewis's former trainer.

"How you feel, Joe?" Wilson asked.

"I'm scared," he replied.

"Scared?" said Wilson.

"Yea," Joe said. "I'm scared I might kill Schmeling tonight."

The Louis entourage arrived at Yankee Stadium at seven o'clock. There was no joking. Joe went to sleep for a couple of hours in the dressing room while outside demonstrators distributed leaflets and more than 70,000 people filed into the hazy, muggy stadium. The crowd included a dozen mayors and governors and a thousand of New York's finest. Another thousand police officers were added to the regular shift in Harlem.

Blackburn woke Joe at nine and got him dressed and taped. "In three rounds, Chappie," he said. "If I don't have Schmeling knocked out, you better come in and get me, because after that, I'm through."

"No, it's all right," Blackburn said. "You can go fifteen rounds."

Joe replied, no, it was going to be all or nothing. The whole world was watching, and his career, his reputation, were in the balance. Normally Joe would shadowbox for ten minutes prior to a fight. This time he blasted the air for a full half hour, right up to the time he was called into the ring.

A sign of the fight's importance was that NBC had combined its Blue and Red Networks to carry the broadcast on 146 stations. The Good Housekeeping Shops featured a special for what was expected to be a record number of boxing fans: a brand new 1939 Zenith Superheteodyne radio was on sale for $14.95. Those who happened to be a little light in the wallet could plunk a buck down and pay fifty cents a week for the chance to hear the fight of the century. Whatever model Americans listened to, they were almost universally tuned into the fight. Later, an industry report estimated that 97 percent of radio owners in New York City listened. Outside the city, nearly two-thirds (63.6 percent) of all radio owners had twisted their dials to the broadcast. Only a pair of President Roosevelt's fireside chats ever drew more listeners. With these kinds of numbers, Buick's decision to pay a whopping $47,000 to air the only two commercials the truncated fight would have time for still proved to be a bargain. In Germany, the 3:00 A.M. curfew was lifted in order that cafes and beer gardens could carry the short-wave broadcast for their customers. Joseph Goebbels invited Schmeling's wife to his home to hear the action, while Hitler preferred to pace back and forth while listening at his retreat, Berchtesgarden.

Mike Jacobs had a last piece of practical advice for Joe. He reminded him that if Schmeling won, they both stood to lose a fortune. "Murder that bum," Uncle Mike said, "and don't make an asshole out of me."

"Don't worry about a thing," Joe replied. "I ain't going back to Ford, and you ain't gonna go back to selling lemon drops on the Staten Island Ferry."

Jacobs didn't tell his fighter that he had hedged his bets, signing a contract with Schmeling to promote his fights should he stage an upset. There was no way Uncle Mike was going to surrender his control of the heavyweight title.

Joe was loose. As he marched to the ring with Roxborough, he noticed his manager gnawing on the first of the twenty or so cigars he would nervously chew through on fight nights. Joe playfully pulled a fistful of stogies out of Roxie's suit pocket and threw them on the floor.

"You'll only need the one in your mouth tonight, John," he said.

The crowd's hostile reaction to Schmeling's entrance had been expected. Twenty policemen surrounded him as he made his way to the ring, during which he was bombarded with fruit, crushed cigarette packs, and paper cups. He finally pulled a towel over his head to protect him from the debris.

Once again the third man in the ring was Arthur Donovan. Curiously, the forty-eight-year-old veteran referee (whose son Art Jr. would gain fame as a Hall of Fame tackle for the Baltimore Colts) wound up refereeing nineteen of Louis's title bouts. But he never had a conversation with him until 1963 when Joe almost ran him over with his car as Donovan absent-mindedly crossed a New York City street.

On this evening it would be Schmeling who would look as if he'd been hit by a car. Donovan instructed both corners that throwing a towel into the ring, a symbol of defeat not recognized in New York, would not be tolerated. He would decide when this fight was over, he explained.

Schmeling, unshaved and with his black hair greased back, stood calmly in his corner while Joe continued to shadowbox in his corner twenty-five feet away. A few moments later the bell rang and Joe shot towards Schmeling, slowly winding his right forearm as if he were cranking Poppa Brooks's old Model T. He and Schmeling circled each other for a few seconds, and then Joe popped two jabs and a left hook to Schmeling's face. As he backed Schmeling up, he practically jumped out of his shoes to launch a left hook that crashed into the side of his opponent's head. They clinched, then Joe delivered a rapid-fire combination of lefts and rights that sent Schmeling into the ropes.

Trapped, the German managed to get off his first punch of the night, a harmless right, before getting blasted by another flurry of short, pistonlike punches to the head and body. "Move, Max, move!" his trainer yelled, just before Schmeling was struck in the face by an overhand right. Schmeling twisted his trunk just as Joe delivered another long right. It struck him in the lower left back, fracturing his third lumbar vertebra and driving it into his kidney. Schmeling gave a short, piercing scream that "sounded like a stuck pig," said Freddie Guinyard. Donovan, who was the boxing instructor at the New York Athletic Club for fifty years, later described it as the most terrifying sound he had ever heard in the ring.

At that point Schmeling was finished. The blow had partially paralyzed his mind as well as his legs. He clung with both gloves to the top rope while Donovan stepped in. "Move away, Joe!" Donovan ordered. Joe backed off while the ref started a standing eight-count. But Schmeling, his head scrambled, lurched off at the count of two, his left arm useless. He was greeted by a hard left, and then a right to the jaw sent him face first to the apron where he rolled over onto his injured back. Schmeling, not knowing what country he was in at this point, got up at the count of three. He was quickly driven to his hands and knees by a right cross. He got up again, and seconds later took a left to the head, a left to the jaw, and a right to the head. Another right to the body and a left to the jaw and Schmeling was down for keeps. A white towel came fluttering into the ring, but Donovan angrily tossed it back out. He started counting but realized Schmeling had been all but finished. Schmeling "looked vaguely around with a helpless silly look in his eyes," reported Stanley Woodward. "He was beaten. He might have got up, but he would have been killed." Seventy thousand open-throated people were on their feet, their screams blending into one continuous, ear-splitting roar.

Donovan breaststroked with both arms to keep Joe away. At two minutes and four seconds of the first round, he signaled the fight over. In what one veteran observer was to call the most concentratedly destructive 124 seconds in two centuries of ring history, Joe Louis had annihilated Nazi Germany's representative with prizefighting's version of the *blitzkrieg*. It would be two weeks before Schmeling was well enough to be moved by stretcher from Polyclinic Hospital to the boat that would take him back to Germany.

Bob Considine's ringside reporting perfectly summed up the slaughter: "Listen to this, buddy, for it comes from a guy whose palms are still wet, whose throat is still dry and whose jaw is still agape from the utter shock of watching Joe Louis knock out Max Schmeling. It was, indeed, a shocking thing, that knockout—short, swift, merciless, complete."

The fight immediately became a cultural touchstone, much as Pearl Harbor Sunday would become three and a half years later. Soon it seemed that everybody had a story to tell about where they were or what they were doing the night Joe Louis beat the hell out of Max Schmeling. Many centered around the fight's brevity. Duke Ellington, for instance, had gotten tickets close to the action. "We're getting settled in our seats just as the fight is about to begin," he recalled, "and I dropped my goddamn straw hat. It's rolling around down by my feet, and I'm trying to pick it up. I'm bending down there looking for my hat so I can settle back in my seat and watch

Joe take that cat apart, and everybody started jumping to their feet, hollering, and I looked up and the goddamn fight was all over."

Entertainer Bob Hope, who as a youth in Cleveland fighting under
the name Packy East had lost twenty-one straight amateur bouts, was with
several friends in the press area near ringside. "Just as the fight began, a guy
behind me yelled, 'Hey, Bob!'" said Hope. "I turned around to talk to him.
A roar went up from those around us. When I turned back to see what had
happened, I saw Schmeling on the floor. Some fight fan, I had missed half
the fight! It was that quick."

Freddie Guinyard was positioned in Schmeling's corner as the Louis
camp's official observer. Years later he asked Joe, "Why'd you knock him
out so fast for? You should've given the crowd a chance to see the fight."

"I wanted to get it over with," replied Joe.

Others emphasized the ferocity of Joe's attack, with many writers
bringing out the shopworn jungle-killer comparisons. One wire-service
reporter, Jack Cuddy, wrote of Joe's "panther-like" attack. The "Detroit
Negro's mask-like face showed its hatred only through the eyes that
gleamed at the former champion like those of an irate cobra."

Some, like Bud Shaver of the *Detroit Times*, ridiculed Schmeling's
claim of being fouled by a kidney punch. Photographs clearly showed
Schmeling turning his back at the moment Joe fired his punch. Joe's own
sportsmanship was hailed. He had not complained when Schmeling had hit
him with that terrible right hand after the bell rang in their first fight. "If
Schmeling had saved his squawk for consumption abroad I would not beef,"
Shaver wrote. "I have no quarrel with what is printed about sports outside
of the United States of America, but I'm deeply concerned about that that
is printed here.

"There is no place for prejudice or politics in sports here, and to me
Joe Louis is an American kid who has fought honestly and fairly to a high
place in American sports. I know he has white, Indian, and Negro blood in
him, and to me that is all good American blood."

But most stories revolved around the fight's symbolism. Some thirty
years later, Studs Terkel interviewed Wilbur Kane, who as a boy had spent
the summer of 1938 at his grandmother's house in Allentown,
Pennsylvania. The night of the fight, Kane and his grandmother were invited to the Stahls, German neighbors who made no secret of their strong pro-
Nazi views.

In expectation of celebrating another Schmeling victory, the Stahls
had traveled to Bethlehem to buy plates of "knockwurst and bratwurst and
all the other kind of wursts you can get," recalled Kane. "And we're all
gonna sit around and we're gonna eat liverwurst and watch this kraut beat
the shit out of this black man, see? And they were gonna rejoice. All I can

remember was praying to God that *somehow* Joe Louis would win. *Somehow* he would win.

"I can remember the faces, how they looked when Joe Louis came out and just *creamed* him . . . They couldn't get the knockwurst in their fat faces, that's how they looked. They couldn't even swallow beer. I was screaming and jumping up and down and my grandmother was whispering to me: 'I know how you feel, but you shouldn't show it. You've got to be polite.'"

Instead the little white boy continued to whoop and holler and carry on, a noisy satellite of triumph far from the craziness of Harlem, Paradise Valley, and the South Side. "It serves you Nazis right!" he yelled as his grandmother dragged him from the house. "It serves you Nazis right!"

America's ghettos exploded in the last truly great celebration of a Joe Louis win. Lines of Harlemites crazily goose-stepped through the mobbed streets while others raced into Yorkville to collect their bets. Detroiters had the foresight to ask police two weeks before the fight to cordon off a section of Paradise Valley for the expected victory party. Tens of thousands of jubilant fans danced, drank, and screamed as a band played a single tune, Slim Gaillard's "Flat-Foot Floogie," over and over again. Above the tumult waved a banner: "Joe Louis Knocked Out Hitler." In Chattanooga, Tennessee, the morning paper ran a picture of two chauffeurs and a doorman counting the $175 they had won betting on Louis. The headline read:

'Dat Boy Joe Louis Done Whup 'Em All'
Ninth Street . . . A few minutes past 8 o'clock . . . A wild, surging crowd . . . Whizzing automobiles . . . Shouts . . . Cheers . . . Laughter . . . Yells . . . Joe Louis.

Joy in Chattanooga's Harlem knew no bounds. Throughout the long stretch of Ninth Street, from the railroad tracks on the east side to Chattanooga's Park Avenue on the west, crowds filled the streets, wildly shouting, good-natured crowds.

Joe Louis wins! Joe Louis wins! Dat boy Louis done knocked him out in the fust round!

Dusky male and dusky female all shouted the tidings at one another. All knew about it, all delighted in telling it over and over again.

Somewhere in the alleys off Ninth Street a parade formed. In disordered formation they swung into Ninth and headed west, a motley array of 200 or more beating on tin pans, buckets, tubs and shouting in wild refrain, "Dat boy Louis, dat boy Louis wins."

Patrolman Ed (Big Ed) Ricketts looked down the street and saw the joyous mob coming. They held the middle of the street, swinging others into their ranks as they moved along. Traffic was blocked but nobody cared; that is, nobody except policemen on the Ninth Street beat, who were expected to keep order in all the chaos.

Policemen put themselves squarely in front of the oncoming crowd. The Negroes scattered good-naturedly, leaving their pots and pans strewn in the street.

There seemed to be conspicuously little betting. Among the exceptions were Sam English, Montgomery Wright, and Sam Stinson, who pooled their money and, of course, bet on Louis.

They won $175. And then joined the happy throng that billowed and flowed along the street.

A woman stood on a street corner and shouted with the rest. Above the din her voice was heard, crying:

"Dat boy Louis, he whups dem all."

And that was the way all Ninth Street felt.

Joe earned nearly $350,000 for his two minutes of work—an astonishing amount of money when one considers that three days later Congress established a new minimum wage of twenty-five cents an hour. However, vindication—not money—was on his mind. As well-wishers and reporters crowded around him in the dressing room, he said evenly, "I'm sure enough champion now."

➔←

Some people worried that Schmeling would be executed upon his return to Nazi Germany. He wasn't. Schmeling is alive today, living near Hamburg and in reasonably good health as he approaches his ninetieth birthday. He is a very rich man, the result of being the owner of the Coca-Cola Corporation of Germany.

Despite the intense nationalism surrounding the fight, its outcome had no visible effect on the march of events that would soon plunge the world into a war that ultimately cost more than fifty million people their lives. Schmeling was a part of that madness, but not always on the same side as his countrymen. In the horrifying evening hours of November 9, 1938—Kristallnacht, the infamous "night of broken glass"—he refused to participate in the orgy of violence that left one hundred Jews dead and many homes, shops, and synagogues in ashes. Thirty thousand Jews were arrested and sent to concentration camps that night.

It was always rumored that Schmeling helped several Jews escape. Asked about his actions on that evening of terror, Schmeling responded, "It wasn't anything dramatic, like an underground. All my wife and I did was to let them hide at our home until they could get out. A lot of other Germans were doing the same thing, and I just had more to lose—especially because I was suspect."

Schmeling had always scoffed at the suggestion that he was a Nazi party member with political connections. He wound up a sergeant in the paratroopers, hardly the kind of plum appointment a former world's heavyweight champion with ties to Hitler could expect. He participated in the massive parachute drop on Crete in 1940 and was captured during the invasion. Schmeling was honest about what the Nazi regime publicized as his "battle wounds." It actually was a bad case of diarrhea. Afterward Goebbels ordered him to give an interview from his hospital bed and describe British atrocities to the still neutral American press. "But when I told the Americans that the so-called 'British atrocities' never took place, he had me court-martialed."

After the war Schmeling returned to the ring, penniless, on his forty-second birthday. In 1954 he visited an old American friend, Jim Farley, in Essen to ask for some help. Farley, the former head of the New York State Athletic Commission and later the head of Coca-Cola International, helped get him started in the soft drink business. "It has been a great pleasure, but also profitable . . . very profitable," said Schmeling, who became a millionaire several times over.

Schmeling had several emotional reunions with Joe in the decades following the war. Joe, true to his nature, never professed any personal hatred toward his former antagonist. Neither felt a need to answer reporters' questions as to who was the greater fighter. "After all," Joe liked to say, "he won one fight, I won one fight—even-steven."

Chapter Eight

Bummin'

Black eye peas ask corn bread
What makes you so strong?
Corn bread says I come from
Where Joe Louis was born.

Rabbit say to the bee
What makes you sting so deep?
He say I sting like Joe
An' rock 'em all to sleep.

—COUNT BASIE, "KING JOE (JOE LOUIS BLUES)" (1940)

A couple of weeks after destroying Max Schmeling at Yankee Stadium, Joe was in the blocks in Chicago, getting ready to race his good friend Jesse Owens between games of a Negro-league doubleheader. The two sports figures were indisputably the most recognizable blacks in America. "Joe and I had been lucky to come along at a time when the imagination of the American public at large was ready to be captured by Negro athletes," reflected Owens. "Because of this, we had unique roles to play in our culture, and it welded us together as friends. Our lives crossed only several times a year, but we understood each other from the beginning."

In 1936, on the strength of his Olympic performance, Owens had briefly eclipsed Joe in the national consciousness. He also succeeded him as the Associated Press's Athlete of the Year. Andrew Young, who would come to prominence as a national black leader in the 1970s, once talked of the pair's influence as symbols of black achievement. "My political education and sense of selfhood really came from people like Joe Louis," he said. "When Joe Louis knocked out Max Schmeling, that was freedom day; when Jesse Owens won the 1936 Olympics, I was only four years old, but I knew what that was about, and my consciousness as a black person came almost entirely from sport."

Although the two were not in competition with each other for the public's affection, there never was any doubt as to which athlete black Americans most closely identified with. A Philadelphia poll taken just a month after Owens's heroics in Berlin revealed that Joe was still the more popular of the two—this despite his recent loss to Schmeling. Three explanations were offered: Joe had reintroduced sportsmanship to boxing; prizefighting was more popular than track; and, through his fists, Joe had proved that the Negro was not cowardly.

But as Paul Gallico admitted, the successful black athlete of the 1930s was considered a "full-fledged citizen" and "a true American" only on the field of competition. "At other times, he remains just plain nigger, and we'd rather he weren't around, because he represents a problem." Owens, his expectations of social advancement raised by the acclaim he received, got a slap of reality when he found out that his parents, in New York to greet him upon his triumphant return from Germany, had been turned away from a whites-only hotel.

Owens's post-Olympics treatment was predictably shabby. At the 1932 games in Los Angeles, Eddie Tolan—a product of Detroit's Brewster Center—had won gold medals in the 100- and 200-meter dashes, but wound up dancing in black nightclubs before finding a job as a poorly paid municipal clerk. Unlike Johnny Weissmuller and Buster Crabbe, a pair of white swimmers who had parleyed their gold medals into Hollywood careers and considerable material wealth, there were no lucrative endorsements, movie deals, or professional job offers awaiting black Olympians. Needing to support his wife and three daughters, Owens dropped out of college, became a playground director in Cleveland, and traded in on his athletic fame the best way he could, accepting money to race against cars, motorcycles, dogs, and horses. Later he toured with the Harlem Globetrotters and the Indianapolis Clowns. "Sure it bothered me," he said of his role as a public spectacle. "But at least it was an honest living. I had to eat."

Which is how he found himself one July day in 1938 lined up for a sixty-yard dash against the most recent destroyer of the myth of Aryan supremacy. As a large crowd, including members of the Chicago American Giants and Birmingham Black Barons, looked on in glee, Owens stumbled and fell down, allowing heavy-legged Joe to lumber across the finish line ahead of him. The stunt was farcical but symbolic. In the eyes of the public, not even the world's fastest human was allowed to surpass the Brown Bomber as America's greatest black hero.

By the late 1930s Joe Louis was indisputably the most famous black the country had ever produced. Proof could be found in almost any direc-

tion one turned. Beyond the usual heavy newspaper and magazine coverage
of his fights and social activities, his image popped up on everything from
hair pomade and a comic strip to clocks and radios. The Nash-Underwood
Company of Chicago came out with a mustard jar shaped like his head;
when it was empty, the slotted top allowed it to be used as a "Lucky Joe
Bank." The champ was charmingly candid about products he backed. Once
a reporter asked him if he had really used Castoria, a bitter-tasting patent
medicine, as a child. He answered yes, but added that he had "sure never
cried for it."

Joe didn't endorse everything thrown his way, however. For many
years he turned down requests from alcohol and tobacco manufacturers to
advertise their products, although Lou Gehrig, Joe DiMaggio, and other
popular athletes of the day heartily praised the alleged health benefits of
cigarettes and pipe tobacco. This drew praise from the press and contributed
to Joe's positive and wholesome public image. When he said no to a cigar
ad, the headline in the *New York Sun* read: "Louis Turns Down Fortune."

While white America tended to view Joe's victories over Carnera and
Schmeling as triumphs of democracy over fascism, millions of Negroes saw
him as the ultimate blues hero, someone whose mythology had surpassed
that of John Henry, the other legendary "hard-drivin' man" of black folk-
lore. While John Henry's exploits were pure fiction, Joe's were deliciously
real. The imagery of a white fighter, head bowed and supplicating on the
canvas to the all-powerful black champion, proved much too strong to
resist. In fact, it was the dominant theme of all such musical tributes,
whether they were work songs, school yard diddies, or formal recordings.
When Joe kayoed Bob Pastor in 1939, kids on 135th Street and Lenox
Avenue in Harlem were heard singing:

> Bob Pastor was on his knees
> Said, "Joe,
> Don't hit me please,
> Just go trucking out of the ring."

After James Braddock fell before Joe's fists, blacks labored on the
docks of Fernandin, Florida, to the following work song:

> Joe Louis hit him so hard he turn roun' and roun',
> He thought he was Alabama bound, Ah, Ah,
> He made an effort to rise agin,
> But Joe Louis's right cut him on the chin, Ah, Ah,
> Weak on his knees and tried to rise,
> Went down crying to the crowd's surprise, Ah, Ah.

Companies like Decca and Okeh issued several 78-rpm recordings singing Joe's praises. "Little Bill" Gaither's "Champ Joe Louis" (accompanied by Honey Hill on the piano) was representative of many blues and jazz numbers produced during the thirties and forties:

> I came all the way from Chicago to see Joe Louis and Max
>   Schmeling fight (twice)
> Schmeling went down like the Titanic when Joe gave
>   him just one hard right
>
> Well, you've heard of the King of Swing, well Joe is the King of
>   Gloves (twice)
> Now he's the World Heavyweight Champion, a man that this
>   whole world loves
>
> It was only two minutes and four seconds poor Schmeling was
>   down on his knees (twice)
> He looked like he was praying to the Good Lord to "Have
>   mercy on me, please!"
>
> If I'd had a million dollars would have bet every dime on Joe
>   (twice)
> I'd've been a rich man this very day and I wouldn't have to
>   worry no more

In addition, Ike Smith released "Fighting Joe Louis," Lil' Johnson came out with "Winner Joe (the Knock-Out King)," and Billy Hicks and the Sizzling Six had a small hit with their "Joe the Bomber." One tune that wore out a good many gramophone needles was Count Basie's 1940 recording of "King Joe (The Joe Louis Blues)." The song represented a remarkable wedding of black talent. The budding author Richard Wright wrote the lyrics; Basie, the legendary jazzman and bandleader, created the music; and the controversial actor-singer-activist Paul Robeson (himself a great college athlete) sang the words, which could be heard in buffet flats and juke joints across black America.

Beyond being a symbol, Joe was a role model to countless youths grappling with the twin burdens of poverty and prejudice. Jimmy Bivins, an eighteen-year-old Golden Gloves champion at the time of the second Schmeling fight, talked of Joe's inspirational effect on a family scraping by in Cleveland during the thirties.

"Joe Louis was an idol to us, somebody to look up to," said Bivins, who was destined to one day face his hero in the ring. "He uplifted us black people, pulled us out of the stream, you know, and put us on top. He gave us a boost to keep on plugging. The harder he fought, the harder we tried to get the Depression over with and try to make a living. People then were down and out.

"I used to tell my kids about the Depression and how we didn't have much to eat. I used to go by the restaurants early in the morning and they'd be cooking all that food. I stand outside there and take a deep breath, sniff real hard, hold my breath, and run all the way home. When I got home, I'd drink a glass of water, then get me a toothpick and start picking my teeth. That's all the food I had for the day.

"Then I'd listen to Joe Louis on the radio, knocking them bums out. When he fought it looked like the whole city would stop moving. The whole world slowed up until that fight was over. If you were walking down the street, that's what you heard on the radios: fight, fight, fight. Then after the fight was over, you heard a lot of yelling, screaming, hollering. Whether he won or lost, you'd hear it."

Berry Gordy Jr. was eight years old when he sat on the curb and watched in fascination as Detroit's Black Bottom erupted after Schmeling was counted out. His father, a shopkeeper, had brought the family up from Georgia several years earlier, and the little boy remembered how older kids on the block would make fun of their own blackness. "If you're white," they'd chant, "you're all right; if you're yellow, you're mellow; if you're brown, you can stick around; but if you're black—get back."

But then, Berry thought amidst the celebrating, "all of a sudden it wasn't so bad to be black. A black man, Joe Louis, was the greatest hero in the universe—at least for the moment. But in that moment a fire started deep inside me; a burning desire to be special, to win, to be somebody."

At first he thought that meant emulating the Brown Bomber. When he was a teenager, Gordy started training under Eddie Futch at the Brewster gym and became a promising 128-pound amateur. One autumn night in 1948, he fulfilled a dream, appearing on the same card at Olympia Stadium as his hero. Gordy decisioned Ciro Montalzo in a four-rounder, then watched Joe take care of Vern Mitchell in a six-round exhibition in the main event. "Looking at him box with such courage and skill," Gordy remembered, "I realized that if I wanted to be a champion I would have to do a lot better than I was doing." Gordy's internal struggle between boxing and songwriting wasn't resolved until one hot August day in 1950 when he quit the gym and dedicated himself to music. The entertainment giant known as Motown Records was the result.

Gordy always gave Joe a good share of credit for his success, saying he was "the first person who made me know what the word hero meant. His phenomenal feats had opened my imagination to the possibility of being somebody in this world."

Malcolm Little of Lansing, Michigan, was thirteen years old when he signed up for his first amateur bout in 1938. "Every Negro boy old enough to walk wanted to be the next Brown Bomber," said the tall, gangly bantamweight, who drew a white novice named Bill Peterson. As Little's family cringed, Peterson repeatedly knocked his scared opponent to the canvas.

"He did such a job on my reputation in the Negro neighborhood that I practically went into hiding," Little recalled. "A Negro just can't be whipped by somebody white and return with his head up to the neighborhood, especially in those days, when sports and, to a lesser extent show business, were the only fields open to Negroes, and when the ring was the only place a Negro could whip a white man and not be lynched."

Humiliated, Little trained hard in the gym. He fared differently in the rematch: this time Peterson knocked him out ten seconds into the fight.

"That white boy was the beginning and end of my fight career," admitted Little. A dozen years later he adopted the Black Muslim faith while in prison and changed his name to Malcolm X. "A lot of times in these later years since I became a Muslim," he said in his autobiography, "I've thought back to that fight and reflected that it was Allah's work to stop me: I might have wound up punchy." Instead the militant social reformer was assassinated inside a Harlem auditorium in 1965, but not before his passionate and eloquent speeches had helped raise the level of black consciousness to heights rarely reached since that magical night when Joe Louis whipped Max Schmeling.

→←

The second Schmeling fight had represented a symbolic prelude to World War II, which the United States formally entered after the slumbering U.S. Navy, docked at Pearl Harbor, was bombed by the Japanese. During the intervening three and a half years, Joe fought so often and was so devastatingly effective that sportswriters regularly referred to his ever-lengthening list of doomed challengers as the "Bum-of-the-Month Club."

Joe's first post-Schmeling opponent was not a bum but a friend in need of a favor. John Henry Lewis had held the light-heavyweight championship for three years but was losing lateral vision in his left eye. He wanted to retire before a blow permanently blinded him, but he wished to bow out with one last big payday. Lewis's manager, Gus Greenlee, was a Pittsburgh numbers racketeer who had long known his counterparts in Detroit and Chicago, John Roxborough and Julian Black. The trio talked

Mike Jacobs into staging a boxing first: two blacks fighting for the heavy-weight championship. The issue of race in the prizefight industry had become so insignificant during Joe's reign that few people saw anything wrong with the match. In fact, with the division cleaned out of any serious contenders, many sportswriters had spent the fall of 1938 clamoring for it.

Jacobs, worried that few people would come to see two black men fight, kept ticket prices low, and as a result, Madison Square Garden was sold out the night of January 25, 1939. Lewis, an eight-year pro who had lost only seven of nearly a hundred fights, was small at 180 pounds, but he was quick and clever. Nonetheless, Joe was confident he would win; the only question in his mind was how he should handle his friend. He didn't want to punish him, so he decided that a swift knockout would be the most merciful approach. He quickly knocked Lewis down three times and at two minutes and twenty-nine seconds of the opening round Arthur Donovan declared the bout over.

"I wasn't happy about that fight," Joe said, "but I knew John Henry was on his way out, and at least he'd had the glory of a fight with the heavyweight champion—and had made a good dollar."

Joe next turned out the lights on Jack Roper in Los Angeles in April. The lanky, 10-to-1 long shot lasted nine seconds less than John Henry Lewis had. "I zigged when I should of zagged," Roper explained to a radio announcer after he had been peeled off the mat.

On the horizon was something more colorful and memorable than Roper's post-fight self-analysis. "Two-Ton Tony" Galento, a rotund, bald-ing, shaggy-chested saloon owner from Orange, New Jersey, illustrated how thin the pool of challengers had become. Galento was on his seventh man-ager, Joe Jacobs, who had taken on the improbably shaped twenty-nine-year-old boxer after Max Schmeling returned to Germany. Mike Jacobs, looking for a fight that could draw a large outdoor crowd that summer, set-tled on style over substance. He signed Galento to fight Louis on June 28 at Yankee Stadium.

Whatever else could be said about him, Galento had always been his own man—to the detriment of his ring career. Once in 1932, for example, he had eaten fifty hot dogs just before a fight just to win a ten-dollar bet. His handlers had to slit the waistband of his trunks to get it around his bloated belly. Galento then waddled out and kayoed his opponent.

For a time he worked between bouts as a $25-a-week bouncer. His heavily jowled face carried the scars of more than a few bareknuckled brawls, including gashes over his eyes and a scar on his chin where he had been hit by a beer bottle. Galento, who like Joe was a sixth-grade dropout who had worked as an iceman, had one more thing in common with his opponent: he was considered a throwback. Galento's personal physician said, "He is the thick-boned, hyposensitive type which does not readily register pain. I doubt if any of the thousands of blows he has stopped really has ever hurt him. He has no nerve or brain injury because he never has been stunned."

Less charitable types might have suggested Galento never suffered a brain injury because there was only wind whistling between his cauliflower ears. He reveled in his role as a neanderthal. He openly endorsed such tactics as head butting and eye thumbing. His favorite expression, one that he had been using since his first pro fight in 1929, was "I'll moida da bum!" No gimmick was too outlandish. He boxed kangaroos, wrestled bears, and claimed to have once choked an octopus to death. While Joe was photographed conscientiously getting into shape, Galento was pictured doing roadwork with a cigar in his mouth, opening bottles with his teeth, and washing down huge plates of spaghetti with a case of beer.

Joe paid little mind to this roly-poly barroom brawler until Joe Jacobs, in a classic case of "steaming" the gate, accused the champ of having concealed a small iron bar in his glove during the Schmeling fight. He told the press that, to protect his fighter, he would insist on Joe's gloves being carefully inspected before his fight with Galento. Mike Jacobs demanded, and quickly received, a retraction. But the intended result was achieved. Interest in the fight picked up. The press fleshed out the actors in this little drama: Galento was the irrepressible lug, Joe the immutable champ. Many of the nearly 35,000 spectators showed up rooting for the underdog.

Galento had never liked to fight blacks, the result of a couple of beatings he had taken early in his career, as well as his own prejudice. Although few people outside of his immediate circle expected him to win, he told a reporter from Charlotte, North Carolina, "I'm gonna knock that nigger out." That was one of the less vile remarks Galento made. Looking back in his middle age, Joe commented, "At first he got on my nerves, but later, you know, I got to like that son of a bitch. He had style and what they're calling 'charisma' nowadays."

Two-Ton Tony entered the ring weighing a bit less than his moniker suggested, carrying 225 pounds on his five-foot-nine-inch frame. There was little to fear, Joe felt, although Galento had a reputation for being able to take a beating and was also known for a powerful left hook, his favorite punch.

During introductions Galento continued to try to psyche Joe out. He told him, "I'm gonna fuck your wife," and added a few other choice remarks in his New Jersey accent. Joe was steaming when the bell finally rang, and before he knew it, he was in a brawl, not a fight.

In the first round Galento, fighting out of a crouch, scored with a left to Joe's jaw and a right-left combination, but the short-armed slugger lacked the boxing skills to follow up on his momentary advantage. Joe escaped and by the second round was ripping open old wounds on Galento's face. One punch practically lifted him off his feet, but Galento got back up. In the third frame, Joe got a bit overconfident. Out of nowhere Galento launched a left hook, and just like that Joe was deposited on the bottom of his silk trunks. It was hard to say who got to their feet quicker: the embarrassed champion or the electrified crowd.

Arthur Donovan was the referee. "When Galento knocked Louis down," he said, "I could see that the champion was badly hurt, even though he jumped onto his feet without a count. If Tony could have landed another left hook, he would have won the title."

But Galento's inability to follow up, plus his own mule-headedness, cost him. Joe, his pride stung, proceeded to savagely work over Galento, who foolishly abandoned his game plan and decided to try and slug it out. In the fourth round, as Galento was buried beneath an avalanche of left hooks and right crosses, Donovan finally stepped in to halt the beating. Joe had earned $114,332 for his sixth straight title defense, but it was Galento who had won the favor of the crowd. The fat man had joined two former world champions, Max Schmeling and James Braddock, as the only men to have knocked mighty Joe Louis down. It had been great theatre, and the loser wound up receiving a flurry of movie, radio, and fight offers as a result, but Galento was distraught. He realized that he had come *that* close to moidering da bum.

"Back in the dressing room," recalled his cut man, Whitey Bimstein, "he is sitting there with blood pouring from his eyes, his nose, and his cheek. He won't let me touch the cuts. He won't let me take off his gloves. He pushes me away every time I try to do something for him and bellows, 'You guys wouldn't let me fight my own fight. I'd've knocked that mug cold!'"

Until he dropped dead of a heart attack in 1979, Galento continued to brood over his missed opportunity to depose the champion and strike a blow for average beer-drinking Joes everywhere. According to Bimstein, Galento "would have licked him if he obeyed orders. We had Tony bobbing and weaving in the first two rounds, and he had Louis dizzy. He even knocked Louis down. Then he thought he was John L. Sullivan and came up straight to slug, and you just can't do that with Louis. If Tony had fought the way he was told, he might have got in another shot that would have kept Louis down for keeps—and I don't think Tony was the greatest fighter in the world, either."

Joe next fought Bob Pastor on a drizzly September night at Briggs Stadium in Detroit. It was scheduled for twenty rounds, the first championship fight of that duration since Jess Willard beat Jack Johnson twenty-four years earlier.

Pastor was just as dissatisfied with their previous meeting as Joe had been. By nature Pastor was a slugger, not a bicyclist. However, this evening the challenger was on the receiving end of most of the punches. Pastor had never been knocked off his feet, but Joe decked him five times in the first couple of rounds alone.

"He always told me that he was out on his feet for five rounds," said his daughter, Roberta Sansiveri. Pastor came to and rallied to win a couple of rounds. But in the eleventh, with one eye closed, he was punched to the canvas, got up, and was soon knocked down again. This time the referee stepped in and signaled another knockout victory. Lillie Barrow, as was her custom, was not in the crowd and probably did not even hear the ring announcer intone those familiar words: *The win-nah and still heavyweight cham-peen of the world—JOE LOU-ISSSS!"*

"She hardly ever listened to the fights on the radio," said Freddie Guinyard. "After Joe would win a fight, Harry Balogh would bring a microphone over to him and ask, 'What have you got to say, Joe?' He'd say, 'Hello, Mom. I had another lucky night.'"

Guinyard snorted in laughter remembering Joe's understatement. "Joe called it luck," he said, "but you couldn't tell it by the guy laying on the floor."

After he left boxing, Pastor owned a restaurant and a sporting goods store before finally retiring as a security guard at the Saratoga Racetrack. Today he lives in a nursing home in upstate New York, suffering from the effects of pugilistic dementia, the medical term for punch-drunkenness. He's blind in one eye, confined to a wheelchair, and only occasionally recognizes the person talking to him. The blows from his two duels with Louis undoubtedly contributed to his condition, but in his lucid moments he wears them almost as badges of pride. Roberta Sansiveri remembered one particularly trying day when she was doing her best to lift her father's spirits.

"Dad, you're tough," she said. "You'll be okay."

"Well," the old fighter conceded, "you don't go into the ring with Joe Louis unless you're tough."

According to Nat Fleischer, that wasn't the case when Johnny Paychek—born Johnny Pacek in Chicago in 1914—was pasted from pillar to post on March 29, 1940, at Madison Square Garden. Paychek, who was floored twice in the opening round before being dropped for good in the second, needed to have a bucket of water dumped on his head in order to be revived. Joe's latest victim was described by Fleischer as "more scared than any pugilist I have ever seen."

This was an unkind and possibly unfair characterization, though Fleischer accurately had observed that "the field of championship contenders is the weakest in the last fifty years."

The time-honored solution was to go outside the country for a fresh opponent. Joe fought Chilean heavyweight Arturo Godoy seven weeks before Paychek at the Garden, but with far less satisfying results. Godoy, stocky and pug-nosed, fought out of an extreme crouch, making it difficult for Joe to open up. Godoy's clinching tactics also deprived Joe of punching room. At the end of fifteen rounds, both combatants were about as unmarked as the 16,000 in attendance. Godoy, an odd bird, hugged Joe and kissed him on the forehead and danced around the ring triumphantly. Joe was given the unanimous decision, while a few boobirds registered their verdict. "This was the worst fight I ever had," he said.

As was his habit, Joe had a vastly improved showing in the rematch. On June 20, in front of 26,000 at Yankee Stadium, he made a 202-pound pincushion out of Godoy, sticking him with an unending series of left hands. The Chilean went down for the third and last time in the eighth round. Beforehand, Godoy had boasted that he would knock Joe out. Asked about this by broadcaster Clem McCarthy, Joe dryly responded, "Any dog can wag his tail."

"I wonder what more Joe Louis must show to prove to the skeptics that he is a great fighter!" Nat Fleischer asked three months after the second Godoy fight. "What did Jack Dempsey, Gene Tunney, Jim Jeffries, and other stars of the roped square exhibit in their public performances that the present champion lacks, other than quick thinking? What other title-holder was willing to face all comers and to place his title in jeopardy eleven times in three years?

"Louis has clashed with sluggers, clever boxers, combination fighters, rugged, strong men, weavers—in fact, every possible variety of opponent, and the result has been the same. In short, even though he failed to stop his opponent in their first engagement, he solved the riddle in a return bout and proved that as he now stands, he is a well-rounded performer, able to cope with any style elected by the opposition. That is what makes him so invincible."

It was when Mike Jacobs scheduled Paychek and Godoy that Jack Miley of the New York Post dubbed this procession of lackluster opponents the "Bum-of-the-Month Club," a takeoff on a recent phenomenon, the popular Book-of-the-Month Club. Before long everybody was using this phrase. Of course, to call these fighters bums is to do them a great disservice. True, they weren't in Joe's league. Then again, who was during his prime?

It's worth noting that Joe never considered his opponents bums. "They were hard-working professionals trying to make a living, too," he said. "I knew the training they went through, and I knew the dreams they had. No different from me. I respected every man I fought. It's no easy job getting up in that ring; you got to have a special kind of balls."

David Levien, a screenwriter based in New York, agrees. He quizzed his grandfather, Johnny Paychek, very carefully during the last fifteen or so years of his life. Paychek, who had taken up boxing as a boy because he was tired of being picked on, either forgot or didn't care to remember the details of his fights. If boxing histories mention his name at all, it's invariably because of a familiar quote belittling his performance against Louis. "Did you ever see a ghost walking?" wrote a reporter at ringside. "I did." The quote became a part of Joe's legend, although at the expense of his opponent.

"He was a more willing talker about his training regimen," Levien said of his grandfather. "Five miles of roadwork, ten rounds of shadowboxing, bag work, skipping rope, the medicine ball for the stomach, two or three rounds of sparring, and more in the weeks before a fight. This was every day. Injuries were treated with ice and liniment. Meals included as much steak as could be afforded. . . . Black eyes and bloody noses and cuts hurt, but they healed. I knew nothing of the lifelong joint stiffness, difficulty breathing due to nose and rib injuries, impaired eyesight, ringing in the ears, and diminished faculties—the kind that cannot be recovered from."

After his boxing career ended, Paychek worked at a small-town high school as a trainer and a custodian. His speech became increasingly slurred with age. In his final year he took to sobbing in his easy chair for no apparent reason. Paychek, who slipped into a coma and died in 1988, was representative of the many journeymen who fell before Joe's fists during the champion's prime, a fate that didn't diminish him in the eyes of his vanquisher or his proud and inquisitive grandson. "As far as I'm concerned," concluded Levien, "if one has to fight, elects to follow that road, becomes a contender, and fights for the championship of the world, and if one has to lose by knockout, then it might as well be to Joe Louis. My grandfather's journey took him closer to greatness than most men ever come."

There was no shame in losing to Joe, who exhibited commendable class in victory or defeat. He was not one to belittle or show up a fellow fighter, and his sportsmanship was regularly hailed by writers and opponents. "Joe never elbowed you in the ring," said Lou Nova, who also went the way of the knockout when the two met in 1941. "He didn't butt. He didn't talk you down. He never pulled a dirty tactic. I never heard Joe use a curse word. I never heard him criticize anyone adversely."

This was in keeping with his personality. To Joe, victory was to be expected and quietly savored, not trumpeted from the highest mountaintop. As Paul Brown, the Cleveland Browns' head coach, would later say of his great running back, Jimmy Brown: "The thing I liked about Jim Brown is that when he went into the end zone, he acted like he'd been there before." In other words, Brown engaged in none of the chest bumping, finger pointing, trash talking, or other end zone theatrics so popular among the less talented. Brown, who grew up on Long Island admiring the deeds of the Brown Bomber, admittedly styled himself after the champ—strong, silent, self-confident. Taunting, strutting, crowing, and other forms of self-aggrandizement were for the insecure.

Joe's confidence level soared after Schmeling II. Before then he had been thin-skinned about anyone who had beaten him. "In the late 1930s I was a thorn in his side," recalled Stanley Evans, one of the few men able to claim a victory over Joe as either an amateur or a professional. "He was not too anxious to greet me. Here was the champion of the world with a group of onlookers and here's this guy Evans who had beaten him."

Later, having wreaked his terrible vengeance upon Schmeling and beaten all challengers, "it was different," said Evans, who had a brief, five-fight fling as a professional in 1938. "When he'd come to Detroit and he'd see me in the crowd, he'd pick me out and say 'Hiya, champ.'" Joe could afford to be magnanimous, for there was no longer any doubt in anyone's mind—especially his—that he was the best fighter alive.

Writers also detected a change: Joe smiled more readily and was more at ease with them. He had matured, both inside and outside the ring, and he no longer had to fret about saying something that conceivably could cost him his shot at the championship. "He used to clam up when talking to white men," Caswell Adams wrote in the *Saturday Evening Post*, "but ever since that Schmeling smashing he's been just as chatty with them as with Negroes."

By 1941 the country had grown comfortable with him as a fighter and as a public figure. Few writers felt the need to identify him as a Negro. His white opponents felt free to criticize him without making his color an issue. That was the case when Buddy Baer lost a fight because of an inadvertent late punch. "Joe's a great fighter and a credit to his race," Baer complained afterward, "but he hit me after the bell."

➤❖

Joe needed to fight to maintain his lifestyle, which in the years leading up to the war grew increasingly lavish. He maintained apartments in Chicago and Harlem's exclusive Sugar Hill district, owned several high-powered luxury automobiles, including a Dusenberg, and continually added to his already overflowing closets. He was a partner in a Chicago jazz club and owned a pair of thoroughbred horses, Flash and Jocko.

Joe's personal vanity grew in proportion to his bankroll. His drawers of socks, underwear, and accessories were meticulously organized, while his dozens of custom-made suits hung on special Italian hangers that prevented them from wrinkling. He was partial to checked, striped, or plaid "swagger-style" suits, two-toned shoes, and brightly colored socks. Green was a favorite color. Bored with what the tailors at favorite New York shops like Billy Taub's and Sulka's were touting, he designed his own creations, including suit coats without lapels and a camel's hair coat with leather piping. He changed clothes two or three times a day; to prevent a fashion faux pas, he taped a running list of what he had worn and when to his dresser mirror. To bring him back to earth, Marva would remind him of the dances he had attended as a teenager, when he would lean self-consciously against the wall for fear of revealing the back of his threadbare pants.

Lillie Barrow, never impressed with the trappings of wealth, would cap off her son's frequent visits to Detroit by baking a sweet-potato pie or a pound cake, frying some chicken, and packing the goodies into wax-lined shoeboxes. "Well," recalled Joe, "now I'm world champion, I can't go carrying around these shoeboxes, but at the same time I want that good food." Marva came up with a solution. Out of Momma's sight, she would wrap the boxes in fancy paper and ribbons, as if they were carrying birthday or Christmas presents onto the train back home. Once they unpacked and Joe was feeling hungry, he would call out to Marva, "Bring on the shoeboxes!"

Given Joe's wealth, paying $2,500 for an English saddle or a diamond necklace was not an outlandish expenditure, though at the time that amount represented a couple of years' wages for millions of ordinary Americans. It was nothing for him to drop that much on a single round of golf or on a night out at some favorite Harlem hangout like the Mimo Club or Johnny Cobb's the Nest. Joe often began a day with a fistful of hundred-dollar bills stuffed into his pockets and ended it by phoning Marva and asking, "Honey, have you got any money?"

"They should have called him 'can't say no Joe,'" remembered one companion. "He was his own worst enemy. He liked fun and laughter and guys clowning around and he paid for all of it. Anyone could give him a hard-luck story and as soon as it was over he'd reach into his pocket and pay."

Joe enjoyed most sports, especially bowling and baseball, but "his vice was that little white ball," said Sunnie Wilson. When he wasn't in training, he was often shooting thirty-six holes of golf a day, sometimes losing thousands of dollars in wagers. "That little white ball will take all your money away," said Wilson, who has a hatful of stories about Joe's losses on the links. "Sometimes Joe would break the sticks and say, 'Get rid of 'em, they're a bad habit.' He was like a man with alcohol. It was an addiction."

When Joe was on the West Coast, he regularly golfed with such celebrities as Al Jolson, Bob Hope, Bing Crosby, Jimmy Durante, and Eddie Cantor. Jolson "was absolutely crazy and funny," he remembered. "He bet that if he beat you, he'd pee on you. I made sure I didn't lose, because I saw him actually pee on some guy after the guy had lost. Between Durante, Jolson, and Cantor, I nearly died of laughing." When he wasn't laughing, he was learning—from black professionals like Bill Spiller and Ted Rhodes, and from black hustlers, like the former Pullman porter who allegedly paid cash for his house, with his winnings. Jack Blackburn, beyond his viewing golf as a silly game for rich white folks and his concern over Joe's gambling losses, was worried that his fighter was developing muscles that were of no use to a prizefighter. But Joe kept hacking away and eventually turned into a near tournament-level player. "He thought his destiny was golf," said Sunnie Wilson.

While many of his Hollywood friends loved to bet on the horses, Joe preferred riding them. He had met several black members of the horsey set in California and wondered why something like them didn't exist in Michigan. In July 1938, he and Marva joined the local black aristocracy in putting on the inaugural United States Negro Horse Show at the Utica Riding Club. Joe was the featured contestant, riding a horse named MacDonald's Choice in the fine-gaited saddle competition. He took third place, receiving a yellow ribbon and $1,500. The following year Marva spent six weeks at the French Lick riding academy in Indiana and became a capable equestrienne, learning to ride both straight and sidesaddle on three-gaited as well as five-gaited horses.

Because of his passion for horses, Joe used part of his purse from the second Schmeling fight to buy a large farm, Spring Hill in Utica. John Roxborough had convinced Joe to pay $100,000 for the historic 477-acre property, which in the last century had been a stop on the Underground Railroad that had helped smuggle thousands of escaped slaves to safety. The giant farmhouse, where Joe enjoyed playing the role of a country squire, was surrounded by endless land over which he and Marva could ride. Eighty Hereford cows, a hundred Poland China hogs, and several dogs shared the quiet, undulating grounds with Joe, Marva, Jocko, and Flash.

Sunnie Wilson, ever the entrepreneur, had a falling-out with Joe's manager over the property's potential. Roxborough wanted a place where his fighter could indulge his passion for dogs and horses and relax. It also figured to be a better investment than another car or closetful of suits. Wilson envisioned an adjacent resort community with people sipping Joe Louis Mineral Water tapped from the local stream. The compromise was a small restaurant and a stable. Before the property was sold to the state in 1946 for use as a park, many blacks had made the pilgrimage to Spring Hill.

The farm was about a ninety-minute drive from Detroit in those pre-freeway days (although Marva could make the trip in about half that time thanks to the chauffeur-driven limousine Joe had provided her). The long ride made for an exciting excursion, recalled Ron Teasley, who grew up on Detroit's northwest side. "It was a big occasion when my father took us there," he said. "Although Joe Louis was famous, he was very accessible. You might see him from a distance. You'd wave to him and he'd wave back."

Marian Jones's father had come to Detroit from North Carolina in 1922 and was hired at Ford. This enabled him to own the only radio on the block, around which neighbors would gather to listen to the Brown Bomber put away another opponent. Naturally, the black and white family dog was named Joe Louis.

"The Joe Louis farm grounds were surrounded by a wooden fence, and had an outdoor restaurant with umbrellas and tables and horse riding for the public," she recounted, "although we couldn't afford to ride the horses. Mama spread a tablecloth on the ground for our picnic. It was an unforgettable Sunday outing, replete with fried chicken, potato salad, freshly baked bread, and a freezer of homemade ice cream! Daddy bought two Baby Ruth candy bars and, with his pocket knife, sliced them into pieces for us children.

"We always looked forward to Sunday afternoon rides in our Model T when we would go to the airport, park on the road, and watch the airplanes take off and land, or go to the Ford Motor Co. and watch coal being converted into coke. But no outing was ever as memorable as the trip to Joe Louis's farm, accompanied by loving parents who took seriously the Bible command about bringing up children in the righteous path."

Unfortunately, Joe himself often strayed off that path. On the surface, he and Marva were the picture of wedded bliss, black America's number-one young couple. Privately, they were waging a battle to keep their marriage alive.

The biggest point of contention was Joe's philandering. To him, sex was as elemental as oxygen. He was "a big man" with "an enormous appetite—"a lover," he confessed. There certainly was no shortage of partners. During his marriage to Marva, he was involved with literally hundreds of women, many of whom were anonymous, others who were well-known names. A partial list of his paramours included lithesome Willamae Johnson, who he squired around the New York World's Fair; Alice "Red" Keyes, a carrot-topped Los Angeles showgirl; actress Fredi Washington; Hortense "The Body" Allen, a dancer at the Plantation Club in St. Louis; Mildred Davenport, a Universal movie studio star known as Acquanetta; New York socialite Muriel Kellogg; nightclub dancer Janet Sayres; and Ruby Allen Dallas, one of the Cotton Club's most popular chorines and later a model for *Esquire* cartoonist E. Simms Campbell. Joe also didn't mind recommending his lovers to good friends. Rhumboogie dancer Edna Mae Holly became the wife of Sugar Ray Robinson, while Joe shared the charms of showgirl Beatrice Ellis with Duke Ellington for many years.

"I knew I had a big appetite," he explained. "It's like I like steaks, lamb chops, chicken, apples, and bananas. I like each at different times but I have to have them all. It was a bad period; I was going through something like what happens to an alcoholic when he falls off the wagon. I got drunk with all these beautiful, exciting women."

He had everything going for him: youth, looks, physical prowess, celebrity, money, and a disarming charm and gentle nature that would have appealed to the opposite sex even if he had been a stevedore or a factory hand instead of the heavyweight champion of the world.

"Joe really was like a big, mischievous kid," said Alberta Barksdale, a vivacious showgirl nicknamed Pudgy because of her short frame. Barksdale anchored chorus lines in Detroit, New York, Los Angeles, St. Louis, London, and elsewhere. It was in California that she got to know the fighter, whose golfing buddy Ted Rhodes had married one of her friends.

"You had to like Joe," she continued. "There were always gobs and gobs of people around him, but when you were alone or in a small group he was at his best. People were always pulling jokes on him, but he'd laugh as hard as the rest of us. I remember he was good with cards. He pulled a card trick on his half-brother, Pat, and his mouth fell open. 'How'd you do that?' he wanted to know.

"Joe liked to play but he liked to win, too. I remember somebody saying once when they were getting ready to play ping-pong, 'You know you gotta let him win. You can't let him lose.' And he had a wonderful sense of humor. I was so proud of my first car. It was a 1928 Model A Ford. Well, you can imagine how that looked in Los Angeles, with all these expensive, brand-new cars. But I asked him, 'You want to go for a ride?' We were driving down Central Avenue in Los Angeles at night when my headlamps went out. They just died. Joe struck a match and held it up like it was a lantern. He was laughing, striking matches all the way back."

Physically, she was attracted to his smooth coffee-colored skin flecked with freckles, his full lips, and his kind, almond eyes. In an era when exceptional muscular development among men was an anomaly, Joe was an impressive physical specimen: broad shoulders, a tautly chiseled chest, powerfully bundled legs and arms, and a washboard stomach. Barksdale delicately deflected questions about any physical involvement. But to borrow a term popular with Peg Leg Howell and other blues artists of the period, it's clear that Joe was "a jelly-rollin' fool."

How tasty was the jelly? Vernon Jordan Jr., a former president of the National Urban League, once recalled a waitress he had caroused around with while in college.

"You've had a lot of boyfriends," he asked one night. "Who's the most exciting man you ever met?"

"Joe Louis," she replied.

Jordan was impressed not so much by her response but "the way she said *Joe Louis*. The body language was there. And she could generate body language. She was quite something in those days. The ladies who sit in the same pew as my momma in church would call her a hussy. Our generation would call her *very sexy*."

One can only imagine what names Marva used. Her marriage to Joe was unraveling, the predictable result of his philandering and neglect. Once he invited a female acquaintance to Spring Hill, totally forgetting that Marva had scheduled a formal dinner for fourteen. She drove up and caught Joe and his girlfriend ambling on horseback through the countryside. Marva gunned the engine, startling Flash whose hoof just missed caving in the windshield. That evening, as the two were getting dressed in their bedroom, she climaxed a long day of feuding by picking up one of his custom-made riding boots and, swinging flat-footed with every ounce of strength she could muster, walloping him in the forehead with it.

Marva tried hard to maintain her dignity. Once she surprised Joe by showing up in Philadelphia where he was being honored by a Negro service organization. Joe, who thought she was back in New York, had brought a girlfriend with him. Marva strode to the stage, hissed "Bitch, move," to the girlfriend, and then, all smiles, accepted the plaque for her husband.

In an attempt to prevent such embarrassing scenes, Joe and Marva eventually came to an agreement. If either one of them should arrive at a restaurant or nightclub and discover the other's car parked outside, the other would not go in. One evening Marva inadvertently entered a club where her husband was entertaining.

"Mr. Louis is here," the maitre d' said. "Would you like to join him?"

"No," replied Marva. "Seat me at the table next to his."

As Marva later said, Joe never left a woman, he simply added another one to his list. The camp secretary, usually Leonard Reed, would see to it that all of Joe's conquests were materially taken care of. One of the secretary's most important duties was mailing rent checks to women in various cities across the country. No matter where Joe traveled, he had an apartment furnished with a girlfriend, to which he could disappear whenever he felt the need. Money was also spent on jewelry, clothes, perfume, and other expensive gifts, which Joe, of course, usually delivered personally. When he felt guilty about his womanizing, which was often, he compensated by sending a gift of equal or greater value to Marva.

Marva rarely saw her husband more than once a week while he was in training. For his part, Joe tried to adhere to the old custom of abstinence while preparing for an opponent, though he often fell off the wagon—or mattress, as the case may be. On fight night, women flew in from cities around the country, checking into Harlem rooming houses or hotels and then sitting in select seats at ringside. Over the course of the next several days, Joe would try to rendezvous with each of them. Sometimes he found himself having to decide between two girlfriends for his night's amusement; he'd make his pick, then give Leonard Reed a hundred-dollar bill and instruct him to show the lady who had been left out a good time.

His immediate postfight routine, attested to by a couple members of his entourage, was to hole up at some hotel and expend weeks of pent-up sexual energy on a succession of willing beauties. On these occasions it was quantity, not quality, that mattered. He might have four or five groupies, spaced twenty minutes to a couple of hours apart, depending on his recuperative powers. Of course, the entire hotel and the surrounding neighborhood would be alive with celebrants, so it was a simple matter to move from room to room a floor ahead of his wife.

Joe's handlers cared about his sexual exploits only to the degree that they worried he might become the victim of a blackmail plot. Mike Jacobs was always trying to get his fighter to choose a downtown hotel for his dalliances, but Joe preferred staying at all-black establishments like Harlem's Theresa or at one of his friends' apartments where he could cavort in relative anonymity.

Judging by the stories told by his followers, Joe was an equal-opportunity lover, bedding down waitresses, actresses, models, cigarette girls, singers, secretaries, showgirls, and society mavens of every race, shape, and creed. His longer-lasting relationships, however, typically were with the same kind of women: elegant, self-assured, and fair-skinned. A strong sense of independence was also desired, for it was vital that these affairs be kept as secret as possible, especially when a white woman was involved.

The first white woman he admitted having a sustained fling with was an unnamed socialite who approached him while he was shopping for a car inside a Detroit showroom in the summer of 1935. According to his recollection, the charming blonde insisted on buying the Buick he was examining. His handlers' warnings about being another Jack Johnson raced through his head. Flustered but intrigued, he nonetheless decided to accept her gift. He promised her a couple of ringside seats at his upcoming fight with Max Baer.

"I got a new Buick every Christmas for the next five years," he said. "The lady was a very important white woman and I was a very important black man. She taught me the word for many of the things I had been doing all along. The word was 'discretion.' And we were 'discreet' the several times we met during those five years."

In 1936 he went to Hollywood to film *Spirit of Youth*. The movie, loosely based on his life (a black dishwasher grows up to be the heavyweight champ), was released shortly after the Braddock fight. Joe recalled the ease with which he slept with a succession of white starlets during this and subsequent trips to Hollywood. "A big movie star would see me, the heavyweight champion of the world, and wonder how I am in the bed. I'd see a big beautiful movie star and wonder how she is in the bed. We would find out very easily. These were just one-night stands. But we both knew to keep it cool. Neither of us could afford to be found out in America in those days."

Sonja Henie, the Norwegian skating star-turned-actress, was among his many tinseltown conquests. "She was a pug-nosed blonde with bright blue eyes and one of the best sports I've ever known. We had a nice thing going, but she was a smart woman and so we kept everything 'undercover,'" he said.

"Undercover" was the operative word with actress Lana Turner, too. "Beautiful girl she was," remarked Joe, "and real likable."

In most cases Joe's liaisons with white women took place in the black enclave of whatever city he was in, which protected both parties from inquisitive white reporters. These entanglements were potentially very dangerous. To a great degree white America's affection for Joe was based not on who he was, but on who he wasn't. He was viewed as the complete antithesis of Jack Johnson. Although mixed couples were considered chic in some circles and simply tolerated in others, it was still a highly inflammatory issue, particularly in the South. Swedish sociologist Gunnar Myrdal, who traveled throughout the South during this period collecting data for his classic study of race relations, *An American Dilemma*, ranked the various forms of segregation considered most important to southern whites. Heading the list was "the bar against intermarriage and sexual intercourse involving white women."

The Negro press, while tacitly acknowledging Joe's affairs of the heart in its gossip columns, continued the fiction that he kept company with black women exclusively. As late as 1951, the many readers of *Ebony*, a popular Chicago-based magazine, were being reassured about his preference for ladies of their own race in a lengthy article about the fighter's near-legendary love life:

> Louis shows a strong inclination to fair-skinned damsels. Most of them could "pass" easily, were they so inclined. Among them have been flaming redheads, brunettes, blondes, chestnuts and auburn-haired beauties. Dark brown-skinned girls have not had much luck in catching the Louis eye, although a scant few have crashed the charmed circle. . . .
>
> The only triumph the female-battered managerial forces of Black and Roxborough were able to achieve from the ruins of their elaborate program to "protect our investment" from women chasing Louis, was avoiding potential trouble on a racial level.

In Chicago when Joe fought Charley Retzlaff at the Stadium in the Winter of 1936, long lines of white women, many with husbands, boy friends, or fathers standing at their sides, broke away as Joe's handlers brought him from the ring after he had fashioned a one-round knockout of Charley. They tried to embrace him, reached out their hands to stroke his sweaty robed arms, let out sighs of delight. The small armies of harassed bluecoats in front and back of Louis and his handlers were unable to prevent the white women from grabbing at the fighter. Black and Roxborough met the problem by successfully taking every precaution in the future to avoid such highly explosive situations as would occur were Louis exposed to the wiles of white women. The record shows Louis was never linked in any way with white women.

A black reporter once broke ranks and took Louis's camp to task, writing that the champ's handlers were consorting with white women. For obvious reasons the main Negro press refused to discuss the issue. It did, however, report on Joe's circumcision in early November 1936. It was unusual for a black male born in the South to have his foreskin removed at birth or anytime thereafter, and unheard of for a newspaper to bring it to the public's attention in any event. But such was the interest in the black community over everything Joe did or said. Because there was no pressing cultural, religious, or medical reason for Joe's operation, one can speculate that he had it to make himself more sexually appealing, particularly to white women, who by and large are accustomed to circumcised partners.

Thankfully for Joe, athletes of his time were often the beneficiaries of a different interpretation of the public's right to know. This was especially true when someone who enjoyed a universally favorable public image was concerned. Joe knew he was playing with fire, but in the absence of a prying press or indiscrete girlfriends, he didn't get burned.

"You didn't step on toes then," said Edgar Hayes. The theory this Detroit writer and his colleagues operated under was that they were guests in the dressing room or clubhouse, "so you didn't repeat what you saw or heard in there. Formal interviews were okay, but what happened in the clubhouse stayed there. The same when you saw an athlete around town. There are all kinds of stories I could tell you concerning big names that will never see the light of day, and that's an attitude most writers had then."

"We respected an athlete's private life," agreed Shirley Povich, the Washington writer whose son, Maury Povich, is one of the leading practitioners of modern trash-and-slash electronic journalism. "We overlooked their peccadilloes, though we knew about them. Joe was a womanizer, a lot of us knew that or had heard the rumors, but we didn't write anything about it, just like we didn't write certain things about Babe Ruth and other sports figures. Those were the mores of the time. I personally didn't feel any hypocrisy. There was no conflict there. The feeling was that it was none of the public's business."

Joe's most intense affair was with entertainer Lena Horne, whose distinguishing characteristics were her unique copper-colored skin, extremely bowed legs, and unladylike vocabulary. "Nice and sweet," Joe said, "but Lord, she had a filthy mouth. Could cuss better than any sailor wished he could."

Horne was sixteen years old in 1933 when she was hired as a chorus girl at the Cotton Club. Two years later her father, numbers racketeer Teddy Horne, took her to Pompton Lakes to visit Joe as he prepared for Primo Carnera. Lena was worldly for her age, having performed in a skimpy costume in front of all-white audiences. Later she suffered a hundred humiliations traveling with the black Noble Sissle Orchestra and working in Hollywood. Horne, who had a hair-trigger intolerance for racism, admired Joe for being "the one invincible Negro, the one who stood up to the white man and beat him down with his fists." Their relationship cooled after both married. But in 1940 it flared up again, as the newly divorced entertainer looked to reestablish herself in Manhattan. One day while Joe was at Spring Hill, getting in shape to face Arturo Godoy, a moving van arrived, filled with Joe's possessions. "Man," said Jack Blackburn, "all your clothes, shoes, ties, underwear, and even your top hat is in there." Marva had come across a love letter from Horne in their New York apartment and decided that if the singer wasn't going to leave Joe's life, *she* would. Joe, heavily embarrassed, sent all of his stuff back to Harlem, along with a new Dusenberg roadster for Marva.

Ironically, while all this was going on, Horne and the Charlie Barnet band had a hit record on the Bluebird label called "Good For Nothing Joe." The title seemed all too fitting to Marva, who clearly was approaching the end of her patience. In early 1939 she had suffered a miscarriage while Joe was away at Pompton Lakes preparing for John Henry Lewis. Her physicians at the Mayo Clinic wrote Joe and his managers, telling them that Marva was being unnerved by their helter-skelter lifestyle. In order for her to have a successful pregnancy, she needed more "stability" in her life and more companionship from her husband.

Joe liked children (Horne had two), but he was in no hurry to have any of his own. He continued his whirlwind lifestyle of fighting, golfing, nightclubbing, and womanizing all over the map. Meanwhile, Marva was expected to be the perfect trophy wife—dutiful, faithful, fashionably attired, and willing to live under a double standard. She received stern rebukes when he deemed that she had danced too close with another man or when she opted to look beyond his immediate circle of cronies for fun and companionship. Joe thought he was merely keeping her safe; she felt that she was suffocating. "Marva, you are so fresh," he told her after one argument. "All you have to do is just be beautiful, gracious, a good mother, and a good wife. Just be my doll-baby."

Many years later Marva explained what it was like being married to "the internationally famous Brown Bomber from Dee-troit," as ring announcer Harry Balogh always introduced her husband.

"Eventually, you tire of it," she said, "the crowds knocking your hat off and pushing you out of the way to reach him. Fame is the most difficult thing that can happen to a relationship. I think a man can handle it more easily than a woman. Your life is just not your own. You always have to be up and on the scene. And Joe was very proud. 'Oh, Marva, you're not going to wear that. Change your clothes.' You see, you represent them, and they want you to be tops. At least, Joe did.

"You're lonely, and you have to be very careful of your selection of friends and acquaintances. You could never go out with somebody that wasn't a part of his entourage or family. Immediately, the columnists would say, 'There's a separation with the Louises, as they do with most celebrities.'"

The pattern of her marriage was set early. Whether Joe was in training or killing large blocks of time between fights, he was rarely at home. He would thoughtlessly fool around, feel pangs of guilt afterward, and try to make up by sending her flowers or an expensive present. Marva received enough gifts to fill a warehouse. However, the one thing she wanted most— a stable home life with the man she loved—was the one thing she never would get. In the spring of 1941, as Joe was halfway through his Bum-of-the-Month tour, she delivered her own blow to the heavyweight champion's considerable pride. She served him with divorce papers.

Chapter Nine

On God's Side

There's a change in fashion that shows
In the Lenox Avenue clothes,
Mister Dude has disappeared with his flashy tie.
You'll see in the Harlem esquire
What the well-dressed man will desire
When he's struttin' down the street with his sweetie pie.

Suntan shade of cream or an olive drab color scheme
That's what the well-dressed man in Harlem will wear.
Dressed up in O.D.s with a tin hat for overseas
That's what the well-dressed man in Harlem will wear.

Top hat, white tie and tails no more
They've been put away 'til after the war.
If you want to know, take a look at Brown Bomber Joe
That's what the well-dressed man in Harlem will wear.

——Production number from *This is the Army* (1943)

It's not entirely correct to say that Joe spent money like there was no tomorrow. To the contrary, he spent money with the full expectation that tomorrow would bring another purse to replenish his bank account. This was the case in late 1940 as Mike Jacobs, anticipating the country's entry into another world war, began scheduling as many fights as possible for his chief client. Thus began a string of seven fights in seven months, December 1940 through June 1941—with a largely undistinguished group of opponents.

Al McCoy, the top heavyweight in New England, was the first to be handed a blindfold and a cigarette. One week before Christmas, 1940, Joe knocked him out in the sixth round at the Boston Garden. On the last day of January, Joe dusted off Red Burman in the fifth round in New York.

Seventeen days later he KO'd Gus Dorazio in the second round in Philadelphia. On March 21 he floored Abe Simon in the thirteenth round in Detroit. On April 8 he toppled the "Baby Tank," Tony Musto, in the ninth round in St. Louis. On May 23 he defeated Buddy Baer, Max's younger brother, in a controversial seven-round affair in Washington. And on June 18 in New York, he rallied to knock out Billy Conn in the thirteenth round of one of the most memorable fights of all time.

It was a remarkable, dizzying pace. Veteran sportswriters used to covering a title match every one or two years were now covering one a month. Joe's domination of the heavyweight division had become almost laughable. On March 30, 1941, just as the Bum-of-the-Month tour was hitting its stride, ABC radio aired a skit on its National Urban League Program lampooning Joe's competition. The dialogue centered around a knock-kneed boxer named Eddie "One-Round" Green, who had just been asked by his manager to imagine his upcoming fight with the Brown Bomber:

> MANAGER: It's the first round. Joe Louis climbs into the ring like a tiger. What do you do?
> GREEN: I climbs out of the ring like another tiger.
> MANAGER: Any other man would run. But you don't.
> GREEN: What's the matter? Am I glued to the floor?
> MANAGER: It's the fifteenth round, and you're crawling around the ring on your hands and knees. What are you doing on your hands and knees?
> GREEN: Looking for a trap door.
> MANAGER: Joe Louis is covered with blood. Your nose is broken. Both your eyes are black, and your jaw is cracked. Now is the time to see what you're made of.
> GREEN: What's he gonna do? Turn me inside out?
> MANAGER: The crowd is yelling to the referee, "Stop it. Stop it." And what do you say?
> GREEN: Okay with me.
> MANAGER: I can't stand to see you take any more punishment, so what do I do?
> GREEN: You close your eyes?
> MANAGER: No, I throw in the towel, and they give the fight to Louis.
> GREEN: Let him have it; I don't want it.
> MANAGER: But you fought so well that they give you a reward.
> GREEN: Oh yeah? What do they give me?
> MANAGER: They give you a return fight with Joe Louis.

GREEN: Oh no they don't.
MANAGER: Oh yes they do.
GREEN: Oh no they don't.

Joe's fight with Billy Conn, immediately recognized as a ring classic, made up for the previous half-dozen bouts, which had been lackluster affairs. The gate told the story. Joe's purses for McCoy, Burman, Dorazio, Simon, Muster, and Baer had totaled just $131,426, an average of less than $22,000 a fight. For facing Conn, he received $152,905. He earned every penny of it.

As Joe would learn, Conn was not a bum, merely young, brash, and Irish. The twenty-three-year-old fighter with the dark Gaelic looks and wisecracking manner hailed from Pittsburgh where street fighting had long been a respected blend of art and pastime. The city of smokestacks coughed up five world champions in the late thirties and early forties alone, including Conn, who in 1940 gave up his title as undefeated light-heavyweight champ to move up to the heavyweight division where the real money was.

A decade earlier Conn had made a similarly bold move, dropping out of eighth grade and eschewing the steel mills for Johnny Ray's gym in the East Liberty section of town. "It was like going to school, learning how to box," he recalled. "I tried to be a real good fighter. I didn't want to be a bum. I wanted to be a real top-notcher."

Thanks to Ray's instruction and guidance, that is exactly what Conn became. Ray was a rummy, but he knew boxing. When he didn't have the youngster sweeping out the locker room or delivering fifteen-cent milk bottles of bootleg whiskey, he had him working out and sparring. His manager "was quiet," Conn said, "but he was a Michelangelo as a teacher. Hell, I didn't know he drank until one day I saw him sober. You know how it is— no Jews drink. I get the one who does. Only I tell you one thing, Johnny Ray knew more about boxing drunk than anybody else did sober."

Louis first met Conn when he came to Pittsburgh to fight Hans Birkie in early 1935. Conn held the spit box for him. "Give that kid twenty bucks," Joe had told one of his handlers, little knowing that six and a half years later the scrawny seventeen-year-old would give him the battle of his life.

The kid turned pro a short while after this 1935 fight. The next year he finally attracted attention in his thirty-sixth money fight when he defeated future welterweight king Fritzie Zivic. Conn then made his name in early 1939 with back-to-back victories over middleweight champ Fred Apostoli in nontitle bouts. That July he decisioned Melio Bettina to earn the world's light-heavyweight championship.

Conn's scheduled fifteen-rounder with Joe had a couple of subplots. One involved a young blonde he was sweet on, Mary Louise Smith, and her dominating father, "Greenfield Jimmy" Smith, an ex-major leaguer and bootlegger who ran one of the plushest drinking joints in the Steel City. Greenfield Jimmy didn't want his daughter marrying a pug, so he shipped her off to a cloistered college in Philadelphia, instructing the nuns in charge not to let the fighter anywhere near. A couple of weeks before the big fight, the two young lovers sneaked off intending to get married. But Greenfield Jimmy found out and went straight to the Catholic bishop in Pittsburgh, demanding that no priest in Pennsylvania marry his eighteen-year-old daughter. "I'm just trying to raise a decent family," he explained, "and I know where these boxers end up."

At the same time, Conn's mother, a hard-toiling Irish immigrant he affectionately called Maggie, was slowly dying of cancer. Prior to meeting Louis, Conn had beaten heavyweights Bob Pastor, Al McCoy, and Lee Savold in succession, using much of his winnings to pay for her treatment. After being stymied in his attempt to marry Mary Louise, Conn visited his mother in the hospital. He tried to give her a diamond bracelet. Maggie, weak and wracked with pain, told her son that it was beautiful but that he should give it to Mary Louise. Maggie, who had supported her son's decision to become a fighter and had sewn his first pair of kelly-green boxing trunks, reminded him that he had always been a good boy and that he should ignore Greenfield Jimmy Smith and marry the girl he loved.

After a few minutes Conn kissed his mother and got up to leave. He was carrying a bracelet and a heavy heart back to training camp. "Maggie," he said, "I gotta go now, but the next time you see me, I'll be the heavy-weight champion of the world."

"No, son," she said, "the next time I see you will be in Paradise."

Joe was unaware of all this melodrama as he prepared for the fight. Concerned with Conn's quickness, and also worried that he would be perceived as a bully picking on a smaller man, he altered his routine in an attempt to get below 200 pounds. Against his trainers' advice, he worked hard up to the final day before the fight and ate and drank sparingly the day of the bout. This helped him pare his weight to 199 1/2 pounds at the official weigh-in, but also left him weak, tired, and dehydrated. When Conn stepped on the scales, the needle stopped halfway between 169 and 170 pounds. Mike Jacobs creatively announced that Conn, a 17-to-5 underdog, weighed in at 174 pounds.

According to boxing lore, Joe had earlier issued one of his typically terse but expressive comments. Asked about Conn's dancing feet, he responded, "He can run, but he can't hide." At least one writer, Shirley Povich, maintained that Joe had first said those same words nearly two years earlier, before the second Pastor fight. In any event, the pithy quote became a part of the hype and a small, integral ingredient of Joe's legend.

The large, boisterous crowd inside the bathtub-shaped Polo Grounds included thousands of Irishmen who, as usual, had chartered a special train—"the Ham and Cabbage Special," they called it—to New York. Back in Pittsburgh, the interest in the hometown boy was so great the Pirates interrupted their night game at Forbes Field to carry Mutual's broadcast over the public address system. Wherever they were seated, fans were treated to one hell of a fight.

As was his style, Conn started slowly. Joe won the first couple of rounds in his usual fashion, methodically stalking his opponent and delivering heavy combinations to the body. Then Conn began to score on his bigger, slower opponent, his quick fists piling up points as he flitted around the ring, safely out of reach of Joe's long leads. The champ looked tired and out of synch. At one point Conn said, "You've got a fight on your hands tonight, Joe."

"I know it," Joe wearily replied.

Although spectators smelled an upset, Joe never surrendered to panic or desperation. He opened a cut above Conn's eye and another on his nose. In the tenth round Conn's right leg gave way as he was being backed toward the ropes. Joe had every right to take advantage of his temporarily helpless opponent. Instead of capitalizing on Conn's slip, however, he stepped back and allowed Conn to regain his footing. This remarkable display of sportsmanship, occuring as it did in the middle of a heated title fight, was much commented on later and solidified Joe's reputation as a clean fighter.

Despite that momentary slip, Conn had clearly wrested control of the fight. Joe was exhausted and had hurt his wrist bouncing a right off of Conn's head. In the eleventh Conn continued to pound away as Joe covered up. In the twelfth he hooked a left to Joe's body, another to his head, and then pasted him in the face with a right cross, left hook combination that put the already frenzied crowd in an absolute uproar. Another left caused Joe to stagger against the ropes. Dazed, he clinched his antagonist and managed to last the round.

The noise was deafening. After twelve rounds Conn was even or ahead on all three officials' cards. One judge had him 6-6, the other scored it 7-4-1 in Conn's favor. The referee also gave the challenger seven rounds. Roi Ottley reported that black Harlemites were tense. "As the fight progressed, there were ominous grumblings, with some near hysteria. The cheers of fifty-five thousand white people in the Polo Grounds, which echoed down the streets of Harlem, heightened the distress."

Nobody at the time, of course, knew what the exact scoring breakdown was, but it was apparent that Conn had the fight won. All he had to do was to continue dancing and pecking away for the final three rounds on this warm summer night, and "the Flower of the Monongahela" would be crowned the new heavyweight champion of the world. "This is easy," he told Johnny Ray. "I can take this son of a bitch out this round."

"No, no, Billy," Ray warned. "Stick and run. You got the fight won. Stay away, kiddo. Just stick and run, stick and run. . . ."

Sometime during the sixty seconds he was sitting on his stool, Conn decided that it wasn't enough to merely beat the reigning world's champion, he had to knock him out. The thought of impressing the two women he loved most in his life factored into his decision, as did the delicious fantasy of strolling through the rest of his life with the admiring comment, "There goes the guy who knocked out Joe Louis," trailing in his wake.

Several feet away in his corner, Joe slumped on his stool and listened to Blackburn. "You're losing on points," he said. "You got to knock him out." Blackburn reminded him that Conn, who always cocked his fist back three or four inches before throwing a left hook, was "beggin' for a right hand."

It was pure bedlam at the Polo Grounds as the bell rang announcing the start of the thirteenth round. Tens of thousands of people were on their feet, screaming and shouting for the brash kid from Pittsburgh. Both fighters alternately connected, then clinched, but now Conn was staying within range, looking to slug it out. Joe, by far the heavier puncher, finally found the opening he was looking for in the last minute of the round. As Conn began to loop a long left, Joe fired a right to the jaw that caused Conn to bend over at the waist. "That was the end of the line," recalled Conn, who was then taken apart by a score of heavy punches to the body and the chin. The final combination of a left to the body, a right uppercut, a left hook, and a right cross, caused Conn to pitch over onto his right side, his curly head bouncing off the canvas. He groggily got back to one knee, then stood, but by then referee Eddie Joseph had counted to ten and waved the wobbly-legged fighter out. There were only two seconds left in the round. "What's the sense of being Irish," Conn bravely cracked a few minutes later in the dressing room, "if you can't be dumb now and then?"

Conn regretted his foolishness for as long as he lived, though an easy smile always disguised his pain when talk of his near miss arose, as it did often. "Gee, what a tough break I got," he once told Joe. "I had your ass beat. I could have won the title, been the champion six months, then I'd let you win it back."

"How was you gonna keep the title for six months," responded Joe, "when you couldn't keep it for twelve rounds?"

That wasn't the end of the story. Shortly after the fight, Maggie died. Conn buried his mother one day and on the next married Mary Louise. He and his new father-in-law continued to feud, even as Conn joined Joe and millions of other Americans in the army after Pearl Harbor. In May of 1942 private first-class Conn got a furlough to attend his newborn son's christening. Despite the war, a rematch with Joe was being planned for the summer. But that wasn't what Greenfield Johnny Smith wanted to talk about as the clan gathered inside his kitchen on the Sunday of the christening. He informed Conn that he had better start attending church more regularly if he expected to remain married to his daughter, then tossed in the remark that, even at his advanced age, he could kick Conn's butt.

It was too much for Conn, who jumped off the stove he was sitting on and fired a left hook at his father-in-law. The punch bounced off the top of Greenfield Johnny's head, and Conn immediately knew that he had broken a bone in his hand. Mary Louise got cut and bruised and a family friend suffered a fractured ankle during the melee in the crowded room. As if all that wasn't bad enough, a few minutes later Conn cut himself when he punched his right hand through a window in frustration over blowing his shot at a rematch with Joe.

As things turned out, the fight was due to be canceled by the government, which thought it unseemly that two servicemen should make hundreds of thousands of dollars from what was being billed as a morale builder for the troops. The country would have to wait until after the war for the sequel. Meanwhile Conn had to live with the indignity of having had more damage inflicted on him by Greenfield Johnny than anybody he had ever met in the ring. For the next several years, Joe would usually begin any conversation with Conn by asking, "Is your old father-in-law still beating the shit out of you?"

Joe's near loss to Conn scared many blacks, whose celebrating was noticeably more subdued. The day after the fight the *Pittsburgh Courier* sought to prepare its readers for that inevitable moment when Joe Louis, superfighter, would prove distressingly human in the ring:

> Can Negro America "take it"? Frankly I don't believe they can. And if they can't take it, I'm preparing them right now for something—which might happen at any time. . . .
>
> We've built out of the mists a "superfighter"—a man who just can't be beaten. We've been selfish in the perpetuation of an ideal which few of us would be willing to live up to. . . .
>
> If—and when—he loses, Joe will take his defeat in stride!
> So will we!
> And so must you!

It was a sign of Joe's nearly universal acceptance that many of his most ardent young fans were white, including Robert Creamer, an Irish

Catholic youngster from New York. The longtime writer for *Sports Illustrated* magazine was thirteen years old in 1936 when he lost a quarter to his grandmother betting on Joe in the first Schmeling fight. "When Louis destroyed Schmeling in the first round of their rematch two years later, I was delighted," Creamer recalled in his memoir of America in the epochal year of 1941.

Creamer acknowledged that there were still "racist pinheads" who wanted Conn to beat Joe because of skin color. "I know that I rooted hard for Louis to beat Conn, to knock him out early, and I was no race-conscious liberal then. I just liked Louis because he was such a good fighter and because he handled himself so well." He didn't mouth off, he took on all challengers, and he beat them convincingly. The Joe Louis that stood supreme in prewar America, Creamer reflected from the distance of fifty years, "was a pleasure to root for."

➤✦

On September 29, three and a half months after beating Conn, Joe returned to the Polo Grounds to face Lou Nova, a tough but thoughtful Californian who claimed to possess a "cosmic punch." Nova was a student of Far Eastern metaphysics, including yoga, the Hindu theistic philosophy that teaches the suppression of all activity of mind, body, and will in order to liberate the spiritual self.

This was some far-out stuff for 1941, and sportswriters had a field day with it. But Nova later insisted his spiritual outlook allowed him to enjoy the otherwise traumatic experience of being thumped by the world's champ. In the fourth round, Joe tagged Nova with one of his classic left hooks. While recovering between rounds, Nova couldn't help reflecting on the contrast between the 56,000 lustily cheering fans and his quiet and impassive opponent, sitting just a few feet away.

"As I sat there and the handlers fussed over me," he said, "I was thinking not about those fans and not about the title. I was thinking that what I'd got hit with was the most beautiful punch I'd ever seen. I could feel everything in Joe's body behind that punch, right from the toes on up.

"Wasn't that odd? I'd got hit by Joe and I just sat like a painter, admiring the fine work of another painter. Then the bell rang and we were on our feet and at it again." Joe, who admitted that he "didn't like all that mysterious shit he was talking about," knocked Nova out in the sixth round and received $199,500, his largest payday since he kayoed Schmeling.

Less than ten weeks later, on December 7, 1941, the rest of the country suddenly became acquainted with the Far Eastern philosophy of Japan, a militaristic society that felt its expansionist policies were being thwarted by the United States. Its surprise attack on the Pacific fleet docked at Pearl Harbor was designed to knock America out of a war that most of its citizens were hoping to avoid. But the bombing, which killed 2,403 sleepy-eyed servicemen, had the opposite effect. Most Americans heard the first radio reports of the attack in the early afternoon, while making their way home from church or sitting around the dining room table. The notion of a sucker punch, delivered on a Sunday morning while Japanese diplomats were still negotiating in Washington, outraged everybody's sense of sportsmanship and fair play. Far from intimidating America and giving a wishy-washy citizenry the reason it needed to stay out of war, the attack galvanized the country. Said one isolationist politician: "There's nothing to do now but lick hell out of 'em."

Joe described his feelings about that infamous day. "I was mad, I was furious, you name it. Hell, this is my country. Don't come around sneaking up and attacking it. If a fighter had done that to me, I would have smashed him. I'm strictly for fair deals and open fighting." A few months earlier, he had registered for the peacetime draft and been classified 1-A by Chicago's Local Draft Board Eight. With war now officially declared, he was certain to be called into the service. As the sole supporter of his wife, mother, and several family members, he might have qualified for a deferment, but he had no intention of avoiding conscription as Jack Dempsey had during the First World War. "I mean, what could I say? 'I have to be exempted so I can work so that my wife can pay the housekeeper.'"

Although he was not the type to think in such terms, the war could not have come at a more inopportune time for Joe. As America scrambled to mobilize its human and industrial resources, some quick number crunching by Mike Jacobs (who *was* the type to think in such terms) revealed that his number-one client was in debt up to his eyeballs. He had been living from fight to fight for some time, spending money like a thirsty man gulps water.

"Joe was the world's softest touch," said Jesse Owens. "I recall how after one fight the world was slapping him on the back and shaking his hand, how reporters couldn't get enough of him until 3:30 in the morning, and how after it was all through he turned to one of his handlers, sheepishly took out an empty wallet, I mean *absolutely empty*, and asked for meal money."

The five ten-dollar bills that were handed to Joe didn't last long, continued Owens. Exiting the building in pursuit of some more after-hours revelry, Joe's entourage came across an old, one-eyed ex-prizefighter. Beat to his sox, as Harlemites liked to describe the down and out, he nonetheless was proudly trying to eke out a living with a shoeshine box.

"Shine, Champ?" he asked.

"Sure," said Joe. As the old middleweight meticulously rubbed polish onto his shoes and snapped a rag across them, Joe asked how life was treating him.

"Oh, you know, Joe," he said. "Sometimes good, sometimes not so good."

"Well, you take care," said Joe, who pressed four ten-spots into the old guy's hand before shoving off into the night.

"I could tell you hundreds of stories like that—I mean *hundreds*," said Owens. "And for every one *I've* got to tell, there are dozens, maybe hundreds more."

These nonstop acts of minor charity, when added to his training camp expenses, lavish lifestyle, and bad investments, portended serious financial trouble for the fighter. Misplaced faith also hurt him. His accountant, Ted Jones, advised him not to pay $81,000 in back taxes, figuring that they could strike a deal with the Internal Revenue Service to pay less a few years down the road. The consequences of that and other similarly bad advice would prove to be disastrous.

Jacobs, figuring that the best way to keep Joe contractually under his control was to have him financially indebted to him, continued to give him large advances against future fights. On one occasion, his cash-strapped fighter accompanied him to the airport, all the while trying to muster the courage to ask for yet more money. When Jacobs walked out to the runway to catch his flight, Joe offered to carry his topcoat. That's when he asked the promoter for another large loan. "For ten thousand dollars," Jacobs laughed as he made out a check, "I could've carried my own coat."

No one needed to remind Jacobs that Joe's future was uncertain. Once inducted, his professional career probably would be put on hold for the duration of the war, and nobody knew how long the fighting would last. Beyond that, there was the problem of continuing to promote cards in any division. How would the public and the government react to boxing—or any other sport—conducting business as usual? It evolved that professional sports would be allowed to continue, albeit with depleted rosters, but in the first few weeks following Pearl Harbor the issue was still very much up in the air. Thinking hard, Jacobs came up with an idea that was both patriotic and self-serving. In mid-December he phoned Joe in Los Angeles where he was golfing at the Hillcrest Country Club. Would he be willing to put his title on the line in a charity boxing event, he asked, with all of his winnings going to the Navy Relief Society? The organization aided the families of sailors killed in combat. Without hesitation Joe said yes. When Jacobs repeated that this meant he wouldn't be paid, Joe told him to go ahead and arrange the match.

It was just like Jacobs to capitalize on the country's patriotic fervor, and just like Joe not to give a second thought to risking his championship for zilch. Of course, Joe didn't view it that way. "Ain't fighting for nothing," he told a reporter as he began training. "I'm fighting for my country."

Joe's generous gesture, offered with no boasting or public relations flummery on his part, inspired a fresh flush of affection among members of the press. Jimmy Powers's comments in the *New York Daily News* were typical. "You don't see a shipyard owner risking his entire business. If the government wants a battleship, the government doesn't ask him to donate it. The government pays him a fat profit. . . . The more I think of it, the greater guy I see in this Joe Louis."

Madison Square Garden was awash in red, white, and blue bunting the night of January 9, 1942. Joe's opponent was considered the underdog but no pushover. Jacobs had arranged a rematch with Buddy Baer, the six-foot-six 250-pounder that Joe had beaten on a technicality the previous May. In that fight, one of Baer's first-round punches had sent Joe flying through the ropes. Joe, despite having his left eye cut and his right one bruised by Baer's punches, recovered to floor his opponent three times in the sixth round. The final knockdown, unfortunately, came a split second after the bell rang. Baer was out cold. His handlers argued that Louis should be disqualified for a late blow, but referee Arthur Donovan awarded the fight to Joe when Baer's handlers refused to vacate the ring and Baer failed to answer the bell for the seventh round.

This time there was concern that Joe's trainer wouldn't answer the bell. Although he was only fifty-eight, Jack Blackburn was battling arthritis, rheumatism, and a weak heart. In the dressing room before the Baer fight, he told Joe that he didn't think he was strong enough to make it up and down the steps to the ring for fifteen rounds.

"If you get up those stairs with me," Joe said, "I'll have Baer out before you can relax."

"Okay," said Blackburn, "and remember, that's a promise."

There were 16,689 people on hand to listen to a drawn-out program of introductions and speeches. Wendell Willkie, a liberal-minded Republican who Joe had actively supported in an unsuccessful 1940 presidential campaign because he felt FDR had not fulfilled his promises to help the Negro race, spoke through the ring announcer's microphone to a national radio audience.

"Joe Lou-ee," Willkie said, "your magnificent example in risking for nothing your championship belt, won literally with toil and sweat and tears, prompts us to say, 'We thank you.' And in view of your attitude it is impossible for me to see how any American can think of discrimination in terms of race, creed, or color."

Joe then proceeded to live up to his promise to Jack Blackburn. He snapped Baer's head back with a succession of fast, accurate punches, knocking him down three times. Baer was still trying to pull himself up by the ropes when he was counted out with four seconds left in the first round. "The only way I could have beaten Joe that night was with a baseball bat," he later said.

The winner's share of the purse was $65,200. After deducting his training expenses, Joe donated the balance of $47,500 to the Navy Relief Society. Baer chipped in a portion of his purse, $4,078, while Jacobs reportedly contributed $37,229. The latter supposedly was Jacobs's entire earnings. But according to Truman Gibson, a close friend of Joe's and a high-ranking War Department aide, Uncle Mike was not entirely forthcoming, holding onto his share of the revenues from radio and film rights.

The day after the fight Joe enlisted in the army. On January 11, 1942, he took his physical at Governors Island, accompanied by a battery of reporters and photographers. The next day newsreel cameramen joined the crowd when Joe reported for duty (via a chauffeured limousine) at Camp Upton on Long Island. There he participated in a staged scene for the cameras. As a clerk nervously typed out a form, he looked up and asked, "What's your occupation?"

"Fighting, and let us at them Japs," replied Joe. The $21-a-month private was then given a pass on his first day in khaki to appear on Eddie Cantor's radio show.

Joe's induction, coming just five weeks after Pearl Harbor, was a public relations coup, though it was hard to figure out from the press coverage which enemy the heavyweight champion of the world was itching to get at first. New York dailies had him disparaging the Japanese as "all lightweights, anyway," while the Chicago Tribune wrote, "Joe has a date for a return engagement with Max Schmeling."

But first his new employer, in an example of the petty interservice rivalries that have always afflicted the military, wanted him to fight for its pet charity, the Army Relief Fund. While Joe underwent basic training with Company C, an all-black unit, Mike Jacobs lined up an opponent. He signed Abe Simon to meet Joe at Madison Square Garden on March 27. Once again Joe would risk his title with all proceeds going to charity, a gesture that caused even southern papers like the Birmingham News to gush that "from almost every angle you can consider, there has never been a champion like Joe Louis in the ring."

The Boxing Writers Association of New York agreed with that assessment. The organization voted Joe its highest honor, the Edward J. Neil Memorial Plaque, commemorating one of its own killed while covering the Spanish Civil War. On January 21 Joe was feted at a black-tie affair at Ruppert's Brewery that included a host of well-known names, including FBI director J. Edgar Hoover and several former heavyweight champions.

Former New York mayor Jimmy Walker presented the plaque. "Joe," he said, "all the Negroes in the world are proud of you because you have given them reason to be proud. You never forgot your own people. When you fought Buddy Baer and gave your purse to the Navy Relief Society, you took your title and your future and bet it all on patriotism and love of country. Joe Louis, that night you laid a rose on the grave of Abraham Lincoln."

Joe's comments weren't nearly as eloquent, but as usual they came straight from the heart. "You don't know how good you make me feel," he said. "The way I feel is good. I'd never thought I'd feel so good as when I won the heavyweight championship of the world, but tonight tops them all. I feel better than I ever felt in my life. Thanks for what you did for me. I want to thank Mike Jacobs for what he did for me. I want to thank the boxing commission for what it did for me. I hope I never did anything in the ring I'll be sorry for in the years to come. I'm a happy man tonight."

His most memorable line would have to wait several weeks, until he attended a dinner given by the Navy Relief Society on March 10 at Madison Square Garden. Wearing his private's uniform, he nervously stood at the dais placed in the center of the boxing ring and honored a request to say a few words. He finished a short statement by saying, "I have only done what any red-blooded American would do. We gonna do our part, and we will win, because we are on God's side. Thank you."

The last line brought a standing ovation and practically overnight leaped into popular usage. President Roosevelt sent him a telegram complimenting his choice of words. "We'll win because we're on God's side" inspired a popular recruiting poster, as well as a poem by ad man Carl Byoir, "Joe Louis Named the War," which enjoyed wide circulation in the *Saturday Evening Post*.

There's some debate as to whether Joe made up the phrase on the spot, memorized the line, or simply mangled a prepared statement. Billy Rowe, a columnist for the *Pittsburgh Courier* and a close acquaintance, claimed that Joe messed up a sentence that he had written for him: "We'll win because God is on our side." In his autobiography, Joe said bandleader Lucky Millander suggested it to him. "We'll win because we're on God's side" wasn't even as original a line as the press made it out to be; Abraham Lincoln, for example, had once said the very same words. But it quickly emerged as one of the most popular phrases of the war.

The army moved Joe to Fort Dix, New Jersey, to train for the Simon fight. The base had a well-equipped gymnasium, and Joe—who had repeatedly turned down offers of an officer's commission before enlisting— enjoyed interacting with the ordinary dogfaces who turned out to watch him train and spar. The segregated barracks, however, bothered him. "Here are all these 'niggers' ready and willing to go out and try to kill Hitler, and maybe get themselves killed, but they can't sleep in the same barracks with the white guys or go to the same movies or hardly get in officer's training." He bought three thousand dollars worth of tickets for the Simon fight and distributed them to his fellow black soldiers.

Their cheering did little to alleviate his concern over Blackburn's deteriorating condition. The ailing trainer had stayed behind in Chicago. Mannie Seamon, Blackburn's assistant for the last five years, took over his duties. Joe, in an effort to fulfill another promise to Blackburn—this time to knock Simon out early—looked wild and awkward, but Seamon calmed his fighter down, and Simon was finally kayoed by a left-right combination in the sixth round. Mutual announcer Don Dunphy used the victory as a symbol of the country's resolve to beat the Germans and Japanese, who in early 1942 clearly had the Allied powers back on their heels. "We won't stop punching," he said, "just as Louis does, till we win."

From his purse of $45,882, Joe deducted his expenses and gave $36,146 to the Army Relief Fund. Jacobs's and Simon's contributions brought the total to about $55,000. Afterward Joe took advantage of Dunphy's microphone to directly address his old friend in Chicago.

"I hope you're satisfied, Chappie," he said.

"I sure am," replied Blackburn, listening to the broadcast eight hundred miles away.

Several days later Joe visited Blackburn at Provident Hospital where he was battling pneumonia. Joe sat at bedside and rehashed old times, old fights. Upon his return to camp, Joe received a terse telegram from Freddie Guinyard. "Chappie's dead" is all it said. Blackburn had recovered from his bout with pneumonia, only to succumb to a fatal heart attack after being released from the hospital. As soldiers in the provost office looked away in respect, the toughest man on the planet broke down and bawled.

Joe received a two-week pass to return to Chicago for the funeral. Ten thousand people tried to get into the Pilgrim Baptist Church where Reverend J. C. Austin addressed the issue of the deceased's legacy. "Think not that Jack Blackburn has left the ring," he said. "Think not that he has deserted the man who was the best work of his genius, his mind, and his soul. He has not! He will be at the next fight, in the corner, leaning over his man's shoulder as usual and whispering in his ear. He has not gone and left his Chappie to carry on alone." Joe was one of the pallbearers. He left Lincoln Cemetery thinking that his life would never be quite the same again.

The two weeks in Chicago gave Joe a chance to mourn his close friend's passing and to focus his attention on Marva. It had been a tumultuous year since she had first filed for divorce in the spring of 1941. Just before the Conn fight, in an attempt to patch things up, Joe had sent her and the wives of John Roxborough and Julian Black on a Caribbean cruise.

Not long after she returned, however, gossip surrounding their relationship grew hotter with the news that taxi driver Joe Gibbons, an ex-beau, was shot to death by Earl Wilson, a Chicago patrolman. The fact that Wilson was a good friend of Joe's fed rumors that Gibbons had been killed in order to squash a blackmail scheme. For a while some newspapers speculated on this bizarre twist, but nobody ever produced any hard evidence of a plot or of Joe's alleged complicity in Gibbons's death.

At the same time new details about their marriage were revealed. Marva accused Joe of neglect and of hitting her on two occasions. Joe responded that he had never used his hands around her, except when he had "peeled off dough," and charged that she had not been a virtuous wife. On August 1, 1941, he published a newspaper ad declaring that he would no longer be responsible for any of her debts. She was awarded temporary alimony of two hundred dollars a week, pending the outcome of the divorce proceedings. On the day the divorce was to become final, the quarreling lovebirds suddenly had a reconciliation; photographs of Joe happily carrying Marva out of the courtroom appeared in newspapers across the country.

This rapprochement was already unraveling when Joe entered the army, though Marva told her husband in the days following Blackburn's burial that his long absences because of military obligations really were no different than those when he had been a civilian. That hurt, he admitted.

Not long afterward, Marva announced that she was pregnant. The joyful news helped take Joe's mind off several recent troubles that seemed to have snowballed in the last couple of years. Just before the start of the war, his comanagers had been indicted on criminal charges arising from their illegal activities. Julian Black was charged with income tax evasion, while John Roxborough had been swept up in an ambitious crackdown on municipal corruption that had netted a former Detroit mayor, the Wayne County sheriff, and eighty-eight policemen. Black's case was dismissed, but Roxie was convicted of running a numbers operation. In early 1943 he began serving a thirty-month sentence at Jackson State Prison where he hung a sign, "Don't give up hope," in his cell.

Although he rarely thought too long or hard about his finances, Joe realized that he was in considerable debt. He reportedly owed Roxborough $41,146 and the Twentieth Century Sporting Club—that is, Mike Jacobs—$59,805. In addition, he owed the government $117,000 in back taxes. Before Joe's 1941 bout with Billy Conn, Jacobs had taken the precaution of signing a contract with the Pittsburgh fighter to promote his bouts. Now, a year later, Conn was $34,500 in debt to Jacobs. Uncle Mike looked to a charity affair to pull everybody out of the hole.

With the War Department's blessing, Jacobs planned a Louis-Conn rematch to benefit the Army Relief Fund. To give it an aboveboard appearance, a committee of sportswriters was organized to copromote the fight with Jacobs under the aegis of War Boxing Incorporated. The match was tentatively scheduled for early October of 1942 at Yankee Stadium. Because of blackout restrictions, the fight would have to be fought in daylight. Nonetheless, a large crowd was anticipated. By late September some $300,000 in tickets had been sold, NBC had agreed to pay a record $71,200 for broadcast rights, and both fighters were in training—Joe at Greenwood Lake, New Jersey, and Conn (his broken hand healed nicely) at Jacobs's estate in Rumson, New Jersey.

Louis-Conn II was shaping up to be a blockbuster, a million-dollar gate. But to the consternation of Secretary of War Henry L. Stimson, the original concept was altered to allow the two fighters to deduct the money they owed Jacobs and Roxborough from the receipts. In addition, Uncle Mike demanded control of the first twenty rows of seats, an audacious money grab by the old scalper. Even with these modifications, the fight still would have produced as much as $750,000 for the Army Relief Fund. But on September 25, Stimson abruptly called the fight off. He carefully avoided criticizing either fighter. He simply explained that it wouldn't be fair to the millions of other soldiers who weren't given similar opportunities to work off their debts while serving their country. Stimson remained adamant even after Joe and Conn offered to fight for free. He soon banned all similar charity projects for Army or Navy Relief. Both agencies were well funded, he said.

To a certain extent, so was Joe. Over the next three years, until he was discharged in October 1945, he continued to borrow against future earnings. He also put off worrying about his outstanding taxes, since it was government policy not to pursue payment or add interest to a delinquent account as long as the taxpayer remained in uniform. By the time Joe was able to return to making a living inside the prize ring, he would owe Uncle Mike and Uncle Sam more than $100,000 each.

➤❦

Boxing, like all industries, carefully blended patriotism and commerce during the war. Promoters put on special war bond tournaments, staged morning shows to entertain night-shift defense workers, and supported the National Boxing Association's 2 percent tax on managers and purses as an appropriate donation to the war effort. More than four thousand boxers served in the military, including several current and former world champions. Ex-leatherneck Gene Tunney was commissioned a captain in the Marine Corps, Barney Ross gained glory and a chestful of ribbons on Guadalcanal, and Jack Dempsey was made a lieutenant commander in the Coast Guard.

One of America's first heroes was a boxer. Mess attendant Dorie Miller, the heavyweight champion of the *West Virginia*, took over a machine gun from a comrade wounded during the attack on Pearl Harbor. Although the navy's discriminatory policies had prevented him from being trained as a gunner, he shot down four Japanese fighter planes. Miller (who later in the war would be reported missing at sea) became the first black to win the navy's second-highest honor for bravery, the Navy Cross.

Dorie Miller remained a long-standing example of what blacks could contribute to their country if given the chance, especially for the Negro press, which in the early stages of the war was accused by the federal government of sedition for its unrelenting attacks on the racial policies of the armed forces. Blacks had every right to protest their treatment. One million of them were drafted during the Second World War, including 700,000 into the army, and millions more worked in war-related industries. In theory, they were to be afforded the same opportunity for training and advancement as their white counterparts. This was because of Executive Order 8802, which President Roosevelt had issued on June 25, 1941, to forestall a massive march on Washington being organized by A. Phillip Randolph, head of the Brotherhood of Sleeping Car Porters. The order created a monitoring agency, the Fair Employment Practices Committee, to ensure that blacks got fair and equal treatment in industry and the military.

In practice, Negroes' gains were slow and fitful, in part because the FEPC lacked muscle, but principally because the government preferred rhetoric over resolve. America's ingrained racism was hard to eradicate. Immediately after Pearl Harbor, Secretary of War Henry Stimson and Secretary of the Navy Frank Knox both went on record questioning the courage and ability of black servicemen—this with the story of Dorie Miller still fresh in the public's mind.

Black troops were trained and housed in segregated units. Most were placed in service or labor battalions. It took a lawsuit to force the army to open a separate air corps training facility for black pilots, and a military calamity—the Battle of the Bulge in December 1944—for black troops to be used in combat in any large numbers. Those few colored outfits that were allowed to get bloodied distinguished themselves in battle. The 761st Tank Battalion, for example, was one of Gen. George S. Patton's finest units, while the 99th Pursuit Squadron—under the command of Brigadier Gen. Benjamin O. Davis, the first black general in the United States armed forces—flew nearly two thousand combat missions.

The majority of training facilities were in the warm-weather states of the South, where prejudice was consistent, across-the-board, and of world-class caliber. Because of this, black servicemen like Lacy Wilson spent more time fighting Jim Crow than the Germans or Japanese.

Wilson, a twenty-five-year-old victim of the peacetime draft in 1941, saw his original six-month tour of duty extended to "for the duration" by the attack on Pearl Harbor. After graduating from Officer Candidate School, the Detroit native was commissioned a second lieutenant and made commanding officer of the Headquarters Company, 364th Infantry Regiment, and shipped to Camp Van Doren, Mississippi. With the exception of Wilson, the all-black 364th was commanded entirely by white officers.

"This was Mississippi before anyone heard of civil rights," said Wilson, today a retired Detroit police officer. "You can imagine what it was like."

After only one evening, trouble began. A white military policeman ("all the MPs were white," reminded Wilson) accosted a black soldier returning to camp for having a sleeve unbuttoned. When the soldier explained he couldn't because the button was missing, the MP said, "Nigger, I said button your sleeve." Soon the two were tussling over the MP's nightstick, at which point the MP told the local sheriff to "kill this nigger."

"So the sheriff did," recalled Wilson. "Shot him dead. This led to a riot of sorts on post. The only way we prevented more bloodshed was by removing the firing pins from all the rifles in our outfit."

On another occasion Wilson, three fellow officers, and their wives stopped to eat on their way to New Orleans.

"We pulled up in front of this little restaurant in some small Louisiana town," he said, "and being black, we knew we couldn't go in and eat. But we thought we could at least get some sandwiches to bring out.

"This one officer named Chet Wilson was with us, and he was very fair-skinned. If you didn't know it, you'd think he was a white person. So Chet went inside with our orders, and we could see the waitress smiling and they're talking. . . .

"Meantime, the sheriff was next door and he saw all of this. Well, when Chet Wilson headed for the restaurant door, that's when the sheriff headed for Chet Wilson. The sheriff came up behind Chet, grabbed him by the shoulders, and spun him around. He pushed Chet out the door, and then pushed him toward our car, saying, 'You niggers gonna fuck around down here and get yourself killed. You know where you're supposed to go eat—you go to the back."

These experiences still visibly pained Wilson as he recollected them several decades later. "What made this so hurting was that the four of us were all second lieutenants, officers in the U.S. Army during the time of war. And there were still places in our country where we couldn't even enter to buy a sandwich to bring out. These are the things that made so many black servicemen bitter back then. You think you're serving your country, saving the world for democracy, but how about us?"

Joe Louis's achievements and tribulations were covered by a wide variety of periodicals throughout his life. (Angelo Prospero)

Because of his reputation as an
amateur, Louis never fought a
preliminary as a professional. Each
of his seventy-one money fights
was billed as the main event.
(Angelo Prospero)

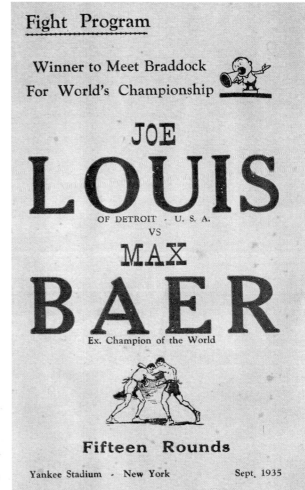

Artists were inspired by the drama and impact of Louis's two fights with Max Schmeling. William Neunheim's primitive wood carving depicted the first bout, in 1936. (Martin Paul)

Robert Riggs's oil on canvas captured the fury of the 1938 rematch. (Capricorn Galleries)

Joseph Golinkin's watercolor of the 1939 Louis–Galento bout shows referee Art Donovan trying to keep the battered challenger from falling through the ropes. (The American Sporting Scene)

Betsy Reyneau Graves included this 1946 oil portrait in her traveling exhibit of notable black Americans. Significantly, Louis was the only athlete depicted. (National Portrait Gallery)

Louis's likeness could be found on a wide variety of products including a mustard jar that doubled as a Lucky Joe Bank. (Martin Paul)

For a penny, Depression-era youngsters could buy an arcade card or trading card of the most famous fighter in the world. (Angelo Prospero)

Hair pomade, soda pop, cigarettes, and instructionals were just a few of the other commercial ventures that Louis lent his name to. (Angelo Prospero)

IN NEW YORK IT'S CHESTERFIELD
...the CHAMP of CIGARETTES *Joe Louis*

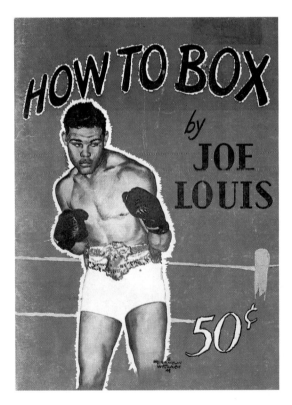

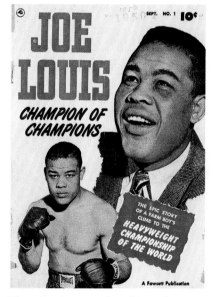

Joe's pithy statement that the United States was "on God's side" was one of the most memorable to come out of the Second World War. (National Archives)

The aging icon was the subject of two staples of American postwar pop culture. In 1950 the story of his life was published in comic book form by Fawcett. Two years later a Topps bubble gum card detailed his career.

Detroit is awash in tributes to its favorite son. The most impressive is the $34-million riverfront Joe Louis Arena, dedicated on the fortieth anniversary of the second Louis-Schmeling fight. (Balthazar Korab)

In 1988 Joe Louis became the first prize-fighter to be depicted on a first-class stamp.

That question was asked more often and more forcefully as the fighting overseas dragged on. While the government was focused on defeating the Axis Powers as quickly as possible, blacks' war aims were broader. To them, the domestic front was the *real* front.

The navy's deeply entrenched racism had caused several Negro organizations to approach Joe about boycotting his fight with Buddy Baer to benefit the Navy Relief Society. Joe, who always preferred the nonconfrontational path in racial matters, refused. By simply going along with the fight as planned, he hoped to have the press expose the hypocrisy of the sea branch's policies. But like Dorie Miller's heroism, Joe's quiet generosity had no immediate impact on the navy. The service did commission its first black officer in 1942, the same year it christened the *Booker T. Washington*, the first of an eventual eighteen Liberty ships named after prominent black Americans. But it continued to relegate its 100,000 black personnel to such menial jobs as messmen and stevedores until the last year of fighting. Additionally, the Marine Corps, a branch of the navy, had only 17,000 blacks wearing the globe and anchor. Few saw combat, but not because they didn't want to.

Although Joe was being used to sell the war to America's nearly thirteen million blacks, the government wasn't always quite sure what to do with him. In June 1942, while plans for a second Conn fight were still up in the air, he used his connections in the War Department to get assigned to Fort Riley, Kansas, a cavalry post. Joe's love of horses, as deep as those of his fellow cavalrymen, wouldn't be enough to delay the outdated unit's replacement by a mechanized outfit. But he "couldn't be happier," he said. The country's most famous private, who had by now been promoted to corporal, was able to use his influence to better the conditions of black soldiers on the base, including a former All-American football player from UCLA named Jackie Robinson.

Robinson, destined to break organized baseball's color line in another five years, had been drafted in April 1942. At Fort Riley he and several other blacks applied for Officer Candidate School. Official army policy called for qualified black candidates to be trained in integrated facilities, but the white command at Fort Riley ignored Executive Order 8802. Rejected candidates like Robinson were privately told that they lacked leadership ability.

William Hastie, the dean of Howard Law School, had been appointed the civilian aide on Negro affairs for the War Department (a post he would soon resign in protest over the military's segregationist policies). Hastie's top assistant was Truman Gibson, Joe's attorney friend from Chicago. Robinson opted to leapfrog the chain of command and in effect asked Joe to pull rank on Fort Riley's commander, Gen. Donald Robinson. Joe called Gibson, who came to Kansas to hear the black candidates' grievances. Within a few days Robinson and eighteen other blacks were enrolled in OCS.

Robinson, never one to close his eyes to racism, almost didn't finish OCS. Gibson remembered: "One day I got a call from Joe. 'Get the hell down here,' he said. 'Jackie's in some real trouble.' A white officer had referred to a black soldier in Jackie's presence as a 'stupid nigger son of a bitch.' When Jackie objected, saying, 'Sir, that's a soldier in the U.S. Army,' the officer said, 'Nigger, that goes for you, too.'

"In addition to being a world-class athlete—basketball, football, baseball, track—Jackie was a tremendous fighter, too. Well, Jackie practically knocked every tooth out of that officer's head and had him on the ground when they finally broke it up. I went out to Fort Riley and importuned the commanding officer to let Jackie graduate. Joe was very persuasive." By that Gibson meant that Joe had offered the CO a bribe—a selection of fine gifts. To Joe, that was what money was for. When Robinson's class graduated, he bought all of the newly commissioned second lieutenants tailored uniforms.

Marva joined her husband at an off-base house, but this time his storied persistence failed him. Homesickness and the Kansas heat made her pregnancy unbearable, and soon she returned to Chicago to have their baby. Jacqueline Barrow, named after Jack Blackburn, was born February 8, 1943. Joe, ecstatic, got leave to visit his newborn daughter. "Oh, such a fussing over that child," he said. The baby's bedroom inside their Chicago apartment was jammed with toys, clothes, and other paraphernalia. Joe, beaming with pride and wonderment, held his firstborn in his big hands and tried to remember not to squeeze too hard.

Not even a child could bond together the rather aimless marriage. In early 1943 Joe was assigned to a duty station near Hollywood where the film version of Irving Berlin's stage hit, *This Is the Army*, was ready to begin production at Warner Brothers. This spoof of camp life featured stars like Ronald Reagan, George Murphy, George Tobias, Alan Hale, Joan Leslie, and Kate Smith, as well as three hundred soldiers who alternately sang, danced, marched, and saluted. Joe, now a sergeant, appeared in uniform as himself in a number called "That's What the Well-Dressed Man in Harlem Will Wear." He gave a short patriotic speech and then was seen smacking a speed bag. Despite the presence of black soldiers in the cast, one number featured white performers in blackface.

In all, Joe spent six months in sun-kissed southern California, a terrific tour of duty when one remembers that GIs a half-world away were then sloughing through the mud of Guadalcanal and Sicily. When he wasn't on the set, Joe played golf, visited troop installations, and drilled a couple of hours each day. He also used the time to bed a variety of starlets and to reacquaint himself with an old lover. Lena Horne, on loan from Metro Goldwyn Mayer, had joined Bojangles Robinson, Fats Waller, and Cab Calloway on the lot of Twentieth Century Fox to make the all-black musical comedy, *Stormy Weather*. Horne sang the title song, which once again seemed to perfectly summarize the events occurring in her life at the time. She was in the midst of another divorce when suddenly good-for-nothing Joe strode back into her arms.

It was a tempestuous reunion. In his memoirs Joe confided that he was seriously thinking of dumping Marva to marry Horne, but the idea made him "feel like a dog." Certainly he was behaving like a hound, sleeping with Lana Turner and other Hollywood beauties while courting Horne and maintaining his usual long-distance telephone relationship with his wife. Horne, who'd had her fill of being used by men, objected to Joe's philandering (except, of course, when the champ was making love to her). The entertainer finally concluded that he could never be faithful to one woman. There was a final, ugly blowout.

It occurred the day before Joe was to participate in a celebrity golf tournament to benefit the USO. Horne had agreed to be the scorekeeper for the stars. But then, mad over Joe's dalliances (possibly with Angelle De Lavallade, a local model with a bit part in *Stormy Weather*), she backed out at the last moment. A phone call from Joe ended with the two arguing. He decided to hash things out in person. When he arrived at her place, she was packing her bags for a trip to Fort Huachuca, Arizona, where she had accepted an offer to entertain the troops. A few years earlier, she had given Joe a gold bracelet with "Joe Louis" engraved on one side and "Lena" on the other. Now Joe took the bracelet off and dropped it into an open suitcase.

Horne exploded. She started cursing him, and he reacted by smacking her onto the bed and starting to choke her. Horne's screams brought her cousin Edwina running into the room. She tried pulling Joe off, but it wasn't until she shouted that she was going to call the police that Joe suddenly snapped back to his senses. He returned to his hotel, so shaken by this passionate and nearly murderous episode that he was unable to attend the next day's tournament.

"I called Lena to apologize and she hung up on me," he remembered. "End of romance."

The army found a better use for Joe's hands. He embarked on a tour of bases around the United States, leading a quartet of fighters known as the Joe Louis Troupe. Accompanying him were his old sparring partner, George Nicholson; a promising black boxer named "California Jackie" Wilson; and *The Ring's* recently selected fighter of the year, Sugar Ray Robinson.

Since leaving Detroit in 1932, Robinson, formerly Walker Smith, had become a two-time Golden Gloves champion in New York. He turned pro in 1940, launching a fabled, flamboyant twenty-five-year career that would see him lose only nineteen of 202 fights and practically every cent he earned in the ring. "I went through four million dollars," he said once, sounding a lot like the man whose gloves he had once carried to the Brewster Center. "But I have no regrets."

The future lightweight and middleweight champion of the world had a great time touring the States with his childhood idol. Dozens of stories, most of them involving women and free spending, came out of their time together. Once in Jacksonville, Florida, the two got into a shoving match over Robinson's last bottle of Coca-Cola, a beverage Joe drank like water when he wasn't in training. Robinson cut his foot on some broken glass, and Joe wound up carrying Sugar Ray into a cab and into the local hospital. However, having attracted the attention of an attractive nurse, Joe suddenly left his buddy in the emergency room to spend the night with his new-found friend.

Robinson, like Louis, was under contract to Mike Jacobs, which meant they both enjoyed a nearly limitless line of credit. Their traveling trainer, Bob Payne, doubled as their treasurer, since neither fighter liked to carry money on their person. Payne had a gold money clip filled with hundred-dollar bills, which he would distribute on demand. One morning Robinson asked him for a fresh infusion of cash.

"You're gonna have to hock this," said Payne, handing over the empty clip, "because that's all that's left."

"We were flat," said Robinson. "We had gone through maybe $30,000 in six months. And we had done it as easy as if it was thirty cents. Picking up tabs, buying presents for chicks, tipping big. But we knew there was more money where that had come from. Mike Jacobs would always stake us. He would give us an advance against future fights."

Despite their privileged position, the fighters still had to contend with many of the same problems facing ordinary black soldiers. Once they found themselves waiting for a bus at Camp Siebert in Alabama.

"No use standin' around here," Joe told Robinson. "I'm goin' to call us a cab." With that he walked over to a phone booth where the white troops were waiting. When he emerged a minute later, he found an MP twirling a billy club in his hand.

"Say, soldier," he said, "get over in the other bus station."

Joe, puzzled, asked him what he was talking about.

"Soldier," the MP explained, "your color belongs in the other bus station."

"What's my color got to do with it?" said Joe, choking back his anger. "I'm wearing a uniform like you."

"Down here," the MP responded, "you do as you're told." With that he poked Joe in the ribs with his club.

"Don't touch me with that stick," warned Joe.

"I'll do more than touch you," barked the MP, who drew back his arm as if to smack him with it.

The policeman either didn't know who he was dealing with or thought himself the baddest cracker in Alabama. In any event, Robinson prevented a possible homicide by jumping onto the MP's back and wrestling him to the ground. In a flash several more MPs charged into the fray while some of the soldiers yelled, "Hey, that's Joe Louis!"

Robinson and Louis were hustled over to the jailhouse where a colonel listened patiently to their stories. According to Robinson, the officer then bawled out the arresting MP. Meanwhile, the scuttlebutt on the crowded base was that the two blacks had been beaten up by MPs and tossed in a cell. To alleviate the growing tension, the colonel asked them to drive around the base in a jeep "to show that you're all right."

Joe was all right, but he was gaining a firsthand education in national race relations. The South was a century behind the times, though the big northern cities he was most familiar with—Detroit, Chicago, and New York—could hardly be considered models of tolerance, either. In 1943 a scuffle between white sailors and black teenagers precipitated a four-day riot that left thirty-four Detroiters dead, including twenty-five blacks. A few weeks later a disturbance in Harlem caused five deaths and five hundred injuries. Joe's approach to dealing with the prejudice he found all around him was to tacitly accept Jim Crow restrictions off base, since he figured to have no chance in changing local ordinances or customs. On base, he quietly but firmly used his position and persistence to effect change. He would privately demand of a commanding officer that the crowd attending one of his exhibitions be integrated or else he would refuse to box. When he came across a particularly egregious example of racism or segregation, he would place calls to his friends in the War Department. In terms of Joe's activism, the brouhaha at Camp Siebert was an aberration in that it got into the newspapers. But the publicity had a positive effect. Soon after, the army ordered all military buses to be desegregated.

Joe was the centerpiece of arguably the most influential U.S. propaganda film to come out of the war, The Negro Soldier. In 1943 the War Department, under fire for its discriminatory practices, ordered Colonel Frank Capra, chief of the Army Pictorial Service, to produce a documentary that would educate all servicemen, particularly whites, about the accomplishments of blacks in American history. During the thirties Capra had won three Academy Awards for best director (It Happened One Night,

Mr. Deeds Goes to Town, and *You Can't Take It With You*) and, after induction, produced for the army the highly acclaimed seven-part film series,
Why We Fight. A populist who was a master at injecting mild social commentary into his films, Capra turned the proselytizing up several notches for
The Negro Soldier. In fact, the documentary was presented in the form of a
preacher delivering a sermon.

Carlton Moss, a young black radio writer recommended by Truman
Gibson, researched and wrote the script and also played the role of the minister. Capra sounded like the heavyweight champion as he sought to cool
Moss's ardor. "Moss wore his blackness as conspicuously as a bandaged
head," said Capra. "Time and again he would write a scene, then I'd rewrite
it, eliminating the angry fervor. He'd object, and I would explain that when
something's red-hot, the blow torch of passion only louses up its glow. We
must persuade and convince, not by rage but by reason."

The finished product began with Moss telling his flock that he'd been
at the second Louis-Schmeling fight, which he presented as an allegory for
the war.

"In one minute and forty-nine seconds an American fist won a victory," Moss said as the screen showed footage from the fight. "But it wasn't
the final victory. Now those two men who were matched in the ring that
night are matched again. This time in a far greater arena and for much
greater stakes."

The screen showed Max Schmeling, then Joe, in military training.
"Max Schmeling, a paratrooper in the German army, men turned into
machines, challenging the world. . . . Joe Louis, training for the fight of his
life. This time it's a fight not between man and man but between nation
and nation. A fight for the real championship of the world, to determine
which way of life shall survive, their way or our way, and this time we must
see to it that there is no return engagement. For the stakes this time are the
greatest that men have ever fought for."

The minister quoted from Hitler's manifesto of hate, *Mein Kampf*, in
which the dictator chided the notion of black progress in the United
States: "it never dawns on degenerate America that it is criminal madness
to train a half ape, till one believes he has made a lawyer of him." The message the government was trying to deliver to blacks through this cinematic
preacher was that to love America's heroic and patriotic Brown Bomber
was to love America itself. Sure, the country still had a long way to go
(Moss carefully avoided any mention of slavery or the Civil War as he
reviewed blacks' participation in past U.S. wars), but as the champ himself
had once observed, "There's nothing wrong with this country that Hitler
can fix."

The film was previewed at the Pentagon's projection room in January 1944 by two hundred skeptical representatives of the black media. As Capra remembered, there was nary a cough during the entire presentation. The audience, accustomed to the stereotypical "Hollywood nigger," was incredulous. Langston Hughes described it as "the most remarkable Negro film ever flashed on the American scene." Abe Hill wrote in the *Amsterdam News*:

> One cannot believe that such dignity and integrity inherent in the script would have ever been accomplished in this generation. When this reviewer saw a preview of the film . . . he kept pondering this fact: Who on earth thought such a thing could be done so accurately—without propaganda, without sugarcoating and without the jackass clowning the movie acting Negro usually degrades himself to. . . .
>
> The movie succeeds in proving that this is the Negro's war. He is too deeply rooted in the making of this great country—he has as much at stake in its destiny as any other waver of the red, white, and blue. If any child, white, black, or blue ever wants to know what in the world the Negro has been doing in this country for the past 300 years, let him spend 40 minutes seeing this picture and he will have learned a life's lesson. . . .

In terms of the sheer number of viewers, *The Negro Soldier* rivaled any of Capra's previous box-office hits. It was released for free to more than 3,500 white-owned commercial theatres and was required viewing for all members of the armed forces. Although the film came in for some criticism, chiefly for exaggerating and glamorizing the Negro's limited role in the war, the reviews were overwhelmingly positive. While it was impossible to precisely gauge the picture's impact on promoting racial tolerance among white viewers, it would seem that, at the very least, most left the theatre enlightened about the oppressed minority within America's own borders.

As the landmark documentary began to appear in movie houses across the country, Joe headed on a tour of military installations overseas. For nearly a year he staged exhibitions and visited hospitals in England, Scotland, Italy, and North Africa. Although he was not a combatant, he occasionally found himself in harm's way. He survived several days of V-12 rocket attacks in London and an emergency landing aboard a crippled bomber. On another occasion he was photographed pulling the lanyard of an artillery piece in Italy; the very next day it malfunctioned, and the barrel exploded, killing several soldiers.

After coming back to the States in October 1944, he was sent to the Aleutian Islands and the Pacific Northwest for further morale-building sessions. By now Marva was back in Chicago, having ended a short-lived attempt at a singing career. To her husband's annoyance she had sneaked off to New York for vocal lessons. She debuted at the Ebony Club on Broadway, after which her manager arranged a schedule of single-night performances in the South to build up her voice and reputation. She made about $15,000 touring thirty-eight cities, less than what she had spent on a wardrobe of gowns. An ordinary voice and her repulsion over the degrading life of the typical black entertainer—eating and sleeping inside cars, being forced to go to the back door of restaurants for food—finished her after only three months on the road.

Their marriage remained as rocky as ever. While he was in London Joe had a heated affair with a buxom Red Cross assistant named Hazel Payne. In Washington he courted Evelyn Penny, a tall, cream-hued secretary in the War Department. Soon rumors were flying that Penny would become Joe's wife, once his wife divorced him. Marva got scant sympathy. When it came to matters of marital discord, the Negro press almost always came out wholly on Joe's side. Many ordinary blacks perceived Marva as a socialite who didn't know how to hold onto her man.

On March 28, 1945, as Patton's Third Army raced through Germany and U.S. Marines prepared to assault the heavily fortified island of Okinawa, Marva was granted a divorce inside a Chicago court. She had charged her husband with desertion, and he had not contested it. "Joe thinks I ought to be happy because I've got all of the material things any woman could want," she said. "But it's no fun being alone all the time." The divorce created no great waves of commentary or protest, only ripples of speculation over who the next Mrs. Louis might be—testimony to the country's preoccupation with the final, decisive battles of the war and the strength of Joe's public image.

Five months later, on September 2, the war officially ended with representatives of the Japanese government formally surrendering to Gen. Douglas MacArthur on the deck of the battleship Missouri. Millions of fighting men were demobilized as rapidly as the government could process the paperwork. On October 1, Joe was discharged at Camp Shanks, New York. With the exception of the occasional ugly incident, he had enjoyed being just plain old GI Joe for his forty-five months of duty. Free from his handlers, he was forced to become more self-reliant. "When I didn't have them around to think for me and tell me what to eat and when to go to bed, I had to figure things out myself," he said. "I grew up in the army."

He had also grown in the nation's consciousness and in its esteem. No longer was he thought of as the expressionless, inarticulate jungle-killer of prewar days. The needs of a country at war with the forces of fascism had humanized him, transforming him into a friendly, dignified, determined, inspiring symbol of patriotism, national resolve, and racial unity. He'd traveled more than 70,000 miles, fought ninety-six exhibitions, visited countless hospitals and bases, and had been seen in person by about five million servicemen. That didn't include the tens of millions of Americans who had seen him featured regularly in newsreels, on recruiting posters, and in such successful propaganda efforts as *This Is the Army* and *The Negro Soldier*. The masses knew that Joe had donated the purses of two title fights and had "named the war" with his statement about America being "on God's side." By the time of his discharge, he had been given the Legion of Merit Medal "for exceptionally meritorious service." He had narrowly lost (to A. Phillip Randolph) the vote for the Springarn Medal for contributions to civil rights and had been glowingly portrayed by *Life* as "a quiet parable in racial good will." It all added up to a practically faultless public image for the thirty-two-year-old ex-sergeant—an image that unfortunately would take several severe hits during the second half of his life.

Chapter Ten

Cruel Twilight

When he got up, Marciano threw two left hooks
that ruined Joe, although he was still on his feet.
Marciano threw a right hand that dropped Joe through
the ropes and onto the apron. One of his legs was inside
the ring, under the lower rope.
I had moved up behind the row of sportswriters,
and as Joe was counted out, I jumped onto the apron.
"Joe, Joe, you'll be all right, Joe," I said, holding
back my tears. "You'll be all right, man."

— SUGAR RAY ROBINSON

*J*oe's army days effectively sliced his career into two sections. "When I came out of the army I wasn't the fighter I was before I went in," he admitted. "Nobody can lay off that long and come back as good as he was."

Four years of cavalier eating and indifferent training had fleshed out his face and added thirty pounds to his frame. His competitive edge, so critical to a champion in any field, also had been dulled by nearly a hundred exhibitions with lackluster opponents. As millions of other discharged veterans who had experienced so much in such a short period of time, he felt restless. Unlike those same veterans, however, Joe re-entered civilian life with a monumental debt load—nearly $350,000, according to one source. This included $41,146 to John Roxborough, $117,000 in back taxes, and as much as $170,000 to Mike Jacobs. He also owed $25,000 to his wife, who originally had agreed to settle their divorce for that amount plus the deed to their Chicago apartment house. However, Marva agreed to a contractual arrangement that made her one of Joe's comanagers. In lieu of alimony and support, she would be paid a percentage of future purses. At least, that's how the settlement agreement was supposed to read, explained Truman Gibson.

Jacobs's accountants, who drew up the paperwork, left out the "support," a legal technicality that would contribute mightily to Joe's future tax woes.

His inner circle had changed. Trainer Jack Blackburn was dead, replaced by Mannie Seamon. Roxborough and Julian Black, whose original ten-year contract with Joe had expired during the war, were out as active managers. Roxborough would be released from prison in October 1946, after which he would quietly drop into the background, unwilling to sully the public image he had helped to craft for his fighter. Black was dropped because he had reportedly refused to loan Joe the $25,000 he needed to pay off Marva. Joe asked Truman Gibson to manage his ring affairs. When Gibson declined, he turned to old friend Marshall Miles, who agreed to do it more as a personal favor than as a profitable business enterprise. To this day, Miles contends that he never made a dime from the arrangement. To the contrary, he just joined the lengthening line of creditors. "Only thing I ever did was give him money," he said.

The top business priority was arranging the long-delayed rematch with Billy Conn, which figured to replenish both fighters' coffers. Because of the onset of cold weather, an outdoor bout was out of the question until the following year. Jacobs scheduled the fight for June 19, 1946, at Yankee Stadium. It would prove to be just one of seven championships frozen by the war to be contested during the year, but none promised to generate as much excitement. With ringside seats going for an unheard-of one hundred dollars apiece, some predicted it would be boxing's first three-million-dollar gate.

Joe knew where the quickest path to financial redemption lay, so despite his age he didn't dread getting up at five in the morning to do the roadwork that would take him there. At the end of 1945 he took off on a month-long exhibition tour of the Pacific Northwest, his 240 pounds jiggling in two- and three-rounders from San Francisco to Victoria, British Columbia. Next was a stop at a resort in West Baden Springs, Indiana, where Seamon tried to melt off more of the excess poundage through a program of roadwork, steam cabinets, and sulphur baths. Then it was on to Pompton Lakes, where he slowly worked out the kinks in the ring.

Visitors to both fighters' camps reported the champ looked rusty in his sparring sessions, while the challenger appeared sharp. "Conn's training for the newspapermen," was Joe's response. "I'm training for a knockout."

Seamon deserves mention for the methodical way he helped Joe restore his pugilistic skills after four years of relative idleness. The short, cheerful Russian Jew had been born Mandel Simenovitch in Chicago in 1897 and raised in poverty in Harlem. A failure as a fighter—he was knocked out in his only two bouts—he switched to training and was in the corner of several world champions, most notably lightweight champion

Benny Leonard, in the years following the First World War. Jack Blackburn hired Seamon as his assistant just before the Tommy Farr fight in 1937, putting him in charge of Joe's sparring partners. Seamon replaced the pushovers with solid performers who followed the same training regimen of the champ. "Joe wants real work," he said, "which he can't get by knocking over slow-motion picture boys."

Joe liked Seamon, who was a perpetual-motion machine in slicked-back hair and double-breasted suits. Seamon loved the horses, enjoyed nightclubbing with entertainers like George Raft and Cab Calloway, and occasionally impressed Joe with his cosmopolitan ways. Once, in France, the fighter watched as Seamon talked to an airport employee in Yiddish. "Mannie," he asked, "since when you learn to speak French so good?"

Seamon's first outing as head trainer was filling in for the ailing Blackburn prior to the Abe Simon fight in 1942. Although no one expected him to replace Blackburn as a confidant or father figure, he was under pressure to keep the wheels spinning smoothly. He knew the routine and rarely deviated from it. As he led Joe down the aisle of Madison Square Garden, he felt his fighter lightly bouncing punches off the back of his sweater.

"I always did that to Chappie, Mannie," he explained.

"Okay, Joe," said Seamon. "Then go right ahead and keep doing it."

When Blackburn died a short while later, Joe told Seamon that he was his and Chappie's personal choice as successor. "I felt honored that a Negro champion had chosen a white man to be his trainer," said Seamon. Later he added, "This is as nice a job as a guy ever had. I take money for it only because my family has to eat."

Although Seamon sometimes seemed bewildered by the bawdy racial humor of Joe's otherwise all-black entourage, he was accepted by everybody in camp. They respected his sincerity, trustworthiness, and devotion to Joe, who was the beneficiary of Seamon's close attention to detail. For example, throughout Joe's postwar career he had him spar on a ring canvas that was three-quarters of an inch thicker than normal. Training on the slower canvas helped put more spring into Joe's legs when he stepped onto the thinner regulation flooring on fight night.

Seamon was a perfectionist when preparing his man for a fight. It took him forty-five minutes to wrap Joe's hands, and he was careful to have separate towels—labeled A, B, and C—for his fighter's face, body, and legs. He also was a slave to routine.

A typical day in training camp began when he woke Joe at 5:30 in the morning for roadwork. Joe, who was as fastidious about cleanliness and personal hygiene as his trainer, brushed his teeth and gargled. Then he alternately walked and ran between five and six miles, occasionally bending over to pick up loose stones without stopping—"very good exercise," explained Seamon, "for the back muscles."

Having done an hour's worth of roadwork, Joe would drink a glass of carrot juice before turning in for a few more hours' sleep. Awakened at ten o'clock, he'd have his first meal of the day: apple juice, three or four lamb chops, ham, or liver, and a couple of boiled eggs, but no bread or potatoes. After eating he'd wait fifteen minutes, then have two glasses of water. To kill time he'd go for a long walk, then play cards or ping-pong before taking a nap.

Joe would report to the gym at three o'clock each afternoon. His workout ritual included five minutes of shadow boxing, four to six rounds of sparring, three to six minutes each on the speed bag and heavy bag, five minutes of skipping rope, fifteen minutes of calisthenics, and finally, five minutes of having a medicine ball thrown into his stomach.

After each workout, said Seamon, "I would undress him, wrap him in a blanket and throw another over him, and put out the lights so that he was in a completely darkened room for fifteen minutes and could perspire freely." Seamon completely dried him off before putting him under a luke-warm shower. Afterward he gave him a massage and dried him off with eucalyptus oil, omega oil, and "a little drop of olive oil." Seamon ended the treatment by applying an eye wash and a foot salve.

Joe sat down to dinner at 5:30. He drank two glasses of water, then dug into a salad, soup with crackers, and a thick, one-pound steak (grilled medium rare) with string beans or corn. He washed it down with tea with lemon or milk, waited fifteen minutes for it all to digest, then had his favorite snack food—a pint of vanilla ice cream. Joe would rest thirty minutes before having another couple glasses of water. He'd play cards or call his many girlfriends around the country. (One associate said his phone bill sometimes reached $1,500 a month while in training.) Once or twice a week he'd go into town to see a movie. Then it was lights out at 8:30 or nine o'clock for eight or nine hours of sleep before getting up early the next morning and doing it all over again.

Joe wasn't always as conscientious about sacrificing his golf game during training, even though Blackburn had repeatedly warned him that the unnatural motion was detrimental to a fighter. During his preparation for Conn he suffered arthritic-like pain in his elbows, a condition caused by his swinging too many clubs. The pain became so intense the fight was in danger of being postponed. But Seamon, using what he later described as "special methods of heat treatment every evening for hours," brought the problem under control. Seamon kept Joe's ailment secret. What the trainer did tell reporters was that the thirty-two-year-old champ, while not the fighter he had once been, was close enough. He was down to 207 pounds, just seven more than he had weighed when he faced Conn in 1941. "Nobody can expect him to be quite the fighter he was when he polished off Schmeling in their second fight," he said, "but I'll go on record that he'll be 90 percent of the best Louis you ever saw. And that will be more than enough."

Five years and a day after they had thrilled America with one of the greatest ring battles ever, the world's heavyweight champion and the number-one contender stepped through the ropes for what everyone hoped would be another classic. Mike Jacobs was disappointed with the turnout, which didn't come close to his prediction of 70,000. Nonetheless, the crowd of 45,266 produced $1,925,564 in ticket sales, a gate exceeded only by the second Dempsey-Tunney fight. Another indicator of the fight's importance was that it was the first heavyweight tilt to be televised. NBC employed specially built RCA "image orthocon" cameras whose turret lenses produced an image equal to what a spectator in the thirtieth row saw. Few receiving sets were in homes yet. But saloon owners, among the first to realize the possibilities of what was then still called "video," did a land-rush business.

Given the sequel's buildup, a letdown was perhaps inevitable. The fight was a "stinkeroo," acknowledged Conn, who was heavier, slower, and less hungry than he had been five years ago. After a flurry of punches in the first round he said, "Take it easy, Joe, we've got fifteen rounds to go," making his opponent laugh.

This time Joe carried the fight to Conn. Less mobile now, and with his left hand rendered ineffective by Joe's unexpected aggressiveness, Conn won only the third round. The crowd yelled for action. In the eighth Joe tagged his twenty-eight-year-old opponent in the jaw with an overhand right. A left hook and a right cross put him on his back, from where he groggily heard the referee count him out at 2:19 of the round. Conn would fight just twice more before settling down to a comfortable life in Pittsburgh with his lovely Mary Louise. "It was a long grind from the sulphur baths and steam baths at West Baden to the eighth round of the Conn bout at the Yankee Stadium," reflected Seamon, "but the payoff wallops were good to see." Especially to Joe's creditors. Of his $625,000 purse—the largest of his career—the winner saw only about $70,000 of it after his obligations were met. He also owed taxes on what he had just earned.

Arthur Daley was one of the nearly 700 journalists on hand to watch Joe successfully defend his title for the twenty-second time. "If the Louis-Conn engagement had been an ordinary main event in the Garden," he wrote in the next day's New York Times, "the customers would have booed it out of the arena. . . . No one can blame Louis for it. He was willing to fight."

The problem was in finding opponents who could draw a crowd. On September 18, Joe met Steve "Tami" Mauriello at Yankee Stadium. The stocky heavyweight with the deformed foot had grown up in the Bronx. This, along with drastically reduced ticket prices, helped boost paid attendance to nearly 40,000. The local boy caused an uproar in the first round when he caught Joe on the chin with a right hand, knocking him into the ropes. He tried to press home his advantage, but Joe covered up, clinched, and quickly regained his bearings. Less than a minute later he knocked Mauriello down with a left hook. Mauriello got back to his feet but was immediately greeted by another left hook that left him draped over the middle strand of the ropes. In a postfight radio interview the disconsolate loser created a minor scandal when he told a national audience, "I got too goddamned careless." Most observers thought he had simply been overmatched. Nat Fleischer wrote in *The Ring* that "Louis continued to prove to the fistic world that he rates so high above the rest of the heavyweights that he is in a class all by himself." Looking back many years later, Joe considered it his last great fight.

The hysteria that had once characterized his victories, however, had tapered off considerably. After the second Conn fight there was not a single reported incident of Harlemites stopping and taunting white drivers, which had been a regular feature of prewar celebrations. The *Baltimore Afro-American* blamed "post-war depression," while others suggested Joe's matter-of-fact victories had lost their novelty. The most likely explanation was the lack of a clear rallying point. With fascism defeated and civil rights progress, much of the old symbolism had been stripped away from his fights.

Not that the jowly, balding, postwar version of the Brown Bomber didn't continue to represent the ultimate in black pride and achievement to millions of American Negroes. Clifton Taulbert has written of his experiences coming of age in the small cotton community of Glen Allan, Mississippi, where "colored heroes" were so few "that the ones we knew by name such as Joe Louis were like the neighbors who lived next door or down the road—a good ol' boy from the plantation that had gone north and made us proud."

On fight nights Taulbert's aunt, Ma Ponk, would bring out an old battery-operated radio, one of the few in the colored section. "It was important to her," recalled Taulbert. "She played it only on Sundays and for special occasions, and this was a special occasion."

A crowd of people started gathering early, bringing their Jax beer with them. Ma Ponk placed the radio in the window and unlatched the screen. She would never let that many people in her house, but her front porch was filled to capacity, and there were grown men sitting on the ground as close to the bedroom window as possible.

With their bottles of beer and laughter, these didn't appear to be tired field hands. Their hard day's work wasn't slowing them down—not on this night. Their hero would be fighting tonight, and Joe Louis with his fists, quickness, and punching power could say for them what they could never say for themselves. It was a sin to miss a Joe Louis fight. They all knew the exact time for the bell to ring, and Ma Ponk knew the exact time to turn on the radio. She didn't want to run the batteries down, which meant most of the prefight announcements were missed.

At eight o'clock someone mildly said, "It's time, Miss Ponk." She hooked the antenna wire into the screen and turned the knob. With a small amount of static, the fight was on. As the crowd listened, ignoring the bites of mosquitoes and night bugs, Joe Louis defended his title.

I remember the men jumping up and down, shadowboxing with each other. They gave step-by-step instructions, as if they were coaches and Joe Louis could hear each word. As they yelled and jumped, Ma Ponk would occasionally throw out her warning, "Don't step on my flowers, or I'll turn this darn thing off." Of course she never did, but for awhile, they were quieted—until a victory punch for Joe was announced.

The radio fight would go on into the night, too late for a little boy like me to hear it to the finish. I'd fall asleep on my cot by the window, while the colored people of Glen Allan successfully coached their hero to another victory.

In between clobbering Conn and Mauriello, Joe reconciled with Marva. She had let him back into her life following his discharge and then, after persistent wooing on Joe's part, accepted his offer to remarry. They retied the knot one July day in 1946. Marva rationalized her decision by explaining that during their divorce she had not met any man as interesting as her ex-husband. Unfortunately, their second marriage was destined to be an instant replay of their first.

>‹

The Mauriello fight earned Joe $103,611. Marshall Miles, one of the few people around Joe who was actively looking out for his welfare, instructed Mike Jacobs to hold onto the purse until after the first of the year. Miles mistakingly thought that the maneuver would ease Joe's 1946 tax burden, but IRS regulations required income be taxed the year it was earned, not when it was dispersed. In any case, when Miles visited the offices of the Twentieth Century Sporting Club in early January 1947 he was shocked to learn that practically none of the money remained. Mike Jacobs, recuperating from a heart attack suffered a month earlier, had left the business in the hands of his cousin, Sol Strauss, an attorney who had helped handle Joe's divorce. Strauss showed Miles a pile of cancelled checks and Western Union money order receipts, all made out in varying amounts to the fighter.

"There was only five hundred dollars left," recounted Miles, who needed three days to track Joe down. Cornered, Joe admitted to pouring $43,000 into his ailing Chicago nightclub, the Rhumboogie, which Leonard Reed managed for him. He couldn't remember where the rest of the money had gone; he'd just spent it, was all. When Miles exasperatingly asked why he'd bothered to leave $500 in the account, Joe just laughed.

Miles had grown accustomed to such shenanigans. A year earlier, when Joe was practically tapped out, Miles had deposited $20,000 of his own money into a joint account at the National City Bank in Times Square. One day Miles got a call from the bank, informing him that Joe had withdrawn half to open an account for a girlfriend. Lickety-split, the new account was drained, the money going for perfume, jewelry, a mink coat, and other expensive items for a statuesque model named Carrolle Drake. One of Joe's friends had spotted Drake at Fritz Pollard's Sun Tan Studios, a Harlem talent agency, and quickly told the fighter of his discovery. A torrid romance ensued, with Joe opening charge accounts for her at fashionable Madison Avenue shops.

"She was a beautiful girl," remembered Miles. "She was from Georgia, and Joe fell hard for her."

The affair was put on hold as Joe embarked on several lengthy exhibition tours beginning in late 1946. He traveled to Mexico and Hawaii, came back to the states for several weeks, then hit the road again, this time fighting throughout Central and South America. Generally he was paid $10,000 plus expenses per fight. All told he made an estimated $157,200, but much of the money was blown covering the costs of the large entourage that accompanied him. Joe could expect a large tax bill due on the amount he had just made. This would be added to what he already owed the government, which was substantial.

Meanwhile, Marva was thrilled to announce to her husband that she was expecting their second child. On May 28, 1947, she gave birth to a twelve-pound baby boy, Joseph Louis Barrow Jr., in Mexico City. As when their daughter was born four years earlier, Joe was on the golf course when he heard the good news. Either he or Thurston McKinney dubbed the oversized infant "Punchy," a nickname that survives.

Joe's revenue stream slowed once the exhibitions ended in the spring of 1947. Having cleaned out the heavyweight division, Joe's prospects for a big outdoor title fight that summer looked dim. In June, as the peripatetic champion made yet another exhibition swing, this time of the West Coast, his handlers shopped around for an opponent. A championship bout with Joe Baksi, the only decent fighter around, fell through after he was pummelled by Swedish heavyweight Olle Tandberg. They finally scratched up an undistinguished black fighter named Jersey Joe Walcott. Walcott's six children and his age (he was a few months older than Joe) inspired the press to dub him "Pappy." The original plan was for a ten-round exhibition. But the New York State Athletic Commission ruled that because the title would be at stake, it had to be an official championship fight of fifteen rounds. Joe's twenty-fourth title defense was scheduled for December 5, 1947, at Madison Square Garden.

The challenger, a religious family man who had been surviving on starvation wages for years, saw his financial prayers answered. Born Arnold Cream, Walcott had been raised in poverty in Merchantville, New Jersey, where he had worked "at every filthy job from cleaning cesspools on up to earn a living," he once said. "And I never did a wrong thing."

Except get sick. He had been a promising welterweight under Jack Blackburn's tutelage at Philadelphia's Arcadia Gym in the early thirties. It was his misfortune to be waylaid by an attack of typhoid just as Blackburn accepted the offer to take on young Joe Louis Barrow as his pupil. Walcott, left behind in Philadelphia, undoubtedly would have benefitted tremendously had he been able to join Blackburn in Chicago, as planned. By the time he recuperated a year later he was all but forgotten, though he was hired to be one of Joe's sparring partners for the first Schmeling fight. Eager to show his stuff, on his first day he angered Joe by giving him a more spirited workout than was necessary. During the following day's session the two tore into each other, Joe knocking Walcott down. Walcott then left camp. Whether he quit or was fired has never been definitely established, but he went away convinced he could beat the champ.

It was eleven years before he was given the chance. During that time he had compiled a mediocre record, getting kayoed by a pair of Joe's nondescript knockout victims, Al Ettore and Abe Simon. Joe, perhaps thinking back to their 1936 run-in, considered Walcott "a tricky fighter with a good right hand," but bettors installed the challenger as a 10-1 underdog. In some corners Pappy was a 20-1 longshot.

While Joe was in training for Walcott, a physician noticed that the champ's reflexes were unequal, that his left side responded with less agility than his right. On occasion there also was slight drooling from the right corner of his mouth. These were signs of reflexive deterioration, but Joe ignored any suggestion that he quit. He needed the money, and the ring remained the quickest and surest way to earn it.

Instead, Joe was unduly worried about his weight. Over Mannie Seamon's strident objections, he decided to dry out the last couple of days before the fight, cutting back on his food and water intake. It was vanity more than anything; the overweight boxer simply didn't want to look sloppy in front of his public. Joe climbed through the ropes weighing a trimmed-down 211 pounds, then proceeded to get his ears boxed off.

Walcott wheeled throughout the fight, firing jabs and doing his best to avoid prolonged exchanges. In the first round he knocked Joe over with a solid right hand to the jaw, then repeated the feat in the fourth round with an uppercut. The second time Joe stayed down until the count reached seven, then endured another flurry as he tried to clear the cobwebs in his head. Despite the two knockdowns Joe was the more aggressive boxer, but he looked sluggish. His counterpunches lacked snap and his combinations seemed out of sync. His reflexes had obviously slowed since his last money fight nearly fifteen months earlier against Tami Mauriello. By the last three rounds Walcott was so sure he had clinched the scorecard he fought not to lose, dancing away from the fatigued champion to avoid the kind of knockout punch that had doomed the overconfident Billy Conn. At the bell ending the fifteenth round there was barely a sportswriter or paying customer present who didn't believe he had just witnessed one of the biggest upsets in boxing history.

Joe was so disgusted with his performance he tried to leave the ring before the decision was announced. Seamon, realizing that this meant an automatic disqualification, held him back. So Joe stood there, drained and embarrassed, his jaw swollen, his left eye closed, and his battered head aching, as Harry Balogh grabbed the microphone to announce the decision: "Judge Frank Forbes scored the fight eight rounds to six, one round even . . . Louis! Referee scored seven rounds to six, two rounds even . . . Walcott!" The cheering was quickly replaced by waves of hooting and booing as Balogh announced the third and decisive vote: "And Judge Marty Monroe scored it nine rounds to six . . . Louis! The winner by split decision and still the heavyweight champion of the world, Joe Louis!"

The decision was so cockeyed that one of Joe's biggest supporters in the press, columnist Jimmy Cannon, remarked that if the winner had been anybody else, there would have been a full-scale investigation into the officiating. The boos rained down as Joe approached the shocked and crestfallen loser. "I'm sorry, Joe," Louis said, before hurriedly leaving the ring. Walcott interpreted the apology as an admission of defeat, but Joe was simply apologizing for his effort. He knew that a rematch would be necessary to salvage his badly wounded pride. However, he held no delusions about his deteriorating skills or his diminished enthusiasm for training. He decided that his next fight would be his last.

In early February of 1948 he, Marva, and the usual complement of handlers and hangers-on sailed to England aboard the *Queen Mary*. Marshall Miles had arranged a series of exhibitions at the Health and Holiday Exposition in Earl's Court in London. Unfortunately, the exposition sponsors went bankrupt, depriving Joe of half of his promised $80,000. A cash-strapped Swedish promoter stepped in with an offer of a Scandinavian tour, but he was shown the door after he proposed paying Joe in ice skates. Joe spent the money he did receive in his usual cavalier fashion, taking extended sidetrips to Brussels and Paris and buying thousands of dollars worth of presents for his girlfriends back in the states. Marva, who had filled her own trunk with expensive Continental goodies, didn't find out about Joe's shopping spree until custom officials opened a second trunk, similarly filled with bottles of perfume and fashionable French clothes.

Joe discovered that, even overseas, he could not escape the injustice of the Walcott decision. A British writer, Peter Wilson, had prepared an article for London's *Sunday Pictorial* with the banner headline: "I'll Swear On Oath That Joe Louis Was Licked!" Somehow Joe had gotten a copy of it. At a dinner party Wilson organized in his honor at the Old Albany Club, Joe suddenly leaned over and said, "So you thought Walcott whupped me?" Wilson, admittedly intimidated, feebly shook his head yes.

Joe nodded thoughtfully. "Well," he said quietly, "mebbe you was right and mebbe you was wrong. But there ain't gonna be no argument when we meets again."

And there wasn't. "I don't care what Joe Louis weighs for this fight," Seamon told a reporter as they prepared for the scheduled rematch on June 24, 1948, at Yankee Stadium. "He can weigh 210, 212, 215 or he can weigh a *ton*. One thing I *do* care about, however, and that is having Joe at the peak of his form. . . ."

There was widespread speculation that this would be Joe's last fight, though the champ had not confirmed that. Rain pushed the bout back to June 25. Joe came in weighing 214 pounds—twenty more than Walcott— and all of them came crashing to the canvas in the third round, the result of a Walcott left-right combination. That comprised most of the action of the first nine rounds, as 40,000 bored fans booed their disapproval over Walcott's evasive tactics and Joe's tedious shuffling. In the tenth, referee Frank Fullam instructed the fighters, "Hey, one of you get the lead out of your ass and let's have a fight." Reluctantly, Walcott quit waltzing and began exchanging shots. Joe started to score and soon the fatigued Walcott was struggling to keep his arms up.

Before the eleventh round Seamon told Joe, "There's only five rounds to go, and I don't want you to forget that you're a million-dollar fighter.

Don't let him get set this round. Go and hit him on the chin. Just get twelve inches away from him, and when you catch him with the first punch give him everything you have." Which is about how the round unfolded. Walcott, absorbing a series of heavy blows to the head and chin, sagged to the floor and was counted out with four seconds left in the round. The crowd gave Joe a standing ovation.

"This was for you, mom," the tired champ announced into the microphone. "This was my last fight." That evening it took thirty minutes and thirty policemen to hustle Joe into the Theresa Hotel; outside, tens of thousands of adoring Harlemites jammed Seventh Avenue all the way from 124th to 125th Street. They dismantled their hero's car and refused to disperse until he appeared and made a short speech.

Joe received more than a quarter-million dollars as his share of the second Walcott fight. Rather than seeing his old problems solved, he found that new ones were just beginning. Carrolle Drake's name had emerged in the papers by this time; in April her husband, Reverend Matthew Faulkner, had sued Joe for "alienation of affections." The cuckolded ex-army chaplain was demanding $500,000 in damages. The case was settled out of court for an undisclosed amount two years later, by which time Joe had been named in another love suit.

Joe, looking to put his troubles behind him, told Marva to pack her bags for another European tour. She responded by telling him, in effect, to pack *his* bags. Weary of his chronic womanizing and his absence from her and their two young children's lives, she was filing for divorce. Joe tried to dissuade her, but he did not contest the action. In early 1949 the divorce became final. Both Marva and Drake moved on to more stable, dependable relationships. Marva married a Chicago internist, Dr. Albert Spaulding, in 1950, while Drake eventually found happiness with singer Billy Eckstine.

Divorce proceedings tied up the Walcott purse, so in September 1948 Joe embarked on a cross-country exhibition tour to drum up some cash. He put off officially announcing his retirement until he could find the right kind of arrangement that would provide him with a regular, guaranteed income after he gave up the title. Joe and his legal adviser and business partner, Truman Gibson, dickered with the Twentieth Century Sporting Club over some kind of settlement. That December, they sat down with Mike Jacobs and Sol Strauss at Jacobs's Florida home and suggested a final championship fight against one of the leading contenders—Ezzard Charles or Lee Savold, perhaps, or even a third fight with Walcott. According to a memo Strauss helped prepare for Madison Square Garden board chairman General John Reed Kilpatrick, this time Joe wanted more than his usual 40 percent of the gate. He also wanted $100,000 under the table, a method of payment with which Jacobs was surely not unfamiliar. The negotiations fizzled, however, when Joe asked what he could expect if he lost. Told that he would be put on Twentieth Century's payroll as a publicist and promoter for $25,000 a year, he responded, "You mean I have to work? . . . I want to play golf, I don't want to work."

If Strauss is to be believed, then Joe's attempted subterfuge is as revealing as it is troubling. The fighter had always been aboveboard in his dealings with the government, though actually he had never done more than sign the tax returns prepared for him by his accountants. The intricacies of finances and taxes mystified and bored him; the concept of saving was foreign to him. Mike Jacobs deserved considerable criticism for not shutting off Joe's easy credit or at least attempting to tutor him in the rudimentaries of personal finance. The tax strategies and decisions that Jacobs, Strauss, and Joe's Chicago accountant, Ted Jones, made in his behalf often were poorly thought out or flat wrong. Additionally, some of Joe's legal advisors became his business partners, an unethical if not illegal arrangement that was bound to cause problems. For example, in a 1950 lawsuit John Roxborough accused Truman Gibson of using the money Joe made on an exhibition tour of South America to start a trade school of which Gibson was a co-investor; as Joe's legal counsel, Gibson should have known that the money would have been more properly applied against back taxes.

Now the pressures arising from his tangled tax situation were causing the usually upright fighter to propose a large *sub rosa* payment to shield the money from the IRS. Although it would take another two years in those precomputer days before a full audit of his past returns would be completed, Joe already suspected that he probably owed the government more than he could ever hope to make back in the ring. "Who Has Joe's Money?" the *Negro Digest* would demand to know once the extent of Joe's indebtedness became public. The answer: Everybody but Joe.

Rich or poor, he remained the world's softest touch. Guileless himself, he rarely questioned someone's intentions when they approached with outstretched hand. Friends, family members, and perfect strangers repeatedly nicked him for money. "Joe was kind of gullible," admitted Marshall Miles. "A dollar didn't mean much to him." All it took was a sob story, pouty look, or flash of leg, and Joe was pulling bills from his pocket. "They really didn't jive me out of my money, I knew what they were doing," the fighter once recalled of the chorus girls who clung to him at one of his favorite afterhours joints in Harlem. "My pockets were full and if it made those pretty little faces light up—what the hell."

"What the hell" could have served as his personal credo. After leaving the army Joe became involved in a number of commercial ventures, nearly all failures. He lent his name to the Joe Louis Restaurant & Bar on 125th Street in Harlem, invested in a vocational training school in Chicago, and helped underwrite a Negro newspaper, the *New York Age*. All died quickly. He continued to pour tens of thousands of dollars into the similarly doomed Rhumboogie Cafe.

Casting about for additional sources of income, he decided he no longer needed to be as protective of his public image. In 1947 he began endorsing cigarettes. Two years later he let it be known that he was "interested in the beer business" or any other industry whose products might benefit from the use of his name. A public relations flack named Al Lockhart sold Joe on the idea of attaching it to a cherry-flavored soft drink. Sales of Joe Louis Punch, which eventually was distributed in thirty-one U.S. cities and throughout South America (where Coca-Cola was king), were modest. All its namesake got out of the transaction was an occasional royalty check, a block of essentially worthless stock, and all the free pop he wanted. He also allowed a Chicago dairy to plaster his name on its milk trucks. The Joe Louis Milk Company was still delivering into the sixties, though payments of $125 a week to Joe apparently halted long before then.

Joe's candor and gullibility cost him at least a couple of potentially lucrative businesses. He and Truman Gibson paid a visit to Henry Ford II to discuss opening an automobile agency. This was a certain moneymaker in the immediate postwar years, when carmakers were working round-the-clock to satisfy the pent-up demand for anything with four tires and an engine. Unfortunately, Joe brought along a defective Ford and indelicately told the tycoon's grandson, "You don't make a car worth a shit." If outspokenness cost him that deal, a closed mouth foiled his and Sugar Ray Robinson's attempt to set up a Canadian Ace Beer distributorship in Illinois. The state licensing bureau denied their application when it learned that the fighters' silent partner, Harry Greenberg, was a racketeer who had once done business with a liquor distributor named Al Capone.

Some business activities did produce dividends. He was the vice president and director of youth activities for the Superior Life Insurance Company of Michigan, a firm owned by John Roxborough. And he continued to earn royalties on the sale and distribution of fight films.

But then there was that little white ball. "Joe was interested in business," said Gibson. "However, his attention span was limited because his interests were always being deflected onto the golf course."

Gibson contradicts the popular view of Joe as a habitual loser at golf. "He won a lot, lost a lot," he said. "He was a golf gambler, sure, but he would win as often as he would lose. He was a hell of a golfer. Oh, shit, yeah. He eventually got his handicap down to a two or three. He'd sink thirty-foot putts to break a guy's heart. Good driver, too. His weak point was giving strokes away." According to sportswriter Shirley Povich, Joe "was taken by hustlers, guys who were better golfers than he was." On one occasion when he was broke, Joe sheepishly approached Sol Strauss for a $15,000 loan to pay off a debt incurred on the links. Povich maintained that Joe "lost a fortune on the golf course"—an assessment shared by most others. Marva recalled one postwar summer when her husband gambled away $90,000.

Today's federal budget deficit could have been modeled after Joe. He would wind up making at least $4.6 million between 1934 and 1951—staggering money in an era of two-cent newspapers and $1,200 Cadillacs—and yet have practically nothing to show for it. At every turn he indulged himself extravagantly and whimsically, only occasionally giving a thought to tomorrow. He borrowed heavily, lent indiscriminately, and spent more than he had on women, gambling, and good times. The rest, as the old joke goes, he wasted.

This could hardly be considered unusual behavior for someone who had in a few short years moved from the mud floor of a sharecropper's cabin to a plushly carpeted apartment on Harlem's exclusive Sugar Hill. By focusing on his immediate needs, on the fleeting surges of pleasure that came from slipping a shoeblack a twenty-dollar bill, wagering a thousand dollars on a single putt, or draping a showgirl in mink, Joe set himself up for the misery waiting around the corner. He knew this and, to his credit, didn't complain or blame anyone but himself. In the 1960s and 1970s it was common for commiserating friends to tell him that it was too bad he had fought when he did. If he'd only come along in the modern era of television and inflated purses, they'd say, he would have made ten or twenty million dollars and been a rich man.

"No," he always replied, "when I was boxing I made five million dollars and wound up broke, owing the government a million. If I was boxing today I'd make ten million and wind up broke, owing the government two million." It was hard for even friends to argue with that math.

><

The nonproductive meeting with Jacobs at the end of 1948 influenced Joe to listen more favorably to an ambitious plan cooked up by Harry Mendel, a roly-poly New Jersey press agent who in the past had helped promote everything from six-day bicycle races to some of Joe's fights. Mendel suggested forming a corporation that would put a clamp on the heavyweight title by signing the top four contenders (Walcott, Charles, Savold, and either Joey Maxim or Gus Lesnevich) to exclusive personal services contracts. Under this scenario Joe would relinquish the belt, then promote a tournament to determine the new titleholder. The contracts would be sold for cash and a share of future earnings to individuals or corporations interested in promoting the bouts. After Florida hotelman Harry Voiler tried unsuccessfully to raise $100,000 capital for a forty-nine percent share of the proposed corporation (Joe would hold the remaining fifty-one percent), Joe had Mendel approach David Charney, a partner in the Tournament of Champions, Inc. The CBS-owned subsidiary promoted and televised Wednesday night fights from New York's St. Nicholas Arena. In little more than a year it had emerged as the greatest threat to the supremacy of the Twentieth Century Sporting Club, which had been in decline since the end of the war. Joe obviously didn't want Mike Jacobs to know what he was up to, at least not yet, but it didn't matter as Charney decided he wasn't interested.

Mendel then suggested Louis and Gibson get in touch with Jim Norris, a multimillionaire with far-flung interests in grain, real estate, liquor, professional hockey, and indoor stadiums, including Madison Square Garden and Detroit's Olympia. Norris, along with his partner, Arthur Wirtz, liked the proposition. In February 1949 they agreed to organize the International Boxing Club in partnership with Louis in exchange for 80 percent of the stock. Joe reportedly was paid $350,000 for his title and the contracts he and Gibson had negotiated with Walcott, Charles, Savold, and Lesnevich. (Some have placed the figure as low as $150,000.) He held onto the remaining 20 percent of IBC stock and was guaranteed an annual salary of $20,000.

On March 1, 1949, in Miami, Joe officially retired in a letter to Abe Greene, commissioner of the National Boxing Association. Joe thus joined Jim Jeffries and Gene Tunney as the only modern heavyweight champions to retire holding the title; the rest had lost it in the ring. He had won 60 of 61 professional bouts, 51 of them by knockout. He had worn the championship belt for eleven years and eight months and successfully defended his title twenty-five times. Both remain records. *

This was not the way he had envisioned the end. "I have held the

---

* In fact, Joe had put his title on the line more often than the eight champions before him combined:

	Won Title	Lost Title	Title Defenses
James Corbett	1892	1897	1
Bob Fitzsimmons	1897	1899	1
Jim Jeffries	1899	1905*	6
Tommy Burns	1906	1908	9
Jack Johnson	1908	1915	9
Jess Willard	1915	1919	2
Jack Dempsey	1919	1926	6
Gene Tunney	1926	1928*	2
Max Schmeling	1930	1932	2
Jack Sharkey	1932	1933	1
Primo Carnera	1933	1934	3
Max Baer	1934	1935	1
James Braddock	1935	1937	1
Joe Louis	1937	1949*	25

* Retired

championship for a long time and I won it in the ring," he said. "I expected to lose it the same way I won it. However, things have developed so that I think I ought to stick to the retirement announcement I made some time ago."

On the heels of this news came the announcement of the Norris-Wirtz-Louis triumvirate. The IBC, of course, was a direct challenge to the Twentieth Century Sporting Club, but Jacobs and his former number-one attraction both viewed the termination of their longstanding professional relationship simply as business. "Joe, I ain't got a kick coming," Uncle Mike said when he saw Louis, throwing his arm around him. "You were always great with me." The ailing Jacobs accepted $150,000 from the IBC to give up his post as boxing promoter at Madison Square Garden and wished the new group good luck.

Joe's retirement left a huge vacuum in the heavyweight division, one that clearly wasn't going to be filled by either Jersey Joe Walcott or Ezzard Charles. The National Boxing Association had deemed the two uninspiring fighters to be the top contenders for Joe's vacant title, which the IBC announced would be contested on June 22, 1949, in Chicago. Ironically, Joe had won the championship exactly twelve years earlier in the same city.

Reporters considered Joe Louis the promoter to be a refreshing change of pace. Radio broadcaster Don Dunphy remembered a press conference prior to the Charles-Walcott fight. "A couple of days before the fight the sportswriters were asking him, 'How are tickets going?' The usual promoter's response would be 'Oh, wonderful. I've got orders from Chicago, New York, and so on.' Joe, new to the promotion game and perpetually honest, said, 'I don't know. We ain't sold none yet.' He fractured everybody."

That was more than either Walcott or Charles did. The twenty-eight-year-old Charles, who once described himself as "just a simple, square sort of fellow, who believed in playing the game by the rules," was a cool ring tactician from Cincinnati who lacked Joe's highly salable knockout punch. After outpointing Walcott in the dull fifteen-round title fight he was called into the center of the ring and pronounced the "new heavyweight champion of the world," which caused one of his managers, Jake Mintz, to faint in the corner.

When Mintz came to he discovered that only the NBA recognized his man as champ. New York State, the British Empire, the International Boxing Union, and most of the public did not. To gain respect, Charles set off on a Louis-style mission to meet all challengers. Unfortunately, they were as uniformly colorless as the new champion. The following summer, when Charles beat Freddy Beshore in Buffalo, only 6,298 showed up—a record low for a title tilt. There was growing sentiment for Charles's promoter—Joe Louis—to come out of retirement. The idea of a comeback appealed to Joe's pride and pocketbook. No heavyweight champion had ever come back to win the title a second time. And the money he made could help satisfy his debt to the IRS.

For the time being, he continued staging exhibitions all over North, South, and Central America to supplement his IBC salary. It was tiring but lucrative freelance work. In 1949-50 he made about $350,000 slapping down second-raters in cities from St. Paul to Havana. But this money, even had he somehow managed to hold onto all of it, still would have fallen well short of meeting his onerous tax burden.

In 1950 the IRS finally finished untangling his past returns. There had been a variety of errors, all of which would now bite Joe in the wallet. Two items on his 1946 and 1947 returns, which accounted for more than $250,000 in deductions, were disallowed. The first was the money Joe borrowed from Mike Jacobs during the war and paid back; the second was the 25-percent managerial share of gross income given to Marva after each fight. Auditors also caught a major mistake on later returns. Joe Louis Enterprises was a dummy corporation set up at the end of 1947 to collect and distribute monies received from exhibitions, fight films, and other commercial ventures. It was perfectly fine and sensible for Joe to draw a regular salary from it and allow the balance to be taxed at lower corporate rates, but he had erred by loaning himself large amounts of money and then deducting them as business expenses. After tacking on penalties and interest, the IRS calculated Joe's total tax liability at more than a half-million dollars. The government quickly slapped a lien against him; froze any revenue he was receiving from his properties; and refused to allow him to sell anything unless the entire proceeds went to pay off his back taxes.

It was "nothing but confusion," Joe admitted. "I had no idea what to do about all these problems; I figured I'd try and ignore them. But I couldn't forget this tax thing gnawing at my brain. Jesus Christ, these tax guys hang onto you. Always calling you up. Showing up where they don't belong. Getting on your nerves."

There really was only one thing to do. Against the advice of Marshall Miles, Mannie Seamon, and most others close to him, in August 1950 he announced his return to the ring. The IBC, looking to stir interest in the heavyweight division, was happy to have him back. A title fight with Ezzard Charles was arranged.

"I didn't want the fight," Charles recalled. "Joe was my boyhood idol. But my manager, Ray Arcel, said that if I wanted everyone to consider me the champ I'd have to fight Joe. I signed, but I wasn't happy about it."

From a conditioning standpoint, Joe wasn't too keen on it either. He had hoped to have several months to prepare, but James Norris scheduled the fight for September 27 at Yankee Stadium, giving Joe just six weeks to round into shape. He weighed 218 pounds the night of the fight, nearly thirty-five pounds heavier than Charles, and later admitted that, as he sat in the locker room, it was all he could do not to call the whole thing off. He was thirty-six years old, ten pounds overweight, and had not fought a professional fight in twenty-seven months.

Although Charles was the reigning champion, Joe commanded 2-1 odds from the bookmakers and a 35-percent share of the gate, which was a disappointing $205,370. (Charles had to be satisfied with 20 percent.) Only 13,562 fans rattled around inside Yankee Stadium.

National television was to blame for the poor turnout. Aired live on the CBS network at 10 P.M. eastern standard time and sponsored by Pabst, the event was one of the IBC's regularly scheduled Wednesday night "Blue Ribbon" bouts. There was no local blackout in New York, so thousands of potential paying customers stayed home or visited their favorite neighborhood bar to watch the action. The fight reached an unprecedented audience of twenty-five million people, thanks to the partially completed coaxial cable that linked the eastern half of the country to many stations in the west. The cable would finally be completed the following September, creating a truly national audience just in time for what would turn out to be Joe's swan song against Rocky Marciano.

Against Charles, Joe started off by stalking his prey, but his quicker, lighter, and younger opponent darted in and out of harm's way. He peppered Joe with hooks and jabs, scoring and cutting him before the former champ could respond in any significant way. "I knew from the seventh round on that I couldn't do it . . . I just didn't have it," Joe said afterward. In the tenth he did rock Charles with a left hook to the jaw, followed by a left and a right to the head. Charles clinched, and by the following round had recovered to resume his methodical beating. In the fourteenth he landed a tremendous right to Joe's jaw, then followed up with a series of head and body shots. Joe basically was out on his feet, but he gamely hung on, even landing a right on Charles' jaw as the round ended. Bruised, bleeding, and bone-tired, he had to be lifted off his stool by Mannie Seamon and Marshall Miles to start the last round. The barrage continued for three more minutes, until the bell mercifully sounded with Joe helplessly backed against the ropes, as Charles drove home the final blows of the night.

Charles had defended the title in convincing fashion, the scorecard showing he had won all but three of fifteen rounds. As the unanimous decision was announced in center ring, tears seeped through Joe's swollen eyes. He had lost for only the second time in his professional career—and to someone who most observers agreed he would have handled easily in his prime. In the locker room the loser was so stiff and battered he needed help to put on his trousers and shoes. Terribly ashamed of his effort and of his appearance, he nonetheless remained a model of dignity and graciousness in defeat. "I enjoyed the fight," he told the press, ice bags pressed to his ballooning face, "and I want to thank you all. I done the best I can. I'll never fight again."

Joe's sorry performance had millions of casual fans wondering about all the hulabaloo surrounding the great Brown Bomber. "Many of them never saw Joe, in the flesh or in the movies, when he was young, quick and lethal," wrote Tim Cohane in *Look* magazine. "To that huge TV audience, the dominant visual image of Joe Louis must be a raked, swollen hulk, wearily, if gallantly and proudly, groping for the top ring rope."

Those who had most closely followed and identified with Joe's career—America's fifteen million blacks—saw their greatest symbol reduced to rubble by a member of their own race. In the ghettos an unexpected backlash arose against Charles, who rightfully expected a measure of respect for defeating the greatest heavyweight fighter in history. Youngsters in his own neighborhood actually booed him. "Louis was proof that a Negro could escape the slums," explained Jimmy Cannon. "They yearned for him to last forever. It made them ache because he could be defeated. It didn't matter that Charles was black. He had beaten Louis, and they would not forgive him. He had stolen something from their lives."

All the kind letters and telegrams Joe received afterward softened the hurt, but he ignored the pleas from his mother and handlers and decided to break his promise. Two weeks after his mauling by Charles he decided that he would continue his comeback. For one thing, he owed a ton of money, far more than the $102,840 (before expenses and taxes were deducted) he had received for the fight. For another, he was in denial. He wasn't convinced that Charles had whipped him but had merely taken advantage of his abbreviated training. Regaining the championship was a possibility, assuming he rebuilt carefully. Any number of mediocre heavyweights could be used to climb back into contention.

"I was an old man now," Joe said in his autobiography, "but still dangerous with somebody who wasn't as good as Charles. The government wanted their money, and I had to try and get it to them. Whether I was some kind of symbol or not didn't matter to them—Jim Norris booked me to fight Cesar Brion in Chicago on November 29."

The lanky Argentinian had scored knockouts in half of his American victories, but his ten-round loss to Louis exposed him as the mediocre fighter he was. Afterward it was back to Pompton Lakes, where Joe continued to shake off years of accumulated rust. He ran five miles a day for five weeks before squaring off with Freddie Beshore on January 3, 1951, at Olympia Stadium. It was his first professional fight in Detroit since he knocked out Abe Simon a decade earlier. Cheered on by a partisan crowd of 13,000, the arena's largest boxing crowd in three years, he was obviously feeling his oats. He looked to be in fighting trim at 210 pounds. He controlled the tempo from the start and landed hard, accurate hooks and jabs almost at will.

Beshore, a twenty-six-year-old ex-sailor from Harrisburg, Pennsylvania, had lasted fourteen rounds with Ezzard Charles the previous August before a cut ear allowed Charles to retain the title. Against Louis he took a methodical beating. His nose was bleeding in the first round, his left eye sliced open in the second, and his mouthpiece knocked flying in the third and again in the fourth. The referee finally stopped the slaughter with twelve seconds left in the fourth frame. Joe, who said he had trained harder than at any time since the second Conn fight, was unmarked and barely panting at the end. Observers called it Joe's most impressive showing since knocking out Tami Mauriello in 1946.

Afterward the victor suggested a telegram be sent to John DaGross. The secretary of the Pennsylvania Boxing Commission had recently stated that Louis be retired "for the good of boxing."

"Ask him how he feels now," Joe laughed.

Joe's apparent return to form had Jim Norris musing of a possible June rematch with Ezzard Charles. "There's no way to compare his improvement over the showing against Cesar Brion in Chicago last month," he cautioned. "I don't know whether Joe's reached his peak or not, but he's come a long way."

Joe's next tune-up scrap was against Omelio Agramonte at Miami Stadium on February 7. Beshore had crowded Joe, letting his heavy legs off easy. Agramonte, who had fought two exhibitions against Joe the previous year, had the benefit of this experience and his mobility. Joe chased the 187-pound Cuban for ten rounds during the outdoor battle, bloodying his mouth, cutting his eye, and staggering him on several occasions. Agramonte was hanging on for dear life when the final bell sounded. Joe won easily on points, but was disappointed in not being able to catch him long enough to measure him for a good-night punch.

Sixteen days later Joe scored a technical knockout of Andy Walker in the tenth round at the Cow Palace in San Francisco. The series of one-night stands continued with a rematch with Agramonte at Detroit's Olympia on May 2. None of the judges gave the bicycling Cuban more than one round. In the second he was belted to the mat—Joe's first knockdown since his comeback began—but he rose at the count of nine and managed to last the fight.

Joe had now won five straight in the wake of his loss to Charles, but veteran observers knew the victories had come at the expense of lesser fighters. "Joe Doesn't Know the Truth, He's That Bad," read the headline in

the next day's *Detroit News*. "Old Joe Louis, in winning his decision, was little more than a clinical study for biologists who might be concerned over
what happens to muscles and reflexes of an aging athlete," wrote Paul
Chandler.

His punch was gone, his footwork was clumsy, he couldn't
defend against a right hand, he telegraphed everything he threw
except light flicks, and was bedazed when he had a knockout
opportunity.

Even on a clinical basis, it wasn't enjoyable, and a psycholog-
ical portion of the study was more discouraging.

When the examiners reached Old Joe Louis after the fight he
seemed to think he had done quite well. "A hard man to fight,"
said the Bomber, in a series of short, panting sentences. "I'm
happy about this one because it proved I can go 10 rounds without getting tired . . . I'm satisfied I can throw my right hand . . .
My right didn't show up much tonight 'cause he weaves away
from a right . . . Sure I want to fight Savold, then Charles . . . He
hurt me just once, with one in the belly."

Here, certainly was evidence that Louis doesn't understand
that he's slipped so far.

Before the second Agramonte fight Joe had signed to meet Lee Savold
in June at the Polo Grounds. The thirty-six-year-old former bartender was
over the hill, but still recognized by the British Board of Control as the
world's champion. Ticket sales didn't figure to top 8,000.

A wonderful thing happened, however. Moved indoors by rain, the
fight drew mobs of late-arriving fans. So many people stormed the Madison
Square Garden box office that the IBC received permission to move the 10
P.M. start back fifteen minutes. When all the heads and receipts had been
counted, it was revealed that some 18,000 had paid more than $90,000 for
the privilege of watching King Joe, who had just turned thirty-seven,
administer a royal beating. It was the biggest gathering at the Garden since
Louis had met Walcott three and a half years earlier. The absence of radio
or TV coverage played a part in the last-minute rush for pasteboards. But
thousands more were driven by a blend of obligation and nostalgia. Fight
fans, by and large, are uncommonly sentimental anyway. Having shared in
Joe's greatest triumphs when he and they were young, they were here at the
end to demonstrate that they still admired him, still appreciated what he
had meant to them when the country and the sport had needed him most.

In his seventeenth year as a professional, Joe once again came through
for his fans. His camp insisted that for the last several fights he had been

saving his hands, pacing himself. On this night his fists were like pistons—firing faster than since before the war, some said. By the sixth round he had mashed his opponent's nose, so that blood covered Savold's face from forehead to chin, was smeared over both men's torsos, and stained the mat. With less than a minute remaining in the round, a left hook deposited Savold on the seat of his pants. He sat there in a dazed heap while the referee flashed fingers: *One . . . two . . . three . . .*

They were on their feet inside the Garden, their ears straining to pick up the count in the din, their outstretched necks poking through shrouds of cigar smoke. The squinty-eyed multitudes could just as well have been peering through the mists of time. For here was the Joe Louis of old, they bubbled as his arm was raised in triumph, the fabled figure whose legend had been gilded by yet another prone body. "Did you see that combination, the old left-right?" one celebrant said excitedly. "Great, absolutely great, Champ," another yelled at Joe. Afterward Milton Berle, Walter Winchell, and other celebrities poured into the noisy dressing room, already swollen with writers and hangers-on. "Can't say I've ever been happier," said Joe, enveloped by the old, familiar tumult. In the mad flush of celebration, few suspected that they had witnessed the last knockout of the Brown Bomber's career.

Joe's purses were averaging about $15,000 in this new edition of the Bum-of-the-Month Club. He had received $13,350 from the Beshore fight, for instance, and about $16,000 (a poor gate swelled by $10,000 in television rights) for the second Agramonte match. Any working stiff would have been overjoyed by these payouts. In 1951, Detroit's auto workers were pulling down $72.45 for a forty-hour week, while the average major-league ballplayer was making $13,300 for the season. But Joe's ring earnings were just spit in the ocean of debt he was floundering in.

"More money I made, the more the government took," he said of this period. "And when my lawyers and the tax people got together, I was really in the dark. I knew I owed the government $50,000 a year just in interest and penalties, and that wasn't even touching the main tax . . . Had to keep working to pay taxes, but the more I worked, the less I had. I couldn't afford to sit on my ass, either."

In July, visions of a second Louis-Charles championship fight evaporated when Jersey Joe Walcott, who had lost all four of his previous title fights, unexpectedly lifted the belt with a seventh-round knockout of Charles. Joe knew that Walcott, having finally scaled the mountaintop, would want to savor the view for a while. All Joe could do was keep on slogging through the ranks and wait his turn at Walcott.

On the first day of August in San Francisco, Joe re-acquainted himself with Cesar Brion, a 12-1 underdog. This time around the crowd of 12,000 got its money's worth, as the two pummeled each other from the opening bell. Game and tough, Brion crowded Joe and scored with left jabs and flurries of body punches. Joe's wallops ultimately wore down the twenty-four-year-old South American, who had initially surprised and confused him by switching from a standup position to a crouch. Up through the halfway point Brion entertained high hopes of foiling his opponent, "but Louis was just too smart," he admitted. Joe got the hard-earned decision, but both fighters left the ring to long applause.

Two weeks later Joe scored a unanimous decision over Jimmy Bivins in Baltimore. He fought at only 203 pounds, his lowest since the Lou Nova fight ten years earlier, but still twenty-three pounds heavier than Bivins. The thirty-one-year-old Cleveland fighter, who in some circles had been referred to as the uncrowned heavyweight champion while Louis was away in uniform during the war, wasn't interested in mixing it up with his boyhood idol, with the result that the Bomber was only able to land a half-dozen decent shots with his famed right. "I was just too light to get that right hand over," Joe told the press. "No question about it, I was five pounds too light."

Most discouraging was his inability to finish off Bivins as he threw everything he had at him in a final-minute flurry. Bivins, still active today training teenagers on the west side of Cleveland, remembered that at the weigh-in Joe had uncharacteristically told him he was going to knock him out in four rounds. Responded Bivins: "You have to hit me first."

"I didn't get angry then," said Bivins. "I knew I wasn't going to stand right there and let him hit me. I respected him as a fighter. But knocking me out—he just wasn't going to do it. A lot of guys go out there and as soon as Joe Louis waves at him, he hits the deck. In order for me to hit the deck, he'd have to hit me on the chin so I could feel it. I wasn't one of those guys who was braggadocios. But I wasn't afraid of him 'cause I could box too. He might have slowed up a bit, but he still could punch. He could punch same as he always did. He never did lose that zip, that punch with that power."

Coming along at this time was a twenty-eight-year-old brawler from Brockton, Massachusetts, named Rocco Marchegiano, a.k.a. Rocky Marciano. Although he hadn't had his first boxing lesson until he was twenty-three years old (an age when Louis had already won the championship), his sledgehammer right hand needed no tutoring. The tenth-grade dropout had fought some amateur bouts during his army days, then kept in the sport while working at a series of manual labor jobs. In 1948 he caught the eye of fight manager Al Weill and trainer Charley Goldman. He was a fireplug of a fighter, with 190 well-packed pounds on a five-foot-eleven frame. He had stubby, muscular arms—his reach was only sixty-seven inches, ten less than Louis's—which forced him to mix things up close. Under

Weill and Goldman he won his first thirty-seven pro bouts, all but five by knockouts. Jim Norris recognized Marciano as a drawing card that could revive the somnolent heavyweight division. He offered Joe a $300,000 guarantee to meet Marciano on October 26 at the Garden.

There was a sense of foreboding among Joe's handlers. "None of us wanted him to fight Marciano," said Marshall Miles. "We begged him to retire. Truthfully, he was over the hill. That's why he held out for the kind of deal we got."

Bookmakers made Joe a slight 6-5 favorite, offering odds of 13-5 that he wouldn't knock out Marciano and 4-1 that Marciano wouldn't kayo Joe. Many on press row were pulling unashamedly for Louis. Mannie Seamon's strategy was for his fighter to try for the early knockout; he knew Joe couldn't go the full ten rounds.

The fight attracted a packed house and a national TV audience. According to Seamon, "I could tell early in the fight that Joe wasn't going to be able to handle Rocky. He wasn't punching with that old zing." At times Joe appeared to be a matador, fending off bull rushes and wildly thrown punches that left Marciano practically pitching onto his face. Meanwhile, Joe's left jab scored, opening cuts below and above both of Marciano's eyes. "Then in the eighth round," continued Seamon, "Rocky caught Joe with a barrage of punches and he went down."

Marciano's second knockdown left the proud but spent former champion sprawled half out of the ring. In the harsh glare of the bright overhead lamps he suddenly looked old, helpless, pathetic, his head hanging over the rope and the light reflecting off his bald spot. Seamon and Sugar Ray Robinson, both choking back tears, jumped onto the apron before the referee finished the count and helped Joe to his corner. John Roxborough later heard Al Weill bragging about Marciano's victory. "My boy knocked out the great Joe Louis," Weill said. "Al," said Roxie, "your boy didn't knock out the great Joe Louis. He beat Joe Louis's shadow."

The coverage of the *Detroit News* was more cruel than clever. Above a spread of three fight photos, all showing Joe in a sad heap on the mat, ran the following head and subhead:

Last Of Unusually Inspiring Star
Lethargic, Old, Unfit, Inept, Sad

Marciano, who had grown up idolizing Joe, said in the dressing room, "I feel sorry for Joe. I'm glad I won, but I feel sorry." The following year he kayoed Jersey Joe Walcott to gain the title. While never a great technical boxer, Marciano would prove a popular champion, taking on all comers before finally retiring in 1956 with a perfect 49-0 record—forty-three by knockouts. Although he was only thirty-one, he vowed never to return to the ring. "I thought it was a mistake when Joe Louis tried a comeback," he said.

During the Labor Day weekend in 1969, Joe was in Charlotte, North Carolina, to referee a wrestling match. He had just walked into his hotel room when a phone call informed him that Marciano had been killed in an airplane crash near Des Moines, Iowa. Shocked to his core—Marciano would have turned forty-six the next day—Joe asked the caller to find out about funeral arrangements.

"I want to be there," he said. "Send flowers for the funeral home and also to his wife."

A couple of days later Joe entered St. Pius Church in Fort Lauderdale to pay his respects to the man who had so convincingly ended his comeback attempt eighteen years earlier.

"When Louis arrived at the church," related Stanley Weston of *The Ring*, "he mingled very briefly with the other celebrities, then walked up to the closed, flower-draped casket and, to the astonishment of all who watched, leaned over and kissed it."

That Joe's gentle buss was not captured by the knot of press photographers on hand, continued Weston, "proves that Joe's gesture was one of impulse and deep emotion, and certainly not for self-serving reasons. When you remember that Marciano had ended Louis's career by brutalizing him as no one had ever brutalized him before, the human side of Joseph Louis Barrow was equal to the legend immortalized by his fists."

This tender scene was in the future, a place Joe rarely visited. In the late hours of an autumn evening in 1951, it was his career that the battered Brown Bomber was kissing goodbye. As the national television audience was shown film of his 1938 demolition of Max Schmeling, he lay on a trainer's table, his pummeled flesh slowly swelling like a zeppelin taking on helium. "An old man's dream ended," Red Smith eulogized. "A young man's vision of the future opened wide. Young men have visions, old men have dreams. But the place for old men is beside the fire."

Chapter Eleven

No Joe Louis, No Jackie Robinson

Somebody'd say, "Yeah, how about that? All those years, man, we was down on the plantation in those shacks, eating just potatoes and fatback and chitterlin's and greens, and look at what happened. We had Joe Louises and Jack Johnsons and Sugar Ray Robinsons and Henry Armstrongs, all that sort of thing."

Somebody'd say, "Yeah, man, Niggers must be some real strong people who just can't be kept down. When you think about it, that's really something great. Fatback, chitterlin's, greens, and Joe Louis. Negroes are some beautiful people. Uh-huh. Fatback, chitterlin's, greens, and Joe Louis. . . ."

— CLAUDE BROWN, *Manchild in the Promised Land*

$\mathcal{T}$hose sizing Joe for an easy chair after his loss to Marciano didn't take into account his overdue taxes, which were growing exponentially because of penalties and interest. Ironically, at the same time his spirit was being assaulted by one branch of the government, another branch—the Defense Department—employed him as a morale builder. In the fall of 1951, with U.S. troops knee-deep in a murderous "police action" in Korea, he went on a tour of military installations around the Far East. One day he fought a half-dozen exhibitions in Tokyo. On another he defied logistics by fighting an exhibition in Sanda, Japan, and then later that day knocking out a boxer named Chang Pulu in Taipei, Formosa. On December 16, 1951, twenty-one long years after he had first signed up for instruction inside the musty Brewster gym, the flabby former champion put on a final three-round show in Taipei with his touring partner, Corporal B. J. DeCordova. Then he left for America, $20,000 richer. When he visited Detroit the following year, he told reporters he wouldn't even know where to find a pair of trunks or gloves.

Retirement proved to be a mixed bag. Joe admitted to missing the cheers of a packed arena and the six-figure checks, but otherwise he enjoyed the prospect of never again having to run five miles at dawn or absorb a fist to the jaw. The problem was making enough money to maintain at least a semblance of the high style of living he had become accustomed to while also taking care of his monumental debt.

It was an impossible task. Joe, who continued to live in New York when he wasn't dropping in on his many friends around the country, derived the bulk of his income from the International Boxing Club, which paid him a $20,000 annual salary, and the small public relations agency on West 57th Street in Manhattan that he had started with publicist-columnist Billy Rowe prior to the Billy Conn fight in 1946. While Rowe managed the day-to-day details of Louis-Rowe Enterprises, Joe's role was to dine with clients. His fame and less-than-onerous duties gave him plenty of opportunities to do what he enjoyed most: playing golf with friends, making personal appearances, glad-handing businessmen, and visiting his mother in Detroit and his two children in Chicago. Marva allowed Joe, who was obligated to pay $5,000 a year in child support, to see Jackie and Punchy whenever he wished. "I was, I'd say, having a good time with no worries except taxes," he said later.

A little over a year after Joe returned from his tour of the Orient, *The Joe Louis Story* went into production in Hollywood. Twentieth Century Fox spent $400,000 on the movie, which was produced by Sterling Silliphant and starred a Golden Gloves champion named Coley Wallace in the lead role. When the production company ran out of money, Billy Rowe invested $15,000 of his own money in the project, which he considered a can't-miss proposition.

Hollywood has always had an affection for boxing, what with its inherent drama and colorful personalities. Since 1910 there have been more than four hundred movies featuring the fight game, including such well-received efforts as *Requiem for a Heavyweight*, *On the Waterfront*, and *Rocky*. A handful of actors, including Robert DeNiro in *Raging Bull* and Wallace Beery in *The Champ*, have earned Oscars for their portrayals of prizefighters. It seemed that Louis's sharecropper-to-champion story would be a natural for the big screen. But Coley Wallace and the storyline were both as stiff as cardboard. The movie opened in New York in the fall of 1953 and, despite a generous review in the *New York Times*, failed to pack theatres. It turned out to be just one more financial flop associated with Joe's name, which remained bankable despite news of his divorce, love suits, tax woes, and many business failures.

Six weeks after *The Joe Louis Story* premiered, Joe's mother passed away. It was just a few days before Christmas when she and Joe had talked of getting the entire family together for a big holiday feast. That evening, Joe was having dinner at a restaurant when a phone call informed him that Lillie Barrow Brooks—"my number-one fan, my number-one advisor, my momma"—had suffered a heart attack. Two days later she died.

"Who ever believes their mother can die?" Joe reflected years later, adding: "It took me a long, long time to get myself together."

The IRS contributed to his fragile emotional state, pressing ahead with its demands for payment. (It eventually seized Joe's share of his mother's estate—$667.) Joe did what he could to get the government off his back. For a while he made appearances for a circus traversing the Southwest. Small-town papers were filled with photos of him warily eyeing a herd of elephants or uneasily brandishing a whip inside a cage of lions. He also was in demand as a wrestling referee. In 1954 he got $2,000 a night and frequently was billed over the wrestlers. For four months' work he received an estimated $40,000, of which a good chunk went to pay current and back taxes.

In 1956 two trust funds that Marva had set up for their children—a total of $65,688—were seized when a federal tax court ruled that the money she had used to establish the accounts had properly belonged to the government. There was growing public sympathy for Joe's plight, with youngsters mailing him dimes and groups as diverse as local Kiwanis clubs and the Harlem Globetrotters staging benefits. The popular opinion was that the IRS was unduly harassing one of America's greatest idols, but Joe didn't see it that way. He'd spent hundreds of thousands of dollars that had legitimately belonged to the government, and like any other taxpaying citizen he was expected to pay it back—no matter how ludicrous that possibility seemed. By now Joe's debt stood at $1,243,097. The *U.S. News & World Report* estimated that Joe would have to earn an average of at least $310,000 a year for the next twenty years to pay this debt (including accumulating interest) and to keep up with current income taxes.

It was no mystery, then, why Joe ignored the protests of friends and family and accepted a promoter's guarantee of $100,000 to go on the wrestling circuit. "We all begged, 'Joe, please don't do it,'" remembered Freddie Guinyard. "We all felt it was beneath his dignity."

It was no use. Forty-one hundred people were on hand on March 16, 1956, at the Uline Arena in Washington, D.C., to watch Joe, his belly sagging over the waistband of his tights, make his wrestling debut. Joe, of course, was always to be cast as the "good guy" in these choreographed morality plays. The "bad guy" his first time out was a 320-pound ex-cowboy named Rocky Lee, who kept Joe wrapped up for most of their ten-minute bout until referee Jersey Joe Walcott (another fighter in dire financial straits) pulled Lee off. The crowd roared in approval as Joe then dispatched the villain with a forearm to the chops.

Joe's new career was short-lived. During a match in Columbus, Ohio, Lee messed up the choreography. Instead of seizing Joe in a headlock, he jumped on him, breaking two of his ribs and bruising his heart. Joe took some time off to recuperate, but when he tried to return he was refused a license. To the relief of his admirers, he quit.

The spectacle of the former world's heavyweight champion, who in the boxing ring had been the symbol of integrity, engaging in such a transparently bogus "sport" had been too painful for many to watch. One observer compared the comedown to "having Edwin Booth switch from the magnificence of Shakespearean roles to slapstick burlesque." Another said it was like "the President of the United States washing dishes." Joe addressed the critics in his typically dignified, pithy way. "It ain't stealing," he said.

For that he could have turned to his partners in the International Boxing Club for some lessons. Throughout the 1950s he should have received some healthy dividends from his IBC stock holdings, but his naivete and disinterest allowed him to be robbed of a small fortune. By the early part of the decade Jim Norris controlled most of boxing's major fighters, arenas, championships, and network television coverage. The IBC's monopoly was so pervasive the press dubbed the organization the "Octopus." By 1955 its tentacles were pulling in $90,000 a week in television revenue alone. But Norris, like Mike Jacobs, had a seamy side, consorting with racketeers like Frankie Carbo and Blinky Palermo to fix matches and arranging with partner Art Wirtz to hide profits. Joe's original role as the IBC's chief promoter had been almost immediately assumed by Truman Gibson, who participated in the shenanigans and wound up taking a good deal of the heat when the Justice Department investigated the inner workings of the Octopus. The IBC was declared an illegal monopoly and ordered dissolved in 1957, a decision upheld by the U.S. Supreme Court in January of 1959. Norris kept Joe on the payroll of a successor company, National Boxing Enterprises. But when that organization folded, Joe was out of a regular salary. The total payout of his promised profits from the IBC, of which he had once been the centerpiece, was zero.

Ben Bentley, who handled the IBC's public relations at Chicago Stadium, regularly crossed paths with Joe during the fifties. "Well, it bothered him," he said of Joe's problems, "but he was the kind of guy who never let it appear to bother him. He didn't think he was going to have to go to jail."

That was Joe's public persona. Close friends Sugar Ray Robinson and Jesse Owens remembered it differently. Both recalled scenes where Joe, discussing his situation in private, broke down and cried. "You don't think they'd put me in jail, do you?" he'd sob.

There was little chance of a national hero landing in the slammer, but the IRS remained resolute that the full amount should somehow be paid. It had already turned down an offer of compromise prepared by Truman Gibson, who argued unconvincingly that the tax code punished prizefighters, whose income tended to fluctuate wildly from year to year. If any good came out of the debate over Joe's indebtedness, it was that it helped highlight such fair and creative ideas as income averaging and deferred taxes, both of which would become a reality in the sixties.

Many people in high places still hadn't forgotten Joe's contributions to the nation. One such person was Representative Alfred Sieminsky. The New Jersey Democrat introduced a bill to erase Joe's debt. It failed to pass, but the IRS soon came to an understanding with Louis. He would be required to pay $20,000 a year toward his unpaid tax bill (which didn't even cover the interest) as well as taxes on his current income.

"I must have been earning about $33,000," he recalled, "and when I paid $12,000 tax on the $33,000, plus the $20,000, I'd only have $1,000 left. You know, something like that can depress a man." Thankfully for Joe, he was not given to long periods of morosity, no matter how bleak things looked. In October 1954, he was inducted into the Boxing Hall of Fame, joining such storied fighters as Jack Dempsey and Henry Armstrong. To Joe, that meant he "wouldn't be forgotten . . . maybe a hundred years from now some little black boy would be thumbing some book or magazine and be glad that I had been born."

About this time his wandering eye settled on Rose Morgan, a tall, curvaceous businesswoman who Joe described as "sweet, open, sensible." Morgan had moved to New York from Chicago several years earlier and opened a large and successful beauty shop in a three-story brownstone on 148th Street near St. Nicholas Avenue. Many considered it Harlem's finest. When he proposed to her one day in 1955, Rose asked him how he knew he'd like to live the rest of his life with her.

"Who said I was going to live the rest of my life with you?" he replied, drawing a laugh from his bride-to-be.

They were married on Christmas Day; in short order she realized that she had made a mistake. Although Rose felt important being around the man everybody in Harlem still addressed as "Champ," and Joe displayed great affection toward his new mate, he clearly viewed the marriage as one of convenience.

His convenience, of course. Although she now took care of his bills, he had no intention of changing his deeply ingrained habits, which generally revolved around playing golf in the afternoon and then hitting the nightclubs with his cronies until the early hours of the morning. Rose, who had a business to operate, sometimes was getting up to go to work scant minutes after her husband had plopped into bed.

"I tried to make him settle down," she once explained. "I told him he couldn't sleep all day and stay out all night any more. Once he asked me why not, and I told him I'd worry and wouldn't be able to sleep. So he said he'd wait till I fell asleep before going out. Well, I stayed up till 4 A.M.—and then *he* fell asleep."

Joe also continued to see other women. He usually rendezvoused with them at his apartment at 555 Edgecombe. In frustration, Rose went there one day and removed all of the sheets. It didn't matter; he still refused to give up his bachelor's sanctuary.

Rose tried to straighten out her husband's finances. Joe, who enjoyed watching quiz shows, was surprised to learn that Rose had written the producers of several of them and arranged for their participation. He appeared on *Masquerade Party*, a nighttime show where well-known celebrities were disguised and then asked questions by panelists attempting to ascertain their real identities. Joe and Rose both appeared on *High Finance*, a Saturday night show hosted by Dennis James. Contestants could win or lose money based on how well they answered questions about current events. Rose and Joe—who had excellent memories to start with—read the newspapers as never before and wound up winning about $60,000 between them in six weeks. The IRS seized Joe's share, but could not legally touch Rose's $30,000. It didn't matter; Joe quickly went through Rose's winnings.

Her husband's free-spending ways exasperated Rose, who for years had had to meet a weekly payroll for dozens of employees. She helped arrange for a cologne manufacturer to produce a Joe Louis men's fragrance called My Man. At the bank where he went to cash a royalty check, he ran into a friend who complained that she needed to have her teeth fixed. When it came to shaking down Joe, any excuse would do. Without further questioning, he pulled $200 out of his pocket and handed it to her.

In the summer of 1957, after a year and a half of living together, the two agreed to an amicable separation. The following year they had the marriage annulled. This meant it had never existed—a legal fine point that in this case was an accurate characterization. That the cosmetics queen of

Harlem was not as financially well off as Joe had first imagined made the split easier for him to take.

When they were married Joe and Rose often invited another well-known couple, Jackie and Rachel Robinson, over for the evening. Robinson's life story had already become as familiar and inspiring to America's blacks as Joe's. Tightly wound and intensely private, he could relax around Joe. Like him, he had been born in the South, the grandson of slaves. When he was a child his family left Georgia for California, where he made a national name for himself as a four-sport star at UCLA. The All American halfback (among other honors) was called "the Jim Thorpe of his race."

In the army during the war, Robinson was called nigger once too often for his liking. After Joe had helped get Robinson off the hook for the 1943 incident in which he had punched out a white officer at Fort Riley, Jackie was transferred to Fort Hood, Texas. There the fiery lieutenant—admittedly inspired by Joe's well-publicized scuffle with MP's at an army camp in Alabama—got into an altercation with a white bus driver on post. He was court-martialed, acquitted, and subsequently discharged "for the good of the service," said Truman Gibson, then a War Department aide.

Meanwhile, the chief executive of the Brooklyn Dodgers, Branch Rickey, was unilaterally deciding to break major league baseball's unofficial color bar. Given the times, he understood the key was not necessarily getting the most talented Negro player available. More important was signing someone who had the courage to walk away from the daily provocation that would be an inevitable part of his game. Baseball's Chosen One had to be nonthreatening, inoffensive, and palatable to whites. According to some accounts, Rickey at one point instructed his chief scout, "Get me someone just like Joe Louis."

Clyde Sukeforth is still alive and well in Maine, where he has been besieged of late for golden-anniversary memories of Rickey's historic signing. He doesn't remember ever receiving that specific instruction, though it's entirely possible that at some point Rickey said those words to someone in the organization. Sukeforth also disavowed quotes attributed to him in a contemporary magazine article that had him unfavorably comparing Louis to Jack Dempsey and several other white champions of the past. "I didn't even follow boxing back then," he insisted. For that matter he hardly followed the Negro leagues, whose success during the war years had demonstrated to his boss the great box-office potential of fielding black players.

Sukeforth watched Robinson play with the Kansas City Monarchs during the summer of 1945. Had anybody bothered to ask Negro leaguers their opinion of the best player available, it's a good bet that nobody would have named the dour, combative, first-year shortstop. Plenty would have been chosen before him, fellows that had spent years polishing their craft and paying their dues. As the fictional Negro leaguer Troy Maxson exploded bitterly in August Wilson's *Fences*: "I done seen a hundred niggers play baseball better than Jackie Robinson. Hell, I know some teams Jackie Robinson couldn't even make! What you talking about Jackie Robinson. Jackie Robinson wasn't nobody. I'm talking about if you could play ball then they ought to have let you play. Don't care what color you were. Come telling me I come along too early. If you could play . . . then they ought to have let you play."

This kind of outburst was not uncommon to Robinson, who impressed Rickey with his intelligence and inner strength. Still, he had to promise Rickey that he would keep his temper in check for his first three seasons before the beetle-browed emancipator finally decided to make him the man who would lead a social revolution.

Robinson's signing on October 23, 1945, was front-page news in every paper in the country. To many of those familiar with how Louis had conducted himself, the integration of organized baseball seemed a natural and overdue progression from his line of work. Reasoned one North Carolina sportswriter: "The Negro and the white man are opponents in the ring, why not the baseball diamond?"

Robinson, who was assigned to Brooklyn's top farm club in Montreal for the 1946 season, was regularly reminded by the black press that he could benefit from following the solid example Joe had set for demeanor and sportsmanship. "None of our scholars, scientists, artists, or writers has received the popular accolades or acclaim" that have been Louis's, stated the *Pittsburgh Courier*. Although many in organized ball grumbled and awaited Robinson's inevitable promotion to the parent club, New York columnist Jimmy Cannon went on the radio and lambasted the national pastime as "a game of prejudice." He added, "Having Jim Crow as an umpire in organized baseball is laughable when you realize what a fine champion Joe Louis has been." Robinson's response to the commotion surrounding his playing was always about the same. "I'll try to do as good a job as Joe Louis has done," he promised. "He has done a great job for us, and I will try to carry on."

Robinson's breakthrough captured the imagination of black America like nothing since the Brown Bomber's march to the championship in the 1930s. He dominated the editorial coverage of the Negro press and caused youngsters to alter the setting of their fantasies from the prize ring to the baseball diamond. Growing up in Detroit, Ron Teasley had patterned himself after the local hero. "I used to try to walk like Joe. I parted my hair like he did. He was the strong, silent type, so I took on that air myself." Most of that went out the window when Robinson was signed. "I started walking pigeon-toed like Jackie," chuckled Teasley, who was good enough to play briefly in the Dodgers' farm system in the early fifties.

Elston Howard was a young sandlotter in St. Louis at the time. "I was sixteen and already dreaming of a baseball career, but not in organized ball," he later told the *Sporting News*. "A friend of mine came into the store and said, 'Ellie, have you heard the news? Branch Rickey has signed one of our boys. His name is Jackie Robinson.' I felt like dancing all over that floor. The path was opening up. Maybe I could become a major league player." Howard's once unthinkable wish came true in 1955, when he integrated the New York Yankees. Deeply rooted prejudice didn't automatically fall by the wayside, however. Manager Casey Stengel remarked of his slow-footed rookie: "Well, they finally get me a nigger, I get the only one who can't run."

In 1946, as Robinson endured beanballs, spikings, and protests during his year of minor league seasoning in the International League, Baltimore sportswriter Sam Lacy wrote that he hoped his son would grow up to be a combination of black America's two greatest role models. "I'd want him to combine the wisdom of Joe Louis with the courage of Jackie Robinson. I'd hope for him to have Jackie's ability to hold his head high in adversity, the willingness to withstand the butts and digs and meanness of those who envy him."

In the spring of 1947 Branch Rickey asked Joe to talk to Robinson in New York. Also present were Paul Robeson and Bojangles Robinson. They were called in to explain to Jackie what might be in store for him as the Dodgers prepared to field the first black major leaguer of the twentieth century.

"We didn't need to say anything to Jackie," Joe said later. "He'd been in the army, he knew just what to look for. He knew he'd have to be strong and take the shit, or he'd close the door for black people in baseball for Lord knows how many more years." Joe admitted that he "felt real good when Jackie said that if wasn't for me and Jesse Owens, he wouldn't be where he was."

Robinson made his big-league debut at first base on April 15, 1947, against the Boston Braves in Brooklyn. From the start he created fans out of thousands of blacks who didn't know a baseball from a turnip, but who nonetheless cheered deliriously whenever he did anything on the field. It got to be embarrassing, people screeching when he gloved a simple pop fly or grounded weakly to the mound. But as Joe had learned, goo-goo-eyed fanaticism was part of the package for racial crusaders.

So were the slurs, hate mail, and death threats. The field microphone at Ebbets Field had to be removed because the vile language directed at Robinson was going out over the air. It was against Robinson's nature not to lash out at injustice and narrow-mindedness, but he choked back his anger, channeling it instead into a brand of daring, creative, hard-nosed baseball that hadn't been seen in big-league parks for years. Bill "Bojangles" Robinson dubbed him "Ty Cobb in Technicolor." He handled his ordeal so courageously millions of Americans, both black and white, openly expressed their admiration and support.

Tommy Henrich of the Yankees played against him in the 1947 World Series. "The first time Jackie got on base he didn't say hello to me and I didn't say hello to him," said Henrich. "Of course, he was that type of guy. I knew he was tough. I knew what he had to take in the International League and I admired him for it. He could take anything and he could hand it out, too. He'd say, 'I'm not afraid of any of you.' That's the way he played ball."

As Robinson went on to carve out a Hall of Fame career, winning a batting title and the MVP award in 1949 and helping to spark the Dodgers to six pennants in ten seasons, he acquired the same Moses-like aura previously attached to Joe. Novelist Ernest Gaines captured this messianic feeling in his 1972 book, *The Autobiography of Miss Jane Pittmann*. "When times got really hard, really tough, He always send you somebody," his heroine observed. "In the Depression it was tough on everybody, but twice as hard on the colored, and He sent us Joe . . . after the war, He sent us Jackie." *

Joe, of course, understood full well the pressures his friend and fellow folk hero had to deal with. During his own career he had never been able to completely escape the specter of racism. When he went into training for the James Braddock fight in 1937, for example, his first pick for a site, Lake Geneva, Wisconsin, had to be scrapped because the local homeowners association didn't want Negroes in their neighborhood. Sunnie Wilson remembered when, shortly after Joe won the title, they were invited to open the annual March of Dimes charity drive in Washington, D.C., but were forced to stay at a segregated hotel. Earlier, Joe had gone on an exhibition tour to Louisiana where his guide had thrown around the word "boy" so freely that he finally had to warn him, "If you don't shut up, this boy's gonna have to kick your ass."

---

* Interestingly, there is a small piece of Joe Louis in the Baseball Hall of Fame. On July 19, 1952, twelve-year-old Joe Reliford became the youngest person ever to play a professional baseball game. That night the Class D Fitzgerald (Georgia) Pioneers were getting pounded by Statesboro, 13-0, when the restless crowd began chanting, "Put in the batboy!"

"You know how people are when the game is lopsided," said Reliford, today a Baptist deacon in Douglas, Georgia. "They were looking to find some other entertainment, and I was a black batboy on an all-white baseball team." To everyone's amazement, the manager inserted the four-foot-eleven, 68-pound youngster into the lineup in the eighth inning. He lined out in his only at-bat and made two marvelous defensive plays as a right fielder. Afterward, said Reliford, the "stands emptied, and they all started running toward me. It scared me. I was a black batboy and I knew I had no business out there with those white folks. I was crying. But they were there to touch me and pat me on the back. They never finished the game. When I went back into the clubhouse, someone told me my back pockets were stuffed full of money."

Little Joe Louis Reliford, of course, had been named by his parents for the heavyweight champion of the world. Today his exhibit at Cooperstown sits directly across from one honoring Jackie Robinson.

Jesse Owens once spoke of an experience in the late 1930s when he and Joe attended a banquet together in Chicago, after which they were invited to a nearby bar. Neither man drank, which was a blessing since most of the time their hands were busy accomodating the steady stream of hellos and autograph requests from the mixed clientele.

Owens remembered the curious ritual that Joe inspired in people meeting the heavyweight champ for the first time: they threw a punch at him. "They'd throw it, not hard enough to hurt but fast enough to make contact. Then they'd be able to say that they had 'hit Joe Louis.' But they never got to say it. Like lightning Joe would block the blow just before it reached him. Then they'd nod their heads in admiration, shake his big bear hand, and walk away satisfied that Joe was indeed the best in the world."

On this particular evening a large, unsmiling white man strode up to Joe's table. "Mind if I throw one at you?" he asked.

"Go ahead, pal," said Joe, obligingly standing up.

The man feinted a left towards Joe's stomach, which was easily blocked. But as Joe turned to find his seat the stranger fired a right into his chin, knocking him against the wall.

The unexpected assault put Joe into a rage, but Owens was able to grab onto his lethal fists while yelling, "What'd you do that for, mister?"

"I can't remember all that he said," related Owens. "He began with his having his 'nigger for the week' and went on from there to just about every obscenity I'd ever heard. He was obviously sick, for some reason full of hate against the Negro, a hate he no doubt had to let out now and then or else. He hated Joe Louis in particular. Through some mental process that only a psychiatrist could explain, Joe had upset this white man's notion of the way things should be."

An anecdotal review of the fifties shows that the "way things should be" was changing dramatically, if fitfully, in postwar America. At the end of 1952, for example, the Tuskegee Institute reported that the year had passed without a single lynching for the first time since it had started monitoring such crimes in 1882. But three years later the nation was sickened by the news that fourteen-year-old Emmett Till had been kidnapped and lynched in Mississippi. His offense was talking to a white woman. In 1953, CBS took *Amos 'n' Andy* off the air, partly because of objections to the show's stereotypical depictions of blacks. But it wasn't until 1956 that the extremely popular Nat "King" Cole became the first black to headline a network television program. The variety show died a year later because major advertisers, afraid of alienating their white customers, backed off from sponsoring it. In 1959 the Boston Red Sox became the last major league team to field a black player. Although baseball was now finally a truly American pastime,

Negro ballplayers on all sixteen big-league clubs continued to be housed in separate hotels on road trips and during spring training.

Events, both trivial and pivotal, were causing well-known blacks like Lena Horne and jazz great Louis Armstrong to uncharacteristically cry out. Horne made headlines around the country by hurling an ashtray and a lamp at a drunk who made a racist remark to her inside a Beverly Hills restaurant. During the crisis in Little Rock, Arkansas, in 1957, when Governor Orval Faubus refused to integrate the school system while President Eisenhower stood idly by, Armstrong told reporters, "The way they are treating my people in the South, the government can go to hell. The President has no guts." After Eisenhower finally ordered federal troops to Little Rock, Armstrong wired his congratulations: "If you decide to walk into the schools with the colored kids, take me along, Daddy. God bless you."

Throughout this period Joe continued to make his own steady contributions to civil rights. He was a quiet revolutionary. Because of his privileged standing he could walk into most places without incident. That didn't mean he was blind to the door slamming shut on the rest of America's blacks. He had always been a "race man" in the same understated, entrepreneurial way practiced by his first adult mentor, John Roxborough. In 1939, he and a friend, Charlie Glenn, opened their Chicago nightclub, Rhumboogie (later called Swingland). It was patterned after Hollywood's Rhumboogie. Joe explained that he was looking for "a place where plain colored folks could go to enjoy and hear their own music and not to have to wait for 'nigger night'. . . ."

Joe didn't mind others capitalizing on his famous name, especially for the sake of advancing the race. The extent of his involvement in Harlem's Brown Bomber Bread Company, which apparently was started in the late thirties, isn't clear. But surely he approved of its objectives. The company proudly advertised itself as "100% Negro owned & operated." A sedan towed a trailer outfitted with a giant two-sided sign. It read:

WHAT EVERY NEGRO SHOULD KNOW

$300,000 a year, that's Harlem's bread industry. What about those 500 jobs in that industry. . . . Demand BROWN BOMBER BREAD & watch the results. . . . If $2/3$ of Harlem's Negroes buy Brown Bomber Bread . . . we guarantee a Negro pay roll of one million dollars a year.

As discussed, during the Second World War Joe was prominently featured in newsreels, recruiting posters, and the widely distributed film, *The Negro Soldier*, causing even nonfight fans to recognize him as a symbol of black achievement and national unity. According to *Time* magazine, there was a nearly uniform reaction among black audiences to Frank Capra's film, which employed Joe's smashing of Max Schmeling as an allegory: "at first they froze into hostile silence. But after 20 minutes they were applauding. For just about the first time in screen history their race was presented with honest respect. Many wanted to know: 'Are you going to show this to white people?' Asked why, they replied: 'Because it will change their attitude.'" The *Time* reviewer went on to call *The Negro Soldier* "a brave, important, and helpful event in the history of U.S. race relations."

Joe's style almost always was of a nonconfrontational and positive nature. Speaking to an assembly of Harlem schoolchildren in 1948, he said they should grow into adulthood in the same fashion that they were sitting there that day: arm against arm, black and white together. Eight years later in St. Petersburg, Florida, he donated his entire purse to the NAACP when he discovered that the audience that had turned out to watch him wrestle had been segregated. He readily accepted invitations from white, black, and mixed organizations to sit on committees that benefitted race relations, including a 1946 benefit to aid a black veteran whose eyes had been gouged out by a South Carolina policeman and a 1948 rally that battled discrimination in the American Bowling Congress.

"Dad didn't call a press conference," Joe Barrow Jr. said of his father's brushes with discrimination. "He simply went to the top, to the person who could change the situation."

Sometimes that approach worked, sometimes it didn't. Once in the late forties local custom caused him to be denied limousine service from a New Orleans hotel to the airport. He protested in writing to the president of the offending party, Eastern Airlines. When he didn't get a reply he vowed never to fly the airline again, even if it inconvenienced him during his many travels. Not only did he keep his promise, he persuaded others to do the same. He hadn't raised his voice. But unbeknownst to Eastern, over the course of thirty years his quiet boycott probably cost the airline tens of thousands of dollars.

Joe discovered the golf course to be a nicely manicured avenue of integration. More than one private club was desegregated by Joe and his entourage, though the Professional Golfers Association steadfastly refused membership to blacks. In January 1952, he was invited to play as an amateur in the San Diego Invitational, a tournament sponsored by the local Chevrolet dealers. To his chagrin he discovered that the PGA barred black pros, which on this occasion meant his buddies Eural Clark and Bill Spiller.

"Getting those fellows in is going to be the biggest battle of my life," he told the press. "I want the people to know what the PGA is. We've got another Hitler to get by." The PGA, embarrassed by the negative publicity, gradually made concessions until it finally dropped its racial barriers for good nine years later. Due in part to Joe's universal acceptance and the country's growing racial consciousness, the National Football League had already started admitting Negro athletes in 1945, followed by the National Basketball Association four years later. Within a generation the racial composition of both leagues, as well as that of major league baseball, would change from all alabaster to primarily black.

Joe's pathfinding role in desegregating sports was not overlooked at the time. One expression that made the rounds of Harlem in the late forties was, "No Joe Louis, no Jackie Robinson." That sentiment was underscored by a newspaper poll taken in Baltimore at the end of Robinson's first season with Brooklyn. Who, the *Afro-American* wanted to know, was the most popular—Louis or Robinson? The answer was not America's newest sensation, but an old favorite: Joe got 60 percent of the votes. Had a similar poll of whites also been taken, the result probably would have been even more one-sided. His image was so nonthreatening that when he fought Jersey Joe Walcott that December, hardly anybody made note of the fact that two black men were fighting for the world's heavyweight championship.

With the fiftieth anniversary of his historic breakthrough approaching, Jackie Robinson soon will be elevated to new levels of mythology. Filmmakers Spike Lee and Ken Burns are just two master storytellers due to release works based on his life. It remains to be seen how much weight Joe Louis's contributions will be given. Not that it has ever really mattered to ordinary blacks engaged in the daily struggle to be seen and heard in postwar America. Assigning credit for advances made in race relations is hardly worth arguing over, as Louis and Robinson would be the first to acknowledge. When it comes to society re-evaluating its prejudice, it's the *result* of the self-examination, not the genesis, that remains most important.

This was cleverly brought out in a cartoon that once appeared in *Negro Digest*. Two black men were talking. Said one: "If we had more Negroes like Joe Louis, things would be better for us."

"Sure nuff," said his friend. "But if we had more white folks like Joe, things would be better still."

Chapter Twelve

Your Whole Life is Your Funeral

"I heard this story," Porter said. "Back when the gas chamber was new, you know? Go back forty years or whatever. First dude they threw in there, one of the first. Somewhere down South, I guess it was. Anyway, they wanted to see how it would go, so they had some kind of a window they could look at him through, and they put a microphone in there with him. To see what he might say, you know, when he saw the gas come rolling in. Last words or whatever . . . You won't guess what he said." Porter's voice was dry, half choking. . . .

"I don't plan to try," Charlie said.

"Save me, Joe Louis," Porter said. "That's all they got. Over and over, just like that. Save me, Joe Louis. Save me, Joe Louis."

— MADISON SMARTT BELL, *Save Me, Joe Louis*

*J*oe's abysmal record as a prognosticator was legendary. His inability to correctly forecast a fight, election, hole card, or even a coin flip bordered on the incredible. During his lifetime he came out on the side of such variegated losers as Wendell Willkie, Fidel Castro, Sonny Liston, Hubert Humphrey, and the Brown Bomber Rib Shack. As a casino employee in Las Vegas he dropped chips with the speed of light—the job, if nothing else, guaranteed him an unlimited supply of house money to play with. Even Joe's personal judgment of his finest fight, the 1935 bout with Max Baer, was rejected by *The Ring*, which explained that "no author is the best judge of his own work." But in selecting his third wife, a woman with a limitless resevoir of strength and compassion, he came up with a winner who would see him through the most difficult chapter of his life.

Tommy Tucker, who for many years operated a Los Angeles bar called Tommy Tucker's Playroom, knew Martha Malone Jefferson was carrying a torch for his friend. "I'm in love with that big guy," she announced one day. "I'm going to marry him."

Tucker relayed the news to Joe: "Hey man, Martha says she's in love with you."

Martha, a year older than Joe, had been born in Texas and schooled at Tuskegee Institute. She earned her law degree from Southwestern University in Chula Vista and became the first black woman to practice law in California. She was married for seven years to Bernard Jefferson, who later became a California Superior Court judge. Always pragmatic, she continued to practice law with him after they were divorced. She later described her first husband as someone who had been "exposed to books, not life," which presumably is why she found someone who had lived enough for twenty-five men so intriguing.

She first met Joe through the efforts of a mutual friend. Martha always considered boxing "silliness." She later kidded him that it was a good thing the date was prearranged "because I never would have stood in line to meet you." Her intelligence and candor made her very formidable, but the sheet-metal exterior disguised a marshmallow interior.

Joe mulled over the news from Tommy Tucker. His favorite activities remained, in no particular order, golf, television, and sex. "I've got one girl in Texas, one in Detroit," he said thoughtfully. "Martha's got the best chance. I want to stay out here and play golf."

And so he did. One day in 1959 they were married in a civil ceremony in Winterhaven, California. Henceforth dunning notices from the IRS were delivered to Martha's ten-room Spanish-style home in Los Angeles. For Joe's viewing convenience she had eight televisions placed throughout the house, including one in the bathroom.

Martha wasn't glamorous like Marva Trotter or Rose Morgan, but she was "easy to be around," said Joe, who nicknamed her "Sergeant." Not long after the wedding ceremony they took off for Hawaii, where she watched Joe perform in a new nightclub act put together by old friend Leonard Reed. A highlight of the skit was when the short, pencil-thin Reed knocked down his much larger buddy. Martha couldn't decide whether the routine was dumb, degrading, or both. A reviewer tried to be kind: "The concensus was that as a song and dance man, [Joe] was a tremendous boxer."

Later that year Joe journeyed to one of his favorite playgrounds, Cuba, where the sexes and races had freely comingled for years under the approving eye of its corrupt dictator, Fulgencio Batista. A year earlier rebel leader Fidel Castro had ousted Batista, a coup that initially drew American approval. However, Castro was soon denouncing the United States and cozying up to the Soviet Union. To the horror of the State Department, the Louis-Rowe public relations agency announced that it had landed what it considered a plum account: promoting Cuba's national Institute of Tourism. At the height of the Cold War, Joe was photographed at a New Year's banquet in Havana, where he was Castro's honored guest. Joe claimed he didn't like Communists and argued to columnist Jimmy Cannon that Castro wasn't one.

"There are Communists in his government," replied Cannon.

"That don't make him one," said Joe. "If he is, I quit. But I don't tell people to believe what Castro says. I say, 'Go to Cuba for a vacation.'" As Joe knew from personal experience, Cuba was a vacationland free of discrimination. In his mind he was helping American blacks as well as making an honest dollar. (It's worth noting that when Castro visited New York in 1995 for the fiftieth anniversary of the United Nations—his first visit to the U.S. since 1960—he was shunned everywhere but Harlem, where an overflow crowd turned out to hear him speak at the Abyssinian Baptist Church.)

Cannon, normally in Joe's corner, criticized the public relations fiasco as "the desperate act of a man hocking his reputation, which is all he has left." The unexpected outcry forced Joe to once again demonstrate his patriotism to the entire nation at the cost of a substantial purse. He resigned the $287,000 account.

The Louis household at this point included two little girls that Martha had attained legal guardianship of when their father, a client, had died. Joe never grew close to his foster daughters. One of them, Candice, remembered that he "never disciplined us or corrected us. Most of the time he was playing golf or he was upstairs in bed." Martha served him lunch and dinner in bed, though he did come down for breakfast, watching *Captain Kangaroo* with Candice's younger sister, Amber.

Meanwhile, his own children by Marva were growing up. Jacqueline resented his absence from her life. Marva's second husband, Dr. Spaulding, was a good man and a fine provider. He gave his stepchildren private-school educations and a sister, Alvita (who died young in 1968). But Jacqueline wanted more—her biological father. In 1956 Joe invited her and Punchy to spend the summer with him in New York, but it was "Momma Rose" Morgan who wound up babysitting them for a month while Joe indulged himself in his usual carefree, vagabond lifestyle. It wasn't until she was a young woman that she finally came to accept her famous father for what he was: "He lived his life the way he wanted to. He lived by his own rules."

Punchy never grew to be his father's size, stopping at five-foot-ten and 170 pounds, but he did acquire his facial features and love of golf. In fact, today Joe Barrow Jr. is vice president of marketing for a Denver golf equipment manufacturing company.

"It was frustrating not to see him for long periods of time," he conceded. "I'd experience a certain level of jealousy when we'd have dinner in a restaurant and he'd spend more time talking with strangers and signing autographs than with me. Dad was the type of person to not have acquaintances, but friends. He was so gracious he could make anyone feel welcome.

"It took me a long time to get over the idea that I had to share him with the world. People would come up to me and say, 'You just don't know what a difference your dad made.' Universally, people of that generation would not only say that but describe in great detail what he had meant to them. Finally understanding all of that did help." But he and his sister could never shake the feeling that their famous father always seemed to be more emotionally attached to casual acquaintances than to his own flesh and blood. It was perhaps his greatest character flaw.

Martha looked for ways that would keep her husband occupied while helping meet his tax obligations, which had now reached $1.3 million. In 1962 she helped set up a boxing promotion company, United World Boxing Enterprises. Among other events, it promoted a closed-circuit telecast of a fight featuring a brash newcomer named Cassius Clay. United World Boxing Enterprises went the way of most of Joe's business ventures, losing $30,000 before folding. The reason? Joe, knowing how bad fighters of his own era had had it, overpaid his boxers.

Meanwhile Martha was negotiating with Dana Latham, commissioner of the IRS. He was still supposed to be paying the agency $20,000 a year, plus taxes on his current income. After the government had seized all but $500 of the $4,000 Joe had made participating in a Las Vegas act, she protested that such actions would merely persuade Joe not to work at all. Worse, the constant harassment was wearing him down emotionally. The IRS, although never officially forgiving Joe's huge tax bill, in essence threw in the towel. It agreed to tax him on just his current earnings, which in 1961 amounted to a mere $10,000. Joe would die twenty years later owing more than $2 million.

No matter what the crisis, Martha found him as unflappable as a flag on a calm day. "You couldn't get a rise out of Joe no matter what you did," she once complained. A bad shot on the golf course came closest to riling him. Then he'd mutter to himself, "Oh, Joseph." When Martha became agitated, he'd chide her: "You should stop that. It wouldn't look good for a big-time lawyer like you to get all worked up."

The Sergeant could get worked up, but the clouds usually quickly blew away. "There's a soul about this man, and a quietness that I love," she once told a writer.

The two made a good pair, but to Joe sex remained something quite apart from marriage. "Move over, honey," Martha would command when she saw a woman too close to her marital property. "I'm Mrs. Louis." Although she eventually gave up trying to stop these dalliances, in the early years of their marriage she sometimes found herself operating like a private investigator, sniffing out leads.

One morning, sensing that Joe was unusually jittery, she suspected an old flame was in town. Later in the day, she called the Beverly Hilton Hotel and asked if this certain woman was registered. She was, but the operator was not allowed to reveal her room number. Martha drove to the hotel, where she was similarly stonewalled by the reception clerk. Unwilling to give up, Martha went to a nearby florist.

"I want to send some flowers to a friend in the hotel," she said. "She's registered, but I don't have her room number. Can you get it for me?"

The florist did: room 417. Martha sent the flowers, then drove home to wait for Joe to return. When he pulled up that evening in a taxi, she icily asked, "How's room 417?"

Joe's deadpan face never changed expression.

"You a regular Dick Tracy," he said.

→←

Joe's nightmare years began with the prick of a needle inside a Milwaukee hotel room in 1958. According to Joe's version of events, he was spending the night with a woman with whom he had been conducting a cross-country romance for several weeks. He was leaning over the side of the bed when she suddenly jabbed him in the buttocks with a syringeful of what was evidently heroin. When Joe jumped up, the woman—who Joe called "Annie" in his autobiography—told him she was just trying to "relax" him. Joe, not inclined to argue under most circumstances, especially with a fine-looking woman, let the incident slide.

After that first taste, however, "she had me good," he admitted. "She was always finding ways to 'relax' me. A little bit of a needle prick and I was feeling good." Joe claimed that the drugs lifted him from his ongoing depression over taxes. Although he was "in funny land," he felt good, as if he were the heavyweight champ and a millionaire again, he said.

Joe should have realized he was walking on the razor's edge. Upon their first meeting he had learned that Annie's husband, a funeral home operator, had recently been shot to death by a disgruntled employee. Later he discovered that she was an actress in pornographic films and was involved in other seamy activities, all of which required her to disguise herself in a variety of wigs and costumes.

According to Joe's account, the FBI stepped in after Annie had given $2,500 of his money to her pimp. The agents explained to him that Annie was running drugs for the Mafia and that he was being used as a shield. Who would ever suspect somebody in the company of Joe Louis to be dealing in dope? Scared of what he was doing to his body, Joe fled to California, where he sought stability in marrying Martha.

Joe's wanderings increasingly placed him in Las Vegas. Nevada, which in 1931 had become the first state to legalize gambling, had never been a model of racial tolerance. In the 1920s, when Las Vegas was little more than a train stop to take on cattle and water, black passengers were warned not to get off to stretch their legs. "Boy, you'd better not get off here," the conductor would say, nodding toward a knot of grizzled cowboys. "Those boys out there are a little rough. Better stay on the train." After the war, as Las Vegas grew into a fantasyland of neon, velvet, and sequins, black entertainers like Sammy Davis Jr. and Nat "King" Cole were welcome at the garish hotel-casinos that lined the Strip, but they had to lodge on the west side of town. Joe, of course, was welcomed everywhere, especially after the city hosted its first title fight in the spring of 1960. With its lure of round-the-clock action, year-round sun, and institutionalized vice, Las Vegas quickly supplanted New York as the boxing mecca of the country. It was a short trip from Los Angeles to Vegas, and Joe made it often. If he wasn't playing golf he was hanging around some fighter's camp, where he usually got "walking around" money from a promoter.

One of his favorite running buddies during this period was a fellow nomad, Charles "Sonny" Liston, a brutal, smoldering man who captured the heavyweight championship in 1962 with a first-round kayo of Floyd Patterson. Liston has come down in ring history as the sport's ultimate bad ass. His background was abysmal. He was the twenty-fourth of twenty-five children born into an Arkansas sharecropping family, though the exact year of his birth remains a mystery. He survived a childhood of beatings from his father and practically no book learning (he was completely illiterate), then drifted into a life of crime in St. Louis. After serving prison time for armed robbery, he became a labor goon. After serving another stretch in jail, this time for breaking a cop's kneecap, he took his ever-lengthening rap sheet to Philadelphia, where he fell under the control of Jim Norris's old associates, Blinky Palermo and Frankie Carbo.

Liston was handy with his fists, having won the national Golden Gloves title and then turning pro while in St. Louis. With the mob's assistance he moved through the ranks. The press dusted off old jungle-killer imagery—"gorilla," "caveman," and "king of the beasts"—to describe his chilling style. "I never saw him smile," Nat Fleischer wrote. "He always seemed mad at the whole world. Like he wanted to get even for things that had been done to him before. I don't think he had one happy day in his life." Liston cooperated with no one, had a glare that could melt lead, and always went his own way, the world be damned. The NAACP, looking for positive role models during this period of incendiary race relations, denounced him. To blacks and whites alike, the menacing, humorless Liston was Godzilla in a porkpie hat.

Liston mistrusted most people, but he grew close to Louis. In 1965, he solidified his relationship with Joe by hiring him as a cornerman. If he didn't exactly consider Joe a surrogate father, he certainly found a kindred spirit. Their backgrounds were similar: uneducated Southern migrants who had saved themselves from a lifetime of manual labor by dint of a scythe-like right hand and a jackhammer left jab. In fact, many veteran observers rated Liston's jab with Louis's as the best of all time. Most important to the relationship was Joe's nonjudgmental nature. "Every man's got a right to his own mistakes," he had once said in response to a reporter's criticism of Jack Johnson's character. "Ain't no man that ain't made none."

As a team Joe and Liston made plenty. About 1964 Martha sold her Los Angeles apartment and bought a house in Denver, where Liston soon took up residence. Martha wound up handling some legal work for him as well. When Joe and Liston were out on the town in Denver or Las Vegas they threw dice, pursued women, stayed up all night, and dabbled in drugs.

During the sixties Joe gradually became hooked on cocaine, a dependency that accounted for, or at least contributed to, his slide into mental illness. Through his show-business friends he had been exposed to the narcotic since the 1930s, but he had never felt the need for it or any other drug, alcohol and tobacco included. He first experimented with coke in the 1950s during a hotel-room tryst with an actress, then became introduced to heroin through "Annie." In 1964 he turned fifty years old. Cocaine, touted as a sexual stimulant, served as a chemical crutch for a libido stalled by advancing age and high blood pressure. Joe's chemically induced tailspin accelerated in Las Vegas, due in part to the corruptive influence of Liston and his Svengali-like advisor, Ash Resnick. Freddie Guinyard, one of many old acquaintances from whom he had drifted apart, thought a close friend's intervention might have made a difference. "I don't know, maybe I should have stayed out there with him," he said sadly.

Resnick had already sunk his hooks into Liston. There was hardly a photograph taken of Liston during his tenure as champ that didn't have his familiar face in the background. Resnick is spoken of in positive terms by some of Joe's family members, who recall his financial support during the fighter's final years, but it's impossible to ignore his history. Widely known as a gambler and bookmaker (he had been barred from several Florida racetracks), Resnick was installed as the director of sporting events at the Thunderbird, a mob-controlled hotel on the Vegas strip. He placed Joe on the public relations staff and set aside a room for him to use whenever he liked. When Resnick moved on to Caesars Palace, he brought Joe along with him.

Liston lost the title to Cassius Clay in Miami Beach in 1964 because of a mysterious shoulder injury that prevented him from answering the bell for the seventh round. Afterward, rumor was rampant that the fight had been fixed. Resnick and other mob figures had had free run of Liston's camp. When Clay (who by now had cast off his "slave name" and adopted the name Muhammad Ali) defended his championship with an infamous phantom-punch first-round knockout of Liston the following May, Liston and his camp were again accused of having arranged a fix. Although no wrongdoing was ever conclusively proved in either fight, the public by and large agreed with the new titleholder's assessment: "Liston's too ugly to be champion."

If Joe's association with Liston repulsed or baffled many people, his quarrels with Ali were understandable and widely supported. It was inevitable that Joe and Ali—who always felt that his self-proclaimed status as "The Greatest" was threatened by the Louis legend—would feud. Ali, a product of Louisville, Kentucky, had won a gold medal in the 1960 Olympics and brashly moved on from there. He was a sleek greyhound of a fighter who also loved to loudly denounce his opponents. His dancing style and big mouth were enough to turn Joe off, but what really rankled him was his religious conversion to the Nation of Islam and his refusal to be inducted into the army. Ali, a gifted self-promoter, was a public relations coup for the blossoming black-pride movement. "Clay means dirt," he said. "It's the name slave owners gave my people. My white blood came from slavemasters, from raping. The white blood harms us; it hurts us." The buildup to the second Liston-Ali bout polarized the public to the point that many of those who disliked Liston still found themselves preferring to have the heavyweight championship in the hands of the mob rather than the Black Muslims.

Joe's response was that he was "against Black Muslims, and I'm against Cassius Clay being a Black Muslim. I'll never go along with the idea that all white people are devils. I've always believed that every man is my brother. . . . The way I see it, the Black Muslims want to do just what we have been fighting against for one hundred years. They want to separate the races and that's a step back at a time we're going for integration."

According to Joe Barrow Jr., in time his father came to respect Ali and his views. "He admired Ali's talent and thought he did a lot to energize the heavyweight division. But he disagreed with Ali's decision to avoid military service. My father had gone in during the Second World War and he felt everybody had an obligation to serve their country. He thought if Ali had gone in, he never would have gone to Vietnam. He'd be placed in kind of a noncombatant role."

In 1967 Joe began his association with Caesars Palace on a freelance basis. It seems his chief duty was being seen with Resnick, whether it was playing golf, making the rounds before a fight, greeting casino guests, or collecting debts. As casino collectors, the pair regularly traveled around the country to gently shake down big shooters for hundreds of thousands of dollars they owed Caesars Palace. It was all very sociable, done over dinner and drinks, though Resnick admitted that it "also didn't hurt to have a former heavyweight champion holding the money." Joe managed to inject notes of high drama into the job. On one occasion they brought along Resnick's two-year-old daughter, using her suitcase to hold the nearly one million dollars in cash they had collected. At a coffee shop Resnick went to the men's room; when he came back he discovered Joe had strolled out the door. Frantic, Resnick raced down the sidewalk after him. "Joe, did you take the money with you?" he asked. No, Joe explained, it was back in the coffee shop. The baby was watching it.

Joe had already had some experience walking out on babies. In December 1967, a woman named Marie Johnson gave birth to a baby boy. After she called Joe to tell him that he was the father, he disappeared, though Martha quickly sized up what had happened. She went to see the mother and the baby. Johnson, a runaway from Ohio who had been working as a waitress when she met Joe, had since drifted into drugs and prostitution. Seeing that she couldn't raise the infant properly, Martha offered to bring him home with her. A few months later Johnson agreed to the arrangement. The boy was named Joe. Martha kept in touch with Marie, who soon afterward had another illegitimate son. This time Joe wasn't the father, but Martha again offered to be the mother. Once again, Johnson agreed. John joined little Joe in the Louis household. In time they were legally adopted.

At the same time Martha began to take careful notice of her husband's strange behavior. He had always been meticulous about his hygiene and wardrobe. Now he was going days without showering or changing his clothes. He was listless and left his golf clubs in the closet for months—probably the surest sign that something was seriously wrong. Cocaine was probably the main culprit for his increasingly bizarre behavior. Of course, heredity—his father had gone insane—and the effects of hundreds of blows to the head during his boxing career can't be discounted.

In his autobiography, Joe admitted he was putting ever-larger amounts of coke into his system. (Truman Gibson and some others familiar with Harlem's drug culture believed he was using heroin laced with cocaine.) "Cocaine was no stranger to me now. I took it whenever I could buy it. I bought it from whoever sold it to me. It made me feel like myself just after the Carnera fight, just like after the Braddock fight, when I became the Heavyweight Champion of the World, like just after I won the second Schmeling fight. I kept telling myself that nothing could be wrong with feeling that good."

One June day in 1969, while he was in New York, he collapsed of abdominal pain after ingesting "some bad stuff." He was rushed to Beekman Downtown Hospital, where his stomach was pumped, probably saving his life. The news of his collapse was tailored by the hospital and his longtime personal physician, a Detroit doctor named Bennett, to protect his image. Scared, Joe laid off drugs for a while, then started up again.

His near-fatal experience foreshadowed the end of bad-boy Sonny Liston, who died of a mysterious drug overdose at his Las Vegas home over the Christmas holidays in 1970. At the time he was broke, his career having ended the year before when a former sparring partner foiled his comeback with an unexpected knockout. Police, who discovered heroin and marijuana in the house, believed he was pushing drugs and doing strongarming for Resnick and other mob types. Liston was found in bed, naked except for a tee shirt, blood coming from his nose. The speculation among veteran detectives was that he had died of a "hot shot," an intentional overdose ordered by Resnick because the loose-lipped Liston was telling people that Resnick had fixed one or both of his fights with Ali.

Resnick and Joe were pallbearers. Passing through the casino on their way to the funeral, a friend at the craps table offered to stake Joe to a game. Joe stopped and pretended to pull off his jacket. "I'm sure Sonny would understand," he joked. But later, as he helped carry his friend's coffin across the cemetery lawn, he appeared shaken. Perhaps he saw in Liston's death something of himself.

→←

While Joe was wrestling with his own personal demons, the civil rights movement blew right past him. Although he occassionally showed up at minor demonstrations when they were convenient—a rally protesting Harlem slumlords, for example—he was never involved in any sustained, significant way in the social revolution that involved so many members of his own race. He drew some criticism for this.

However, his example as a national hero palatable to whites had influenced the early course of events. Early on, civil rights leaders looking to personalize their cause realized that the "correct" image had to be projected in the media if mainstream whites were to be won over. The history books tell us that Rosa Parks sparked the modern civil rights movement on December 1, 1955, when she was arrested for refusing to yield her seat to a white man on a Montgomery, Alabama, bus. What's often left out is that she was the fourth person considered by Edgar Nixon, an activist lawyer in search of the perfect defendant to be the centerpiece of his test case. Three other black females, including an unmarried, pregnant fifteen-year-old, had previously been arrested for exactly the same "crime." None seemed sympathetic enough to be able to raise the expected half-million-dollar defense fund, much of which would have to come from white supporters. In the quiet, dignified seamstress, however, Nixon found someone cut from the same inoffensive cloth as Joe Louis. The ensuing year-long Montgomery bus boycott brought the city to its knees and ended in a Supreme Court decision in favor of the protesters.

The principle of nonviolent protest and massive civil disobedience— sit-ins, boycotts, voter registration drives, the 1963 march on Washington—stalled against those bulwarks of the Old South, Mississippi and Alabama. In 1962 two people were killed and 5,000 troops were called in as James Meredith attempted to become the first black to enter the University of Mississippi. The following year NAACP field secretary Medgar Evans was murdered in front of his Jackson home; Birmingham police chief "Bull" Connor turned fire hoses and attack dogs loose on marchers; and a black school was bombed in Birmingham, killing four little girls. The three networks fed televisions across the country with images that challenged the conscience.

So much was going on. Assassinations . . . riots . . . drugs . . . psychedelia . . . Vietnam. As the sixties roared on Joe Louis suddenly became quaint to younger, more militant blacks. His name was shrouded in the mists of his recent but suddenly irrelevant past. Older blacks and those with a sense of history still spoke of him in almost reverential tones. Before he was gunned down in 1968, Reverend Martin Luther King invoked the symbolism of his name from time to time, including a story (possibly apocryphal) where a frightened young Negro about to be executed inside a southern prison pleaded over and over, "Save me, Joe Louis . . . Save me."

It was the younger generation, impatient with the pace of change, that attached radically different meaning to the symbol of a clenched fist. Black power no longer meant huddling around a communal radio, savoring a vicarious knockout of some pasty-faced Bum of the Month. Now it was pursuing a vigorous movement of dissent and confrontation that found its inspiration in such apostates as Muhammad Ali, Malcolm X, Angela Davis, H. Rap Brown, and Bobby Seale. At the 1968 Olympics in Mexico City, Tommie Smith and John Carlos became the ultimate symbols of defiance and racial pride, bowing their heads and raising their clenched fists on the medal stand as the national anthem was played. Joe, watching along with the rest of the world on TV, later said their gesture brought tears to his eyes.

During the long, hot summer of 1967, Joe had to get on the phone to make sure family members were safe in the wake of a riot that destroyed whole neighborhoods and killed forty-three Detroiters. It was the worst civil disturbance in the country's history. As scores of similarly bloody urban uprisings made too clear, the children of those who had once raced from their living rooms to celebrate another knockout by "the winner and still champion" were taking to the streets for different reasons. When a historical precedent was required, they reached past Joe and pulled up that ultimate anti-establishment hero, Jack Johnson. In 1969 Papa Jack enjoyed a renaissance that surprised anyone old enough to remember the racial hysteria he had helped stoke. Howard Sackler produced a long-running Broadway play, The Great White Hope, which later was turned into a feature film starring James Earl Jones. A documentary of Johnson's life was also produced. Its musical score was created by Miles Davis, who released it on one of his most popular albums, Jack Johnson. Muhammad Ali openly professed his admiration for Papa Jack, not just for his boxing skills, but for having had the audacity to tweak and taunt white America.

"Jack Johnson was the most influential person in my career," he said. "He did things in the ring defensively that I saw on film and tried to copy. He came along at a time when black people felt they had nothing to be proud of, and he made them proud."

Some black athletes did use Joe as a role model, but for all the wrong reasons. Several cited his humiliating tax problems when vowing never to go broke. Willie Mays, impressed by Joe's easy Las Vegas lifestyle, would later disassociate himself from major league baseball and became a casino shill in Atlantic City. Jimmy Brown, who retired at the top of his game to pursue an acting career, once explained why he resisted repeated attempts to have him return to the gridiron. "I hated the fact Joe Louis stayed too long," he said. "All the guys in history who stayed too long, I thought it was embarrassing. People had sympathy for them. Champions should never, ever stay too long."

Gerald Early grew up in Philadelphia's ghetto during the fifties and sixties. The essayist and educator observed that it was difficult "to picture the old man with the receding hairline and paunchy belly who was predicting George Foreman would destroy Ali in Zaire as anything more than a tired old man."

This was a new generation that admired Ali and was not even born when Louis was an active fighter. Every time Louis predicted Ali would lose . . . the men on the stoops would say, "Joe talkin' crazy again. He ain't never called a fight right in his whole motherfarmin' life"; or, "If Joe say the other guy gonna win, then all my money goes on Ali." It was hard for those of us of the generation of civil rights marches, black power, and the Eastern approaches of exotic names and religions to believe our fathers and grandfathers who told us he was not only the greatest fighter in America but the most famous black man in history at that time.

Because of his problems, Joe in his middle years often appeared foolish, weak, pathetic. His inoffensive and accommodating style caused Ali and others to label him an "Uncle Tom," though few people bought the charge. Barney Nagler described a dinner conversation among Jimmy Brown and several other Americans who were in Frankfurt, West Germany, for the Ali-Karl Mildenberger title fight in 1966. "In his time, Louis did as much for the black cause as Muhammad Ali," one of the whites present innocently offered. "I don't buy that," Brown shot back. "You like Louis because he's the kind of Negro you want him to be. He could have been, should have been, more outspoken on the problems of blacks."

Joe understood his limitations better than his critics. He knew he was neither a gifted orator nor an original thinker. As a boxer he had demonstrated a knack for the pithy quote. His "He can run but he can't hide" and "We'll win because we're on God's side" have survived as classics of the American lexicon. Unfortunately for his legacy, he couldn't come up with a bumper-sticker quote to satisfy the needs of the civil rights generation. He left it to others more flamboyant and energetic to lead the charge for change.

"Jackie is my hero," he said shortly before Jackie Robinson, burned out from years of personal heartbreak and public struggle, died young in 1972. "He don't bite his tongue for nothing. I just don't have the guts, you might call it, to say what he says. And don't talk as good either, that's for sure. But he talks the way he feels."

The way Robinson and the rest of his generation felt about Joe was always clear, if not often expressed in the firestorm of the era. Said Robinson: "When I went up to the majors with the Brooklyn Dodgers, people asked me if I would have made it if there hadn't been a Joe Louis before me. I think so, eventually. If I hadn't made it, some other black player would have. But Joe, by his conduct, cleared the way. And it's a funny thing. Joe himself has never really realized the impact he had on the black community and the fight against prejudice."

Robinson may have been wrong about that. More than once, when the chances for racial harmony seemed particularly bleak, Joe was heard to grumble, "Didn't I count for nothin'?"

➤←

By the late 1960s Joe was showing signs of paranoia. They were out to kill him, he told Martha, "they" being Annie, the woman who introduced him to heroin a decade earlier, and her partner in crime, the Mafia. Soon he wouldn't eat Martha's meals, afraid that the food was poisoned. He began to tape over air conditioning ducts and heaters, convinced that the Mafia was trying to pump poison gas into his room. He spread mayonnaise over cracks on the ceiling. He slept fitfully, often creating a makeshift cave from pillows and furniture into which he could retreat.

He was sure people were following him, waiting for a chance to harm him. In Las Vegas, he threatened to knock a couple of casino guests "right on your ass" if they didn't quit tailing him. Those who knew and loved him despaired. He seemed certain at some point to hurt somebody or himself. The problem was that Joe refused to submit himself to treatment.

However, Colorado law provided for the involuntary medical treatment of a person if immediate family members requested it. Joe Barrow Jr., who had moved to Denver a few years earlier to attend college and was now working in the city, signed the commitment order. Martha tricked Joe into leaving Las Vegas. On May 1, 1970, three sheriff's deputies and a probate officer arrived at the Louis home to take Joe to Colorado Psychiatric Hospital. Joe, realizing what was happening, tried calling President Nixon, then settled for an impromptu press conference. News of his mental illness slipped into the papers. By the time he was transferred to the local Veterans Hospital he was receiving about 100 letters a week from well-wishers. Many enclosed money.

Doctors determined that his mental illness had not been caused by boxing. Joe responded to treatment, the street drugs in his system replaced by five fifty-milligram doses of Thorazine each day. In his outsized slippered feet and robe he lumbered around the ward like a big, kindly bear, encouraging other patients and giving away his last cigarettes. But his softened face still grew tense on occasion. A visitor caught him staring out the wire-meshed window and asked if everything was okay.

"Ain't worried," he replied. "I'm just thinking about them assholes blowing gas in on me."

On August 12, 1970, while Joe was undergoing treatment in Denver, Martha traveled to Detroit to represent Joe in a "Salute the Champ—Joe Louis" benefit held at Cobo Hall. In a marvelous show of support, 10,000 people showed up although they knew in advance that the object of their tribute couldn't appear. The event raised nearly $100,000 to help pay his bills.

In the middle of September Joe's doctors were talked into letting him visit Las Vegas for a weekend. Joe was a people person, Martha said. The crowds and bright lights would do him good. It was a gamble—once out of Colorado he was beyond the court's jurisdiction—but he came back. On October 16, he was discharged with the provision that he would continue to return for therapy on an outpatient basis. He faithfully returned for his twice-weekly appointments until his physician, Dr. Martin, grew ill himself in December. Joe lost confidence and quit going. He never returned to Colorado.

At fifty-six, Joe had approached the foothills of old age. Back in his old surroundings, he soon felt well enough to resume golfing. He even hit the banquet circuit. Alex Karras, a football player-turned-actor, described a series of banquet dates he did with Joe in 1970. As Karras tells the story, his main function was to introduce his more famous partner to the crowd: "And now, ladies and gentlemen, the fabulous, the wonderful, the legendary Brown Bomber—let's hear it for the former world heavyweight champion . . . Joe Louis!"

The room would fill with applause, Joe would say a few inconsequential words before sitting down, and then the master of ceremonies would introduce that evening's main speaker, Karras. At which point, Karras recalled, people in the crowd would look at each other and ask, "Who the hell is he?"

"I didn't mind," Karras said. "I'd talk for an hour, mixing humor and straight talk, finally getting the audience to enjoy my routine. But the fact that Joe Louis never spoke one word to me during the entire banquet swing—that hurt."

As the rubber chicken circuit concluded with a final date in Canada, Karras decided to forego the usual pleasantries.

"Ladies and gentlemen," he said this time, "when I was a small boy in Gary, Indiana, my greatest dream was to grow up to be the heavyweight champion of the world. You see, I had someone to emulate. That man was Joe Louis. Everything he said, I believed. Because he was so terrific. Now, Joe used to sell a drink called Joe Louis Punch . . . and I would drink gallons of it every week."

At this point Karras turned to face his former idol.

"Joe," he said, "I just want to say this. Your pop gave me a million pimples. It was the worst pop I ever drank in my life. It changed my attitude about boxing, Joe. And especially about you. The only one who saved me from being scarred for life was Tony Zale, the ex-middleweight champ. One day I saw him on television . . . doing an Ex-Lax commercial. And because he comes from my hometown, Joe, I went right out and bought some Ex-Lax. And I shit all your pop away."

The room filled with gasps and screams of laughter. Joe, who had always been a merry prankster in training camp, hiding snakes under sheets and administering hotfoots, was nonplussed. He enjoyed having his tail twisted.

"I like you," he said after Karras had returned to his seat. "What's your name?"

Berry Gordy Jr., the fabulously rich creator of Motown Records, often saw Joe after the Vegas clubs started booking the Supremes, Temptations, Four Tops, and other Motown acts in the sixties. Sometimes when they played golf together he could barely contain his excitement. "Every now and then, I had the urge to just shout out right there on the green to whoever was passing by—Hey, people, this is Joe Louis! I'm playing golf with my hero!!"

It was this kind of gushing, coupled with Joe's equanimity, that influenced Caesars Palace to announce on February 15, 1971, that Joe had been hired as a full-time employee. It's not hard to sort out the casino's motives, which were a blend of altruism and public relations. Bill Weinberger, who had been in charge of concessions at Cleveland's Municipal Stadium when Joe wore the heavyweight belt, had long been a Louis fan. Now as the head of Caesars Palace, he was in the position of offering Joe something more substantial than his affection. Joe also had old friend Ash Resnick in his corner. He was put on the payroll as "casino greeter" and given a salary of $50,000 a year.

Veteran Detroit sportswriter George Puscas recalled Joe's duties. "He'd sit by the blackjack table opposite the number-one crap table for three or four hours, signing autographs and talking to whoever came up to him. Everybody knew him, of course, and so it was always, 'Hello, Champ,' or 'I remember when you knocked out Schmeling,' or Conn. He liked the attention."

Joe was always given a few thousand dollars of house money to play with, which he promptly lost or gave away. Puscas told of one evening when Joe paused in their conversation to whisper to a nearby friend, to whom he had been slipping some chips. After a few seconds he turned to Weinberger. "I need some more chips," he announced.

"You've already gone through your allotment today?" Weinberger asked. "I know what you're doing, Joe. You're giving the chips away to people when they come by your table."

Joe mumbled something that sounded like a denial, but Weinberger could only smile helplessly. "Tell 'em I said to give you another five thousand dollars," he finally said. Joe smiled, winked to his friend, and whispered, "I'll have it for you in a minute."

To the tourist from Kalamazoo or Des Moines, who walked away from a brief encounter with the champ feeling as if they were old friends, Joe appeared to have recovered from the illness that he had read about in his local paper. Whether shaking hands, posing for snapshots, listening for the five millionth time to someone describe how they had listened to the Billy Conn or Max Schmeling fight, he seemed like the old Joe Louis, maybe even better.

"I don't know about better," argued Truman Gibson, who now saw him only two or three times a year. "He was not himself. He had a different direction in his bad habits. By that time he was drinking cognac and smoking cigarettes. He was not the Joe Louis I knew."

Some walked away secretly saddened. What was a national hero doing on the Las Vegas strip, lurching along on the fumes of his fame, wearing a cowboy hat and surrounded by oceans of polyester and plastic hair? The reaction among some was as if Joe DiMaggio had been discovered working at a flea circus.

This was unfair, said his son.

"Those who criticized him didn't understand that Las Vegas gave him new life," said Joe Barrow Jr. "He was in his element again. He was earning a salary, traveling, and meeting people. He was loved by Caesars Palace and the people who visited there. Those who felt that Las Vegas somehow demeaned his stature have got it wrong. They wanted him to retire in some pristine house, but that's not the way he lived his life. He'd always had an exciting, worldly life, and Las Vegas was just an extension of that life. It might not be what you or I would do, but it clearly made him happy. Las Vegas doesn't take away anything that he had accomplished before."

He continued to be afflicted by spells of paranoia and delusion, although his outbursts and panic attacks were usually pretty well covered up. Most of the time he was his usual genial, generous self and functioned perfectly well in public.

As the seventies ran their course, Joe's damaged heart continued to deteriorate. His coronary problems reached the crisis stage. In October 1977, Houston heart specialist Dr. Michael Debakey performed an arterial graft to correct an aneurysm. While Joe was in the hospital recovering, he suffered a debilitating stroke.

For the last three and a half years of his life Joe's world was largely confined to a sprawling ranch-style house at 3333 Seminole Circle, located on a cul-de-sac just a mile east of the Vegas strip. He shared living space with Martha, a housekeeper, a nurse, and what now numbered four children. Marie, the fertile New York prostitute, had given birth to two more babies, Joyce in 1972 and Janet in 1975, and Martha had taken both of them in.

A therapist visited eleven times a week—twice each weekday and once on Saturday mornings—to work with him. On those rare occasions when he felt strong enough, he would agonizingly attempt a few steps on the exercise bars in the living room. A hot tub and a private pool were available, as was a small fleet of motorized and manual wheelchairs. But most days were spent in bed. On the dresser next to it were arranged dozens of bottles of medication and pills.

"He has his good days and bad days," sighed Martha. "Some days I can't even understand him, but on other days he's just fine. We try to make things as pleasant as possible . . . but it's not easy. Some of the doctors suggested I put him in a home, but I wouldn't do that to a dog. We'll keep him right here at home. That's where he should be."

Martha saw to all her husband's needs. All the steps in the house were replaced with ramps and the doors to the bathrooms were widened to provide Joe wheelchair access. She paid a steep price for her deathwatch. Her law practice suffered and finally she just abandoned it completely. Her savings drained, she was forced to accept the largesse of Joe's many friends, most notably Frank Sinatra and the management of Caesars Palace. In fact, the house, previously occupied by late-night talk show host Johnny Carson, was an outright gift of the casino. Few thought the arrangement unusual. "Why shouldn't his bills be paid?" said one casino employee. "He's an American institution." It was exactly the kind of reasoning Joe had employed throughout his post-ring life.

On those rare occasions when he did venture out—typically for a big fight, tribute, or a checkup at Houston's Methodist Hospital—he would follow the same ritual. He would conserve his strength for several days and then have his nurse give him one of his infrequent shaves. "Of course, he can't go any place by himself," Martha explained. "But he can get in and out of a car with hardly any help at all." The therapy, she said optimistically, was designed not to maintain him at a certain level but to improve his condition.

On November 9, 1978, Caesars Palace hosted a gala tribute to him, with 1,500 people paying $500 hundred dollars a plate. Frank Sinatra was chairman of the testimonial dinner, which attracted a variety of leading entertainment and sports figures and was designed to benefit the Joe Louis International Sports Foundation. The tax-exempt Houston-based charity had been formed earlier in the year to develop sports programs and scholarships for youngsters. Sinatra had become a Louis fan in the late forties, when a boxing show he was promoting bombed financially. Joe waived his fee, a gesture Ol' Blue Eyes never forgot. It was his money that helped cover Joe's medical bills and other expenses in his final years.

In late February 1980, just a week after the U.S. hockey team had shockingly whipped the Russians enroute to capturing a gold medal at the winter Olympics, Joe visited Detroit for the last time. The occasion was a civic tribute to the aging champ, who to the keen disappointment of thousands of admirers was too sick to attend the black-tie affair. Earlier, *Detroit News* columnist Mike O'Hara had been one of a steady procession of old friends and new acquaintances who passed through his hotel suite, eager to pump the hand of the man who, like those exuberant young Olympians, also had once shaken the world.

"Those hands," O'Hara marveled in print. "They are still a fighter's hands, huge and meaty, and the grip remains firm and sure. The palms spread like a pair of catchers' mitts, wider than the hands of two normal men. They are the hands that beat Braddock and Schmeling and Walcott. They are Picasso's brush, Casel's bow, Shakespeare's quill."

His condition continued to deteriorate. One October night in 1980, Budd Schulberg was seated for the Larry Holmes-Muhammad Ali fight when Joe was wheeled down the aisle and placed alongside him. Forty-two years earlier, Schulberg had been ringside for the second Schmeling fight, so close he later told his friends that he "could hear the blow that almost removed the German's head." Afterward he had gone to Harlem to join in the "democratic carnival" that surged through the streets, dancing and goose-stepping behind a coffin draped with a Nazi flag. "Everybody laughed and we hugged each other, and the closest thing to it I would ever know was V-E night in London," he said of the massive, unbridled merriment.

Now he glanced to his side and jotted his impressions into a notebook: "Joe Louis wheeled in—mouth hangs open—eyes staring—what is he seeing? He holds his head in his hands. An attendant wipes spittle from his mouth. His head sags. He sees nothing. The crowd cheers as Ali comes down the aisle. Louis doesn't see him. Doesn't hear the cheers."

Two days before Christmas, doctors implanted a pacemaker in Joe's chest. This seemed to improve his condition. But internal forces were well on their way to claiming a final victory. Early in the morning of Sunday, April 12, 1981, Joe collapsed while walking to his bathroom and was rushed to Desert Springs Hospital. He arrived at 9:35 A.M. in full cardiac arrest. Thirty minutes later, despite the best efforts of a team of specialists frantically working to revive him, he was pronounced dead. He was a month shy of his sixty-seventh birthday.

Despite his years of poor health, the end, when it came, was swift and shocking. According to Martha, he appeared to be recovering, even talking of attending a Diana Ross concert. The night before he had been wheeled to ringside at Caesars Palace to watch Larry Holmes successfully defend his

World Boxing Council heavyweight title against Trevor Berbick. His entrance had inspired a long standing ovation from the 4,000 people on hand. If it was any consolation to Budd Schulberg, Joe had checked out of this world with the cheering still ringing in his ears.

In Atlantic City, where much of the fight crowd had gathered for the Hilmer Kenty-Sean O'Grady lightweight fight, tears rolled down trainer Walter Smith's eyes as the bell sounded ten times in tribute to the departed champ. "When I was a kid," said Joe Frazier, also in attendance, "he had a great influence on my career. Because I was sort of stocky, my father and uncle used to say, 'He's going to be another Joe Louis.'"

"Boxing lost one of its great champions," said promoter Teddy Brenner, former president of Madison Square Garden. "He opened up boxing to every black fighter. He even led the way for guys like Jackie Robinson in other sports. Every black athlete that followed owes a debt of gratitude to Joe Louis."

While editorial writers and columnists worked to put Joe's life in its proper historical and cultural perspective, reporters looking for an angle visited his birthplace. That his passing came during spring planting time didn't concern Turner Shealey, who nearly seventy years earlier had been driven into the woods by his second cousin's incessant wailing. Shealey was retired now—or at least too old to work in the fields—giving him plenty of time to sit in the shade of an oak tree and reflect on the roads one travels in life.

"Can you imagine it?" said Shealey, who during his ninety years would never stray more than a few miles from his corner of Alabama. "He was born in this little house and died in Las Vegas. That's some moving."

Mourners flew into Las Vegas from all points on the map. The evening before Reverend Jesse Louis Jackson was to deliver the eulogy, Freddie Guinyard appealed for moderation. "If Joe isn't in heaven yet," he firmly told Jackson, "don't you put him there."

Where Caesars Palace had put him, with the permission of the family, was inside a boxing ring in the cavernous Sports Pavilion. An honor guard was posted by his open copper casket. A practically nonstop file of the respectful, grieving, or just plain curious wound past it. The send-off offended some who questioned its taste. "Just when you thought the Joe Louis story could get no sadder," wrote Dave Kindred of the *Washington Post*, "they put him dead in a boxing ring in a tin warehouse."

Martha Louis thought such criticism missed the point. "Your whole life is your funeral," she said. If true, then the third Mrs. Louis ended up being terribly shortchanged. She would spend most of the next ten years alone in a succession of nursing homes, dying broke and unsung before being buried alongside her husband.

More than three thousand people attended the morning funeral service on April 17. In his eulogy Rev. Jackson, who owed his middle name to the fighter, reminded them that Joe had outlived other powerful black figures, such as Martin Luther King and Malcolm X. "We could have lost Joe when we truly needed him," he said. "When we were vulnerable. When the stench of oppression and the lynch mobs filled our nostrils. He was our Samson, our David who slew Goliath, but he did it with kindness, with tenderness. He soothed our wounds."

His voice rising, he spoke powerfully of the rich meaning of Joe's life. "God sent Joe from the black race to represent the human race," he said. "He was the answer to the sincere prayers of the disinherited and dispossessed. Joe made everybody somebody . . . Something on the inside said we ought to be free, something on the outside said we can be free.

"Joe, we love your name. To all the witnesses gathered here, you leave and tell the story. Turn out some more editions—Extra! Extra!—the way they used to do.

"We all feel bigger today because Joe came this way. He was in the slum, but the slum was not in him. Ghetto boy to man, Alabama sharecropper to champion. Let's give Joe a big hand clap. This is a celebration. Let's hear it for the champ. Let's hear it for the champ!" By the end the crowd was on its feet, clapping hands and then slowly waving their arms in the air, saying goodbye.

On Sunday, April 19, Joe's body was flown on an Air Force jet to Washington, D.C. It lay in state for two days at the Nineteenth Street Baptist Church, a small church whose pastor, Reverend Jerry Moore, had grown up in Louisiana inspired by his fights. On April 21, a nippy but bright spring day, he was finally laid to rest at Arlington National Cemetery. Eight hundred people attended the chapel service.

As the casket was being lowered into the ground, a young black man broke the officious solemnity by clanging a cow bell.

"Time for low profile, brother," muttered one of the military guards.

"We been low profile a long time, brother," was the reply. "This is the bell of liberty, rung for Joe Louis."

>✦<

Nearly twenty years after his death, Joe's ranking as one of the top heavyweights of all time remains indisputable. In seventeen years as a professional he fought seventy-one times and won sixty-eight of them. He knocked out fifty-four opponents, including six (Primo Carnera, Max Baer, Jack Sharkey, James Braddock, Max Schmeling, and Jersey Joe Walcott) who at one time or another held the heavyweight title. His first two defeats were spaced more than fourteen years apart. His only three losses were, in order, to a former (Schmeling), current (Ezzard Charles), and future (Rocky Marciano) champion. He wore the belt longer and defended it more often and more successfully than anyone else in the history of the division.

"The greatest heavyweight I've ever covered was Joe Louis," maintained Jimmy Cannon. "The hands were quick, and a left hook or a right hand would stun the other guy and then he would put the combinations together with a rapid accuracy. The big feet were slow but he herded the guy he was fighting. Once he got his hands on a guy it was all over. He could be knocked down, but he came up quickly and his head was clear once he was on his feet."

Harry Salsinger once appraised his impact on the sport. "Louis did for boxing what Babe Ruth did for baseball, only more so. Joe came into the fight game when it was controlled by the survivors of the bootleg wars. Fixed bouts were the order of the day. Boxing had reached its lowest level, and Louis pulled the game out of the gutter. Louis set a standard for ring conduct and boxing decency. He came closer to being the perfect champion than any man before him. He always did the right thing, instinctively and not by design."

How would Joe have done if placed in the ring with Jack Johnson or Jack Dempsey or Muhammad Ali, other contenders for the title of the all-time best heavyweight? Barroom arguments and computerized matchups are fun, but unfortunately these fantasies can resolve nothing. Joe, of course, was always confident of the outcome of the dream encounter most fight fans during the sixties and seventies liked to speculate about, the one involving him and Ali. What if these two had met in their prime?

In the early sixties, when their relationship was soured by Ali's conversion to the Nation of Islam and his refusal to enter the military, Joe told a reporter, "Clay had a million dollars worth of confidence and a dime's worth of courage. He can't punch; he can't hurt you; and I don't think he takes a good punch." He cited the lack of talent in the division and rated him with the likes of Johnny Paychek, Abe Simon, and Buddy Baer.

"A lot of guys would have beaten him if he was around when I was around," he continued. "I would have whipped him. He doesn't know a thing about fighting on the ropes, which is where he would be with me. I would go in to outpunch him rather than try to outbox him. He'd be hit into those ropes as near a corner as I could get him. I'd press him, bang him around, claw him, clobber him with all I got, cut down his speed, belt him around the ribs. I'd punish the body, where the pain comes real bad. He would ache. His mouth would shut tight against the pain, and there would be tears burning his eyes."

Ali got his say in. "What's this about Joe Louis beating me? Slow moving, shuffling Joe Louis beat me? He may hit hard, but that don't mean nothing if you can't find nothing to hit. I'm no flat-footed fighter. Joe Louis, you're really funny . . . The men that Joe Louis fought, if I fought them today in Madison Square Garden, they'd boo them out of the ring. Fat bellies, out of shape, awkward, had no stance, no stamina, no footwork . . . Would Joe Louis have beat me? How would Joe Louis have knocked me out? What's he gonna do when I'm jumping and sticking and moving? And don't say I can only do it for a minute, because I can keep it up for fifteen rounds, three minutes a round. Now, how is Joe Louis gonna get to me? I just can't see how Joe Louis, who is shorter than I am, fought at a lighter weight than I did, and wasn't half as fast, could knock me out. Would I just quit dancing that night and stand there and let him hit me?"

The two later patched up their differences, though Ali continued to poor-mouth the caliber of Joe's competition. During a network sports program featuring the pair, Joe was talking about his career. "When I was champion, I went on what they called the Bum-of-the-Month tour," he began.

Ali interrupted. "You mean I'm a bum?"

"You would've been on the tour," said Joe.

Less problematic is Joe's standing as a cultural figure. He is unquestionably the greatest metaphor the American prize ring has ever produced.

"What made Louis a unique figure was not simply his great talent as an athlete," Thomas Sowell wrote in a column following his death. "He appeared at a time in American history when blacks were not only at a low economic ebb—but were also the butt of ridicule. . . .

"In this kind of world Joe Louis became the most famous black man in America. What he did as a man could reinforce or counteract stereotypes that hurt and held back millions of people of his race. How he fared in the ring mattered more to black Americans than the fate of any other athlete in any other sport, before or since. He was all we had. . . ."

In keeping with his iconic place in our culture, Joe's name and image pop up all over the map. Las Vegas has an impressive tribute: a 4,500-pound statue cut from solid marble taken from the same quarries that supplied the stone for many of Michelangelo's works. Hewn in Italy, the seven-and-a-half-foot work stands at the entrance to the Olympiad Sports Book at Caesars Palace.

Detroit has its share of tributes to its favorite native son, including an oil portrait that hangs over the entrance to the Brewster-Wheeler Center, where he first learned his craft in the early 1930s. Nearby is the $34-million riverfront arena, home to the Detroit Red Wings since 1979, that Mayor Coleman Young wryly said he named after "that great hockey player from

Black Bottom, Joe Louis." Seven years later, Robert Graham's controversial "Monument to Joe Louis" was unveiled at the intersection of Jefferson and Woodward avenues. The two-ton, twenty-four-foot-long arm and fist, which seems poised to punch the neighboring Canadian city of Windsor directly in the snout, was deemed a bit too menacing by those involved in trying to soften the city's hardcore image. But the city and the Detroit Institute of Arts gladly accepted the $350,000 bronze sculpture as a gift from *Sports Illustrated* on the occasion of the museum's centennial. Moreover, the magazine and the museum have joined forces to recognize a member of the local sports community who best "exemplifies the humanitarian spirit" of the sculpture's namesake. Each year the fighter's son flies in to hand the honoree a handcast bronze miniature of what has become known simply as "The Fist."

On June 22, 1993, in ceremonies marking the fifty-fifth anniversary of his greatest moment in the ring, the U.S. Postal Service made the Brown Bomber the first prizefighter to appear on a first-class postage stamp. Significantly, the Postal Service had previously considered John L. Sullivan and Jack Dempsey for the honor, but neither boxer could garner the necessary support. In anticipation of a record demand from stamp collectors and fight fans from around the world, some 140 million copies of the stamp were printed.

A good gauge of Joe's stature is his standing in the collectibles market. An autographed picture demands about $750, while a tin of his hair pomade typically sells for about $50. A 1952 Topps trading card, depending on its condition, can bring as much as $300. Fight programs, ticket stubs, on-site posters, even milk cartons from the Joe Louis Milk Company, are all snapped up when they become available. At what has been described as the largest boxing memorabilia auction in history—held March 18-19, 1995, at Superior Galleries in Beverly Hills, California—Joe Louis items were the most eagerly sought after. Of the scores of fight posters sold, one of his rematch with Schmeling fetched the highest bid: $4,600. Another poster, his 1940 bout with Red Burman, sold for $1,495. Fifteen original magazine cover paintings by C.R. Schaare for *The Ring* also went on the block, with the priciest ($1,955) featuring Louis and Tony Galento. The single most expensive item was Joe's championship belt, presented to him by *The Ring*. It brought $74,750, nearly triple the amount paid for the belts of James Braddock and Sonny Liston.

Against this backdrop of stamps, statuary, soaring oratory, and twenty-five-dollar milk cartons, America's Brown Bomber is best remembered as being, by his own choosing, decidedly unheroic. "I used to spar with Joe when we were coming up together at Brewster, and I knew him after he was the champion of the world," said Walter Smith. "He never acted like he was a big shot or pretended that he was better than anybody else." Confidantes and perfect strangers saw the same person: proud, honest, generous, gullible, nonjudgmental. He was a powerfully built man in a cruel profession, but he never set out to intentionally hurt anybody in his life, even in the ring. His desire to live for the moment made him a wonderful companion but a poor husband and father. To compensate he was blessed with an innate decency and timely spurts of common sense, though almost never when it came to women and money. He was also a loyal friend and a true patriot, and for that most people liked him and remember him fondly.

Fame, the famous know, has everything to do with chance and circumstance. Joe Louis Barrow had the bad luck to be born into a world that measured worth by the amount of melanin in one's skin, but the extreme good fortune to be placed in the position of knocking the bejesus out of Jim Crow and fascism. If Primo Carnera had been a Korean and Max Schmeling a Mexican it would have made no difference to him, though of course history would have treated him differently. He was uncomfortable at first with being a cultural curio, but in time he grew into the role. He eventually became what people kept telling him he was. If somebody wanted to view him as a symbol, to live vicariously through his victories, to pronounce him a great black hope and a credit to his race ("the human race," Jimmy Cannon hastened to add)—then that was okay, that was their business. He was the simple son of a poor, insane Alabama sharecropper, who had gone broke and crazy himself, but to the very end people still crowded around and called him Champ. Life for a black man in twentieth-century America could have been a lot worse—and usually was.

"In a way, I don't think it made much difference to him that he was heavyweight champion of the world," Marshall Miles, his old friend and former manager, said a few years after his death. "He was proud because of the prestige and the attention, but I think inside of him he just didn't care."

Eddie Futch, in Las Vegas for a fight, dropped by Joe's house not long before the end. He was bed-ridden and couldn't talk, but an occasional nod of the head told the visitor that he was following the conversation. After an hour or so Joe suddenly turned over.

"He's tired," Futch told the nurse. "I think I'll leave now."

The nurse stared at the bulky figure crumpled beneath the ornately carved headboard. "When I was a little girl," she said softly, "my father used to take me to see newsreels of his fights. I just thought he was wonderful. And now here I am taking care of him."

Touched, Futch decided to linger. He told her of golden days at Brewster's gymnasium, fifty years and a half-country away, when Joe insisted on using his 140-pound buddy as a sparring mate. He told of how Joe could

never solve Futch's lightning-like combination of a left feint to the body—
which drew Joe's right hand—then following with a left hook to his suddenly unprotected head.

One session, Futch recalled, Joe stopped dead in his tracks.

"What are you doing?" Futch asked.

"I'm trying to see where you throw that flukey left hook from."

"What do you care?" responded Futch. "I can't hurt you."

"I want to see how you do it," insisted Joe. "Because if you can hit me
with a left hook, somebody who can hurt me with a left hook can hit me."

"Joe," said Futch, "as long as I'm working with you, you'll never know
how I do it."

Futch smiled at the warm memory. "Telling that story to Joe's nurse,"
he reflected later, "I thought Joe was asleep. But when I got to the part
about us talking about the left hook, I heard Joe chuckling."

Appendix

The Professional Ring Record of Joe Louis

The following is a complete list of all of Joe Louis's seventy-one professional fights between 1934 and 1951, including the date, site, opponent, decision, and his purse. An asterisk (*) indicates a title fight. His overall record was 68–3, 54 knockouts.

Date	Site	Opponent	Decision		Purse
1934					
July 4	Chicago	Jack Kracken	W-KO	1	$59
July 11	Chicago	Willie Davis	W-KO	3	$62
July 29	Chicago	Larry Udell	W-KO	2	$101
August 13	Chicago	Jack Kranz	W	6	$125
August 27	Chicago	Buck Everett	W-KO	2	$150
September 11	Detroit	Alex Borchuk	W-KO	4	$106
September 24	Chicago	Adolph Wiater	W	10	$200
October 24	Chicago	Art Sykes	W-KO	8	$280
October 30	Detroit	Jack O'Dowd	W-KO	2	$111
November 14	Chicago	Stanley Poreda	W-KO	1	$300
November 30	Chicago	Charley Massera	W-KO	3	$1,200
December 14	Chicago	Lee Ramage	W-KO	3	$2,200

Date	Site	Opponent	Decision		Purse
1935					
January 4	Detroit	Patsy Perroni	W	10	$4,227
January 11	Pittsburgh	Hans Birkie	W-KO	10	$1,900
February 21	Los Angeles	Lee Ramage	W-KO	2	$4,354
March 8	San Francisco	Reds Barry	W-KO	3	$3,270
March 28	Detroit	Natie Brown	W	10	$6,589
April 12	Chicago	Roy Lazer	W-KO	3	$11,212
April 22	Dayton	Biff Benton	W-KO	2	$750
April 27	Flint	Roscoe Toles	W-KO	6	$1,250
May 3	Peoria	Willie Davis	W-KO	2	$750
May 7	Kalamazoo	Gene Stanton	W-KO	3	$750
June 25	New York	Primo Carnera	W-KO	6	$60,433
August 7	Chicago	King Levinsky	W-KO	1	$53,752
September 24	New York	Max Baer	W-KO	4	$240,833
December 13	New York	Paulino Uzcudun	W-KO	4	$39,612
1936					
January 17	Chicago	Charlie Retzlaff	W-KO	1	$23,065
June 19	New York	Max Schmeling	L-KO	12	$140,959
August 17	New York	Jack Sharkey	W-KO	3	$36,506
September 22	Philadelphia	Al Ettore	W-KO	5	$52,897
October 9	New York	Jorge Brescia	W-KO	3	$8,411
December 14	Cleveland	Eddie Simms	W-KO	1	$20,000
1937					
January 11	Buffalo	Steve Ketchell	W-KO	2	$3,100
January 27	New York	Bob Pastor	W	10	$36,000
February 17	Kansas City	Natie Brown	W-KO	4	$11,000
June 22	Chicago	James J. Braddock*	W-KO	8	$103,684
		(Louis won the heavyweight championship of the world)			
August 30	New York	Tommy Farr*	W	15	$102,578
1938					
February 22	New York	Nathan Mann*	W-KO	3	$40,522
April 1	Chicago	Harry Thomas*	W-KO	5	$16,659
June 22	New York	Max Schmeling*	W-KO	1	$349,228
1939					
January 25	New York	John Henry Lewis*	W-KO	1	$34,413
April 17	Los Angeles	Jack Roper*	W-KO	1	$34,850
June 28	New York	Tony Galento*	W-KO	4	$114,332
September 20	Detroit	Bob Pastor*	W-KO	11	$118,400

Date	Site	Opponent	Decision		Purse
1940					
February 9	New York	Arturo Godoy*	W	15	$23,620
March 29	New York	Johnny Paychek*	W-KO	4	$19,908
June 20	New York	Arturo Godoy*	W-KO	8	$55,989
December 18	Boston	Al McCoy*	W-KO	6	$17,938
1941					
January 31	New York	Red Burman*	W-KO	5	$21,023
February 17	Philadelphia	Gus Dorazio*	W-KO	2	$18,731
March 21	Detroit	Abe Simon*	W-KO	13	$19,400
April 8	St. Louis	Tony Musto*	W-KO	9	$17,468
May 23	Washington	Buddy Baer*	W-DQ	7	$36,866
June 18	New York	Billy Conn*	W-KO	13	$152,905
September 29	New York	Lou Nova*	W-KO	6	$199,500
1942					
January 9	New York	Buddy Baer*	W-KO	1	$65,200[a]
March 27	New York	Abe Simon*	W-KO	6	$45,882[b]
1946					
June 19	New York	Billy Conn*	W-KO	8	$625,916
September 18	New York	Tami Mauriello*	W-KO	1	$103,611
1947					
December 5	New York	Jersey Joe Walcott*	W	15	$75,968
1948					
June 25	New York	Jersey Joe Walcott*	W-KO	11	$252,522
1949					
March 1	Louis announced his retirement as heavyweight champion				
1950					
September 27	New York	Ezzard Charles*	L	15	$102,840
November 29	New York	Cesar Brion	W	10	
1951					
January 3	Detroit	Freddie Beshore	W-KO	4	$13,350
February 7	Miami	Omelio Agramonte	W	10	
February 23	San Francisco	Andy Walker	W-KO	10	
May 2	Detroit	Omelio Agramonte	W	10	$16,000
June 15	New York	Lee Savold	W-KO	6	
August 1	San Francisco	Cesar Brion	W	10	
August 15	Baltimore	Jimmy Bivins	W	10	
October 26	New York	Rocky Marciano	L-KO	8	$132,736

[a] Donated purse to Navy Relief Society
[b] Donated purse to Army Relief Fund

Bibliography

Ali, Muhammad, with Richard Durham. *The Greatest: My Own Story*. New York: Ballantine Books, 1975.

Anderson, Dave. *In the Corner: Great Boxing Trainers Talk about Their Art*. New York: Morrow, 1991.

Andre, Sam, and Nat Fleisher. *A Pictorial History of Boxing*. New York: Bonanza Books, 1981.

Angelou, Maya. *I Know Why the Caged Bird Sings*. New York: Random House, 1969.

Astor, Gerald. *". . . And a Credit to His Race": The Hard Life and Times of Joseph Louis Barrow, a. k. a. Joe Louis*. New York: Dutton, 1974.

Bak, Richard. *Turkey Stearnes and the Detroit Stars: The Negro Leagues in Detroit, 1919-1933*. Detroit: Wayne State University Press, 1994.

—. "The Toughest Cop Who Ever Lived." *Detroit Monthly*, June 1986.

Baker, William J. *Jesse Owens: An American Life*. New York: Free Press, 1986.

Barber, Red. *The Broadcasters*. New York: Dial, 1970.

Barrow, Joe Louis, Jr., and Barbara Munder. *Joe Louis: Fifty Years an American Hero*. New York: McGraw-Hill, 1988.

Batchelor, E. A. "Joe Louis Has His Punch But Can He Take It?" *D.A.C. News*, September 1936.

Bell, Madison Smartt. *Save Me, Joe Louis*. New York: Harcourt Brace, 1993.

Berkow, Ira. *Red: A Biography of Red Smith*. New York: Times Books, 1986.

Belknap, Tim. "Detroit's Purple Gang." *Detroit Free Press Magazine*, June 26, 1983.

"The Blow That K.O.'ed Joe Louis." *U. S. News & World Report*, January 25, 1957.

Blum, John Morton. *V Was For Victory: Politics and American Culture During World War II*. New York: Harcourt Brace Jovanovich, 1976.

Brewster Old Timers Souvenir Journal. Detroit, 1988.

Brown, Claude. *Manchild in the Promised Land*. New York: Macmillan, 1965.

Buchanan, A. Russell. *Black Americans in World War II*. Santa Barbara: Clio, 1977.

Burley, Dan. "Love Life of Joe Louis: Romances of the Most Eligible Negro Bachelor Have Involved Beautiful Women Around the Nation." *Ebony*, July 1951.

Bushell, Garvin, with Mark Tucker. *Jazz From the Beginning*. Ann Arbor: University of Michigan Press, 1988.

Byoir, Carl. "Joe Louis Named the War." *Collier's*, May 16, 1942.

Cannon, Jack, and Tom Cannon, eds. *Nobody Asked Me, But . . . The World of Jimmy Cannon.* New York: Holt, Rinehart & Winston, 1978.

Cannon, Jimmy. "Say It Ain't So, Joe." *The American Weekly,* April 17, 1960.

Capra, Frank. *The Name Above the Title.* New York: Macmillan, 1971.

Coburn, Mark D. "America's Great Black Hope." *American Heritage,* October/November 1978.

Cohane,Tim. "The Sad Story of Joe Louis." *Look,* February 27, 1951.

Collier, James Lincoln. *Duke Ellington.* New York: Oxford University Press, 1987.

Creamer, Robert W. *Baseball in '41.* New York: Viking Penguin, 1991.

Crow, Bill. *Jazz Anecdotes.* New York: Oxford University Press, 1990.

Dancy, John C. *Sand Against the Wind: The Memoirs of John C. Dancy.* Detroit: Wayne State University Press, 1966.

Davis, Lenwood G., ed. *Joe Louis: A Bibliography of Articles, Books, Pamphlets, Records, and Archival Materials.* Westport, Connecticut: Greenwood Press, 1983.

Deford, Frank. "The Boxer and the Blonde." *Sports Illustrated,* June 17, 1985.

Donovan, Arthur J., and Bob Drury. *Fatso.* New York: Morrow, 1987.

Drake, St. Clair, and Horace A. Cayton. *Black Metropolis: A Study of Negro Life in a Northern City.* Chicago: University of Chicago Press, 1993.

Durant, John. *The Heavyweight Champions.* New York: Hastings House, 1976.

Early, Gerald. *Tuxedo Junction: Essays on American Culture.* Hopewell, New Jersey: Ecco Press, 1989.

Edmunds, A. O. *Joe Louis.* Grand Rapids, Michigan: Eerdmans, 1973.

Edwards, Harry. *The Revolt of the Black Athlete.* New York: Free Press, 1969.

Falkner, David. *Great Time Coming: The Life of Jackie Robinson from Baseball to Birmingham.* New York: Simon & Schuster, 1995.

Fine, Sidney. *Frank Murphy: The Detroit Years.* Ann Arbor: University of Michigan Press, 1975.

Fleischer, Nat. "Cassius Clay: 'Louis Clobber Me? He Must Be Joking!'" *The Ring,* May 1967.

Fried, Albert. *The Rise and Fall of the Jewish Gangster in America.* New York: Columbia University Press, 1993.

Fried, Ronald K. *Corner Men: Great Boxing Trainers.* New York: Four Walls Eight Windows, 1991.

Gallico, Paul. "The Private Life of Private Joe Louis." *Liberty,* May 23, 1942.

Gilmore, Al-Tony. *Bad Nigger! The National Impact of Jack Johnson.* Port Washington, New York: Kennikat Press, 1975.

Gordy, Berry, Jr. *To Be Loved: The Music, the Magic, the Memories of Motown.* New York: Warner Books, 1994.

Gorn,Elliott J. *The Manly Art: Bare-Knuckle Prize Fighting in America.* Ithaca, New York: Cornell University Press, 1986.

Gowdy, Curt, with John Powers. *Seasons to Remember: The Way It Was in American Sports, 1945-1960.* New York: Harper Collins, 1993.

Gross, Milton. "The Emancipation of Jackie Robinson." *Sport,* October 1951.

Haskins, James, and Kathleen Benson. *Lena: A Biography of Lena Horne*. New York: Stein & Day, 1984.

Hauser, Thomas. *Muhammad Ali: His Life and Times*. New York: Simon & Schuster, 1991.

Heller, Peter. *In This Corner . . . ! Forty World Champions Tell Their Stories*. New York: Simon & Schuster, 1973.

Higgins, Chester. "The Joe Louis Story Nobody Talks About." *Jet*, May 28, 1970.

John Holway. *Voices From the Great Black Baseball Leagues*. New York: Da Capo Press, 1992.

Holtzman, Jerome. *No Cheering in the Press Box*. New York: Holt, Rinehart & Winston, 1974.

"How Joe Louis Lost Two Million." *Ebony*, May 1946.

Hughes, Langston. "Need for Heroes." *The Crisis*, June 1940.

Kahn, Roger. *The Boys of Summer*. New York: Signet, 1973.

—. *The Era: 1947-1957, When the Yankees, the Giants, and the Dodgers Ruled the World*. New York: Ticknor & Fields, 1993.

Karras, Alex, with Herb Gluck. *Even Big Guys Cry*. New York: Holt, Rinehart & Winston, 1977.

Katzman, David M. *Before the Ghetto: Black Detroit in the Nineteenth Century*. Urbana: University of Illinois Press, 1973.

Kieran, John. *The American Sporting Scene*. New York: Macmillan, 1941.

King, Martin Luther, Jr. *Why We Can't Wait*. New York: Harper & Row, 1964.

Kubit, Don. "The Man Who Whipped Joe Louis." *Monthly Detroit*, March 1980.

Lemann, Nicholas. *The Promised Land: The Great Black Migration and How It Changed America*. New York: Knopf, 1991.

Levine, David Allen. *Internal Combustion: The Races in Detroit, 1915-1926*. Westport, Connecticut: Greenwood Press, 1976.

Levien, David. "A Grandson Remembers Johnny Paychek." *The Ring*, July 1995.

Levine, Lawrence W. *Black Culture and Black Consciousness: Afro-American Folk Thought From Slavery to Freedom*. New York: Oxford University Press, 1977.

Libby, Bill. *Joe Louis: The Brown Bomber*. New York: Lothrop, 1980.

Louis, Joe. "My Toughest Fight." *Salute*, December 1947.

—. "How I Would Have Clobbered Clay." *The Ring*, February 1967.

Louis, Joe. As told to Meyer Berger and Barney Nagler. "My Story." *Life*, November 8, 15, 1948.

Louis, Joe, with Edna and Art Rust, Jr. *Joe Louis: My Life*. New York: Harcourt Brace Jovanovich, 1978.

Lutz, William W. *The News of Detroit*. Boston: Little, Brown, 1973.

Malcolm X with Alex Haley. *The Autobiography of Malcolm X*. New York: Grove Press, 1964.

Manchester, William. *The Glory and the Dream: A Narrative History of America, 1932-1972*. Boston: Little, Brown, 1973.

Mandell, Richard D. *The Nazi Olympics*. New York: Macmillan, 1971.

Mann, Arthur. *The Jackie Robinson Story*. New York: Grosset & Dunlap, 1951.

Marks, Carole. *Farewell, We're Good and Gone: The Great Black Migration*. Bloomington: Indiana University Press, 1989.

Martin, Paul. "When the 'Second City' Was First in Boxing: An Informal History of Chicago's Ring Wars." *The Ring*, February 1993.

McGehee, Scott, and Susan Watson, eds. *Blacks in Detroit*. Detroit: Detroit Free Press, 1980.

McNamee, Laurence F. "A Rare Interview with Max Schmeling." *Boxing Illustrated*, October 1992.

Mead, Chris. *Champion: Joe Louis, Black Hero in White America*. New York: Scribner's, 1985.

Miller, Margery. *Joe Louis: American*. New York: Current Books, 1945.

Mitchell, Luther. "Harlem Reconsidered." *Freedomways*. Fall 1964.

Morrison, Ian. *Guinness Boxing: The Records*. Great Britain: Guinness Books, 1986.

Moses, Wilson Jeremiah. *Black Messiahs and Uncle Toms: Social and Literary Manipulations of a Religious Myth*. University Park: Pennsylvania State University Press, 1993.

Motley, Mary Penick. *The Invisible Soldier: The Experience of the Black Soldier, World War II*. Detroit: Wayne State University Press, 1975.

Mullane, Deirdre, ed. *Crossing the Danger Water: Three Hundred Years of African-American Writing*. New York: Doubleday, 1993.

Myrdal, Gunnar. *An American Dilemma: The Negro Problem and Modern Democracy*. New York: Harper & Bros., 1944.

Nagler, Barney. *Brown Bomber*. New York: World Publishing, 1972.

—. *James Norris and the Decline of Boxing*. New York: Bobbs-Merrill, 1964.

Paul Oliver. *Blues Fell This Morning*. London: Cassell & Co., 1960.

—. *Aspects of the Blues Tradition*. New York: Oak Publications, 1970.

Owens, Jesse, with Paul G. Neimark. *Blackthink: My Life as Black Man and White Man*. New York: Morrow, 1970.

—. *I Have Changed*. New York: Morrow, 1972.

Rader, Benjamin G. *American Sports: From the Age of Folk Games to the Age of Spectators*. Englewood Cliffs, New Jersey: Prentice-Hall, 1983.

Rice, Grantland. *The Tumult and the Shouting: My Life in Sports*. New York: A. S. Barnes, 1954.

Richards, E. G. *Reminiscenses of the Early Days in Chambers County*. LaFayette, Alabama: Court of County Commissioners of Chambers County, 1942.

Roberts, Randy. *Jack Dempsey: The Manassa Mauler*. Baton Rouge: Louisiana State University Press, 1979.

—. *Papa Jack: Jack Johnson and the Era of White Hopes*. New York: Free Press, 1983.

Robinson, Jackie. *I Never Had It Made*. New York: Putnam, 1972.

Robinson, Sugar Ray, with Dave Anderson. *Sugar Ray*. New York: Signet, 1969.

Roxborough, John W. "How I Discovered Joe Louis." *Ebony*, October 1954.

Rust, Art, Jr., with Edna Rust. *Recollections of a Baseball Junkie*. New York: Morrow, 1985.

Sammons, Jeffrey T. *Beyond the Ring: The Role of Boxing in American Society.* Urbana: University of Illinois Press, 1988.

Schmeling, Max. *Erinnerungen.* Frankfurt: Verlag Ullstein, 1977.

Schulberg, Budd. *Sparring With Hemingway.* Chicago: Ivan R. Dee, 1995.

Sheed, Wilfred. "And Playing Second Base for Brooklyn . . . Jackie Robinson." *Esquire,* December 1983.

Skehan, Everett M. *Rocky Marciano: Biography of a First Son.* Boston: Houghton Mifflin, 1977.

Stark, Al. "Flashback to Paradise." *Michigan: The Magazine of The Detroit News,* December 4, 1988.

Sugar, Bert Randolph, ed. *The Ring Record Book and Boxing Encyclopedia.* New York: Ring Publishing Co., 1981.

Suster, Gerald. *Champions of the Ring: The Lives and Times of Boxing's Heavyweight Heroes.* London: Robson Books, 1992.

Talese, Gay. "Joe Louis: The King as a Middle-Aged Man." *Esquire,* June 1962.

Taulbert, Clifton L. *Once Upon A Time When We Were Colored.* Tulsa, Oklahoma: Council Oak Books, 1989.

"Ten Biggest Lies About Joe Louis." *Ebony,* August 1953.

Terkel, Studs. *Hard Times: An Oral History of the Great Depression.* New York: Pantheon, 1970.

Tygiel, Jules. *Baseball's Great Experiment: Jackie Robinson and His Legacy.* New York: Oxford University Press, 1983.

—. "The Court-Martial of Jackie Robinson." *American Heritage,* August/September 1984.

Ward, Arch. "Negroes in the Golden Gloves." *Ebony,* March 1951.

Williams, Juan. *Eyes on the Prize: America's Civil Rights Years, 1954-1965.* New York: Viking Penguin 1987.

Woodward, C. Vann. *The Strange Career of Jim Crow.* New York: Oxford University Press, 1974.

Woodford, Frank B., and Arthur M. Woodford. *All Our Yesterdays: A Brief History of Detroit.* Detroit: Wayne State University Press, 1969.

Young, Coleman, with Lonnie Wheeler. *Hard Stuff: The Autobiography of Mayor Coleman Young.* New York: Viking, 1994.

Young, Alexander T. "Joe Louis: Symbol, 1933-1949." Unpublished Ph.D. dissertation, University of Maryland, 1968.

Index

Note: An "n" following page numbers indicates footnotes; "i" indicates illustrations.

Other titles of interest